For Indigenous Minds Only
A Decolonization Handbook

Edited by Waziyatawin
and Michael Yellow Bird

School for Advanced Research Press

Santa Fe

SAR
PRESS

School for Advanced Research Press
Post Office Box 2188
Santa Fe, New Mexico 87504-2188
www.sarpress.org

Managing Editor: Lisa Pacheco
Editorial Assistant: Ellen Goldberg
Designer and Production Manager: Cynthia Dyer
Manuscript Editor: Judith I. Hoffman
Proofreader: Barbara Feller-Roth
Indexer: Catherine Fox
Printer: Versa Press

Library of Congress Cataloging-in-Publication Data

For indigenous minds only : a decolonization handbook / edited by Waziyatawin and Michael Yellow Bird.
    p. cm.
  Includes bibliographical references and index.
  ISBN 978-1-934691-93-9 (alk. paper)
1. Indians of North America—Ethnic identity. 2. Indians of North America—Politics and government. 3. Indians
of North America—Social conditions. 4. Self-determination, National—United States. 5. Decolonization—United States.
6. Postcolonialism—United States. 7. Cultural property—Protection—United States. 8. United States—Race relations.
9. United States—Politics and government. I. Yellow Bird, Michael. II. Wilson, Angela Cavender.
  E98.E85.F68 2012
  323.1197—dc23
                    2012039532

Library of Congress Catalog Card Number: 2012039532
International Standard Book Number: 978-1-934691-93-9
First edition 2012. Second paperback printing 2014.

FSC
www.fsc.org

MIX
Paper from
responsible sources
FSC® C005010

Cover illustration: *Releasing the Spirits of the Mind*
by Monte O. Yellow Bird Sr. AKA Black Pinto Horse
www.blackpintohorsefinearts.com

About the Image:
This work was specifically created for the book, *For Indigenous Minds Only: A Decolonization Handbook*. The image is designed on a US Cavalry recruiting ledger circa 1800s to demonstrate the resilience and persistence of the People over colonization. The picture illustrates the process of change (the releasing and decolonizing of the mind and brain through ceremony). The horses moving upward from the different parts of the brain towards the lodges represent the streams of thoughts of the People about the necessity of returning to traditional beliefs, values, practices, and living. The woman represents "She that makes all things grow," and has always been there for the People to nurture change and inspire growth. When the People call on her for help, she extends a finger to point at, and touch, all the possibilities of decolonization, which exist in the four directions. Change is coming. Be ready.

The School for Advanced Research (SAR) promotes the furthering of scholarship on—and public understanding of—human culture, behavior, and evolution. SAR Press publishes cutting-edge scholarly and general-interest books that encourage critical thinking and present new perspectives on topics of interest to all humans. Contributions by authors reflect their own opinions and viewpoints and do not necessarily express the opinions of SAR Press.

CONTENTS

Figures and Tables

Figures

Tables

For Indigenous Minds Only

James F. Brooks

General Editor

Contributing Authors

George Blue Bird is a Lakota language speaker, writer, and artist from the Pine Ridge Reservation in South Dakota. He is also a part of the Lakota/Dakota/Nakota Spiritual Group at the State Penitentiary in Sioux Falls, South Dakota.

Gregory A. Cajete, PhD (Santa Clara Pueblo) holds the Native American Studies Chair and is Associate Professor of Education at the University of New Mexico. His work is dedicated to honoring the foundations of Indigenous knowledge in education. Dr. Cajete is a Tewa Indian from Santa Clara Pueblo, New Mexico. He has served as a New Mexico Humanities scholar in ethnobotany of northern New Mexico and as a member of the New Mexico Arts Commission. In addition, he has lectured at colleges and universities in the United States, Canada, Mexico, New Zealand, England, Italy, Japan, and Russia. Dr. Cajete has authored five books: *Look to the Mountain: An Ecology of Indigenous Education* (Kivaki Press, 1994); *Ignite the Sparkle: An Indigenous Science Education Curriculum Model* (Kivaki Press, 1999); *Spirit of the Game: Indigenous Wellsprings* (Kivaki Press, 2004); *A People's Ecology: Explorations in Sustainable Living;* and *Native Science: Natural Laws of Interdependence* (Clearlight Publishers, 1999 and 2000).

Ngaropi Diane Cameron (Iwi: Ngāti Mutunga, Ngāti Kahungunu ki Wairoa) has five children and eleven grandchildren. She is a New Zealand registered general and obstetric nurse, registered Whānau, Hapū, and Iwi practitioner, and a member of the New Zealand Association of Counselors. She has worked in the social service area in a variety of environs for thirty years. Throughout this time she has been involved in numerous local and national community development projects implementing a variety of Kaupapa Māori services, trainings, and resources. She is a founding member of Tu Tama Wahine O Taranaki Inc. (TTW) and currently serves as its Chief Executive and Senior Program Facilitator and Educator for Family Violence, and has been a member of the Māori Reference Group to the National Taskforce on Family Violence since 2007. Her work in the family violence arena was recognized in 2011 by the Nursing Network on Violence Against Women International (NNVAWI) when they awarded her the Excellence in Nursing Award. TTW has several research projects currently under way, one of which is *An Investigation into the Origins of Family Violence within Taranaki Whanau*, with Dr. Leonie Pihama.

Chaw-win-is (Ruth Ogilvie) is Nuu-chah-nulth aht and a mother of two. Chaw-win-is has been involved in both learning and regenerating the culture and practices of the Nuu-chah-nulth Peoples, and maintains a deep and heartfelt commitment to confronting the ways in which colonialism has affected our lives and our lands. She is a former member of the West Coast Warrior Society and currently upholds the position of Witwaak (warrior) by her Chief Hyuushtuulth and Head Chief Witwaak Tuutah. Chaw-win-is also earned an MA in Indigenous Governance from the University of Victoria in 2007.

Jeff Corntassel (Cherokee Nation) is an Associate Professor in the Indigenous Governance Program at the University of Victoria. Dr. Corntassel is the author of *Forced Federalism: Contemporary Challenges to Indigenous Nationhood* (University of Oklahoma Press, 2008), and his next book is a co-edited volume (with Professor Tom Holm) entitled *The Power of Peoplehood: Regenerating Indigenous Nations* (University of Texas Press, forthcoming), which brings together Indigenous scholars from across Turtle Island to discuss contemporary strategies for regenerating Indigenous communities. Dr. Corntassel's research has been published in *Alternatives, American Indian Quarterly, Human Rights Quarterly, Nationalism and Ethnic Studies,* and *Social Science Journal.* He lives with his family on Wsanec Territory.

Scott DeMuth is a Dakota descendant, Dakota language student, graduate student in the Sociology Department at the University of Minnesota, and grand jury resistor. He has been involved in several prisoner support projects, including the Anarchist Black Cross and EWOK! (Earth Warriors are OK!), a Twin Cities group supporting earth and animal liberation defendants and prisoners. He is currently a board member of Oyate Nipi Kte, a group dedicated to the reclamation of Dakota land and the revitalization of traditional ways of life, and a member of the editorial collective for the Dakota community journal, *Anpao Duta*.

Na'cha'uaht/Kam'ayaam (Cliff Atleo Jr.) is Ahousaht of the Nuu-chah-nulth People and Kitselas of the Tsimshian People. He has worked on the inside as a Treaty Manager for the Nuu-chah-nulth Tribal Council, but has abandoned his bureaucratic efforts in favor of education and community-rooted activities. A former member of the now-disbanded West Coast Warrior Society and a graduate of the Indigenous Governance Master of Arts Program at the University of Victoria, he is currently pursuing his PhD at the University of Alberta.

Leonie Pihama, PhD (Iwi: Te Ātiawa, Ngā Māhanga ā Tairi, Ngāti Māhanga) is the mother of six children and has had extensive involvement in Māori Education, with involvement in Te Kōhanga Reo, Māori language immersion units, and Kura Kaupapa Māori. She has been involved in a wide range of research and evaluation projects in the area of family and domestic violence. Dr. Pihama is currently Senior Research Fellow at the Te Kotahi Institute at the University of Waikato, New Zealand. She is also Director of Māori and Indigenous Analysis Ltd, an Independent Māori Research Company. Her current research includes *Marae-a-Kura: Understanding the Pedagogy of School-based Marae, He Kakano: Investigating Historical and Intergenerational Trauma upon Māori Wellbeing*, and she is co-investigator with Ngaropi Cameron on the Māori Health Research Project.

Waziyatawin is a Dakota writer, teacher, and activist committed to the pursuit of Indigenous liberation and reclamation of homelands. Her work seeks to build a culture of resistance within Indigenous communities, to recover Indigenous ways of being, and to eradicate colonial institutions. She is currently writing on the topics of Indigenous women and resistance and Indigenous survival in the collapse of industrial civilization. Waziyatawin comes from the *Pezihutazizi Otunwe* (Yellow Medicine Village) in southwestern Minnesota. After receiving her PhD in American History from Cornell University in 2000, she earned tenure and an associate professorship in the history department at Arizona State University, where she taught for seven years. Waziyatawin currently holds the Indigenous Peoples Research Chair in the Indigenous Governance Program at the University of Victoria. She is the author or co-editor of five additional volumes, including *Remember This!: Dakota Decolonization and the Eli Taylor Narratives* (University of Nebraska Press, 2005); *Indigenizing the Academy: Transforming Scholarship and Empowering Communities* (University of Nebraska Press, 2004); *For Indigenous Eyes Only: A Decolonization Handbook* (SAR Press, 2005); *In the Footsteps of Our Ancestors: The Dakota Commemorative Marches of the 21st Century* (Living Justice Press, 2006); and *What Does Justice Look Like? The Struggle for Liberation in Dakota Homeland* (Living Justice Press, 2008).

Molly Wickham is a member of the Gitdumden (Bear/Wolf) clan of the Wet'suwet'en Nation in northern British Columbia. She is the proud daughter of June Wickham, granddaughter of the late Emily Isaac and Jimmy Skin, and great-granddaughter of the late Paddy and Julie Isaac. Wickham is also a proud mother to her young son, Liam. She grew up with her mother and sister, Jennifer, in northern British Columbia. Wickham earned both her undergraduate degree in Sociology and her MA in Indigenous Governance at the University of Victoria. Throughout her education she has worked with young Indigenous people in custody and holds a special place for them in her heart. Her research focuses on revitalizing the Wet'suwet'en clan governance system through the repatriation of displaced people. Wickham has published and presented at conferences on her youth justice work, child welfare, and, most importantly to her, the empowerment of Indigenous youth and families.

Michael Yellow Bird (PhD, University of Wisconsin) is a citizen of the Sahnish and Hidatsa Nations. He is a professor and Director of Graduate Education in the department of social work at Humboldt State University, Arcata, California. He has authored a number of scholarly articles and book chapters, and has presented workshops, scholarly papers, and keynote addresses related to Indigenous Peoples in numerous academic and non-academic venues. Dr. Yellow Bird is the co-editor of two books: *For Indigenous Eyes Only: The Decolonization Handbook* (with Dr. Waziyatawin, SAR Press, 2005) and *Indigenous Social Work around the World: Towards Culturally Relevant Education and Practice* (with Professors Mel Gray and John Coates, Ashgate Press, 2008, 2010). His research, activism, and lectures focus on Indigenous Peoples, war, spirituality, culturally informed mindfulness, and mindfulness-based interventions for Indigenous communities, neurodecolonization, critical and intuitive thinking, and mind-body health.

Chapter 1

INTRODUCTION
DECOLONIZING OUR MINDS AND ACTIONS

Waziyatawin and
Michael Yellow Bird

A. Introduction and Background

B. Definitions of Colonization and

Decolonization

C. The Context and the Topics

D. Ramping Up Resistance

A. Introduction and Background

In 2005, eight Indigenous intellectuals created the volume *For Indigenous Eyes Only: A Decolonization Handbook*, to offer hands-on suggestions and activities for Indigenous communities to engage in as they worked to develop decolonizing activities. Beginning from the assumption that Indigenous Peoples have the power, strength, and intelligence to develop culturally specific decolonization strategies to pursue our own strategies of liberation, we attempted to begin to demystify the language of colonization and decolonization. Through a step-by-step process, we hoped to help Indigenous readers identify useful concepts, terms, and intellectual frameworks that will assist all of us in our struggle toward meaningful change and self-determination. The handbook covered a wide range of topics including Indigenous governance, education, languages, oral tradition, repatriation, images and stereotypes, nutritional strategies, and truthtelling.

In this volume, a number of new Indigenous scholars, writers, and activists have collaborated for the

> **"The most potent weapon in the hands of the oppressor is the mind of the oppressed."**
> **—Steve Biko**

creation of a sequel to the *Decolonization Handbook*. The title, *For Indigenous Minds Only*, reflects an understanding that decolonizing actions must begin in the mind, and that creative, consistent, decolonized thinking shapes and empowers the brain, which in turn provides a major prime for positive change. Undoing the effects of colonialism and working toward decolonization requires each of us to consciously consider to what degree we have been affected by not only the physical aspects of colonization, but also the psychological, mental, and spiritual aspects. Kenyan intellectual Ngugi wa Thiong'o, in his book *Decolonising the Mind*, describes the "cultural bomb" as the greatest weapon unleashed by imperialism:

> The effect of the cultural bomb is to annihilate a people's belief in their names, in their languages, in their environment, in their heritage of struggle, in their unity, in their capacities and ultimately in themselves. It makes them see their past as one wasteland of non-achievement and it makes them want to distance themselves from that wasteland. It makes them want to identify with that which is furthest removed from themselves; for instance, with other peoples' languages rather than their own. It makes them identify with that which is decadent and reactionary, all those forces that would stop their own springs of life. It even plants serious doubts about the moral righteousness of struggle. Possibilities of triumph or victory are seen as remote, ridiculous dreams. The intended results are despair, despondency and a collective death-wish.

The planting and igniting of this "cultural bomb" by the colonizing forces has been essential to the colonization process, for if our minds are contaminated with self-hatred and the belief that we are inferior to our colonizers, we will believe in both the necessity and virtue of our own colonization. We will begin to

diminish the wisdom and beauty of Indigenous ways of being and embrace the ways of the colonizers as inherently superior. When we believe in their superiority, our motivation to fight for our own liberation is splintered and eventually seriously damaged. However, we do not believe that it can be killed. That destiny lies within each of us. Still, if we accept the cultural bomb, why would we fight for something we perceive to be undesirable?

Working toward decolonization, then, requires us to consciously and critically assess how our minds have been affected by the cultural bomb of colonization. Only then will we be positioned to take action that reflects a rejection of the programming of self-hatred with which we have been indoctrinated. We will also learn to assess the claims of colonizer society regarding its justification for colonization and its sense of superiority. When we regain a belief in the wisdom and beauty of our traditional ways of being and reject the colonial lies that have inundated us, we will release the pent-up dreams of liberation and again realize the need for resistance to colonization. This volume is dedicated to facilitating the critical thinking that will help us work toward our collective decolonization.

From the song "Ancestors" (2007)
by Savage Family
from Skokomish (Tuwaduq):
If our ancestors came back and
asked us who we are/
would we be too far gone
to recognize them/
through the stars and the
stripes of the flags/
living our lives as they say?/
If our ancestors came back
would we fight them today?//

B. Definitions of Colonization and Decolonization

Colonization generally refers to the process that is perpetuated after the initial control over Indigenous Peoples is achieved through invasion and conquest. Perpetuating colonization allows the colonizers to maintain or expand their social, political, and economic power. It is detrimental to us because their power comes at the expense of Indigenous lands,

COLONIZATION refers to both the formal and informal methods (behavioral, ideological, institutional, political, and economical) that maintain the subjugation and/or exploitation of Indigenous Peoples, lands, and resources. **DECOLONIZATION** is the meaningful and active resistance to the forces of colonialism that perpetuate the subjugation and/or exploitation of our minds, bodies, and lands. Decolonization is engaged for the ultimate purpose of overturning the colonial structure and realizing Indigenous liberation.

resources, lives, and self-determination. Not only has colonization resulted in the loss of major rights such as land and self-determination, most of our contemporary daily struggles are also a direct consequence of colonization (poverty, family violence, chemical dependency, suicide, health deterioration). Colonization is an all-encompassing presence in our lives.

Decolonization is the meaningful and active resistance to the forces of colonialism that perpetuate the subjugation and/or exploitation of our minds, bodies, and lands. Its ultimate purpose is to overturn the colonial structure and realize Indigenous liberation. First and foremost, decolonization must occur in our own minds. The Tunisian decolonization activist, Albert Memmi, wrote, "In order for the colonizer to be the complete master, it is not enough for him to be so in actual fact, he must also believe in its legitimacy. In order for that legitimacy to be complete, it is not enough for the colonized to be a slave, he must also accept his role." The first step toward decolonization, then, is to question the legitimacy of colonization. Once we recognize the truth of this injustice, we can think about ways to resist and challenge colonial institutions and ideologies. Thus, decolonization is not passive, but rather it requires something called *praxis*. Brazilian libratory educator Paulo Freire defined praxis as "reflection and action upon the world in order to transform it." This is the means by which we turn from subjugated human beings into liberated human beings. In accepting the premise of colonization and working toward decolonization, we are not relegating ourselves to a status as victim, but rather we are actively working toward our own freedom to transform our lives and the world around us. The project that begins with our minds, therefore, has revolutionary potential.

Michael Yellow Bird has created a **Conceptual Model of Decolonization** in which he defines decolonization as both an event and a process:

Event – As an event, decolonization concerns reaching a level of critical consciousness, an active understanding that you are (or have been) colonized and are thus responding to life circumstances in ways that are limited, destructive, and externally controlled.

Process – As a process, decolonization means engaging in the activities of creating, restoring, and birthing. It means creating and consciously using various strategies to liberate oneself, adapt to or survive oppressive conditions; it means restoring cultural practices, thinking, beliefs, and values that were taken away or abandoned but are still relevant and necessary to survival; and it means the birthing of new ideas, thinking, technologies, and lifestyles that contribute to the advancement and empowerment of Indigenous Peoples.

In the first *Decolonization Handbook,* as the first activity we encouraged readers to work within their own cultural traditions to develop words in their own Indigenous language for both colonization and decolonization. This exercise provides an opportunity for individuals and communities to think consciously and critically about the meaning of the terms from within their own cultural framework. If you have not yet engaged in this activity, it is a good place to start. Identifying the literal and figurative meanings of both these terms will allow you to consciously understand your culture's view of them.

Michael Yellow Bird's conceptual model provides an analytical tool with which we can facilitate understanding and create strategies for decolonization in various ways and contexts. With this framework in mind, contributors to this volume attempted to address the following questions as they pertain to their particular topic: (1) how has colonialism affected our lives, and (2) what strategies for decolonization might we employ to not only challenge colonialism at its core, but also to undo, counter, or reverse the effects of colonialism. These are questions you may also keep in mind when thinking about the realities, struggles, and hopes of your family and community.

C. The Context and the Topics

This *Handbook,* more so than the first volume, is written with a sense of urgency. We are heading into a new era in which we will no longer be able to deny the effects of industrial "civilization's" grave damage to the diverse zones and ecosystems of our planet. As Indigenous Peoples we know that this devastation has been occurring on Turtle Island for the last five centuries; and, for that length of time, our ancestors have continued to sound the alarm to the ongoing, un-restrained feeding frenzy of non-renewable resources by the corporate-led, capitalist engines of colonial society. We know from the stories and prophecies of our ancestors that this mindless consumption activity portends a future of deep hardship and dramatic change for all forms of life on the earth. We are now bearing witness to the collapse of major ecosystems, the extinction of many species, the desertification of fertile lands, the

rise in infectious diseases, a decline in fisheries, and a staggering increase in the toxicity of the lands, waters, and air.

Moreover, we now have become even more aware of how this collapse is contributing to the suffering of all Indigenous life. What is happening now differs from the natural declines of species and changes to the earth in that the planet has now reached a "tipping point" that will undoubtedly threaten the foundations of industrial civilization and the survival of much of life. The whole earth will reap the effects of hyper-exploitation, exceeding the carrying capacity, and wide-scale ecological degradation or destruction. To be clear, this present and impending disaster was not the making of our ancestors who maintained ingenious, sustainable ways of life—ways that were considered to be backward, primitive, and undeveloped by our colonizers. Still, the cultural bomb has infected many, but not all, Indigenous Peoples in the current generation, making us apologists and cheerleaders for the unfettered corporatocracy that continues to bring about the rapid decline of our planet. Our uncritical participation in this colonial system undoubtedly increases the rate at which we are falling and failing.

In his recent volume, *Red Alert: Saving the Planet with Indigenous Knowledge,* Daniel Wildcat asserted, "Many political leaders throughout Indian country and around the world continue to speak of sovereignty, self-determination, economic development, and occasionally even democracy. As important as these topics are in the everyday lives of humankind, in the big picture of life on the planet, such talk is beginning to appear meaningless unless explicitly related to the climate changes we are observing." Likewise, in his article "American Indian Studies in the Time of Global Warming," Michael Yellow Bird addresses his comments to Indigenous scholars. In discussing why he chose to play off the title of Gabriel Garcia Marquez's best-selling novel *Love in the Time of Cholera,* which regarded lovesickness as an actual disease like cholera, Yellow Bird writes, "Similarly, I look upon global warming (climate change) as a self-inflicted illness that is overriding and overshadowing all that we are doing, planning, and hoping for in our little human lives. Unless we keep this enormous planetary event at the center of our reality and immediately engage in effective antidotes, the future of our world, including American Indian/Indigenous nations studies, will surely be more fleeting than it might have been if 'natural' events were allowed to unfold."

Global climate change is not the only crisis with which our people will be contending in the coming decades, however. Other practices resulting from a faulty belief in unlimited growth and progress are now proving to be failures. We are witnessing the endgame of capitalism. As the US debt grows by over a million dollars every minute (for an update, visit www.usdebtclock.org) and we reach the point of peak debt—our borrowing limit—we find ourselves on the verge of an economic collapse from which a recovery does not look possible. Furthermore, peak debt will only be compounded by the issue of peak oil use (not to mention peak natural gas, peak coal, peak uranium, etc.). We are about to run headlong into a number of simultaneous crises.

Thus, when we discuss strategies for decolonization, we also cannot afford to ignore our current predicament. While addressing colonialism in our lives, it is important for us to understand how that struggle influences, interacts with, and is affected by these other global emergencies. It is an awareness of these impending crises that must foreground all our visions, thoughts, and actions related to decolonization. All of this means that as Indigenous people, we can no longer pretend that it is in our best interest to get on board with the project of modernity and economic development as a pathway to self-determination. That ship is quickly sinking. It is in this context that we present the following discussions.

For this volume, we have taken on a host of new topics and offered some additional perspectives on some of the old topics. Included in this volume are discussions of global collapse; what to consider in returning to a land-based existence; neurodecolonization; demilitarization for imperial purposes and re-militarization for Indigenous purposes; survival strategies for tribal prisoners; moving beyond the nation-state model; a land-based educational model;

methods for developing healthy family relationships; decolonization strategies for youth in custody; and the decolonizing of gender roles. As with the first volume, we do not intend to provide universal solutions for problems stemming from centuries of colonialism. Rather, we hope to facilitate and encourage critical thinking skills while offering recommendations for fostering community discussions and plans for purposeful community action.

Chapter 2 by Waziyatawin and chapter 3 by Na'cha'uaht/Kam'ayaam (Cliff Atleo Jr.) focus on Indigenous responses to global crises. They both raise questions about our current level of preparation and offer ideas about how we might successfully weather the coming storms by revitalizing our ancient relationships with our territories. Waziyatawin's chapter, "Indigenous Survival in the Coming Collapse," provides an overview of the impending crises such as depletion of resources, declining per capita food production, global climate change, economic collapse, and increased political instability. Given the American and Canadian dependence on cheap oil, she then spells out why peak oil, in particular, threatens the foundations of American and Canadian societies with no viable alternatives that will allow for the continuation of this way of life. In discussing the "promising" alternative energy sources—many of them labeled "green energy" or "clean energy"—Waziyatawin explains why those too do not provide long-term solutions because of their dependence on fossil fuels. The dispelling of myths regarding the dominant society's capacity to continue this way of life raises questions about a whole host of lies fed to us by colonizing society that most of us have come to accept. Once we shed our misconceptions (and the sooner the better), we become open to strategizing about how to respond to collapse. When we realize how our future survival will be intimately linked with the health of our land base and the integrity of our ecosystems, it quickly becomes apparent that as Indigenous Peoples we must take much more seriously our role as defenders of the land.

Waziyatawin then offers a seven-point Indigenous Action Plan for responding to economic, ecological, and fossil-fuel collapse that encourages Indigenous people to return, first and foremost, to our own spiritual and cultural foundations. Since many Indigenous people have stories, prophecies or teachings about the coming times, as well as Original Instructions about how we are supposed to live on the land, understanding and living those teachings will be an important component in facilitating the rebirth of our nations at the same time settler society is collapsing. Waziyatawin then calls for all of us to diligently work to "ignite the flame of revolution" within our communities by building a culture of resistance. She encourages individuals, families, and communities to get armed so that we may work in defense of our people and lands. She advocates "life-boat building" in which Indigenous people shed dependency on settler society and seek to establish food, water, and land security. For those who do not have a sufficient land base for survival, she recommends developing a plan for the reclamation of lands. Her Action Plan's last two steps include working to dismantle the existing systems and institutions that are destroying our homelands and planet and committing to defending the land at all costs. Ultimately, she says, preparing for collapse calls us to "live the meaning of indigeneity."

Na'cha'uaht continues the discussion of crisis preparedness in his chapter, "Returning to the Land: What Does It Take and Are You Ready?" He begins with the provocative statement, "It is said that Vancouver Island has only three days of supplies at any given time." This stark reality requires Indigenous people on the island to consider what would happen if the flow of supplies were interrupted as a consequence of any disaster. Na'cha'uaht addresses the issue of crisis preparedness in the context of his father's people, the Nuu'chah'nulth community of Ahousaht. By examining the potential for short- and long-term survival within his own context, he provides a framework for us to begin asking questions about the capacity for survival within our own communities.

In the age of increasing natural disasters due to climate change, it is quite practical to assume that any of our communities might be subjected to natural disasters, and aid may not come in a timely manner (or might not come at all). One need understand only that New Orleans is still attempting to recover from Hurricane Katrina, which devastated the region in 2005. For example, in the United States, 2011 was an unprecedented year for natural disasters (such as drought, tornadoes, and flooding), causing fourteen different billion-dollar weather disasters that devastated region after region. On the global level, seven countries and one territory suffered the hottest temperatures on record in 2011. Indigenous communities may be particularly vulnerable to natural disasters and disruptions in services. During the 2010–2011 winter, Alaska experienced record snowfalls and northern villages were iced in, unable to receive needed fuel oil that would get them through the long, harsh winter (with temperatures hovering at –45ºF). It was not until January that a Russian tanker was able to break through the Bering Sea ice and deliver 1.3 million gallons of oil to the town of Nome.

While all our ancestors were obviously self-sufficient and practitioners of sustainable ways of living—our occupation of the same land base over thousands of years without destroying it is proof of this—Na'cha'uaht points out that under colonial rule our capacity for self-sufficiency has been undermined and diminished, leaving us in tenuous and dependent positions today. He encourages us to take inventory of our current ability to meet our basic needs, especially shelter, water, food, and security, and recommends that we develop and hone our survival skills now, so that we do not have to learn by trial and error while in the midst of a crisis. Recognizing how deeply our lives have been altered through colonization, Na'cha'uaht calls on us to be flexible in our thinking about our futures and to reject a dogmatic adherence to "tradition," which may not have the same relevance to our lives and may actually hinder our capacity to survive in certain situations. Still, he says, there are core values by which we must live if we are going to help ensure the long-term health and viability of Mother Earth. While not all Indigenous people may yet be prepared to take up this task, Na'cha'uaht reminds us that it is important that some of us do so right now.

In chapter 4 we move from discussions of crises and survival to a discussion of "Neurodecolonization:

Using Mindfulness Practices to Delete the Neural Networks of Colonialism." Anti-colonial thinkers, writers, and activists have long understood the importance of decolonizing the mind, and Michael Yellow Bird's latest research reveals that colonized people can successfully transform their neural networks in positive ways that will allow us "the personal resources, strengths, talents, and abilities we need to overcome the oppressions of colonialism." In breaking down the latest neuroscience research and explaining his experience with mindfulness practice, he teaches us that we can improve our mental and physical well-being by shedding unconstructive negative thinking, feelings, and behaviors. We can then strengthen weak neural pathways and create new ones associated with positive attributes and behaviors.

Yellow Bird explains how the constant stresses of colonialism—the effects of which we experience in our daily lives—take an enormous toll on Indigenous health. But, he explains, we have the power to limit or reverse the negative effects of past trauma and harms through consistent mindfulness practice. This alone does not alter the colonial relationship we endure, but it strengthens our capacity to create additional positive change in all aspects of our lives, including challenging colonialism more forcefully and effectively. While many of us today may think mindfulness practice is something that comes from another culture, Yellow Bird reminds us that it is also an Indigenous practice, one that has been a part of both traditional and contemporary ceremonies among Indigenous Peoples. Thus, in engaging mindfulness practice, we are part of an ancient tradition practiced by our ancestors who benefited from such practices. He tells us, "Whether it is mainstream or traditional cultural mindfulness practices that we engage in, we will change the function and structure of our brains for

> "No matter how briefly colonization may have lasted, all memory of freedom seems distant; [s]he forgets what it costs or else [s]he no longer dares to pay the price for it.... Everything has been brought into play to destroy [her]his courage to die and face the sight of blood."
> —Albert Memmi,
> *The Colonizer and the Colonized*

the better.... It will increase our compassion, patience, creativity, emotional intelligence, and courage." In this way we might achieve freedom from the hold that trauma has had on us while simultaneously attaining the highest levels of brain performance and well-being that we can.

In chapter 5, "Living in a Longer Now: Moving Beyond the State-Centric System," Jeff Corntassel builds on the notion of Indigenous populations renewing our relationships to our territories, including our relationship of accountability. He roots his discussion in the Tsalagi teaching to "Live in a longer 'now'—learn your history and culture and understand it is what you are now." This philosophy, he says, urges us "to remember our histories by strengthening and revitalizing our relationships." Renewing our roles and responsibilities within our own communities, however, calls into question many of the ideas we have uncritically accepted under colonial rule.

Corntassel reveals the myths behind terms such as "sovereignty," "nation," "state," and "globalization," and teaches us to see beyond the rhetoric and institutions of colonizing society toward a responsibility-based relationship with our homelands. For example, in discussing the inappropriateness of Indigenous Peoples seeking something called "sovereignty" within a nation-state framework, Corntassel tells us that in denying our self-determination, states are actually exposing their inherent violence against Indigenous nations. He further states that "acts of state-building are also actions of Indigenous nation-destroying." Because our self-determination cannot be granted by an outside entity or negotiated with a colonial state, he reminds us that self-determination is something that we must take for ourselves. He tells us, "this is about Indigenous Peoples re-asserting our responsibilities, not rights. Then we can once again say that we are defenders of our homelands." Furthermore, because "self-determination is asserted, not negotiated," he recommends we cease trying to define self-determination through state-centered forums like the United Nations, and instead define it on our own terms and according to our renewed relationship with our homelands. Finally, Corntassel closes with the hopeful reminder: "Indigenous Peoples are persistent and resilient—we are nations that existed well before states were created and our nations will outlast them."

Scott DeMuth begins chapter 6, "Colonization Is Always War," by describing how any Indigenous challenges to state authority today, even peaceful challenges, are met with threats of police violence, arrests, and heavy surveillance. This serves as a useful reminder to Indigenous people who have come to believe that because we do not observe open repression on a daily basis, we have made progress in our relationships with our colonizers, or that colonization at its core is not still serving the same purpose it always has. DeMuth asserts that because colonization is inherently a war for territory and resources, "If colonization continues today, then it follows that war continues to be waged against Indigenous Peoples and territories." In this context, it is imperative that Indigenous people develop a proper response to warfare, requiring the development of an organized resistance movement. Rather than viewing a potential resistance movement as an offensive action, however, DeMuth points out that decolonization is actually a self-defensive action against the war that is colonization.

DeMuth argues that once we have a foundational understanding of the colonial relationship and the need to engage in resistance efforts, we can then work on building a resistance movement. Drawing from the writings of British officer Frank Kitson on the basic tactics of counterinsurgency, DeMuth uses his analysis to walk us through three phases of resistance movements and how they are typically suppressed by the state. In understanding counterinsurgency efforts, we can learn more about effective insurgency tactics. Warning of the dangers of COINTELPRO (counter intelligence program) tactics used by the state, he encourages us to develop counter measures, including the development of a strong security culture, and to employ successful methods of asymmetrical warfare. Furthermore, rather than bogging the resistance movement down with divisions over the use of violence or nonviolence, DeMuth encourages Indigenous resistance movements to embrace a diversity of tactics. Arguing a sense of urgency, DeMuth relates, "The longer we wait to stand and defend ourselves, the more we will lose."

One possibility for building a culture of resistance within our communities is to train a new generation of Indigenous people committed to the cause of Indigenous liberation. Waziyatawin addresses this topic in chapter 7, "*Zuya Wicasta Naka Icahwicayapi* (Raising New Warriors)." Indigenous youth continue to be problematized in our society, but rather than seeing their struggles as a symptom of the colonial condition or a reflection of the sense of meaninglessness imbued in their lives, society often blames our youth, our families, and our communities for some kind of failure. It is true that we could do more to support our youth, but not in the sense that colonizer society might suggest. Rather than offering a different way of living and a commitment to indigeneity, we have been forced under threat of colonial violence to teach indigeneity as a sort of supplement to the teachings of settler society. Most of us, for example, turn over our children to the colonizers' educational system for seven hours a day to be indoctrinated with values and teachings that are often in direct opposition or in contradiction to many Indigenous values and teachings. Under colonial rule, we have failed to offer them a meaningful alternative to acquiescing to settler society, and they have suffered as a consequence.

We currently risk jail time or the loss of custody of our children if we withhold them from the educational system, but there are other options for young people once they have either graduated or passed the age requirement for compulsory education. In chapter 7, Waziyatawin discusses the concept of a cultural immersion camp to train the next generations of warriors. These camps could be embraced within Indigenous communities at the present moment to undo the colonial teachings of settler society and re-ignite a fierce commitment to defending Indigenous Peoples and homelands. She has outlined a plan for a two-year program for young adults, dedicated to decolonizing all the ways in which we are affected by colonial rule. The program would entail a critical assessment of these effects and conscious efforts to replace colonial ways with reclaimed Indigenous ways of being. Such warrior training, if supported by a community, would provide a communal living experience in which young adults could practice physical strengthening and discipline, self-sufficiency and sustainable living, and service to the People and homelands. If a group of new warriors were honored and celebrated by the broader community, it would set these young people on a new pathway to self-determination in this era of major changes. Waziyatawin reminds us, "Our youth will be the ones to lead this struggle and we need to prepare them the best that we can. If our Peoples are to survive, we must teach our young people to live the mantra, 'For the People! For the Land!'"

Gregory Cajete, in chapter 8, also examines the education of our young people, but seeks to intervene and make changes at a much earlier stage in the educational process by offering a land-based educational alternative. In his chapter, "Decolonizing Indigenous Education in a Twenty-first Century World," Cajete asks us to "critically analyze the effects modern education has had on our collective cultural, psychological, and ecological viability," which inevitably leads us to the realization that the mainstream educational system has failed to serve our interests and honor our ways of being. Indeed, he argues that the system in the United States has failed all Americans as it has lead to a crisis of identity and disconnection from the natural world: "Those who identify most with the 'bottom line' more often than not suffer from image without substance, technique without soul, and knowledge without context: the cumulative psychological results of which are usually unabridged alienation, loss of community, and a deep sense of incompleteness."

Traditional Indigenous education, on the other hand, offers a powerful antidote to the current educational crisis because it emphasizes the interconnectedness and interdependence of all beings, both human and nonhuman, and is therefore a profoundly environmental education. This is "education for life's sake." Cajete explains the stages of a traditional education, from the first recognition of spirit and orientation to place that occurs at birth, through the seventh stage of deep understanding, enlightenment, and wisdom. He then provides ten essential characteristics of Indigenous education that exemplify its transformational nature. While this life-affirming educational approach would also serve as a useful model for mainstream educational systems, Cajete says that ultimately it is most important that we revitalize our expressions of education for our future generations. "As we collectively 'Look to the Mountain,'" he tells us, "we must truly think of that seventh generation of Indigenous children, for it is they who will judge whether we were as true to our responsibility to them as our relatives were for us seven generations before."

In chapter 9 we shift gears as Michael Yellow Bird challenges us to think critically and make decisions about another institution with which Indigenous people are intimately acquainted—the military industrial complex that continues to serve imperial interests. His chapter, "A BROWN PAPER on the Iraq War," is written in a report format with Indigenous interests at heart to "expressly solicit consultation from Indigenous, native, tribal, and aboriginal communities on a major public policy issue." Arguing that under colonial rule our capacity and will to carefully deliberate over decisions regarding both war and peacemaking has been diminished or undermined, Yellow Bird encourages us to resume these inherent powers of self-governance. Citing data about the cost of the Iraq War in dollars, human lives, damage to infrastructure, relationships between Indigenous Peoples, and devastation to the land, he convincingly argues that this war does not serve Indigenous interests, yet few Indigenous nations have declared a position about whether they agree with the US-led invasion of Iraq. This silence, along with our people's continued presence serving in the US military, means that our nations "are in de facto agreement with the Bush administration's reasons for this war," however trumped up or illegitimate these reasons may be.

To address the issue of the Iraq War and avoid being drawn into immoral or unjustified future wars of aggression by imperial forces, Yellow Bird discusses what actions we can take within our own communities. He provides step-by-step directions for initiating broad discussions within our communities and between nations to consciously develop an informed, thoughtful, and collective position on the Iraq War, as well as a political and moral code for evaluating all stages of future wars. This type of thoughtful deliberation of warfare was practiced by our ancestors, and it can be resumed by our Peoples today, but it will require a shift in our perceptions about our role in the world and our capacity for self-determination. Yellow Bird tells us, "Perhaps most important is that Indigenous governments regard themselves as legitimate political bodies within the international community who must participate in all affairs that concern the well-being of all nations on the planet." He closes his chapter with suggestions for how all people within our communities—from tribal leaders to tribal youth—may participate and assist in this project.

> **"Jails and prisons are designed to break human beings, to convert the population into specimens in a zoo—obedient to our keepers, but dangerous to each other."**
> —Angela Davis,
> ***The Black Scholar***

Chapters 10 and 11 address the topic of our populations in custody. Given the reality that Indigenous people continue to be disproportionately represented in prisons and detention centers, we felt it important to speak to our incarcerated relatives, as well as the people who work with those who are incarcerated. Molly Wickham has developed programming in British Columbia designed to help young people understand their experience within the larger colonial context, while also encouraging a sense of empowerment rooted in their indigeneity. In chapter 10, "Initiating the Process of Youth Decolonization: Reclaiming Our Right to Know and Act on Our Experiences," she begins by relaying her own personal experiences with what she calls "the intergenerational effects of residential schools, foster care, and displacement" and the development of her own

commitment to decolonization. Wickham rejects the pathologizing of Indigenous youth by governmental programs, which, she says, "focus on individualistic remedies that deny the greater context of colonization and imply that there is something inherently wrong with Indigenous youth." In contrast to this approach, Wickham relates how Indigenous families and communities have been systematically torn apart (literally in many cases, as children were ripped away from their families) and explains the current social problems as a direct outcome of those genocidal governmental policies. Understanding the legacy of colonization is only one part of the process, however. As Wickham points out, "Once youth have been introduced to colonization, it is critical that they also be introduced to resistance efforts and decolonization."

One counter to the devastating disconnection from family and community is the conscious rebuilding of Indigenous relationships. This is the first theme Wickham addressed in her pilot project developed and facilitated by a group of Indigenous adults for youth in custody. Throughout the program they continued to collectively explore relationship building as it applies to the themes of land, spirituality, and family. To engage the youth on these topics, the team used a series of activities, including physical and visual activities, to facilitate openness, communication, and learning. Wickham provides activities in this chapter that youth workers may utilize or adapt for work in their own communities and institutions. Through these efforts, she has experienced a remarkable receptiveness among the youth, which bodes well for future efforts in this area: "By mentoring youth and building relationships, a positive sense of community will provide an alternative way of viewing their past experiences and help them imagine a different future." This transformation is essential if we want to help prevent our young people from transitioning from the juvenile (in)justice system to the adult "correctional" system.

This is a particularly urgent issue in the United States context. The rapid expansion of the prison system in the last few decades of the twentieth century caused scholar and activist Angela Davis to dub the phenomenon the Prison Industrial Complex (PIC) in 1998: "Taking into account the structural similarities of business-government linkages in the realms of military production and public punishment, the expanding penal system can now be characterized as a 'prison industrial complex.'" PIC refers to not only the rapid expansion and privatization of prisons, but also the exploitation of inmate labor and building prisons as a source of job creation. In 2002 the prison population passed the two million mark, which meant that one in every 142 citizens in the United States was imprisoned (with males and people of color bearing the disproportionate brunt of that reality). By 2008 the number reached 2.3 million with one in every 100 adults imprisoned. Today, the United States has the dubious record of the highest rate of incarceration in the world. This has severe implications for Indigenous populations.

Chapter 11, "Decolonization Lessons for Tribal Prisoners," is written from the perspective of someone inside the prison walls. George Blue Bird has been incarcerated since 1983 and is currently in the Jameson Annex of the South Dakota State Penitentiary in Sioux Falls, South Dakota. As a lifer in a maximum security prison, Blue Bird lives within the confines of the most tangible manifestation of colonialism—the prison. Conscious of the way the prison has been used as a weapon by colonial powers to ensure our subjugation from the earliest periods of white invasion, Blue Bird understands the linkages between past generations of Dakota, Lakota, and Nakota people imprisoned in jail cells and concentration camps and our populations trying to survive in prisons today. Furthermore, he has wisdom to share based on his experience: "Anyone serving a life sentence without parole or anything over twenty years must live with the bitter realities that are everywhere in prison. Visits are far and few in between. Contact with the outside world fades in and out. We grow old and live without the crucial elements of our families and people. Time becomes a yearly test

of survival and hope." Because his wisdom is born of experience that may help others survive imprisonment, his chapter in this volume is primarily offered as a message to other tribal prisoners. It is filled with suggestions about how to maintain sanity, integrity, humanity, and a spirit of resistance, all while doing time in an inhumane environment. Through his writings, we witness how he has learned to survive decades of confinement.

In his chapter, Blue Bird pays tribute to the life of "Nisko" Iron Moccasin, who he believes modeled a code to live by in prison. By explaining the way Nisko did time, Blue Bird illuminates the important details of day-to-day prison life that can make it tolerable, while also building a sense of unity among tribal prisoners. He then addresses issues that tribal prisoners frequently have to endure, such as administrative segregation (the "hole"), infiltration by informants, and the loss of spouses on the outside. But he also emphasizes ways to stay strong. For example, he focuses on the importance of practicing our spirituality, learning to find joy in small pleasures, and the necessity of maintaining discipline. Blue Bird also describes his commitment to activism, which is based on the understanding that our suffering as Indigenous Peoples is ongoing, and that tribal prisoners can work for the People while imprisoned, including working toward the improvement of their own prison conditions.

Finding ways to recover from debilitating circumstances, initiate healing, and restore well-being to our families and communities is an important decolonizing project. The value of these undertakings is illuminated in chapter 12, "Kua Tupu Te Pā Harakeke: Developing Healthy *Whānau* Relationships," contributed by Māori women Leonie Pihama (researcher) and Ngaropi Diane Cameron (service provider). They contend that Indigenous people may draw from traditional knowledge as a means of healing contemporary issues, and they provide an example from their home territory of Aotearoa (the place referred to in colonial terms as New Zealand). Specifically, they focus on how to repair the damage done to relationships (family relationships, intimate relationships, and friendships) by returning to their traditional teachings. Beginning with the story of Niwareka and Mataora, they illustrate how Indigenous ancestors have passed on knowledge to us about how we are to live with one another in a good way, and they demonstrate how often-overlooked teachings embedded in the story offer lessons that can be applied today. However, because many of our stories have been translated and interpreted by the colonizers (usually men who overlook and diminish the role of women in the stories), only through delving more deeply into this particular story were they able to reveal the power and importance of the female ancestor, Niwareka, who challenges and leaves her abusive partner to return to the support of her people.

Pihama and Cameron then describe how similar traditional teachings have been an essential component in service programs dedicated to decolonization, particularly programs from the organization headed by Cameron, Tū Tama Wahine O Taranaki, which addresses the issue of domestic violence. Many Indigenous academics were introduced to the concept of *Kaupapa Māori* (Māori philosophies, Māori approaches, and Māori ways of being) as a tool for research through Linda Tuhiwai Smith's book, *Decolonizing Methodologies*, and in this chapter we learn that Kaupapa Māori may also be applied to a wide range of community services, programs, and initiatives. Like Wickham (chapter 10), Cajete (chapter 8), and Yellow Bird (chapter 9), who argue that help for Indigenous people will not be found in the colonizers' institutions, Pihama and Cameron argue that transformation will not occur through programs of the colonial government "as they have no interest in our people affirming our language, our culture, and our cultural identity." Thus, they say, "the work remains with us as Indigenous Peoples globally to decolonize and reassert those cultural ways of being that will bring well-being to this and future generations." By incorporating language, values, stories, and other teachings into programming that services Indigenous communities, they initiate healing in a way that genuinely supports self-determination.

The final chapter in this volume, "Remaking Balance: Decolonizing Gender Relations in Indigenous Communities" (chapter 13), is contributed by Nuu-chah-nulth intellectual and writer, Chaw-win-is (Ruth Ogilvie). In addressing issues of gender within contemporary Indigenous communities, Chaw-win-is begins by situating herself within her own community politics, stating, "This disclosure is important anytime an Indigenous woman acts politically or changes personally. Her 'credibility' is questioned and she may become a target for lateral or physical violence." Unfortunately, given the high rates of gender oppression within our communities, Indigenous women need to be conscious of the potential consequences for our political actions or decisions to step outside gender boundaries, traditional or not, in a way that few heterosexual men ever need to think about. Furthermore, if we do not step outside those prescribed roles or become politically active, we also fall prey to frequent expressions of patriarchal violence stemming from our experience under colonialism. It is precisely because our cultures have been detrimentally impacted by colonization that rigid teachings about gender roles, even traditional ones, are often difficult to reconcile with our present circumstances. Thus, Chaw-win-is emphasizes our need to *remake* gender balance as an act of decolonization, rather than viewing this process as a simple "recovering of" or "reviving of" traditional roles.

Chaw-win-is argues that "the task of decolonization under our current conditions may require that we de-gender our traditional roles as we re-make them." This requires a critical evaluation of what we perceive as traditional gender roles and an understanding of how they might be influenced by experiences with colonial institutions like boarding or residential schools. To engage such a critical assessment, she encourages open communication as well as a renewed emphasis on competency or capability over gender, especially in regards to leadership roles in the community. Furthermore, she demonstrates that we can conceptualize ways to defend and protect abused women and children while also strengthening the best of our institutions and capacity for self-determination. Chaw-win-is also recognizes the importance of practicality and common sense in the lives of our people, both past and present, reminding us that "our actions must make sense in our homelands." She encourages us to ask fundamental questions about our traditions and practices so that we may consciously understand when we are clinging to ideas simply because someone told us to or because they fulfill an idea of unexamined tradition, or if we can identify the heart of a teaching and determine how best to practice it in today's context. Having embraced her own role as *witwaak* (warrior), she offers a useful model by which we can see how this seemingly gender-role defying responsibility was negotiated within her family and community.

All the chapters in this volume seek to illuminate some aspect of our struggle as colonized people and suggest ways we might effectively challenge, or at least mitigate, the worst effects of colonization. We have attempted to refrain from using a lot of academic jargon and have largely eliminated academic citations as a way to make the book more accessible to a wider audience. The exception is Michael Yellow Bird's "BROWN PAPER" chapter, which required endnotes because of the large amount of data included in his analysis. We recognize that our efforts build on the efforts of generations of Indigenous people who came before us—people who resisted colonization on their watch, in their own way. We are attempting to carry on that five-hundred-year-old tradition in defense of our homelands and Peoples. We do not claim to provide universal solutions, nor do we think that every community suffers from identical problems. What we do know is that colonized populations tend to suffer similar effects of colonization and share common struggles. Thus, we encourage readers to utilize what makes sense in your particular context, and to adapt, improve, or throw out what does not make sense.

> **"The struggle for decolonization requires us to identify clearly our objectives and to critically question whether they are constrained by the parameters of thought set by colonialism, or whether they traverse those parameters and reflect our desires as free, Indigenous Peoples of the land. We can be free, but only if we first imagine, and then seek our freedom."**
>
> **—Waziyatawin, *What Does Justice Look Like? The Struggle for Liberation in Dakota Homeland***

D. Ramping Up Resistance

In the first volume of the *Handbook, For Indigenous Eyes Only*, we wrote, "As Indigenous intellectuals concerned about the survival of our Peoples, we have included exercises and activities that we felt we could responsibly advocate as beginning decolonization strategies. We are not advocating the immediate taking up of arms or the organization of an Indigenous militia. Instead, we are advocating peaceful, intelligent, and courageous challenges to existing institutions of colonialism as well as questioning our own complicity in those institutions." We also wrote, "But, make no mistake: Decolonization ultimately requires the overturning of the colonial structure. It is not about tweaking the existing structure to make it more Indigenous-friendly or a little less oppressive. The existing system is fundamentally and irreparably flawed."

For this second volume, at least some of us are now prepared to actively encourage ramping up our resistance and organizing a resistance movement. Not only do some of us believe it is something we can responsibly advocate, we recognize that it would be irresponsible for us to recommend otherwise given the numerous crises our populations will face in the coming decades. If you are not yet willing to mobilize a serious resistance effort for your people, practice decolonization in whatever way you can. If you are willing, know you are not alone. Seek out those who are like-minded, and work to build your movement. But be careful. For example, in addition to being a colonial power, the United States is increasingly becoming a totalitarian police state. When President Obama signed the National Defense Authorization Act, he made it legal for the military to indefinitely detain without trial any US citizen perceived to be a terrorist or an accessory to terrorism. Of course, anything that threatens the state or corporate capitalism will be construed as terrorism. Our people have a long history of being labeled as terrorists precisely because Indigenous interests directly challenge colonial authority. Today is no exception, but the state has greater capacity for surveillance and suppression of resistance than at any time in the past. Still, with so much at stake, it is essential that we find ways to resist, just as our ancestors did.

For more than five hundred years, Indigenous populations have experienced the ravages of imperial powers as they annihilated our people and plundered our homelands. We observed the insanity, knowing it was suicidal to destroy the earth in that manner, and we knew that kind of pillaging could not continue indefinitely. Now, the failure of colonizer ways is written in every collapsing economy, every effect of climate change, and in every "peak" fossil fuel. Never before has the untenable nature of colonialism been so apparent here on Turtle Island. Colonial rule will come to an end. We need to prepare to take back our freedom.

Below is an excerpt from the song "Rain" by Savage Family. This particular song is a collaboration between Dakota, Nataysha, Derek, and Anthony. According to their biography, like all Savage Family lyrics, these lyrics "represent a voice of Indigenous revolution for social change in communities that are plagued by the social ills created through colonization and genocide."

Why's there so much love and yet so much pain / Let the rain wash it all away/

Ancestors call in the thunder hear them coming / Let the rain wash it all away/

Why's there so much love and yet so much pain / Let the rain wash it all away/

Ancestors call in the thunder hear them coming / Let the rain wash it all away//

What if we went back in the time living with our ancestors /

Hearing the stories of our people knowing everyone has blessed us /

Fam I'm restless, trying to find my life in this world so cold /

Searching for traditions that most boys and girls don't know /

Most never grew up with it, most never learned to live it /

But what were we supposed to do when the Cavalry came to burn the village /

Buried and burned, is anybody very concerned /

Ancestors sacrificed their lives for this we're meant to return /

Stronger than ever our connection won't be broken /

This the prophets foretold and by the unspoken for the hearts that've been stolen /

And hold in hostage by the pain, thinking it will never be the same /

Patiently waiting for the rain to wash it all away /

And I mean all away creator bring us right back /

To the traditions, back to the wisdom, we need to listen to the past /

In these times of turmoil how much longer will we survive /

How many more of our people will die in this genocidal lie (Native why) //

Chapter 2

INIDIGENOUS SURVIVAL IN THE COMING COLLAPSE

Waziyatawin

A. Are We Still Defenders of the Land?

How have our relationships to our homeland changed under colonial occupation? Do we still cherish the land as our mother, or do we see her today as a resource to be exploited for economic development? Do we still envision ourselves as protectors of the land, or have we fallen prey to a belief in our own helplessness? Do we still believe in the value of our traditional ways of existing, or have we succumbed to the belief that those ways are inferior to those of colonizing society? Are we aware of the impending threats to the planet caused by industrial civilization and the changes that will come with the end of oil, or have we embraced the belief that technological innovation will solve all current problems? To what extent have we allowed a belief in progress to impact our vision of the future? To what extent have we allowed colonizing society to define our conception of ourselves and our place in the world? To what extent have we, as Indigenous Peoples, forgotten our obligations to our homelands?

After returning to my home territory of *Minisota Makoce* (Land Where the Waters Reflect the Skies) in 2007, I became involved in the struggle to prevent the expansion of Big Stone's coal-burning power plant at the headwaters of the Minnesota River. Every day I look out over the expanse of the Minnesota River Valley, a beloved place to Dakota people, and it pains me to know how badly the integrity of the river has been compromised in the last 150 years of white occupation of Minnesota. In addition to the damage to the river valley caused by toxic runoff from farmers' fertilizers and pesticides, as well as their drain-tiling of the entire region, the first Big Stone power plant has continued to pollute the valley with mercury and other contaminants since 1975, while also contributing to global warming because of its CO_2 emissions. According to Duane Ninneman and Mary Jo Stueve of Clean Up the River Environment (CURE), the 630 megawatt plant expansion that Big Stone was proposing would have released an additional 16,448 tons of nitrogen oxide, 13,278 tons of sulfur dioxide, 348 tons of particulate matter, 4.7 million metric tons of carbon dioxide, 13,305 pounds of hydrochloric acid, and 399 pounds of mercury into the environment each year.

Yet in spite of the current contamination of the river and the potential for considerably more harm that would have been caused from Big Stone's expanded operations, it was difficult to rally any interest in resisting Big Stone among Dakota people in Minnesota. Even the tribal council from my home community would not pass a resolution formally opposing Big Stone II, although we are the closest Indigenous community living directly downwind, downgrade, and downstream from the coal-fired plant. Our tribal leaders were clearly aware of the toxins emitted from the existing Big Stone power plant and the damage it has caused to our land base and river system. Perhaps they were suffering from a sense of disempowerment and helplessness and consequently believed that none of their actions would have any impact on the proposed expansion of Big Stone. Or perhaps they believed in some way that the electric power produced from the plant was really necessary and that we, like other Americans, must accept the realities of the modern world and its voracious energy appetite. Either way, this kind of thinking is a consequence of how colonialism has impacted our minds. The end result, immobilization (no action), clearly serves the interest of the colonizer.

Fortunately, the plans for Big Stone II were squashed through a combination of environmental activism, withdrawal of investor support, and growing sentiment against coal-burning power plants. While that was a victory, it in no way affected the ongoing release of toxins by the original Ottertail Power Company's Big Stone Plant. According to the 2010 Toxic Release Inventory, Big Stone released 1.3 million pounds of toxic emissions in 2009 alone, not including dioxins or dioxin-like substances. It continues to harm all life in the Minnesota River Valley every single day.

The struggle for the river raised a fundamental question in my mind regarding our obligation to our homeland: If we will not fight to defend our land and river, what kind of Indigenous people are we?

I began to think about what is at stake for us if we continue along this trajectory and what our resistance might look like in the face of environmental catastrophe. This intellectual journey compelled me to examine literature on the end of oil, global collapse, and the fight to save the planet, and to further think about the Indigenous role in the impending struggle.

B. Global Collapse or 2012 Predictions

Given the crises facing the world community today, many of us believe we are on the cusp of major changes, whether they are environmental, economic, or spiritual. Predictions regarding the year 2012 surround us and the media bombards us with stories about NASA's solar storm warning, Armageddon, the Bible Code, galactic alignment, and magnetic polar shift, all of which indicate that the world as we know it is coming to an end. In this environment, it is difficult to sort fact from fiction, especially when many of the 2012 discussions take on a religious fervor.

Yet many of us come from Indigenous traditions that suggest major changes are upon us and our nations are on the cusp of rebirth. While Mayan prophecies are the best known in popular culture, many other Indigenous nations carry prophecies about the coming changes. As we think about the current situation, it is important for us to consider these changes in the context of the worldviews and traditions from which we come. Those worldviews and traditions will help us shape our responses to current and future threats to our nations and our homelands, as well as develop potential solutions.

Richard Heinberg, in *Powerdown: Options and Actions for a Post-Carbon World*, identifies the major challenges facing us in the twenty-first century as:

- Resource depletion
- Continued population growth
- Declining per capita food production
- Global climate change and other signs of environmental degradation
- Unsustainable levels of US debt and a potential dollar collapse
- International political instability

He states, "These problems are related to one another in complex, often mutually reinforcing ways. Taken together, they constitute the most severe challenge our species has ever faced. They represent not merely a likely culmination of human history; in their ongoing and potential environmental impacts, they also may collectively signal one of the most momentous events in all of geological time."

C. Twenty-first Century Challenges

This chapter will not address hypothetical threats to our future survival, but rather it will address some of the particular challenges we currently face in the twenty-first century largely as a consequence of industrial civilization. It is not intended to address all crisis scenarios or provide comprehensive solutions, but is intended to provoke serious discussions in Indigenous communities, however they might be defined, about Indigenous roles in the coming crises. Because everyone living today has grown up in an era of unprecedented resource extraction that has supported rapid technological innovation, we have taken the notion of progress for granted. Colonizing society has trained us to believe that American and Canadian societies represent advanced civilizations and that technology will solve any existing problems. We expect conditions to systematically and continuously improve. We expect our children to have better lives than we have had and our grandchildren better lives still. When we come from populations that have actually experienced a loss of freedom and a loss of quality of life since invasion and colonization, however, this notion of progress does not make sense. Furthermore, when we put the industrial age in broad historical context, we can quickly recognize the flaws in that kind of limited thinking. Ronald Wright, in *A Short History of Progress*, states, "Our age was bankrolled by the seizing of half a planet, extended by taking over most of the remaining half, and has been sustained by spending down new forms of natural capital, especially fossil fuels." We have created societies and ways of life utterly dependent on the continued exploitation of an endless supply of fossil fuels. Richard Heinberg in *Powerdown*, for example, describes the twentieth century as "the petroleum century, a one-time special event in human history."

Thus, the wealth and power accumulated by "advanced" industrial societies is not a product of ingenuity or superiority, rather it is the product of the massive exploitation of the natural world on an unprecedented scale. We are about to experience the devastating consequences of such harmful actions. Author James Kunstler explains:

> Today, after roughly two centuries of fossil fuels, and with extraction at an all-time high, the planet supports six and a half billion people. Subtract the fossil fuels and the human race has an obvious problem.

James Hansen, the NASA scientist who brought global warming to the attention of the world when he testified before the US Congress in the 1980s, wrote in 2009:

"The urgency of the situation crystallized only in the past few years. We now have clear evidence of the crisis.… The startling conclusion is that continued exploitation of all fossil fuels on Earth threatens not only the millions of species on the planet but also the survival of humanity itself–and the timetable is shorter than we thought."

—*Storms of My Grandchildren*

The fossil fuel bonanza was a one-time deal, and the interval we have enjoyed it in has been an anomalous period of human history. It has lasted long enough for the people now living in the advanced industrialized nations to consider it absolutely normative. Fossil fuels provided for each person in an industrialized country the equivalent of having hundreds of slaves constantly at his or her disposal. We are now unable to imagine a life without them—or think within a different socioeconomic model—and therefore we are unprepared for what is coming.

Since Kunstler wrote those words, the human population has actually crossed the threshold of seven billion and we have depleted fossil fuels further. What this means is that we do not live in a world of infinite bounty, and human societies can continue along this current trajectory only as long as cheap fossil fuels remain accessible.

More importantly, even if we continue along the current trajectory as long as the fossil fuels hold out, our survival is still in jeopardy. In fact, the future survival of all life on the planet is in jeopardy. Access to cheap fossil fuels has afforded the unsustainable burgeoning of the population of the planet, unprecedented human-caused CO_2 emissions, and the likelihood of increasing political violence. Disruptive climate change will lead to extreme weather events, humanitarian crises, and violence over remaining resources. We have what Christian Parenti has labeled a "catastrophic convergence," which means not only that several disasters (political, economic, and environmental) happen simultaneously, but that these problems also compound and amplify one another.

Challenges include not just the depletion of fossil fuel, but also the depletion of fresh and saltwater resources, as well as topsoil. For example, in spring 2009, in the farm region of southwestern Minnesota, we experienced near brown-out conditions from topsoil blowing across the farmlands. The Minnesota River Valley near Upper Sioux was covered in such a thick haze, it initially appeared that a bad prairie fire had erupted in the valley. As we drove toward Minneapolis that day, visibility in some sections was so greatly diminished that it was hard to see beyond the car directly in front of us. In their desire to plant every square acre of land, many farmers have eliminated the natural wind buffers, adding to the topsoil devastation already occurring from monoculture agribusiness. This has become a dangerous, though often overlooked, global problem. One of the major causes of poverty in parts of the world such as sub-Saharan Africa is the degradation of the soil. Populations that rely on local agriculture simply cannot feed themselves without healthy topsoil. Even in the United States, topsoil in croplands is eroding ten times faster than it is being replaced.

Similarly, in the not so distant future, water will become much more precious than oil or minerals. Maude Barlow and Tony Clarke in *Blue Gold* write, "According to the United Nations, 31 countries in the world are currently facing water stress and scarcity. Over one billion people have no access to clean drinking water and almost three billion have no access to sanitation services. By the year 2025, the world will contain 2.6 billion more people than it holds today, but as many as two-thirds of those people will be living in conditions of serious water shortage, and one-third will be living with absolute water scarcity. Demand for water will exceed availability by 56 percent." Even in 2010, the United Nations released a report stating that polluted waters kill more people each year than all forms of violence, including war. Because we often cannot see the pollution of our waterways, however, we can lull ourselves into believing, at least temporarily, that water shortages will not affect us in the United States and Canada. Yet 40 percent of the streams and rivers in the United States are already too toxic for fishing, swimming, and drinking, and aquifers are now drained far faster than they can replenish themselves. A 2007 Associated Press headline read, "U.S. water supplies drying up: Government projects at least 36 states will face water shortages within five years." Drought, pollution, population growth, urban sprawl, waste, and excess are all factors contributing to threatened water supplies.

As populations continue to grow and oil becomes more expensive, the capacity for enough food production to meet global demand will also continue to diminish. Graeme Taylor, author of *Evolution's Edge*, argues that the food crisis has already begun: "In 2007 reserves of the world's three main grains—rice, wheat and corn—fell to their lowest levels in more than two decades.… In early 2008 the World Bank said that average global food prices had risen 83% in three years. The United Nations warned that nearly 40 countries were facing critical food shortages and blamed dwindling food supplies on the combination of crop failures caused by global warming, natural disasters, wars, and farmers increasingly growing grain for animal feed and biofuels instead of food crops." Food riots, such as those we have seen in other parts of the world, will become commonplace.

Human beings are not the only ones impacted by human activities, however. The devastation humans have wrought also affects all other life on the planet. Daniel Wildcat has pointed out in *Red Alert* that "The uniquely calamitous feature of this culture is that we are killing ourselves by ending the lives of many of our other-than-human relatives on which our own lives depend." Most Indigenous cosmologies, if not all, reflect this understanding of interconnectedness. Among the Dakota, we use the phrase *mitakuyapi owas'in* (all my relations) to reflect the interrelatedness of all beings, and we understand that if one species is harmed, we are all harmed. When the biodiversity of any ecosystem is endangered, that, in turn, will serve to threaten all of us. More than a decade ago, the great twentieth century Indigenous intellectual, Vine Deloria Jr., warned us that unless pollution is controlled, mankind may extinguish itself within a generation, jeopardizing the entire planet. "Outside of massive repentance and a society turned completely around," he told us, "there appears to be no solution to modern problems." Other experts have begun to speak of the threat to the planet as the "omega point."

D. Peak Oil

On some level, we all understand that oil is a finite resource and, eventually, it will run out. Disagreements occur, however, over when the oil will run out and whether alternative sources of energy will be developed before it does. Mainstream society encourages us to be optimistic about an end to oil that will occur decades—or even centuries—into the future. As the story goes, by the time that occurs we will have developed technological solutions that will allow us to maintain our existing civilization indefinitely. There are other perspectives, however, that are not so optimistic.

The notion of peak oil was developed in the mid-1950s by an oil geologist who worked for Shell Oil Company, Dr. Marion King Hubbert. He argued that after we depleted oil reserves halfway, production would continue to drop until the reserve emptied, charting the life span of oil extraction as a bell curve. The apex of oil extraction became known as Hubbert's Peak. In 1956, much to the chagrin of the administration at Shell, he gave a seminal speech in which he predicted that peak oil in the United States would occur about 1970, after which oil production would begin to decline (see David Room and Steve Tanner, "Shell Execs Briefed on Peak Oil in 1956"). He was correct. Furthermore, Hubbert plotted oil production on a 10,000-year chart, demonstrating that industrial civilization's use of oil is "a unique event in human history, a unique event in biological history. It is non-repetitive, a blip in the span of time." His continued analysis suggested that the year 2000 would be the moment of global peak oil. Subsequent analysts amended Hubbert's model after his death in 1989

> "According to Hubbert's model, and assuming at least current levels of world petroleum consumption at 27 billion barrels a year (and notwithstanding a still hugely expanding world population and the continued rapid industrialization of China), then the world has only about thirty-seven years of oil left, in the ideal case that every last drop is pumped out."
> —James Kunstler, *The Long Emergency*

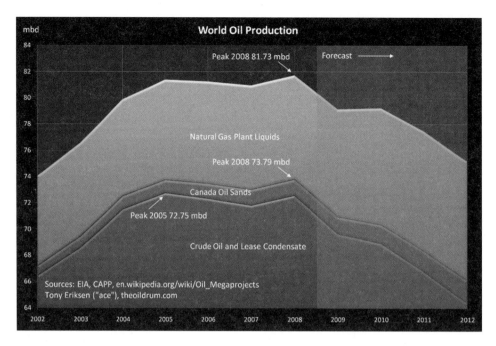

Figure 2.1. World Oil Production to 2012. From The Oil Drum website (http://www.theoildrum .com/node/5177). Chart by Tony Eriksen, courtesy of The Oil Drum and Tony Eriksen.

and estimated global peak between 2000 and 2010. Because peak oil can be confirmed only in hindsight, in the next few years we should see agreement among experts regarding the precise year of global peak oil. Many analysts already agree that it occurred sometime between 2005 and 2008. We can anticipate that world oil reserves will continue to be depleted at a rate of about 2%–4% every year.

For example, according to Tony Eriksen from the website The Oil Drum, "World oil production peaked in 2008 at 81.73 million barrels/day (mbd) shown in the chart (figure 2.1). This oil definition includes crude oil, lease condensate, oil sands and natural gas plant liquids. If natural gas plant liquids are excluded, then the production peak remains in 2008 but at 73.79 mbd. However, if oil sands are also excluded then crude oil and lease condensate production peaked in 2005 at 72.75 mbd."

Furthermore, the oil that remains on the declining side of Hubbert's peak will be harder and more energy-intensive to extract, if it can be extracted at all. At some point, if the remaining oil requires more energy to extract than is returned, ongoing drilling

will be pointless to pursue. Most of the easily accessible and best quality oil has been pumped already, and most remaining oil reserves require deeper drilling in more difficult locations, or advanced processing (as in the Alberta tar sands, for example). To compound the situation, oil resources will be running out at the same time that world demand is expanding.

What does this mean? This essentially means that the world as we know it is coming to an end. This does not necessarily mean that all life on the planet will end (or that your life will end), but that our lifestyles based on cheap fossil fuels will be impossible to sustain. Yet mainstream society continues to deny this reality.

At the Earth Summit in 1992, then president George H. W. Bush forcefully declared, "The American way of life is not negotiable." Ten years later at the follow-up summit, George W. Bush sent Colin Powell to state that "the American way of life is a blessed one." During his inaugural speech, even current US president Barack Obama praised the American way of life and promised to defend it. Americans, especially, are trained by politicians and corporate-controlled media to believe in the righteousness of this way of life

Major Products of Oil Refineries include *Asphalt, Diesel Fuel, Fuel Oils, Gasoline, Jet Fuel, Kerosene, Liquefied Petroleum Gas (LPG), Lubricating Oils, Paraffin Wax, Tar, and Petrochemicals.*

In addition to supporting the manufacturing and transportation of goods, as well as major infrastructures in industrialized nations, petroleum is also used to make thousands of other products, many of which we use every day. The partial list below is from the Ranken Energy website, but many energy companies provide similar lists used to demonstrate how pervasive our use of oil is.

Some additional petroleum products include *Solvents, Ink, Upholstery, Bicycle Tires, Sports Car Bodies, Nail Polish, Fishing Lures, Motor Oil, Bearing Grease, Floor Wax, Ballpoint Pens, Football Cleats, Sweaters, Boats, Insecticides, Dresses, Tires, Golf Bags, Perfumes, Cassettes, Dishwasher Parts, Toolboxes, Shoe Polish, Motorcycle Helmets, Caulking, Petroleum Jelly, Transparent Tape, CD Players, Faucet Washers, Antiseptics, Clothesline, Curtains, Food Preservatives, Basketballs, Soap, Vitamin Capsules, Antihistamines, Purses, Shoes, Dashboards, Cortisone, Deodorant, Footballs, Refrigerant, Panty Hose, Dyes, Putty, Percolators, Life Jackets, Rubbing Alcohol, Linings, Skis, TV Cabinets, Shag Rugs, Electrician's Tape, Tool Racks, Car Battery Cases, Epoxy, Paint, Mops, Slacks, Insect Repellent, Oil Filters, Umbrellas, Yarn, Fertilizers, Hair Coloring, Roofing, Toilet Seats, Fishing Rods, Lipstick, Denture Adhesive, Linoleum, Ice Cube Trays, Synthetic Rubber, Speakers, Plastic Wood, Electric Blankets, Glycerin, Tennis Rackets, Rubber Cement, Fishing Boots, Dice, Nylon Rope, Candles, Trash Bags, House Paint, Water Pipes, Hand Lotion, Roller Skates, Surf Boards, Shampoo, Wheels, Paint Rollers, Shower Curtains, Guitar Strings, Luggage, Aspirin, Safety Glasses, Antifreeze, Football Helmets, Awnings, Eyeglasses, Clothes, Toothbrushes, Ice Chests, Footballs, Combs, CDs & DVDs, Paintbrushes, Detergents, Vaporizers, Balloons, Sunglasses, Tents, Heart Valves, Crayons, Parachutes, Telephones, Enamel, Pillows, Dishes, Cameras, Anesthetics, Artificial Turf, Artificial Limbs, Bandages, Dentures, Model Cars, Folding Doors, Hair Curlers, Drinking Cups, Soft Contact Lenses, Movie Film, Cold Cream, Fan Belts, Car Enamel, Shaving Cream, Ammonia, Gasoline, Toothpaste, Golf Balls, and Refrigerators.*

because there is still too much money for companies and individuals to make in this capitalist, consumer-driven society. As author Pat Murphy explains, "To Americans, consuming more products and services is the critical measure of both national and personal success—even freedom." As oil becomes more and more scarce, these consumerist values become increasingly impossible to sustain. The only hope of survival in the coming years will stem from a reworking of the existing values of settler society—what we might call an indigenizing of values. The longer settler society takes to transform its values the worse will be the consequences for all of us.

Right now, all major systems and institutions in the United States and Canada are oil-dependent.

Not only is our transportation system and agricultural system entirely oil-dependent, so are the systems of modern medicine, national defense, resource extraction, communications, industry, and water. We also rely on petroleum for all our plastics, computers, and manufacturing, including the manufacture of high-tech products. For most of us who grew up in the late twentieth century, it is hard to conceive of a life without plastic because its use is so prevalent today. In addition, even the alternative sources of energy we tout as possible technological solutions for the end of oil, such as solar panels and wind turbines, require oil to produce. Essentially, all modern technology is based on oil. In other words, when the oil runs out, this way of life will not exist.

ACTIVITY:

To understand your own oil dependency, for one day attempt to document the different ways in which you use oil in your everyday life. For example, what petroleum products do you use in your home? At work? Remember, even foods consumed from industrial agriculture and feedlots are made from petroleum. David Pimentel from Cornell University has found that in North America, we use an average of ten calories of fossil fuel to produce one calorie of food energy.

_____

_____

_____

_____

_____

In addition, most of us use fossil fuels for our vehicles, to heat and cool our homes, and for electricity. Where does your energy come from? What fossil fuels are used?

_____

_____

_____

_____

The decline in oil production will be compounded by the challenges mentioned previously, particularly global climate change, water and food shortages, and the likely rise of epidemic diseases. Sustained exponential growth in the human population would not have occurred outside the context of cheap oil. The planet, without fossil fuel exploitation, has a human carrying capacity of about one billion people and probably less since our ecosystems are now so degraded. That means that at least five and a half billion human lives will be in jeopardy over the next century, as well as billions, even trillions, of non-human lives. In addition, given the wars already waged by the United States and other world powers over oil and other resources, we can anticipate that violent struggles will continue to escalate in the coming decades.

E. Alternative Energy Solutions

Few of the proposed substitutes for oil offer any real possibility of maintaining the existing daily standard of living in the United States and Canada. We have especially high hopes for renewable alternatives such as wind and solar, as they represent apparently endless sources of power that offer a logical counter to finite fossil fuel resources. Few of us stop to contemplate, however, the origin of materials for solar panels and wind turbines, or how we might access those materials, as well as manufacture, transport, and install them without oil. Even if we devoted all our remaining oil resources to the manufacture and installation of these alternative sources of energy, they would provide a solution only for the duration of the life of the panel or turbine as we would have no means to replace them. They would postpone the collapse of the existing system by only a few decades. As a consequence, analyst James Kunstler concludes, "Solar electric and wind power therefore might be viewed as accessories of the fossil fuel economy."

In the agricultural regions of the American Midwest, biodiesel was heralded as an answer to our dependency on foreign oil and farmers have turned every available acre in Dakota Territory to growing corn for ethanol. This, too, has proven to be disastrous, as biofuels have contributed to a sharp rise in food prices and the reduction in global food production, while also eliminating biodiversity and degrading both soil and water. Furthermore, like wind and solar, biofuel production is heavily oil-dependent, as are all forms of industrial agriculture. Petroleum is used for the fertilizers and pesticides, to manufacture and run the farm machinery, for irrigation pumps, and for food processing, storage, and transportation.

Even if we (foolishly) overlooked the devastating harm caused by the burning of coal and the production of toxic waste by nuclear power companies, and we decided to pursue coal and nuclear energy as viable alternatives to oil, we would find that they, too, are oil-dependent. Modern coal production requires oil for mining, processing, and shipping. Similarly, nuclear energy production is also dependent on oil for the mining of uranium and the building of nuclear reactors. Furthermore, coal and uranium are both finite resources that will also run out in the relatively near future. We have already mined the coal that is easiest to access and the best quality. The remaining coal beds will be harder to access and will require an increasing energy investment to extract. If we turned to nuclear power as a replacement energy source for oil and built the necessary power plants, uranium resources would also be depleted in a matter of decades.

There is no technological fix that will allow industrialized civilization to continue. We have been part of the most rapacious and destructive human era in history. While Indigenous nations have not set the course of this history, many of us have succumbed to myths promoted by this society. We have come to believe in the capacity of technology to solve the world's problems (most of which were created by colonizing society's technological advances). Many of us have come to accept the permanency of the United States and Canadian governments. In the context of global collapse, the sooner we shed these misconceptions, the better able we will be to conceptualize our roles in the coming collapse and strategize for the survival of our nations and our homelands.

In *Endgame*, Derrick Jensen asks us when we will fight back:

"Maybe you don't yet love the land where you live enough that you will fight for it. But what if fascists toxify not only the landscape but the bodies of those you love? What if their actions put dioxin—one of the most toxic substances known—and dozens of other carcinogens into the flesh of your lover, children, mother, brother, sister, father? Would you then fight back? What if the fascists toxify your own body? Would you still cling to the illusion that their edicts carry more weight than that brought to bear by their secret and not-so-secret police? Would you work for this regime? Would you teach others its virtues? Or would you fight back? If you will not fight back when they toxify your own body (and toxify your mind with propaganda leading you to believe their edicts carry moral weight), when, precisely, will you fight back? Give me—and more importantly yourself—a specific threshold at which you will finally take a stand. If you can't or won't give that threshold, why not?"

ACTIVITY:

When contemplating Indigenous futures in the context of collapse, it is important for us to identify which aspects of our lives are beyond the control of an oil-based society or oil-based economy. What aspects of your current lifestyle can survive without oil? Which of your activities do not require oil?

_____

_____

_____

_____

_____

_____

What aspects of your traditional culture might help you survive and thrive in a post-oil world?

_____

_____

_____

_____

_____

F. Renewing Our Roles as Defenders of the Land

Derrick Jensen, in his 2006 two-volume work, _Endgame_, relentlessly reminds us about the tremendous harm to the planet caused by industrial civilization. He creates a sense of urgency about our need to take action, an urgency that I have increasingly felt in the last few years. When reading his work, I was particularly affected by a brief statement at the head of one of his chapters:

> In the last 24 hours, over 200,000 acres of rainforest were destroyed. Thirteen million tons of toxic chemicals were released. Forty-five thousand people died of starvation, thirty-eight thousand of them children. More than one hundred plant or animal species went extinct because of civilized humans.
>
> All this in one day.

What this means is that every single day we allow this society to continue, the more endangered all Indigenous life becomes. Every single day we allow this society to continue, we jeopardize our own future survival and the survival of all we say we hold dear.

We all should be aware of threats to our homeland. Just as the Big Stone coal-burning power plant and industrial agriculture have been toxifying the Minnesota River Valley, all Indigenous homelands are under similar assault. Yet how many of us are taking direct action to challenge the perpetrators of harm to our homelands? How many of us have become so complacent in our acceptance of the actions of mainstream society that we no longer engage in acts of resistance to defend our lands? How did that happen?

At one time I believed we might be able to effect major changes by working with settler society, beginning with truth telling efforts and eventually achieving

> **Ronald Wright, in _A Short History of Progress_, explains the Paleolithic era of human existence:**
>
> **"It spans more than 99.5 per cent of human existence. During most of that time, the pace of change was so slow that entire cultural traditions (revealed mainly by their stone tool kits) replicated themselves, generation after generation, almost identically over staggering periods of time. It might take 100,000 years for a new style or technique to be developed.... The human world that individuals entered at birth was the same as the one they left at death. There was variation in events, of course—feasts, famines, local triumphs and disasters—but the patterns within each society must have seemed immutable. There was just one way of doing things, one mythology, one vocabulary, one set of stories; things were just the way they were."**

land return and reparations. I no longer believe we can wait for settler society to come to its senses and do the right thing. The magnitude of harm to the earth is too great for us to continue to allow its daily destruction. In addition, our colonizers will not likely voluntarily relinquish their power and control over our Peoples, lands, and resources. Yet we know the current way of life in North America cannot persist because it is hopelessly unsustainable. The oil is running out and changes are coming. What are our obligations amidst the growing crises?

G. Indigenous Obligations

At the 2009 Indigenous Leadership Forum at the University of Victoria in British Columbia, Blackfoot intellectual Leroy Little Bear reminded all of us that at one time Indigenous people did not have a choice about who we wanted to be. In contrast, today Indigenous people can choose to deny their Indigenous traditions or embrace them, and there is tremendous diversity among any Indigenous community or nation. We often speak different languages, practice different spiritual traditions, and hold different visions of the future. But it was not always so. Many of us have embraced a notion of change and evolution of culture that our ancestors would be hard-pressed to understand. For the vast majority of our ancestors, the nation they were born into dictated where they lived, the language they spoke, the food they ate, and the way they prayed. It was, in fact, this way for all human populations at one time. The period we live in is actually the exception. In that older context, we knew who we were, we understood our relationship to all of creation, and we knew how to survive in our homelands in a good way. Colonialism has disrupted all that, and most Indigenous people in the United States and Canada no longer adhere to those ways of being. In the context of colonialism, it is essential for all of us to consider how far we have strayed from our original directions about how we are to live in our homelands, and to work toward recovering those ancient relationships with the land and all the non-human beings that are also Indigenous to the land. Now we must also negotiate those obligations in the context of unprecedented environmental destruction and the collapse that will accompany the end of oil.

All of this places an incredible responsibility on the current and future generations to take action for the survival of our nations. The young people, in particular, face such a difficult future that they have become what I refer to as the "do or die generation." What steps should we be taking to help ensure our continued existence?

H. Indigenous Preparation

Dmitry Orlov, author of *Reinventing Collapse: Soviet Example and American Prospects,* explores the political collapse of the Soviet Union and the restructuring of Russian society as they weathered economic, social, and political crises. Drawing comparisons between the demise of the Soviet Union and the decline of the American empire, Orlov's analysis makes it clear that the United States is likely to fare much worse than the USSR in the projected collapse scenario. In the context of this collapse, the obvious priorities for everyone will be food, shelter, transportation, and security, but the United States will be particularly challenged to meet even these basic needs. Indigenous Peoples will certainly have to meet those challenges as well, but what additional concerns might we also have?

One concern is the increasing urbanization of our population. Today in the United States, about six out of every ten Indigenous people live in a city, and in Canada more than half of the Indigenous population is urban. In Aotearoa, more than eight out of ten Māori live in urban areas. Of course, even in the cities

Indigenous Action Plan

- Seek spiritual and cultural foundation
- Develop a culture of resistance
- Arm yourselves
- Assuming a sufficient land base–build your lifeboats
- Without a sufficient land base–prepare to reclaim a land base
- Work to dismantle existing structures
- Defend the land at all costs

our people are still on Indigenous homelands—they are all Indigenous homelands. But they are now areas in which surviving from the land is virtually impossible, as lands have been so paved over and polluted that ecosystems have been destroyed. Given the unsustainability of city living, there is no question that as crises ensue, most urban populations will face extreme difficulty meeting basic needs, in part because it is hard to maintain Indigenous food practices—indeed, sometimes it is even challenging to find a patch of grass to stand on! If indigeneity centers on relationship to land, then it may be time for our urban relatives to leave the cities and find ways to reconnect with earth, plants, animals, and waters. This may mean returning to reservation lands (which is also complicated by toxification and destruction of the land, as well as shortage of land) or to establish new communities within the boundaries of our traditional territories where we can seek sustainable ways to live and position ourselves so that we can more effectively challenge those who continue to harm our homelands.

Seek Spiritual and Cultural Foundation

As we begin to develop a plan of action within our communities, it is essential that we first seek a spiritual and cultural foundation. Perhaps it is most useful to begin by examining and listening to the needs of our homelands. Since our cultures were created in a specific context, it helps for us to return to that original context and redevelop our relationship with the land. As Indigenous Peoples, we probably all come from traditions that require us to care for the land, as we would care for our loving mothers. Yet in our lifetimes, all of us have witnessed humans perpetrating the most extensive harms to the land in recorded history (either oral or written). How many of us have challenged these harmful actions to our beloved homelands?

Derrick Jensen and Aric McBay, in their recently published collaboration, *What We Leave Behind*, pose some of the most challenging questions to human beings in the current age. They ask all of us, "What will be your legacy? What will you leave behind?… Will your legacy be a world who is healthier, stronger,

more resilient, more diverse, than had you never lived?" When they pose these questions, they do not mean in a cultural, spiritual, or intellectual sense. In other words, they are not asking us if we have positively affected the lives of other human beings, through our love, kindness, or charity, or whether we have made significant contributions to humankind through our benevolent actions. Rather, they are asking us, in a very physical sense, if we have left the world in a better condition because we lived. "If not," they tell us, "then the world would have been better off without you. If not, then the world would have been better off had you never been born."

If we are honest with ourselves, we know that very few of us can answer their questions positively. Our participation in industrial society, no matter how unwilling, has meant that our existence has contributed to the harm caused to Mother Earth. How many tons of garbage is each of us personally responsible for? How much have our actions contributed to CO_2 emissions? How do we participate in the destruction of the planet in a thousand different ways? How much harm to the land have we never tried to stop? And how much of this has occurred while we espouse our beautiful teachings about our sacred relationship to the land?

When I initially posed these questions at the 2009 Indigenous Leadership Forum, several Indigenous people were clearly offended at the suggestion that they might have harmed the planet. Some began to speak to the group about their cultural work (in practicing or transmitting language, spirituality, songs), which is all-important and wonderful, but it does not negate the physical harm we have perpetrated. Others spoke about our lack of choices as Indigenous people under colonial rule, as though this too absolves us of responsibility. Anyone who understands colonialism knows that any time we step out of our prescribed roles as colonized people, settler society will attempt to crush us, so this is no small point. However, if we are willing to allow harm to our homelands out of fear for our own lives, we are placing our own lives above the lives of the animals and plants, above the life of the waters, and above the life of the land. We have discontinued believing that our fate is intertwined with the fate of the land and that our lives will be forfeited if our land base is destroyed. Or we have decided that our comfort is more important today than the lives of our future generations. We have considerable work to do to leave a positive physical legacy and a healthier, more diverse planet before we die. Our success in this endeavor will largely be determined by our capacity to restore Indigenous ways of being.

Many of us contemplate how our ancestors will recognize us when we meet them in the next world. While we may possess many elements that we think will make ourselves recognizable to them, we might also possess aspects that they will not recognize or that they will have no desire to claim. They might not understand, for example, how we have become destroyers and exploiters of the lands they held dear. They might wonder where our hearts have been or where our courage has been. The sooner we begin to ask ourselves these difficult questions and engage in actions that demonstrate our commitment to an ethical way of living, the sooner we might strive to become the descendants they will proudly claim, lest "our fathers, from their tombs, *reproach* us as slaves and cowards," as Tecumseh once admonished his contemporaries.

ACTIVITY:

Where was your nation originally created? What are the needs of your homeland? How has your home territory been harmed? What are the most immediate threats to the well-being of the land and its Indigenous plant and animal life?

_____

_____

_____

_____

When we begin listening to our homelands and renew that spiritual relationship, it will help remind us of our original instructions. We can also re-examine our oral tradition and our original directions for guidance about our fundamental obligations to our homelands. It is only through this re-examination that we can take stock of how far we have strayed from those directions and what action is required for us to begin a new era of contributing to a positive legacy for the planet.

ACTIVITY:

What stories exist in your nation about the future of the planet and our role in the coming changes? What stories exist in your tradition regarding the rebirth of your nation?

_____

_____

_____

_____

_____

Develop a Culture of Resistance

As Michael Yellow Bird has outlined in his "Model of the Effects of Colonialism," one of the psychological adaptations to colonization is that the colonized have "low or no commitment to resisting different forms of racism." Colonization normalizes the oppression we experience, and even if we desire to escape the oppression, it crushes our sense of hope. The acts of resistance we do perform are frequently and violently repressed. Our defiance is paid back with severe repression by a colonizing society dedicated to maintaining control over our bodies, lands, and resources. After decades or centuries of colonization, whatever cultures of resistance many of our communities once maintained have been replaced with complacency and resignation.

To survive the collapse of industrial civilization, we will need to shed this collective complacency. We must work diligently to ignite the flame of revolution within our communities. We cannot wait for everyone to be on board before we take action, however. Actions, by whoever is willing to take them, matter most in this context. The actions of a few can inspire and mobilize a community.

Jensen and McBay define a culture of resistance as "a group of people with an understanding of the root causes of their predicament and a willingness to work together in opposition to authority to address those causes." As Indigenous Peoples under colonial rule, we know that we must work to overturn colonial authority, along with its accompanying systems and institutions, but we must also factor in the harm to our homelands. This means identifying the root causes of the devastation to the land and working to eradicate them. It also means seeking solutions to repair the damage done. However, we cannot do everything as individuals; that is why it is essential that we create a critical consciousness within our communities about the impact of colonialism on our lives, the devastation the existing society and social order is causing to ourselves and our homelands, the impending crises resulting from environmental damage and the end of oil, and the ways in which the truth of these realities is continuously denied or suppressed. Developing this critical consciousness will assist in building a culture of resistance, with the intent that individuals, families, communities, and nations will be compelled to take action to challenge the social order.

ACTIVITY:

What steps can you take to build a culture of resistance within your community? For example, are there specific media outlets or creative mediums you might use? Are there existing venues for facilitating discussions about important issues?

_____

_____

_____

_____

_____

Arm Yourselves

Taking up arms can be a frightening prospect for colonized populations who have experienced or witnessed violent state repression. Settler society, for example, so violently suppressed the last Dakota effort at military resistance—initiating a campaign of forced removals, ethnic cleansing, mass lynching, concentration camp imprisonment, and bounties—that the terrorism we experienced has strangled our dreams of liberation. We were so thoroughly traumatized by the ruthlessness with which settler society attacked our nation that each generation has carried with it the shackles of our own submission.

Yet we must remember that when we lived as free and independent nations, we were never without weapons for the protection of our lands and Peoples. It is only in the colonial context that we have been trained to believe that physical defense of our lands and Peoples is wrong. We are bombarded by messages almost daily about the moral purity of non-violence in America, yet we live under the boot of the largest purveyor of violence in the world. Who do we help by laying aside our weapons?

If, as Scott DeMuth reminds us elsewhere in this volume, colonization is war, we must also begin to broaden our conception of defense. If corporations, for example, are waging war against our homelands, we must, in defense of the lands, attack the perpetrator of harm.

Recommending that you arm yourselves does not necessarily mean that armed resistance is always a necessary or desirable component of every step of an anti-colonial struggle. Rather, it means we need to arm ourselves with an arsenal that will allow for a diversity of tactics. It does not mean we always reject non-violent action, but rather it means we are intelligent about our use of tactics, including the use of violence.

For those of us who have dreamt of revolution, weapons are a natural component of that dream. The

Lierre Keith, in a discussion on "Effective Action" (previously posted at www.inthewake.org), stated: "The most militant or extreme action isn't necessarily the most radical. The question is: what's most effective? Where are the vulnerable targets on this monster that's devouring our planet alive?" We need to learn to strategize effective use of arms in our struggle for liberation.

context of the coming collapse presents an urgent challenge for us to prepare for a worst-case scenario in which our existing land bases and resources are under additional threat as cities empty and food shortages trigger widespread panic. Given the number of weapons held by other segments of the population, it would be wise for Indigenous individuals and communities to maintain a diverse collection of weaponry.

Fortunately, Indigenous communities today remain well armed, if only because of the large percentage of hunters within our communities. This is a good beginning. We need to take inventory of our current stock of weapons and actively consider our own national or community defense to increase our possession of arms. Given the coming collapse, it would also be wise for us to consider actively reviving our pre-industrialized weaponry or those weapons we can build by hand. For some of us this might mean reviving bow and arrow making, for example. It also means critically questioning the morality of nonviolence, especially dogmatic nonviolence, since nonviolence in the post Wounded Knee era has not sufficiently kept our Peoples, lands, and waters safe from harm.

Assuming Sufficient Land Base—Build Your Lifeboats

In an interview on UCF Global Perspectives, Winona LaDuke gave a brief inventory of the resources available to people in her community at White Earth: "We have 25,000 tribal members. We have enough wild rice to feed our community, and enough deer and enough agricultural products and forest products to support those people, and enough wind energy to create a pretty strong export economy." She and others in her community have worked persistently to build their local economy and develop self-sufficiency. In terms of Minnesota populations, they may enjoy the most food security.

Most Indigenous populations, including LaDuke's neighboring Dakota communities, are not so well situated. Even among those who are seemingly prepared for global collapse, no one can entirely plan for changes resulting from global warming or invasion and other threats to additional lands and resources by surrounding non-Indigenous populations. About the

survival of Indigenous populations, Richard Heinberg wrote, "Indigenous people who have not lost their life-sustaining traditions may do well, if they live in places that have few covetable natural resources. However, the number of relatively undisturbed indigenous societies is dwindling year by year. And global climate change will challenge the survival skills of even the most tenacious tribes."

Building lifeboats means that we develop self-sufficiency so that when settler society collapses, we are not dependent upon them for our physical survival. It assumes that we already have a sufficient land base to provide for our resource needs. These needs most immediately include a large enough land base to support the population. The land base needs to be able to provide enough harvestable food (as in the case of wild rice for the Anishinabe), enough land to grow what remaining food supplies are needed to support the population, and enough land to support an animal population for sustainable hunting and fishing. If not, when we can no longer rely on the food transportation networks of settler society, our populations will starve.

Furthermore, we need to ensure a sufficient clean water supply to support our populations, as well as the animal and plant populations who will also require clean water. Because of the toxicity of the waters in North America, many of us can no longer drink from the rivers, streams, and lakes in our homelands. It may mean that in building our lifeboats, we have to work now to dig wells that may be hand-pumped, develop methods of water filtration, or build cisterns for rainwater catchment. We will need to develop filtration methods for both immediate water use and the long-term cleansing of rivers or streams, perhaps by restoring plant life that provides water filtration, for example.

Finally, we need to have a sufficient land base with resources to fulfill our shelter and clothing needs. We need to consider our environment, taking an inventory of what is plentiful and what is scarce. We may be able to rely on our traditional practices to produce shelter and clothing, or we may realize that those traditional resources no longer exist and we will have to develop new ways to create shelter and clothing.

If we do not have these basic needs met, we will need a surplus of some resources that may be used to trade with other communities to obtain what we, or our land base, cannot produce. It is important for all of us to take stock of our community's capacity for self-sufficiency. Urban populations are especially vulnerable, in that few people living in cities have access to their own water or food supply. If Indigenous people are committed to staying in urban areas, it is best to organize communities so that together they might mitigate the worst effects of urban chaos and ensure food and water security. It is important that people consider what steps might be taken now toward self-sufficiency in this context. For example, my daughter who lives in the Phillips neighborhood of Minneapolis is currently working with others to help build a food co-op. They have built raised garden beds in their front and back yards and have organized a food-share program already. In building their networks now, which in this case draws on cooperation among the Indigenous, Somali, Hispanic, and Black families inhabiting the area, they hope to have a solid system in place before any crisis hits. They encourage guerilla gardening (recovering vacant lots to grow food), and they advocate that cities and neighborhoods plant edible landscapes. Sugar maples have now been planted along Franklin Avenue in Minneapolis, the street that runs in front of the American Indian Center, and those trees will be available to tap for maple syrup in future years. These are actually the same kinds of steps that can be taken in any community, whether urban, rural, or rez, and they emphasize the need for people to work together to build community.

ACTIVITY:

What food sources does your community's land base or your neighborhood currently produce?

_____

_____

_____

Is your current source of water sufficient for your community's survival? Can you access it without electricity? If your current water source is insufficient, what steps can you take to create alternatives? Is rainwater catchment a possibility where you live?

_____

_____

_____

_____

What resources are available on your land base for producing your shelter and clothing? What will your community need to provide these basic necessities during collapse? Or, if you live in an urban area, how might you acquire supplies in a crisis context?

_____

_____

_____

_____

Prior to invasion and colonization, our lifestyles were in balance with our homelands. The lands and waters provided all our basic needs, and we were adept at surviving in that context. The recovery of our traditional knowledge, then, offers the best hope for sustainable survival on the same land base in the future. It is in our own best interest to re-learn and re-value the pre-industrial survival skills of our ancestors, as well as the traditional knowledge about our local ecologies. In the current context, however, it is unlikely that this will be enough. The introduction of non-Indigenous plant and animal species and the destruction or transformation of the land under the period of colonial rule mean that some traditional knowledge is no longer applicable, and there are lessons we must learn from contemporary society that may be useful to our own survival. For example, in the Minnesota River Valley, many of our traditional food sources are no longer available or no longer edible because of toxicity in the waterways. Thus, the fish, mussels, and water plant life that traditionally helped sustain us are threatened or toxic. Yet non-Indigenous plant species can provide food for us if we are able to recognize and harvest them. Today, for instance, Dakota people can eat a host of greens of varying tastiness that may or may not be indigenous to our territory but now grow in abundance (such as Virginia waterleaf, curly dock,

lambs-quarters, nettles, wood sorrel, ramps, dandelions, milkweed, and plantain). When we are hungry, it will matter little whether available food sources were part of our traditional diet. Similarly, if we need medicine, we will want to utilize all knowledge of both Indigenous and non-Indigenous plants.

While it is important for us to build our lifeboats at the individual and family level, that will likely not be enough in the context of collapse. Certainly, our ancestors knew that the greatest chance of survival and quality of life was ensured through kinship and community. In general, there is also a consensus among survival writers regarding the need for lifeboat building to occur at the community level. Heinberg tell us, "The strategy of individual survivalism will offer only a temporary and uncertain refuge during the energy downslope. True individual and family security will come only with community solidarity and independence. Living in a community that is weathering the downslope well will enhance personal chances of surviving and prospering far more than will individual efforts at stockpiling or growing food." Or, as my colleague Jeff Corntassel has pointed out, "This cannot be about each of us becoming 'Mad Max' and emulating the possessive individualism that pervades settler society. Rather, it's about deepening the way we live as Indigenous Peoples."

Cody Lundin, in *When All Hell Breaks Loose*, states:

"A friend of mine who teaches primitive living skills put together a 'primitive living' experiment on her land. Several people, all well versed in the hard skills it takes to live from the land, joined her for the event. For months prior, each prepared what they felt would be required to give them a fighting chance. They dried deer and elk meat, made baskets, buckskin clothing, extra footwear, hunting and fishing implements, pottery cookware, shelters, and on and on the list went. When the experiment finally commenced, more than 75 percent of the people washed out before the first week was over, many due to headaches suffered from caffeine and nicotine withdrawal! My friend ended up alone with her eight-year-old daughter for the next several weeks.

"Regardless of her knowledge and the fact that she was on her own turf, she was unable to advance beyond eating and using the stores she had initially prepared for the experiment. She couldn't gather enough new calories to break even with what she started with, let alone store a surplus for the coming weeks. The trial was conducted in late summer in northern Montana, a land where calories were not going to get any easier to find as autumn hit and winter followed.

"As she recounted her experience, she stated that the reason she failed to make any progress toward a self-sustaining lifestyle was because she had to do everything herself."

In reviewing the literature on surviving global collapse, even non-Indigenous writers usually agree that our best chance of survival will result from community cooperation. This is perhaps the most challenging aspect of lifeboat building, as it requires, first and foremost, a recognition that we are about to enter a stage of crisis. We may need to begin by implementing community discussions about the coming changes and the inevitability of the collapse of unsustainable ways of being. Like much of settler society, many Indigenous people still believe that even if problems have resulted from our reliance on fossil fuels, there will be a technological solution that will save society. The sooner we abandon this fantasy, the better prepared we will be to weather the coming changes.

Collectively committing to re-simplifying our lives, shedding materialist values, and recovering Indigenous knowledge will naturally contribute to a renewing of our relationship with our homelands. This will compel a return of the profound understanding that our survival is intertwined with the survival of the land, and that one of our fundamental obligations as Indigenous Peoples is in ensuring its health and protection. Jensen and McBay remind us that we have to move beyond ourselves in thinking about the coming changes: "Far more important than our own personal survival is the survival of the land. Far more important than making

a lifeboat for me and mine is doing something to protect the land where I live, to make it so that not merely I and mine will have a somewhat better chance of surviving, but doing something so that everyone—human and nonhuman alike—has a better chance of making it through that imperfect storm."

Increase Your Land Base

When you consider the current status of your land base and whether it can support your population post-collapse, if you determine that it cannot it is imperative that you begin to conceptualize ways to increase your land base in the immediate future. Indigenous populations have experienced the genocidal policies of colonial governments for centuries, but in the coming decades we will feel more poignantly, once again, the harm caused by our confinement to small reserves or reservations. If we exist on a land base that cannot support our population, colonial governments will be issuing another wave of death sentences to Indigenous populations. If we cannot eat, we will starve.

This is the reality that Dakota people face within our *Minisota* homeland. Our four tiny reservations, amounting to several thousand acres, are not sufficient for our populations to survive global collapse. Our populations are heavily dependent upon food from grocery stores and medicines prescribed from doctors' offices. The exception is our wealthiest community, the Shakopee Mdewakanton Sioux Community, which has used its gaming resources to acquire land, seed wild rice in the lake on their reservation, and build a Tribally Supported Agriculture (TSA) system, modeled after the Community Supported Agriculture (CSA) alternative food networks. Through their vast financial resources, they have been able to employ a team of biologists, water resource specialists, technicians, and other people with skills in land and natural resource management to work toward self-sufficiency and sustainability. But they are the exception.

Most of our Dakota communities are lacking self-sufficiency. When the collapse of transportation networks or even the increased price of gasoline affects the capacity of our people to buy food and medicines, our populations will suffer. Our options will be extraordinarily limited if we remain confined to our small parcels of land.

In this context, we have to create our own alternatives. As I have argued elsewhere, Minnesota maintains nearly twelve million acres of public land, all of which could be returned to Dakota people tomorrow without touching a single acre of privately held land. The fact that the vast majority of our nation still lives in exile because there is no land base within our homeland for them to return to is an example of ongoing colonial injustice. By not providing a land base for Dakota people, each generation of Minnesotans has prioritized recreation for its citizens over justice for Dakota people. There are literally millions of acres in state park lands, national forest lands, and tax forfeited lands that could provide a land base for Dakota people to resume our traditional subsistence practices and renew our relationship to our homeland. In the context of impending collapse, we cannot afford to wait for settler society to dispense justice to Dakota people. We will need to take action on our own.

Reclaiming land is an immediate priority for Indigenous populations facing a limited land base, including those currently living in urban areas who seek self-sufficiency and a closer relationship with the land. To prepare for land reclamation, you must first identify your land needs. Then, you will need to

target areas and plan for occupation. Finally, organize yourselves and prepare for action. Given the escalating social, political, and economic challenges around the world, there will be increasing windows of opportunity for taking action. When the windows open, we will need to mobilize immediately. Prime opportunities will occur when the government is mired in other crises, or when other anti-statist populations—including other Indigenous populations—engage in direct action. If five, ten, twenty, or fifty other Indigenous communities initiate land reclamation efforts simultaneously, we all exponentially increase our chances of success.

Dismantle the Existing Structure

Decolonization requires two components. The first component involves the work in which we need to engage within our families, our communities, and ourselves. That includes recovering our traditional knowledge and ways of being, understanding how colonialism has distorted our existence, and struggling to free ourselves from the bounds of our colonized existence. The second component involves challenging colonizer systems and institutions that serve to maintain the colonial relationship so they are eventually eradicated completely. These two components must be engaged simultaneously as one cannot occur without the other.

If, for example, we take one area of the recovery of traditional knowledge, such as the recovery of our spirituality, we can very quickly see how we cannot fully practice our spirituality if we do not simultaneously work to challenge settler society. Because our spirituality is land-based, it requires that we have full, unencumbered access to our sacred sites. It requires that our land base not be toxic. It requires us to restore and maintain a spiritual relationship with our homeland and all the plants and animals sharing the land with us. It requires pristine water. It also requires that we have the freedom to engage in practices without religious imperialists from colonizing society shoving their religions down our throats. If we live our spirituality, we will bump up against settler society at every turn. It is thus imperative that we work on challenging the colonial system that prevents us from living our birthright.

Similarly, if we work on eradicating colonial systems and institutions without recovering our traditional knowledge, we will not be able to replace them with Indigenous ways of being. When it is time for us to rebuild, we must do so from an Indigenous philosophical and spiritual center so that we do not reproduce hierarchical and oppressive systems and institutions. Thus, we must restore ways of living based on the mutual interconnectedness of, and respect for, all beings. This is impossible, however, under the current colonial relationship.

Colonizing society has conditioned most of us to assume the permanency of the nation-state and industrial civilization. We have come to view the dismantling of the American and Canadian states as an impossibility. Our ancestors were not encumbered with such psychological baggage. Before invasion and conquest, our capacity to live as free people was taken for granted. Now we must face the psychological task of challenging our assumptions about the nation-states that have held us under their boots. And we must think about how they might be strategically dismantled. If we are serious about committing to the path of decolonization, we must also be serious about challenging the nation-states that perpetuate our colonized existence. We must dare to think about how we might achieve a decolonized existence in the fullest sense of the word—a monumental psychological leap for people who have been under colonial occupation for generations.

Given the crises that will emerge even if we take no action in the coming decades—that is, even if we do not work to bring on collapse—the nation-state will become increasingly stretched and weakened. We can use those crises points to push our own agendas for land reclamation, or we may also work to help bring about the demise of industrial civilization more rapidly. We may do this by working to strategically target vulnerable areas, particularly infrastructure. This means first assessing how major networks and systems function and determining how they would best be interrupted, disabled, or dismantled. For example, the destruction caused by this society's endless appetite for energy also indicates major sites of weakness. American and Canadian societies would have a difficult time functioning without constant fuels feeding the fires of industrial civilization. Any actions we can take, then, to interrupt the production, flow, or distribution of energy will contribute to the breakdown and eventual dismantling of these societies. Our best efforts will ideally also serve to help our animal and plant relatives survive. Dams, coal-burning power plants, relay stations, pylons, transmission lines, oil and gas refineries, fuel storage sites, pipelines, oil tankers, and transmission lines would all be strategic targets. Similarly, transportation and shipping systems, communications networks, and the economic infrastructure may be disrupted through both large and small actions, especially if we focus on the bottlenecks and levers. Even minor acts of destruction to industrial civilization's infrastructure performed consistently by increasing numbers of people are costly to repair and replace, and have the potential to eventually render it inoperable. This will require us to decide that our obligations to the natural world supersede our obligations to the protection of the ongoing exploitation and destruction of our homelands. Given the current threats to the planet, this should be an easy decision for Indigenous populations, but the commitment to act on this decision will require tremendous courage, clear-mindedness, and fortitude.

ACTIVITY:

What are smaller potential actions you could take to disrupt industrial civilization's systems, institutions, and networks?

_____

_____

_____

_____

Who are the larger perpetrators of harm in your territory? How might they be disrupted, eradicated, or dismantled?

_____

_____

_____

_____

Note: While you may need to initially write down ideas and strategies for planning purposes, destroy any written records of your plans long before taking action. Furthermore, be aware that plans should not be circulated over e-mail or cell phones (like iPhones or Blackberries) because messages may be monitored and recovered.

Obviously, everyone who decides to act will need to make the moral decision about whether they are willing to put human lives at risk in our efforts to facilitate the breakup of colonial society. But even if we are personally unwilling to directly threaten or place at risk human lives for the sake of stopping this destructive and rapacious way of life, we must remember that all of life on earth is currently under threat. Our homelands and Peoples have experienced unprecedented violence perpetrated by the invaders to our homelands, and as those invaders learned to exploit greater and greater resources, the violence to our lands escalated exponentially. Indigenous Peoples did not initiate the violence, but we must take action if we want to halt or impede the continu-ing destruction. Our task is to begin by simply deciding which side we are on: the side of life, or the side of destruction of the planet.

Defend the Land at All Costs

Daniel Wildcat, in his most recent book, *Red Alert: Saving the Planet with Indigenous Knowledge*, reminds us, "In many American Indian traditions, the inalienable responsibilities we are born with require us to act, lest the Earth, our mother, and all of her children remember us as the people who forgot their relations and their relatives." Almost of us have been raised with the beautiful rhetoric regarding love of land and have cultivated a spiritual relationship with the land based on our indigeneity, yet far fewer of us are raised to take action in defense of the land and all of her children. Or, if we are compelled to take action, settler society (and previous generations of Indigenous people, including many Indigenous scholars) has con-ditioned us to channel those efforts into legal avenues for resolving harms to the land and land claims. For decades, Indigenous people have signed petitions, written letters, brought our grievances to the court-room, attempted to elect politicians who would be more Indian-friendly or environmentally friendly, and worked to shift governmental policy to protect specific land bases. In spite of all these efforts, threats to our homeland and planet have only increased.

An honest reading of the historical record sug-gests that our efforts to appeal to the goodwill of settler society have failed. Rather than conditions improving over centuries of colonization, not only are our popula-tions still suffering with alarming rates of sickness, dis-ease, incarceration, and early death, the destruction to our lands and planet has never been worse within the broad scope of planetary history. How much longer will we continue to delude ourselves into believing that the very societies and ways of life directly responsible

> "If we are the caretakers of this land, then the obligation to alter the destiny of this society is our collective responsibility. The damage done to our home-land is our collective burden."
> —Lee Maracle, *I Am Woman: A Native Perspective on Sociology and Feminism*

for these assaults on all living beings will be compelled to act morally because we have successfully appealed to their better nature, especially when there is still a profit that can be drawn from exploitation and destruction? If all our efforts to work within the legal strictures have failed to produce results, we must change our strategy and embrace the philosophy "by any means necessary" to achieve liberation for ourselves and the planet.

A much smaller population of Indigenous people in the United States and Canada has breached the legal strictures established by set-tler society in protection of the land and our capacity to live as Indigenous Peoples within our homelands. These are the people who have demonstrated a willing-ness to step outside the parameters of permissible behavior set by the colonizers seeking to keep us subjugated, and who have conse-quently risked imprisonment or death. These are the people who have blockaded roads and bridges, laid down in front of bulldozers and semi-trucks, taken up armed occupations, will-ingly stepped in front of guns aimed at themselves or animals and lands they love, sabotaged corporate or state projects, and practiced indigenous spirituality and traditions in violation of settler laws. While many of these actions are depicted as destructive or offensive by settler society, all of them may be more accurately viewed as defensive actions by Indigenous people who are trying to protect the land and ways of life that nourish the land. These are the people who place protection of the land above their own immediate personal safety and comfort. Few of us who value the old ways would question the morality of our ancestors who took up arms in defense of our lands and Peoples. More of us now need to similarly take up tactics that can most effectively put an end to the assaults to indig-enous life.

One of the reasons that I embrace the term "Indigenous" over others is that I love the notion of coming from the land or being of the land. This aligns with my understanding of our origins as Dakota people. According to our oral tradition, we did not come from anywhere else; rather, we were created from the clay of Mother Earth at the place where the Minnesota River joins the Mississippi River. In the most vital sense, we are the earth. We are Indigenous to *Minisota Makoce*.

In our age, we will witness the ultimate vindication of Indigenous ways of being through the failing of Western civilizations. For centuries, our cultures were diminished by colonizing society because we did not hold the same beliefs regarding the exploitation of the environment, about a hierarchy of creation, about progress. Yet we knew how to live sustainably on a land base for thousands of years. Now our colonizers are reaping the stupidity of their own values and ways of being as they are destroying the very planet upon which our survival depends. Our complicity as colonized populations has contributed to the harm to the earth. Ironically, now that the age is finally upon us, many Indigenous people have succumbed to the lure of materialist values and have become accustomed to a way of life disconnected from the land. It is not too late, however, for us to revitalize the ways of our ancestors and return to our traditional values of respect for all of creation and living in balance with the land.

Essentially, we must now live the meaning of indigeneity. We need to no longer exist as if we are separate from the land, as if our fates are not intertwined. When we embrace this aspect of our identity, when we resume the kinship relationships with our mother and the rest of creation, we will allow ourselves to feel more acutely the harm this society is causing creation. When we complete that reconnection, just as a mother bear would defend her cubs from harm, we will use whatever means are necessary to defend our land base. We will do whatever it takes to protect our mother.

I. Resources

Global Collapse

Barlow, Maude, and Tony Clarke. *Blue Gold: The Fight to Stop the Corporate Theft of the World's Water.* New York: New Press, 2003.

Deloria, Vine, Jr., *For This Land: Writings on Religion in America.* New York: Routledge, 1999.

De Rothschild, David. *The Global Warming Survival Handbook: 77 Essential Skills to Stop Climate Change—or Live Through It.* New York: Live Earth, 2007.

Estill, Lyle. *Small is Possible: Life in a Local Economy.* Gabriola Island, BC: New Society Publishers, 2008.

Hansen, James. *Storms of My Grandchildren: The Truth About the Coming Climate Catastrophe and Our Last Chance to Save Humanity.* New York: Bloomsbury, 2009.

Heinberg, Richard. *Blackout: Coal, Climate and the Last Energy Crisis.* Gabriola Island, BC: New Society Publishers, 2009.

———. *Peak Everything: Waking Up to the Century of Declines.* Gabriola Island, BC: New Society Publishers, 2007.

———. *Powerdown: Options and Actions for a Post-Carbon World.* Gabriola Island, BC: New Society Publishers, 2004.

Jensen, Derrick. *Endgame, Volumes 1 and 2.* New York: Seven Stories Press, 2006.

Jensen, Derrick and Aric McBay, *What We Leave Behind.* New York: Seven Stories Press, 2009.

Keith, Lierre. "Effective Action." http://www.inthewake.org.

Kunstler, James Howard. *The Long Emergency: Surviving the End of Oil, Climate Change, and Other Converging Catastrophes of the Twenty-First Century.* New York: Grove Press, 2005.

LaDuke, Winona. Interview on UCF's *Global Perspectives.* http://www.youtube.com/watch?v=62QHVOB96L0.

Layton, Peggy. *Emergency Food Storage & Survival Handbook: Everything You Need to Know to Keep Your Family Safe in a Crisis.* New York: Three Rivers Press, 2002.

Lundin, Cody. *When All Hell Breaks Loose: Stuff You Need to Survive When Disaster Strikes.* Salt Lake City: Gibbs Smith Publishers, 2007.

Manning, Richard. "The Oil We Eat: Following the Food Chain Back to Iraq." *Harper's Magazine,* February 2004, 37–45.

McBay, Aric. *Peak Oil Survival: Preparation for Life After Gridcrash.* Guilford, CT: The Lyons Press, 2006.

McBay, Aric, Lierre Keith, and Derrick Jensen. *Deep Green Resistance.* New York: Seven Stories Press, 2011.

Murphy, Pat. *Plan C: Community Survival Strategies for Peak Oil and Climate Change.* Gabriola Island, BC: New Society Publishers, 2008.

Orlov, Dmitry. *Reinventing Collapse: Soviet Example and American Prospects.* Gabriola Island, BC: New Society Publishers, 2008. In addition, view his slideshow at: http://www.slideshare.net /rksprst/closing-the-collapse-gap-presentation.

Parenti, Christian. *Tropic of Chaos: Climate Change and the New Geography of Violence.* New York: Nation Books, 2011.

Room, David, and Steve Tanner. "Running Out of Oil: Shell Execs Briefed on Peak Oil in 1956." May 5, 2008. The Cutting Edge News. http://www.thecuttingedgenews.com/index.php?article=476.

Ruppert, Michael. *Confronting Collapse: The Crisis of Energy and Money in a Post Peak Oil World, A 25-Point Program for Action.* White River Junction, VT: Chelsea Green Publishing, 2009.

———. *Crossing the Rubicon: The Decline of the American Empire at the End of the Age of Oil.* Gabriola Island, BC: New Society Publishers, 2004.

Shiva, Vandana. *Soil Not Oil: Climate Change, Peak Oil and Food Insecurity.* London: Zed Books, 2008.

Spigarelli, Jack A. *Crisis Preparedness Handbook.* Alpine, UT: Cross-Current Publishing, 2002.

Stein, Matthew. *When Technology Fails: A Manual for Self-Reliance & Planetary Survival.* White River Junction, VT: Chelsea Green Publishing, 2000.

Taylor, Graeme. *Evolution's Edge: The Coming Collapse and the Transformation of Our World.* Gabriola Island, BC: New Society Publishers, 2008.

Weaver, Andrew. *Keeping Our Cool: Canada in a Warming World.* Toronto: Viking Canada, 2008.

Wildcat, Daniel. *Red Alert: Saving the Planet with Indigenous Knowledge.* Golden, CO: Fulcrum, 2009.

Wright, Ronald. *A Short History of Progress.* New York: Carroll & Graf, 2005.

Yellow Bird, Michael, "A Model of the Effects of Colonialism." Office for the Study of Indigenous Social and Cultural Justice. School of Social Welfare, University of Kansas, 1998.

Documentaries on Global Collapse

A Crude Awakening: The Oil Crash. Dir. Ray McCormack and Basil Gelpke. DVD. Zurich, Switzerland: Lava Productions AG, 2006.

End:Civ Resist or Die. Dir. Franklin Lopez. DVD. Oakland: PM Press/subMedia.tv, 2011.

The Power of Community: How Cuba Survived Peak Oil. Dir. Faith Morgan. The Community Solution. DVD. Gabriola Island, BC: New Society Publishers, 2006.

Food Harvesting

Elias, Thomas S., and Peter A. Dykeman. *Edible Wild Plants: A North American Field Guide.* New York: Sterling, 1990.

Thayer, Samuel. *The Forager's Harvest: A Guide to Identifying, Harvesting, and Preparing. Edible Wild Plants.* Ogema, WI: Forager's Harvest, 2006.

Websites

Center for Climate and Energy Solutions (http://www.c2es.org/).

ClubOrlov (http://cluborlov.blogspot.com/).

Deep Green Resistance (http://deepgreenresistance.org/).

Exploratorium (http://www.exploratorium.edu/climate/index.html).

Hubbert Peak of Oil Production (http://www.hubbertpeak.com/).

Indigenous Environmental Network (http://www.ienearth.org/).

OilCrash.com (http://www.oilcrash.com/).

The Oil Drum (http://www.theoildrum.com/).

The Wolf at the Door (http://www.wolfatthedoor.org.uk/).

Chapter 3

RETURNING TO THE LAND
WHAT DOES IT TAKE AND ARE YOU READY?

Na'cha'uaht/ Kam'ayaam (Cliff Atleo Jr.)

A. Introduction

It is said that Vancouver Island has only three days of supplies at any given time. This includes food, fuel, and other necessities. Notably, Vancouver Island produces only 6 percent of its annual food needs. This is significant when you live on an island. It is more significant when you consider that Vancouver Island is not far from a major fault line and vulnerable to earthquakes and tidal waves. Vancouver Island is located off the coast of what is now commonly known as the province of British Columbia in western Canada. It is a little more than 32,000 sq km in size— approximately three times the size of the big island of Hawai'i—and home to more than 700,000 people. The Indigenous Peoples of Vancouver Island include Coast Salish, Kwakwaka'wakw, and Nuu-chah-nulth Peoples.

My Tsimshian name from my mother's people of Kitselas is Kam'ayaam. My Nuu-chah-nulth name from my father's people is Na'cha'uaht. My father's family is from the village of Ahousaht, and it is from the perspective of this locale that I write. Based on the three-day-supply scenario, I will discuss Nuu-chah-nulth Peoples' readiness for disaster and capacity for survival. I choose this scenario because it is the most realistic and should give us reason enough for concern. It would not take much to test the limits of self-sufficiency for the residents of Vancouver Island. In a globalized world fueled by cheap oil, this test will become more and more common everywhere. In this chapter I examine both the short-term capacity for survival in the wake of a disaster, as well as the longer-term viability for self-sufficiency in Nuu-chah-nulth Territories on the west coast of Vancouver Island. As I look at each aspect of survival, I invite you to ask similar questions about your own nation's survivability capacity in your traditional territories. It is important to remember that more than 60 percent of Indigenous people, including my fellow Nuu-chah-nulth-aht, live outside their home territories, usually in large cities. And while it is not my intention to ignore this reality, I choose to focus on survival in both the short and long term, in the context of our Indigenous homelands. In truth, I cannot imagine genuine decolonization without a serious reconnection with our homelands.

Nuu-chah-nulth people thrived in great numbers on the west coast of Vancouver Island for thousands of years. Access to abundant seafood, along with inland foods, provided Nuu-chah-nulth people and other northwest coast Indigenous Peoples with much to be thankful for. Tremendous wealth led to the development of unique societies, cultures, and intricate art forms that are still alive today. The Nuu-chah-nulth people currently number approximately eight thousand. Like most Indigenous Peoples, our numbers were reduced from 60 percent to 95 percent by the end of the nineteenth century—mostly due to succumbing to colonial diseases. Although we share many cultural similarities with our Indigenous neighbors, Nuu-chah-nulth-aht are unique among coastal Peoples for being the only ones who hunted for whales (the Inuit living near the Arctic Circle also hunted whales). All of this has changed since the arrival of settlers.

Most Nuu-chah-nulth people are now disconnected from our traditional lands and waters—living either in cities far away from our traditional territories or confined to small reservations but still cut off from our territories. Over the generations of colonization, fewer and fewer children have been taught the cultural, spiritual, and physical skills that served our ancestors

well for thousands of years. Even our participation in what some might interpret as adaptive or mixed economic activities like commercial fishing and seafood harvesting are in dramatic decline. In short, we no longer live as people of the sea as our ancestors once did. This way of life has resulted in reduced physical, mental, and social health as well as an increased dependence on government social programs. We go to grocery stores for food and to shopping malls for clothing and household goods. We have been caught up, along with others around the world, in the rise of globalization as an economic phenomenon that has increased exploitation and dependence. While we have lost many of our traditional ways of living and providing for our families, we have grown accustomed to cheap consumer goods made by underpaid Indigenous Peoples from other parts of the world. We have arrived at (and not by accident) a place where we can no longer feed ourselves from our own territories. Furthermore, our lands and waters continue to be threatened by capitalist exploitation.

Modern civilization is frighteningly dependent on an oil-based economy for food, clothing, and shelter. Increasingly efficient inventory and distribution systems have linked producers and consumers all over the world—usually in uneven and exploitative relationships—leading to our present three-day-supply scenario. One response has been the awareness by some people of the need to retain and reclaim local food knowledge. People are talking about "food security" or "food sovereignty" issues, which refer to securing access to food or maintaining local control of food. But since we only grow 6 percent of our annual food needs on Vancouver Island, we have a long way to go before achieving any real security or sovereignty. From an Indigenous perspective, food security also involves hunting, fishing, gathering, and growing—the latter being a tribute to our southern and eastern sisters and brothers who practiced various forms of agriculture more widely known than our own. From a Nuu-chah-nulth perspective, food security involves a reassertion of our rights *and* responsibilities to fish, hunt, gather, trade, and protect. The primary purpose of this chapter is to outline what our basic needs are, determine our ability to meet them independently of outsiders, and explore how we might revitalize our local food knowledge and survival skills and therefore increase our capacity for short- and long-term self-sustainability.

B. On Indigeneity, Tradition, Authenticity, and Practical Survival

Before I get into details, I want to make a short comment about the philosophical and practical orientation of this chapter. It is not my intent to examine current Nuu-chah-nulth survival skills from a strictly traditional perspective. It is my belief that being Indigenous is not dogmatically tied to a particular set of practices and traditions. I do believe, however, that Indigenous Peoples have many core principles that are sacred and inviolable such as the duty to respect all life—but our practices can adapt *and* remain consistent with an Indigenous ethic. In my view, the essence of Indigeneity is living in a way that makes sense for a particular place. This will vary from the west coast shores of the Nuu-chah-nulth people, to the eastern woodlands, rivers, and lakes of the Haudenasaunee, to the dry mesas of the Pueblos, and to the rolling plains of the Blackfoot and Dakota. All Indigenous Peoples, if they are to survive, must live in ways that respect and protect their homelands. This is what it means to be Indigenous.

When I speak of adaptation, I should mention two key contexts. The first is adaptation as a means of survival. What I mean by this is that all creatures, when faced with a changing environment like a drought, must adapt or risk being wiped out. Sometimes, our environments change so dramatically that we have to adjust our practices so that we can survive and stay in harmony with the new landscapes. My second view on adaptation is more in the context of colonization. I do not suggest that we reject everything brought over from the colonizers. Many of our ancestors utilized European tools and assimilated them *into* Indigenous practices while still respecting Indigenous worldviews. This is not to say that all things were consistent or even helpful in the long run. I am saying that, in some cases, our ancestors adopted European-based technologies without significantly altering their

ways of living. We would do well to heed this possibility now.

Traditions come about through time-tested learning, observation, and refinement. To live an authentic Indigenous life is to live in a way that allows us to fulfill our responsibilities to the land and all the living creatures that share it with us. This responsibility demands that we do not overhunt or overfish *or allow others to do so.* Keeping this in mind ensured that Nuu-chah-nulth people lived in groups that were dispersed enough so that no river system was too heavily fished. It is also important to remember that substantially more Nuu-chah-nulth people lived on the west coast of Vancouver Island than live there now, including settlers. Resources were abundant, but we also had to manage our conduct carefully.

I raise these issues to illustrate the fact that we need not limit ourselves to specific traditions to remain authentically Indigenous. Traditions require critical examination for a number of reasons. First, time and colonization have made it virtually impossible to know exactly how our people lived five hundred years ago. Second, there is no way to determine exactly how many of our traditions have been influenced or contaminated by colonial society because traditions are established and persist when they are relevant to our daily lives. Third, the issue of practical survival means that our first priorities must be shelter, water, and food access for our loved ones. This does not mean that in the long term we neglect everything else, especially our languages, cultures, and spirituality. In a disaster scenario, however, we must address our most pressing needs if we are to make it to the point where we can rebuild our communities. We must also be open to using whatever physical materials we can find to help us survive. In contemporary times that means we may have access to many kinds of implements that our ancestors did not have access to, like certain manufactured materials and firearms. Let us first consider the basics of sustainability.

C. The Basics

I used to assume that the top three priorities for human survival in order of importance were water, food, and shelter. I've since reconsidered that it might be shelter, water, and food. According to survivalist Stuart Goring, from his article, *The Reality of Food in the Bush,* human beings can survive forty days without food before any "irreparable damage is done." Comparably, we can survive for only three to four days without water. According to Goring, caloric intake *and* expenditure are vital in survival situations. He recommends, "If you are healthy, use the first few days to provide shelter, warmth, water and seek rescue." Shelter is critical because of the calories we expend to heat our bodies in colder conditions, while warm conditions require shade and access to water.

What are the basics of shelter, water, and food in a Nuu-chah-nulth context? Although Nuu-chah-nulth territory does not experience the climatic extremes of other places, the weather of this temperate rainforest is often wet and chilly, and the need for warm, dry shelter should not be underestimated. While the temperature rarely drops below freezing, visitors will tell you that we have our own unique brand of bone-chilling cold. The wind and rain factor heavily, especially during the winter months. This necessitates that shelters be sturdy, dry, warm, and well ventilated.

In the old days prior to power tools, I am told that Nuu-chah-nulth house builders used an ingenious method of splitting long, thin planks off of old growth trees while leaving the tree in place and alive. Around old village sites where some of the old growth trees remain intact, you can still see signs of this house-building activity. These trees, along with those stripped for cedar bark, have come to be known as "culturally modified trees." When I learned of this, I was inspired by the fact that contemporary Nuu-chah-nulth people could employ similar methods in the absence of chainsaws, lumber mills, and the fuel needed to run them, although immediate survival needs might necessitate the use of modern tools if we have access to them.

In the very short term we would be wise to prepare in advance and at the very least maintain access to some rugged camping equipment—tents, tarps, sleeping bags, and so on. Another factor to consider is that my Nuu-chah-nulth ancestors were semi-nomadic—moving with the seasons. They did this for easier access to resources during the optimal food gathering and preserving months as well as to seek more protected living spaces during the harsher winter months. If contemporary Nuu-chah-nulth people sought, or were forced, to return to living on the land, we would do well to follow our ancestors' semi-nomadic example. Different foods were gathered at different times from the spring to the fall, which mainly included different types of fish and shellfish.

D. Water

Now the easy part: water. Fortunately, the west coast of Vancouver Island receives an average annual rainfall of 326 cm. Compared with other places in British Columbia—84 cm for Victoria, 115 cm for Vancouver, and 27 cm for Osoyoos—we have plenty of access to the most vital aspect of human survival. That being said, the town of Tofino, which is located in our traditional territories, did experience a water shortage in the summer of 2006 that forced many tourist-oriented businesses to shut down temporarily. The Tofino example gives us a lesson in sustainability. Even in an area that receives tremendous amounts of rainfall all year long, it is still possible to live beyond our means. For the purposes of our survival scenario, however, we are blessed with plentiful access to clean water. The west coast of Vancouver Island is also full of small streams and river systems that descend from remote, mostly uninhabited mountains.

Today, aside from gathering water from rivers and streams (which is not as safe as it used to be due to increased development, particularly by mining companies), we would have to employ a system of gathering and storing fresh water. Most survival handbooks give plenty of advice on collecting and storing fresh water from a wide variety of regions and climates. Some water may have to be boiled by using contemporary means such as a gas stove and pot, as well as traditional methods, such as wooden boxes or vessels and fire-heated stones. Again, the challenge of survival may demand that we not limit ourselves to strictly traditional methods. Given that oil is a finite and destructive resource, however, we would be wise to adopt cleaner and more sustainable practices in the long term.

ACTIVITY:

Are there natural sources of clean water where you live (springs, streams, rivers, lakes)? If they are not clean, what kinds of bacteria or toxins do they contain? Can you effectively filter or cleanse the water? If so, how?

_____

_____

_____

_____

It is wise now to also investigate a water catchment system. How much rain usually falls in your territory? What methods can you use to catch and store rainwater?

_____

_____

_____

_____

E. Learn Now, Practice Now

Increasing the likelihood of survival will come from familiarity with the lands and waters of our territories. As mentioned previously, most Indigenous People live disconnected from their traditional homelands, although some still retain important knowledge of water, plant, and animal life. If we cannot learn from these people because of the physical distance between us, we will have to learn on our own. In either case it makes sense to prepare in advance by acquiring what knowledge we can from elders or contemporary sources, and practicing what we learn on the land while we can still afford to make mistakes. Some Indigenous people—particularly youth—engage in these activities via culture camps, while others continue to return to the land to hunt, trap, and gather. There are not many people who rely on these traditional activities for their complete—or even partial—subsistence, but some people are able to meet the basic food needs of their families with these traditional activities.

Goring makes an interesting point about hunting, stating that often more physical energy is expended by the individual or small group of hunters than the energy obtained from the meat, resulting in a "calorie debt" for the hunter. But at the same time, hunting makes an important contribution to the collective unit, and the hunters benefit from more efficient methods of trapping, gathering, and growing of other foods carried out by other community members. Goring suggests that because hunting is an important source of food, shelter, clothing (in the form of hides), and tools (in the form of bones, antlers, teeth, and hooves), it is best to target large game. Large land-based game in Nuu-chah-nulth territory would be limited to deer, elk, and black bears. There are cultural taboos against hunting wolves, and cougars are among the most dangerous animals to stalk and hunt. I do not suggest that you ignore small game, which may also be important especially in the context of training younger hunters, but your community considerations will adjust over time and to some extent be dictated by the urgency of your community needs. Again, many of the survival guides can provide information on hunting, trapping, and snaring animals that we may not be able to learn from our own traditions and practices. Extensive preparation and practice make sense in developing and honing these skills, especially if our traditional foods are not as plentiful as they once were, requiring us to make adjustments to the kinds of foods we eat and how we obtain it.

More plentiful than land-based game on the west coast of Vancouver Island is seafood. Nuu-chah-nulth people traditionally gathered, fished, and hunted a wide range of seafood from clams, mussels, and crabs to salmon, halibut, and cod, to larger sea mammals like seals, sea lions, and even whales. Many of these gathering activities are seasonal, however, and it is critical to know where and when to seek various species, as well as how best to preserve food for the cool winter months when harvesting is less intense. The main exception is that most shellfish are gathered during the cooler months, as they can become poisonous during the summer.

Fishing can involve a variety of methods from spearfishing in the rivers to the use of fishing weirs, nets, and simple poles with reels. While resting on shore after a canoe journey, one of my uncles actually kicked a salmon onto the beach when he noticed it swimming close to shore and had no other means of capturing it! He did have a knife, however, and was able to clean the fish and roast it over a fire for a delicious and unexpected dinner. Cod and halibut do not swim upstream, so catching them would require the use of lines, lures, and hooks. You can buy these from local outdoor stores or make them using natural implements and traditional methods. Fishing hooks can be made from animal bone or even certain hardwoods. Obtaining local knowledge about where, when, and how to capture various fish species is also critical. Access to this kind of information would greatly increase the efficiency of fishing for food. Otherwise, if we are forced to rely on the relatively random process of trial and error, our techniques might be immensely inefficient. The need for information about fishing strategies and methods highlights the importance of intergenerational knowledge sharing while it is still possible, and the urgency of learning however we can if it is not.

As Goring pointed out, if you are going to hunt, it might as well be for big game. In Nuu-chah-nulth territories, game does not get any bigger than whales. Nuu-chah-nulth people hunted mainly gray, humpback, and right whales. Other species may have been too fast or dangerous to hunt, but it has been documented that young whalers would sometimes take killer whales as proof of their whaling prowess. Just a few whales hunted annually would make a significant contribution to the nutritional needs of a community. The whale hunt of the Nuu-chah-nulth epitomizes the maximum risk of caloric expenditure, not to mention personal safety, for the potential windfall for the community in meat, oil, and tool materials. The decimation of whale populations as a result of European and Asian commercial over harvesting, in combination with assimilative government policies and international laws, resulted in disconnecting Nuu-chah-nulth people from our whaling traditions. Many whale species have returned to healthy population levels, however, and Nuu-chah-nulth people are once again reviving our whaling traditions.

After more than a century of whaling inactivity, our Nuu-chah-nulth relatives in Washington State, the Makah, successfully captured a whale in 1999, invoking an 1855 treaty with the United States. After years of preparation, they had a successful hunt using mostly traditional technology (canoe and handheld harpoons), although the US government demanded that the Makah use a large-caliber rifle to kill the whale after it had been harpooned. The Makah were successful despite a media circus and vigorous opposition by environmental groups who came up with the slogan "Save a Whale, Harpoon a Makah." I do not raise the case of the Makah because I think we have to do the same thing on Vancouver Island. The benefits would have to outweigh the costs, and Goring and others seem to suggest that a hunt of this scale would be very risky. According to family history, my great-great-grandfather, Keesta, captured only three whales in his lifetime. It is inspiring to know, however, that the Makah were successful just a few years ago. It reminds me that even skills that were thought long lost can be recovered.

ACTIVITY:

What sources of protein are abundant in your territory? How many people in your family and community are adept at hunting and fishing? What steps can you take to develop your skills in this area?

_____

_____

_____

_____

How aware are you of the abundance or scarcity of game in your area? Where would you go to find this information?

_____

_____

_____

_____

Plant food, including seaweed and various shoots, berries, and roots, are also important to the traditional Nuu-chah-nulth diet. Late Ahousaht chief Earl George remembered collecting thimbleberry shoots, salmonberry shoots, and "wild celery" as a child. People hardly do this anymore. Instead they opt for the convenience of their local grocery store. Nancy Turner, an ethnobotanist at the University of Victoria, has worked extensively with many coastal Indigenous Peoples and remains an authoritative repository of Indigenous plant knowledge. If we are to relearn all we can about edible plants in our territories (especially which poisonous ones to avoid), we must have access to the traditional knowledge retained among ourselves *and* seek the advice and support of people like Turner. Again, this kind of knowledge is extensive and will require that we prepare in advance and spread the knowledge among many people.

ACTIVITY:

Who in your community has retained knowledge about and uses traditional plants for food and medicinal purposes? Similarly, are there other non-Indigenous people who have developed knowledge about plants in your territory? How can your community begin to collectively, or even individually, recover this knowledge?

_____

_____

_____

_____

F. Contamination, Climate Change, and Traditional Foods

Scientists have been telling us for years that tuna is not safe to eat in large quantities because of mercury contamination. Other species of fish, as well as larger mammals and birds, are also showing higher levels of toxicity in their meat. Thomas Child, a Kwakwaka'wakw graduate student in Environmental Sciences at the University of Victoria, researches the degree and type of contamination in traditional west coast foods. If we begin consuming traditional foods again, we would do well to heed the findings that come from such research. In general terms, the smaller the animal—particularly for seafood—the safer it is to eat. Larger animals that feed on smaller animals typically accumulate greater amounts of toxins and contaminants.

Not only are contaminants in the food supply an immediate concern, but the long-term effects of industrialization must also be considered. Based on an emerging scientific consensus on climate change, the potential and likely impact on our traditional foods is very troubling. According to Terry Glavin, rising ocean temperatures are negatively impacting the food that salmon feed on (small, drifting organisms, or *microzooplankton*), salmon migratory routes, and spawning success. Scientists are now predicting that a further increase in ocean surface temperatures of just a few degrees will be enough to completely devastate salmon populations. It is not a stretch to say that this will have an equally devastating impact on all the species that depend on the health of the salmon—eagles, bears, seals, and humans, to name a few. The gravity of this situation demands two responses. First, we need to reassert our responsibilities by actively protecting our homelands from environmental harm. Second, in certain cases life in our territories may be irreparably harmed, requiring that we consider alternatives for our food supply.

Some of these alternatives will come from both our Indigenous and non-Indigenous allies, primarily in the area of agriculture. Peter Goodchild, in his book *Survival Skills of the North American Indians,* points out that "the gap between cultivated and wild plants was not always great. What is sometimes called 'semi-agriculture' was fairly common." Perhaps most well-known are the maize (corn) fields of Latin America or the Haudenasaunee's "three sisters" of corn, beans, and squash. Goodchild also refers to the wild rice gathering and conservation methods of the Ojibwe of the Great Lakes region as "incipient agriculture." Waziyatawin writes in *For Indigenous Eyes Only* that Indigenous Peoples throughout the Americas cultivated over three hundred major food crops (with thousands of different varieties) and that "these foods comprise about three-fifths of the food crops now under cultivation in the world."

Because Indigeneity is place-based, some methods of subsistence will not make sense on the west coast, but others may. So bountiful were the sea resources years ago, my ancestors did not have to consider other forms of subsistence, but a changing environment necessitates that all species—including humans—adapt or risk extinction. For example, many non-Indigenous settlers have been participating in local food movements, usually involving small-scale farming and organically grown vegetables. There is no reason why we cannot learn from these potential allies as well. In the Nuu-chah-nulth territories there are plenty of inland spaces like the Alberni Valley that are more conducive to agriculture than the coast.

ACTIVITY:

What species of plants can successfully be cultivated in your territory? Are there potential allies with whom you could work to either develop agricultural skills or collaborate on agricultural projects?

_____

_____

_____

_____

I have covered the major areas of food acquisition in a Nuu-chah-nulth context, but just as critical as acquisition is food preservation. Because many of the foods are gathered seasonally, it is important to know how to preserve meat and other foods for the cold winter months when very little gathering will be done. The climate on the west coast is not as extreme as other places on Turtle Island, but careful preservation cannot be ignored. According to the literature, meat was preserved primarily through smoking and drying. Whale oil was also used to preserve certain foods. In this regard, it would be prudent to learn all the effective methods of food preparation and preservation, including those from other Indigenous and non-Indigenous Peoples. In the short term this might include canning if we have access to the materials, but over the longer term we will more than likely have to resort to more traditional methods.

ACTIVITY:

What methods of food preservation did your ancestors use?

_____

_____

What other methods might you use to store foods over the relatively short and long terms?

_____

_____

What materials and skills do you need to effectively store food for your family and community?

_____

_____

Although the focus of this chapter is survival in a disaster scenario, a word or two about spirituality is important. Strictly speaking, culture and spirituality are not luxuries unimportant to long-term sustainability. They may not be so apparent as we struggle to survive in the short term, but if we are to survive indefinitely as Indigenous Peoples, our cultures and spiritual beliefs will need to re-emerge or become reformulated to meet our changing needs. The Nuu-chah-nulth believe that *heshookish tsawalk* (everything is one). Simple yet profound, this principle guides our daily actions and will inform our decisions as we look toward the future of our people. My intent here is not to discuss Nuu-chah-nulth culture and spirituality in detail, but to convey how they are inherent in all our thoughts and actions, especially as we work to rebuild self-sustaining communities. An issue that I have thus far neglected, however, is that of safety and security.

G. Safety and Security

Our struggles for healthy, self-sufficient communities would be all for naught if our communities were unnecessarily vulnerable to outside aggression or additional environmental calamities. Two major environmental threats that come to mind for the coastal territories are earthquakes and tidal waves. If all our housing was made of wood (a flexible material) and consisted of no more than one or two stories, we would be immune from most of the urban-related dangers—namely crumbling buildings. I understand that most of our people live in cities, but this scenario focuses on either living in our home territories or retreating to them in the event of a disaster. There are storms on the west coast, but not of the hurricane or typhoon variety, at least not yet.

Tidal waves, or tsunamis, on the other hand, have been a problem in the past. Many coastal peoples speak of "flood stories" that may be related to tsunamis. As recently as 1964, a tsunami generated from an Alaskan earthquake damaged nearly four hundred homes in the Alberni Valley, located thirty-two miles inland at the end of the Alberni Canal. The only precaution I can think of at present would be to ensure that our primary dwellings have relatively quick access to higher ground. Waziyatawin has reminded me of the Andaman Island natives who were able to reach safety when the 2004 tsunami hit their lands because they were attuned to warning signs. I feel certain that if our peoples made a more sustained return to our homelands, then over the next generations we too would enhance our connections to the land and be able to observe signs that now often go unnoticed until it is too late.

ACTIVITY:

What kind of natural disasters have the potential to impact your community? How did your ancestors deal with these dangers? How might you minimize the effects of these dangers?

_____

_____

_____

_____

Concerning the matter of security, our first priority would be to ensure that other Nuu-chah-nulth people could return to Nuu-chah-nulth lands. Even under dire circumstances, I cannot imagine denying recently returned Nuu-chah-nulth people access to their homelands. Fortunately, on the west coast of Vancouver Island there are still relatively few non-Indigenous people, with the exception of about three thousand people living in the towns of Tofino and Ucluelet. Port Alberni, in the traditional territories of the Tseshaht and Hupacasath tribes, is another matter.

There are about eighteen thousand people living in the Alberni Valley, with about a thousand to fifteen hundred of them being Nuu-chah-nulth. Securing the Alberni Valley would be much more difficult, but there are refuges away from the urban centers that both the Tseshaht and Hupacasath people could travel to that would be easier to secure. The primary desire for staying in the valley, however, is access to the Somass River salmon fishery and, as mentioned previously, to the fertile agricultural lands of the Alberni Valley.

ACTIVITY:

What kind of non-Indigenous presence is there in your region? If your community needed to think about defending itself from outside aggression, where would you go? What would it take to create a secure area?

_____

_____

_____

_____

Defense at its most basic level requires people who are committed and trained to protect their homelands and the means to do so. In a contemporary context, this can mean access to weapons such as firearms. In addition to the utility of the smaller hunting calibers (.223–.308), it would also be useful to have larger caliber rifles for longer ranges (.338–.50). The .223 round is effective to about 300 meters. The .308 round is effective out to 800 meters, and the .338 round is effective out to 1,500 meters. The .50 round, however, has been used in wartime to distances over two kilometers and is also effective in disabling equipment and vehicles. If you are getting a bit nervous about

this, do not worry; I am too. But I am comforted by something Waziyatawin stated in chapter 2: "Indigenous nations have never been without weapons." At this point, I am not talking about offensive actions against anyone, but merely our right to self-defense. Nuu-chah-nulth people have always been prepared for war and self-defense and there is no reason—despite decades of pacifying Christian influence—why we should not consider self-defense in our scenario here. I would like to note that defense and security are not necessarily synonymous, and I do not mean to oversimplify the issue. The broader concept of security also includes diplomacy and good relations with neighbors.

By defense, I am speaking of preparedness against outside aggression.

Ideally, we would have a fully trained, motivated, and professional force of young Nuu-chah-nulth *wit'waak* (warriors, meaning those without fear; *wii'uk* is the singular) before we *needed* them, but that is not presently the case. The experiences of the now-defunct West Coast Warrior Society, not to mention the Oka Crisis, Ipperwash, Burnt Church, or Wounded Knee II, have taught us that the Canadian and American states do not take kindly to Indigenous Peoples training for, or acting in, self-defense. However, there are other, inconspicuous approaches to training that can be taken. A key characteristic of the rugged west coast is its unique and seemingly inhospitable terrain. Familiarity with the lands, waters, mountains, and valleys of Nuu-chah-nulth territory, by any defense force, would yield significant advantages. This familiarity can be achieved, quite simply, through spending more time on the land—picking berries, gathering cedar bark, or hunting and trapping game. Add to this competent leadership and the basics of individual and group strategies, and you have the beginnings of a small but formidable defense force.

H. Fulfilling Medical Needs

Another element of safety that I want to touch on briefly concerns medical care. In a defensive context it would be important to have trained medics or first-aid attendants, but it would also be smart to have each wii'uk (warrior) familiar with the basics of first aid, including non-combat related conditions such as broken or sprained limbs and heat exhaustion. For more serious injuries and overall community health concerns, it would also be important to have experienced medical physicians. Of course, all Indigenous Peoples have extensive traditions of medicine people, which we should not overlook, but along with the warrior, the medicine man was one of the first Indigenous roles to be discouraged by the colonizers. Revitalizing a strong medicine person tradition may take more time than to train modern medical doctors.

In addition, we cannot overlook the less extreme but no less important aspects of human health care such as midwifery, elder care, and dental care. Also, our communities would benefit from a revitalized knowledge of "natural" remedies such as those derived from plants and roots. This kind of Indigenous knowledge has not been completely lost, but it will take commitment and time to ensure that it is shared again with younger practitioners for the benefit of future generations.

I. What Next? Getting from Here to There

Exploring this hypothetical scenario has been gratifying, but the reality is that most Nuu-chah-nulth people are so disconnected and disillusioned that they no longer consider a sustained return to our traditional homelands as something remotely viable. Taiaiake Alfred states that, "Ongoing Indigenous struggles against colonialism consist mainly of efforts to redress the fundamental injustice of being forcibly removed from the land or being denied access to the land to continue traditional cultural activities." The processes of colonization and Indigenous land dispossession have resulted in what Alfred calls "double-barreled psycho-physical effects" and "profound alienation." We exhibit generational trauma from having our lands taken away from us. The answer is obvious. Alfred concludes, "The message from traditional teachings and from the academic research is consistent and clear: *return to the land and re-learn how to live as Indigenous people according to the original teachings that sustained people and the earth for thousands of years.*" Just because the answer is obvious and straightforward does not mean it is easy to do. Waziyatawin and Michael Yellow Bird wrote in the beginning of *For Indigenous Eyes Only*, "When others invaded our lands and stole them from underneath our bodies, when they destroyed our ways of life and injured our peoples, they prevented us from living the way we were intended to live." Perhaps, the best we can hope for and count on is a small group of committed people who will undertake their responsibilities to relearn how to live in harmony with the land.

I have several aunts who still know how to gather cedar bark and various grasses for weaving. While they do it mostly for crafting purposes now, their skills in knowing the land and their art are still valuable. I have uncles and cousins who hunt and fish. I still have my father and others who speak the language fluently. I also have the examples of my friends Marika Swan and John Rampanen, two young Nuu-chah-nulth people who have independently returned to the lands of their ancestors in their own unique ways. Both Marika and John have concluded that an urban, Aboriginal Canadian existence—exemplified by banal consumerism and social dysfunction—is not fulfilling or healthy. Although their return to Tla-o-qui-aht and Ahousaht Territories, respectively, is at this time seasonal, they both speak of the regenerative effects of their reconnections and a commitment to eventually make their moves permanent. Others, including myself, also plan to make similar returns to our traditional territories. In this way, we hope to keep alive a few burning embers that might be reignited into a great communal flame in the future, even if only out of necessity. It is not a popular road at this time, but one we think is important, both to address our present health concerns, and not just physical but spiritual and psychological as well.

Once you gather your small group of committed individuals, you can begin the process of relearning the practical skills you will need to survive on the land. Many of the skills are generalist in nature and should be learned by everyone, but other skills may be more specialized and acquired by only a few individuals, such as advanced medicinal knowledge. Marika and John and their families have already begun this process and may be in a position to teach others what they have learned.

Again, it is unrealistic to expect masses of Indigenous people to do as you do and work to develop the practical skills to live on the land sustainably. Most of our people are too used to their hot coffee and showers and television and convenience stores to readily accept a radical change in living conditions. This does not mean that all Indigenous people living urban, Aboriginal existences are happy and fulfilled, but it does mean that if you live in the city you can still take measures to prepare for a potential disaster, and you can also prepare for the longer-term goal of decolonization that

will return you to the land of your ancestors. Many of my friends living in cities grow their own vegetables, and a few even raise chickens in their backyard.

I use the term "Aboriginal" in the same way Taiaiake Alfred and Jeff Corntassel do, implying a negative, co-opted, and acquiescent state of being. You only have to talk to Aboriginals for a short while about meaningful things to appreciate the appealing yet insidious nature of Canadian life or the "American dream." It can only help the collective if you encourage others to join you in your efforts to live a healthy, righteous Indigenous life. You can set a powerful example simply by the life you choose to live.

Jeff Corntassel speaks about "sustainable self-determination," renewal, and the need to return to an ethic of *responsibility* rather than the ethic of the rights-based *entitlement*. He concludes his paper, *Toward Sustainable Self-Determination*, with the observation, "As ancient nations, we have proven to be persistent because of our shared commitment to responsibility—we are nations that predate the rights-based state and will outlast it. Ani-yun-wiya power arises from Gadugi and *responsibilities* to our territories, families, and communities." Alfred and Corntassel remind us in their writings on "Being Indigenous" that change happens in small increments, "one warrior at a time.… The movement toward decolonization and regeneration will emanate from transformations achieved by direct-guided experience in small, personal, groups and one-on-one mentoring towards a new path." The time to forge a new path is now, even if others are unwilling to follow just yet. We cannot afford to wait for others. We must be willing to lead by example.

J. Conclusion

At the conclusion of Waziyatawin's chapter on decolonizing Indigenous diets in *For Indigenous Eyes Only*, she writes, "Our well-being is connected to the well-being of the land and all of its inhabitants. When we devote our time and energy to truly understanding those rhythms and cycles, we are closer to truly understanding who we are as Indigenous Peoples." From her book, *Lighting the Eighth Fire*, Indigenous scholar Leanne Simpson observes, "If we are to continue on a

Nishnaabeg pathway, we must choose to live as Nishnaabeg, committing to *mno bimaadziwin* (the good life or continuous birth), and committing to building resurgence. We have a choice, and that choice requires action, commitment, and responsibility. We are not simply born Nishnaabeg, even if we have "full blood." We must commit to living the good life each day. We must act. We must live our knowledge."

Again, it is unrealistic to expect great numbers of Indigenous people to embrace this path, but increased vulnerability through colonization and globalized dependence necessitates that some of us, at least, act sooner rather than later. As Leroy Little Bear states, perhaps the problem is too much choice. A few hundred years ago, we simply lived Indigenous lives, albeit in contention with settlers in some cases. Today we are overwhelmed with the sicknesses of colonization and settler society, but we cannot rely on the "advancements" of Western technology to save us. In fact, Western settler society has brought this planet to the brink of global collapse. No one can predict if collapse is imminent or hundreds of years away. What we do know is that this way of life—this "First World" existence—is killing us, our animal relatives, the planet, and any hope for a healthy future. Indeed we do have choices, but not many that will ensure the long-term health and viability of Mother Earth. If we are to save her, and ourselves, our way must be the Indigenous way. In a Nuu-chah-nulth context, we are not yet ready to resume all of our responsibilities again. We have a long way to go, but we can get there if we begin to act now.

K. Resources

Alfred, Taiaiake. "Colonialism and State Dependency." National Aboriginal Health Organization Project: Communities in Crisis, 2009.

Alfred, Taiaiake, and Jeff Corntassel. "Being Indigenous: Resurgences Against Contemporary Colonialism." *Government and Opposition* 40, no. 4 (2005): 597–614.

Corntassel, Jeff. "Toward Sustainable Self-Determination: Rethinking the Contemporary Indigenous-Rights Discourse." *Alternatives* 33, no. 1 (2008): 105–132.

Drucker, Philip. "Nootka Whaling." In *Indians of the North Pacific Coast*. Ed. Tom McFeat. Toronto: McClelland and Stewart, 1966.

Glavin, Terry. *Last Call: The Will to Save Pacific Salmon: A Report of the Pacific Salmon Forests Project*. Vancouver: David Suzuki Foundation, 1998.

Goodchild, Peter. *Survival Skills of the North American Indians*. Chicago: Chicago Review Press, 1984.

Goring, Stuart. "The Reality of Food in the Bush." *Bulletin of Primitive Technology* 37 (2009): 20–27.

Harkin, Michael. "Whales, Chiefs, and Giants: An Exploration into Nuu-chah-nulth Political Thought." *Ethnology* 37, no. 4 (1998): 317–332.

Monks, Gregory G., Alan D. McMillan, and Denis E. St. Claire. "Nuu-chah-nulth Whaling: Archeology, Species Preferences, and Cultural Importance." *Arctic Anthropology* 38, no. 1 (2001): 60–81.

Rampanen, John. Personal interview, December 1, 2008.

Reaveley, Travis. "Nuu Chah Nulth Whaling and its Significance for Social and Economic Reproduction." *Chicago Anthropology Exchange Graduate Journal of Anthropology* 28 (1998): 23–40.

Simpson, Leanne. "Our Elder Brothers: The Lifeblood of Resurgence." In *Lighting the Eighth Fire: The Liberation, Resurgence, and Protection of Indigenous Nations*. Ed. Leanne Simpson. Winnipeg: Arbeiter Ring Publishing, 2008.

Sullivan, Robert. *A Whale Hunt: Two Years on the Olympic Peninsula with the Makah and Their Canoe*. Toronto: Scribner, 2000.

Swan, Marika. Personal interview. November 30, 2008.

Turner, Nancy J. *The Earth's Blanket: Traditional Teachings for Sustainable Living*. Vancouver/Toronto: Douglas & McIntyre, 2005.

Waziyatawin. "Decolonizing Indigenous Diets." In *For Indigenous Eyes Only: A Decolonization Handbook*. Ed. Waziyatawin Angela Wilson and Michael Yellow Bird, 67–85. Santa Fe: School of American Research, 2008.

———. "Reclaiming Indigenous Homelands." Lecture given at the Indigenous Leadership Forum, Victoria, BC, May 13, 2009.

Waziyatawin and Michael Yellow Bird. "Beginning Decolonization." In *For Indigenous Eyes Only: A Decolonization Handbook*. Ed. Waziyatawin Angela Wilson and Michael Yellow Bird, 1–7. Santa Fe: School of American Research, 2008.

Websites

CBCNews. "Visitors scramble as water shortage shuts Tofino businesses." http://www.cbc.ca/canada/british-columbia /story/2006/08/30/tofino-water.html.

Environment Canada (http://www.climate.weatheroffice.ec.gc.ca /climate_normals/index_e.html).

Chapter 4

NEURODECOLONIZATION
USING MINDFULNESS PRACTICES TO DELETE THE NEURAL NETWORKS OF COLONIALISM

Michael Yellow Bird

A. Introduction and Background

This chapter* focuses on a new mind brain science called *neurodecolonization*, which refers to how the human brain (figure 4.1) functions in a colonial situation and how specific mind and brain activities can change important neural networks to enable a person to overcome the myriad effects of colonialism. The *mind* can be thought of as our perceptions, higher order thinking, and consciousness. Our *brain* is the physical organ that changes its structure and function according to the needs of our mind.

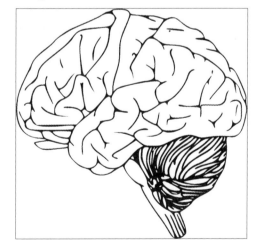

Figure 4.1. The Human Brain, Open Clip Art Library (OCAL).

*Another version of this chapter will be published in the forthcoming book *Decolonizing Social Work*, Burlington, VT: Ashgate Press.

Neurodecolonization advocates that Indigenous Peoples engage in mainstream, secular, contemplative practices such as mindfulness, as well as their own contemplative practices that may be traditional, contemporary, secular, or sacred. Although there are a number of important mind brain strategies that can change our brains, this chapter focuses on mindfulness meditation practices since they are (1) easy to implement; (2) low to no cost to undertake; (3) culturally appropriate and in line with many contemplative practices of Indigenous Peoples; and (4) proven to be highly effective in changing the mind and brain in profound and positive ways. In the activity sections, this chapter asks the reader to investigate and discuss with others which traditional contemplative practices of their community might be used to decolonize the mind and brain from their unhealthy attachments and experiences. You can even make a list that you think distinguishes colonized behaviors, thinking, and feelings from those that you consider to be decolonized.

In the introduction of this book we state that in order for decolonization to be successful it must begin in our minds. We believe that creative, healthy, decolonized thinking, actions, and feelings positively shape and empower important neural circuits in our brain, which in turn provide us with the personal resources, strengths, talents, and abilities we need to overcome the oppressions of colonialism. We believe that a healthy, well-balanced mind and brain are essential to helping one to engage in proactive, creative, and successful decolonization activities. On the other hand, we are convinced that unconstructive, negative thinking, feelings, and behaviors dampen and short-circuit our brain's creativity and optimism networks, and increase our susceptibility to the many stresses that arise in everyday life; we believe that these "regular" stressors are made even worse by the additional traumas of colonialism.

We are not alone in our position. A large body of neuroscience research shows that our brains have the capacity to change throughout our lives based on our experiences. Science writer Sharon Begley says that how our brain changes depends on how we train our minds to engage the world. Our brain's capacity to change to accommodate our wishes and experiences is referred to as *neuroplasticity*, which is discussed later in this chapter. For now, just remember that scientific research shows that when we engage in healthy, constructive thinking, feelings, and behaviors, our brains (and our lives) change for the better. Many sophisticated brain imaging studies show that neural circuits associated with well-being and other positive attributes become activated and strengthened when we purposely engage in positive thinking and behaviors. The longer, more frequently, creatively, and intensely we engage in these constructive activities, the stronger and more capable these neural networks become.

Of course the reverse is also true. A life that is filled with negativity, stress, and destructiveness actually damages our brains and bodies and ushers in greater levels of mental and physical suffering and dissatisfaction. And, as we remain in the states of negativity and engage in faulty thinking, feeling, and behavior, we strengthen our brain's neural circuits of despair, fear, anger, and helplessness. Norman Doidge, neuroscientist and author of the best-selling book *The Brain That Changes Itself: Stories of Personal Triumph from the Frontiers of Brain Science,* refers to our brain's ability to stubbornly retain and display our bad habits and disorders as the "plasticity paradox."

This chapter begins with a short discussion on negativity and how the human brain is strongly wired for this emotion. I am initiating this dialogue because many of us may mistake our negativity as only a product of colonialism, which I believe gives colonialism too much credit and power. In the next section I share a mindfulness practice exercise and allow you to process your experience by contemplating some questions that I ask. Following this, I provide a definition and discussion of neurodecolonization and share a mindfulness neurodecolonization exercise. In the next two sections I discuss what mindfulness is, the neurobiology of mindfulness (what happens to your brain when you meditate), and how I have used mindfulness practices as a neurodecolonization tool. I explain what this means for your well-being and how it contributes to decolonization, and end the chapter by providing some suggestions for an Indigenous Peoples' mind brain policy. Throughout this chapter I include mindfulness exercises that can be practiced and discussed in terms of their relevance for personal and community decolonization.

B. A Special Note on Negativity

It does not take colonialism to create feelings of deep negativity in us. The oppressions from colonialism certainly make our negativity much worse, but from our traditional trickster stories that long preceded European and American colonialism, many of us realize that we humans can be a fairly egotistical and negative species. The importance of understanding the risks of negativity and an overinflated ego are undoubtedly one of the many reasons that our ancestors urged us to practice deep introspection and humility in our daily lives. We are also an optimistic species, but as the brain science will show later in this chapter, the *compassionate feelings* and *self-awareness* (both situated in a younger part of the brain), which we need in order to graciously interact with others, can be easily overridden by *negative feelings* and *aggressions* (situated in the oldest part of the brain). In order to successfully decolonize our harmful, obstructive emotions, thoughts, and behaviors, we must understand this imbalance and have the courage to confront it.

From neuroscience studies we know that the human brain is wired for negativity. While we humans do display many acts of compassion and respect toward the people and other beings that we have come to trust and love, in most cases we are much more likely to take the low road of negativity when we get annoyed or upset. In the book *Buddha's Brain: The practical neuroscience of happiness, love, and wisdom*, Rick Hanson, PhD, and Richard Mendius, MD, discuss the human brain, its functions, and its evolutionary history. While they delve into the many beautiful attributes of our brains, they are quick to conclude that we are programmed for negativity, which is a bit depressing. Oops, there goes my negativity.

Still, there is strength in our brain's negativity. According to Hanson and Mendius, without it, it would be difficult for our species to survive. For instance, imagine one of our ancient ancestors hiking

home along a riverbank after a long visit with relatives downstream. After many miles and hours of not eating, she or he suddenly comes upon a bush that is loaded with bright, beautiful, plump berries, which have never been seen before. Two alarms in the brain go off. The first is "Wow!" "Food!" The second is more measured, thoughtful, and pessimistic: "*Hmmmm. They look tasty but what if they're poisonous? Better to wait and eat when I get home.*" In the second scenario, negativity certainly becomes beneficial if, in fact, the berries are poisonous: disaster averted. I often think about our negative brain bias as functioning like an on and off switch that is mostly turned on, or easily flipped to the on position (in other words, usually negative).

While negativity resides in our feelings and behaviors, it is most abundant in our thoughts. For instance, according to a study by the US National Science Foundation (NSF), it is estimated that we humans have 12,000 to 50,000 thoughts a day; some folks may have as many as 60,000. It is also estimated that up to 80 percent of those thoughts are negative—some of them little irritants like "I don't like Mom's fry bread, Grandma's is better," or "geez that jingle dress looks pretty tight on her," or "I don't like the color of the paint on my bedroom walls," or "I don't like how his cologne smells," or "I don't like how my teenager wears his pants." As you can see, these "little" negatives can add up very quickly.

On the flip side, negative thoughts can be horrifying beyond belief. A person can have sustained, intense traumas creating the belief that he or she may have contracted a deadly illness, or that the world is going to end in a fireball of destruction in the year 2012, or after death she or he will be doomed to spending an eternal afterlife in extreme heat, pain, and suffering, while shoveling coal without any breaks for a drink of cool water. These last examples, in my opinion, represent the times when negativity crosses over to become a liability, a burden, and unhealthy since the brain has wandered into an imagined future that may never be. This kind of flawed thinking is regarded as *cognitive bias*, which refers to our patterns of perceptual distortions, inaccurate judgment, and irrationality. How often do you find yourself in the loops of negative thinking and cognitive bias?

In a 2003 article "Why We Love Bad News," published in the magazine *Psychology Today*, the negativity bias is discussed through the research of Dr. John T. Cacioppo, a distinguished professor and the director of the Center for Cognitive and Social Neuroscience at the University of Chicago. Dr. Cacioppo used sophisticated imaging technology to show that the brain reacts more strongly to stimuli that is considered negative. His studies show that there is a greater surge in electrical activity when one is exposed to what is perceived as negative versus what is considered to be positive or neutral. In other words, our views are much more likely to be shaped by pessimistic news than positive news.

The last bit of information that is important for us to know about our negative brain bias is that it has been around for hundreds of millions of years. Evolutionary brain biologists refer to the oldest part of our brain as the *hind brain* or *reptilian brain,* which we share in common with all other species that have a backbone. So, our ancestors were right—we are related to all life.

Our reptilian brain is on duty 24/7 and is in charge of our survival. It controls our body functions such as breathing, heart rate, balance, and body temperature, which are essential to life.

This part of the brain is regarded as being reliable but rigid and compulsive. It is most often associated with what some neuroscientists refer to as the five F's: fighting, feeding, fearing, fleeing, and fornicating. Defending territory, ideas, beliefs, and your girlfriend or boyfriend, husband or wife, from other suitors using aggression is a key function of this part of the brain. In other words, "might is right!" Sexual behavior is instinctive, responses are automatic, our emotions are more stimulated, and negativity and anxiety flow easily.

When our reptilian brain is in charge, which is a good part of the time for most of us, it is much harder to access the neural networks in our brains that are in charge of compassion, self-awareness, and emotional intelligence. This is also true for the part of the brain

that is referred to as the limbic system, which I will discuss later on. In the book *How God Changes Your Brain: Breakthrough Findings from a Leading Neuroscientist,* authors Andrew Newberg and Mark Robert Waldman tell us that the *anterior cingulate* is a special part of our brain that is involved with some of our deepest levels of humanity. For instance, our compassion, social awareness, and ability to recognize the feelings of others (emotional intelligence) are located here. This region of our brain is associated with our ability to decrease our propensity to express and react with anger and fear. It is where our deepest feelings of love reside.

Newberg and Waldman are quick to point out that the neurons in this area are very vulnerable to being overridden by our reptilian or limbic part of our brain, which has been around much longer. In their view, we are much more likely to engage in fighting, aggression, anger, and fear than we are in acts of love, compassion, generosity, and acceptance. Newberg and Waldman report that the neurons in the anterior cingulate have been around for only about fifteen million years, while the "amygdala" (responsible for generating fear and aggression) in the reptilian part of the brain has been around for four hundred and fifty million years. In terms of strength of influence on our behavior and attitudes, the reptilian brain is thirty times older (and stronger) than the compassionate, empathetic, socially aware anterior cingulate part of the brain.

There are many ways out of our negativity brain bias. Some of them are as old as Indigenous culture itself: practicing positive thinking, speech, actions, and feelings; engaging in mindfulness meditation; stopping ourselves from ruminating on the hurtful past and uncertain future (this is where the constant thinking about and discussions of *historical trauma,* without effective neurodecolonization strategies, has, in my opinion, become a liability for decolonization); and, finally, engagement in contemplative prayer that is personally loving and extends love to all creatures and sentient beings on the planet.

But be careful how and to whom you pray. According to Newberg and Waldman, prayer that centers on the fear of retribution and punishment from a critical, "I'm going to get you, my pretty (and your little dog Toto)," or a "fire and brimstone" kind of God, activates the neural circuits of fear and negativity in the reptilian brain, blocking access to the compassion, love, and acceptance that reside in the anterior cingulate.

ACTIVITY:

What things or experiences do you feel contribute to your negativity? How much (what percent) of your thinking do you feel is negative and positive? When is negativity helpful or unhelpful? What traditional practices does your community use to reverse the negativity of individuals or of the community?

_____

_____

_____

_____

_____

_____

_____

_____

C. Sitting Mindfulness Practice

My oldest daughter, Arundhati (figure 4.2), was two and a half years old when her mother took this picture. She is now nearly five years old at the writing of this chapter. Since she was about a year and a half, she has been engaging in mindfulness meditation practices. I understand the neurobiology behind her meditation and how good it is for her brain and well-being, so I have persisted in making sure that she practices every day.

> "Every single person has within, an ocean of pure vibrant consciousness. Every single human being can experience that— infinite intelligence, infinite creativity, infinite happiness, infinite energy, infinite dynamic peace."
>
> —David Lynch, interview, *The New York Times*

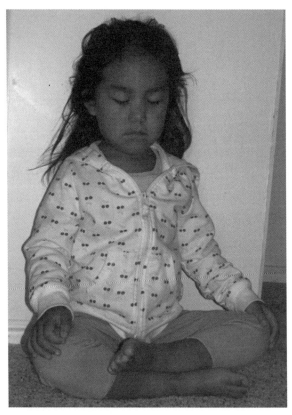

Figure 4.2. Arundhati Yellow Bird, two and a half years old, practicing mindfulness. Photo from author's collection.

ACTIVITY:

Here is a mindfulness practice that you can try at home. This is an exercise that we do at home each morning. At the end of the practice, write down what this experience was like.

1. What you need: stopwatch with a timer, ten minutes to do this exercise. Read each point completely before attempting. As you work on this practice, you can gradually increase the number of minutes.

2. Find a quiet place.

3. Get into a comfortable position sitting in a chair or cross-legged on the floor. If you choose the floor, you can sit on a pillow or a cushion to help support you and to reduce the strain on your knees.

4. As you get into your sitting position, make sure that you keep your back straight but relaxed and your neck aligned with your spine. If you choose to sit in a chair, sit away from the backrest.

5. If you are sitting on a chair, make sure that both feet are resting on the floor. Relax your shoulders and put your hands, palms down, on the top of your legs. If you are sitting on the floor, rest your hands on your lap. One hand can rest inside the other, with palms facing upward, fingers slightly and gently curled up, and thumbs lightly touching.

6. Take a deep breath and settle into a relaxed, balanced position that feels grounded and calm. Relax your jaws and allow the tip of your tongue to be in light contact with the back of your top teeth.

7. Close your eyes and bring your attention to calming your breathing. Settle into your breath but do not force it. Just allow it to be as natural as possible. Allow yourself to experience what this natural, relaxed breathing feels like for a bit. When you are ready, gently shift your attention away from the sensations of your breathing and imagine your breath as it leaves your nostrils and returns to you in the form of new, fresh air. What does it look like? Is it soft or hard? Is it a different color when you breathe in and breathe out? Spend a moment to see if you can see a picture of what your breath looks like.

> **"What you think you become."**
> —**Buddha**

8. When you are ready, see if you can feel any difference in the temperature of your breath as it leaves your nose and as it comes back in. Does it feel slightly warmer when it leaves your nose because it has been warmed by your body? Does it feel a bit cooler as it enters the tips of your nostrils? Again, allow yourself to experience this for a bit.

9. If any thoughts come up that distract you away from observing your breath, that's fine. Regard them as teachers of what you are or have experienced. Observe their content and how they make you feel, but do not get attached to them or judge them. Just allow them to be and then simply return to your breathing as soon as you remember to do so. Gently remind yourself to connect a bit more deeply with being aware of your breath after you have let go of each distraction. It is important not to get frustrated or judge yourself when you get distracted. Just stay relaxed and continue to return to your breathing, remembering that it is your anchor.

10. When you are ready, gently open your eyes and continue to let your breathing be relaxed and natural. Take a deep, cleansing breath and observe how you feel and what your surroundings look like. Write down what this experience was like. Was it pleasant, difficult, or relaxing? In what ways? What was happening in your mind or body? Can you say what thoughts, feelings, and beliefs might have come up that are related to having a colonized mind? For instance, colonial society may have imposed the beliefs in you that your Indigenous culture, language, or beliefs are inferior.

_____

_____

_____

_____

_____

D. Neurodecolonization Defined

Neurodecolonization involves understanding how the mind and brain function and are shaped by the stresses of colonialism. Some stressors include, but are certainly not limited to, racism and hate crimes; loss of territories, culture, and pride; high levels of mortality, poverty, and poor health; and disregard of Indigenous Peoples' sovereignty and rights. Neurodecolonization concerns the deliberate and systematic use of particular exercises and activities that can be used to transform one's mind and brain structures and functions to attain the highest levels of performance and well-being. Neuroscience research shows that deep reflective prayer and sacred ceremonies and practices; positive thinking and concentration exercises; and using visualization or creative imagery and meditation are just a few on a long list of practices that can create positive changes in our brains.

The goal of neurodecolonization is to delete old, ineffective brain networks that support destructive thoughts, feelings, memories, and behaviors—not only those that occur for most people, but also those that are intimately connected to the past and contemporary oppressions associated with colonialism. For instance, a past colonialism that may create negativity, sadness, and anger in us (and activate our brains' networks of feelings of helplessness) might be our memories of our parents' or grandparents' awful treatment in Indian boarding or residential schools. A current colonialism that may activate our neural networks of intense emotions and boiling anger might be someone calling us a racist name such as a "squaw" or "redskin."

ACTIVITY:

Make a list of as many other stressors that you can think of and how you think they affect the feelings, beliefs, and behaviors of Indigenous Peoples.

_____

_____

_____

_____

_____

_____

The goal of neurodecolonization is also to encourage the growth of new beneficial brain networks, which enable us to engage in a level of optimistic thinking that permits us to believe that we can overcome the oppression of colonialism, develop the courage to confront it, and cultivate the creativity we need to use novel, effective approaches to change it. Neurodecolonization does not say that we should not think or have intense feelings about the past or present events of colonialism. It merely informs us that we can change the way we think, feel, and behave; and that when we do spend time thinking, feeling, and reacting to the events in unproductive ways there are consequences: we actually strengthen the unproductive neural networks and become even more proficient at being an angry, depressed, and frustrated victim. Indeed, as Grandma and the Buddha have both said, "Be careful how you think and what you think about because you will become what you think!"

The neurodecolonization framework has been influenced by many recent discoveries in the neurosciences that demonstrate the powerful role that the mind and brain can play in improving one's health, performance, and well-being. Powerful brain imaging technologies have led the way, enabling us to see what happens to the brain when it is given different tasks, senses different emotions, processes different experiences, makes decisions, or is at rest. For instance, fMRI (functional magnetic resonance imaging) uses powerful magnets to record blood flow to functioning areas of the brain that become activated during different experiences, while EEG (electroencephalogram) tests can allow us to see electrical changes in the brain (as brain band waves) when the brain is engaged or at rest.

The first part of the term "*neuro*" (in neurodecolonization) refers to neurons, which are specialized cells in our nervous system (brain and spinal cord) that send and receive electric signals throughout our bodies. *Decolonization* refers to activities that weaken the effects of colonialism and create opportunities to promote traditional practices in present-day settings.

The neurons in our brains are responsible for organizing and processing our five senses, thoughts, moods, and emotions. Neurons assemble themselves into neural networks in our brains, which enable them to communicate and work together on a particular task. For instance, if we want to learn something new (creating a neurodecolonization meditation application for your iPhone that you listen to three times a day) or remember something old (empowerment words from your Indigenous language that your grandmother taught you), we call upon our neurons to help us do so. There are about one hundred billion neurons in the brain and one hundred billion in the rest of the body constantly communicating and taking action or remaining in the state of readiness.

A healthy functioning mind and brain are the greatest assets we have to promote healthy, intelligent, and mindful decolonization processes. As internationally known clinical neuroscientist and best-selling author Daniel Amen, MD, writes in his book *Making a Good Brain Great,* our brains are involved in all that we do. Dr. Amen says that our brain determines how effective we will be in our lives. When our brain works right, we work right. On the other hand, when our brains are troubled we are much more likely to experience trouble in our lives. Numerous health care professionals, researchers, scientists, government and private organizations, and self-help specialists agree with Dr. Amen's position, and many are advocating and implementing programs to improve the functioning of the brains of the populations they serve. In fact, changing the brain to make it more happy and healthy has become somewhat of a major for-profit industry. Bookstores, magazines, newspapers, newsletters, advertising signs, and websites are flooded with the latest research (good and bad) of how one can change his or her brain to improve relationships, lose weight, develop washboard abs, improve memory, heal from trauma and other illnesses, sleep better, and (you guessed it) make lots of money from the abundant universe!

ACTIVITY:

A Neurodecolonization Mindfulness Exercise

Think of an *experience, problem,* or *emotion* that you can attribute to the effects of colonialism or that you feel has been made worse by colonialism. Do not pick something that will trigger excessive negative, sad emotions or re-create trauma. Pick something that you know you want to work on. (As a refresher, think of colonialism as policies, practices, attitudes, beliefs, and values of a colonizing society that have been personally damaging).

Silently repeat the experience, problem, or emotion to yourself as you sit quietly on the floor or in a chair. Make sure you keep your back straight but relaxed and your neck aligned with your spine. Close your eyes if you would like, or you can keep them slightly opened as you focus on an area in front of you or on the floor. If you are sitting in a chair, make sure that both feet are resting on the floor. Relax your shoulders and put your hands, palms down, on the top of your legs. If you are sitting on the floor, rest your hands on your lap. One hand can rest inside the other, with palms facing upward, fingers slightly and gently curled up, and thumbs lightly touching. When you are ready, begin breathing in and out, silently repeating the twelve statements below. To begin with, spend about one minute on each (twelve minutes total). As you get better at it, you can increase your time. These exercises are adapted from Ken McLeod's "Seeing from the Inside" meditation:

Breathing in I feel this experience/problem/emotion

Breathing out I feel this emotion

Breathing in I feel my reactions to this experience

Breathing out I feel my reactions to this experience

Breathing in I am calm in this problem

Breathing out I am calm in this problem

Breathing in I understand how this emotion arises

Breathing out I understand how this emotion arises

Breathing in I creatively overcome this emotion

Breathing out I creatively overcome this emotion

Breathing in I see the fading of this problem

Breathing out I see the fading of this problem

Overall, how do you feel after practicing these exercises? Were any parts easier or more difficult? Can you say why you may have reacted more or less to the different exercises? If you could choose to eliminate an experience, problem, or emotion, which would it be?

_____

_____

_____

_____

_____

E. What Is Mindfulness?

Mindfulness is an activity that is credited with helping to heal and improve our health, minds, brains, and bodies. The two exercises you have done so far are mindfulness practices. There is a large and growing scientific literature that describes how the practices of mindfulness are being successfully used with a number of different populations to treat many medical and mental health conditions. Mindfulness practices are also used to help adults and children enhance their intelligence, self-esteem, life satisfaction, optimism, creativity, compassion, ability to focus and relax, and acceptance of where one is in life. This last statement should not be thought of as being satisfied with staying where one is in life, especially if circumstances are difficult. Rather, it means that you are not spending your time wishing that things were different and despising where you are. It means that you learn to be okay with where you are at the moment,

> **"To the mind that is still, the whole universe surrenders."**
> **—Lao Tzu**

but understand that you have opportunities for growth that you can act on when you are ready.

Mindfulness is a very powerful tool for liberating the mind and brain from oppressive thinking, feelings, and actions. It is an ancient practice that engages the mind and brain to enter into states of deep, sustained wakefulness for the purpose of gaining greater awareness and insight into one's life and reality. In mindfulness practice we do not judge any thoughts, feelings, or memories that arise, nor do we try to hold on to them or push them away; instead we work on being with them just as they are.

Mindfulness refers to being deeply aware of what is happening from moment to moment, outside and inside us, without judging or attaching to the content, feelings, and emotions that arise. It refers to living deeply and richly in the present moment and not responding to life in a distracted and mechanical manner. For instance, when we eat mindfully we slow down the pace of our eating and become deeply aware of the taste, texture, smell, temperature of the food, and feeling of fullness. When we eat mindlessly we miss most of these rich experiences with our food; many times we do not taste it and end up overeating or maybe eating something that is bad for us. After mindless eating we often end up not feeling well. Mindless eating is one of the major reasons why there has been such a meteoric rise in food-related obesity, hypertension, cancer, heart disease, and diabetes among Indigenous Peoples.

ACTIVITY:

Mindful eating is an exercise that is a core practice in learning mindfulness. It can help you to build your mindfulness meditation skills and help you to eat a healthier diet. The following exercise to promote mindful eating is adapted from Thich Nhat Hanh's book *Peace Is Every Step: The Path of Mindfulness in Everyday Life*. Make sure that you try this activity in a quiet place, on your own.

Choose a time and place that promote mindful eating. Try eating in a quiet, distraction-free environment. This means no eating in front of the television or reading while you eat. Your only task is to eat in an unrushed, deliberate manner.

Before you begin, look down at your food. Take in what it looks like, and how it smells, and think about where it came from. Before you take a bite, see if you can notice the urge to eat (e.g., your mouth watering, the feeling of hunger).

Put a bite in your mouth. Notice how the food feels in your mouth and what it tastes like. Before you swallow, notice the things that happen in your mouth when you put food in. Notice how you salivate, notice the urge to swallow, notice the sensation of chewing.

As you swallow your food, notice what that feels like. How does your stomach feel now that it is one bite closer to being full?

Repeat your mindful eating for each bite until your meal is finished. Try to decide when the meal is done based on the sensations in your body (e.g., the feeling of fullness in your belly, no more sensation of hunger) rather than on whether your plate is clean.

Write down what you noticed about this exercise. Was it difficult? Did your food taste any different? What was your brain saying to you?

_____

_____

_____

_____

_____

Developing mindfulness involves systematic training and practice and is a process that takes place over time. Aside from mindful eating, mindfulness can be deepened through formal practices such as mindful sitting (meditation), walking, doing an exercise called the *body scan*, or almost any other activity that we are willing to bring the full scale of our focus and attention to. Mindfulness is a journey that is well worth the trip because it enables us to enter into states of deep awareness and understanding of our world and experiences; in doing so our lives become much richer, less fearful and angry, and more vivid, creative, peaceful, and healed.

> **"Your worst enemy cannot harm you as much as your own unguarded thoughts. But once mastered no one can help you as much. Not even your own mother or father."**
> **—Buddha, from the *Dhammapada***

What is most exciting is that research shows that mindfulness practices profoundly and positively influence our biology and can significantly help improve our health and well-being. In the book *Mindfulness-Based Treatment Approaches* (edited by psychology professor Ruth Baer), the contributors to this text share how depression, anxiety, eating disorders, chronic mental illness, cancer, chronic pain, and violence have all been successfully treated using mindfulness treatment approaches. In a separate study, neuroscientists Richard Davidson and Jon Kabat-Zinn showed the positive effects that mindfulness practices have on the brain and immune system. Their research showed that mindfulness helps one to deal with difficult emotions under stress and supports and improves the function of the immune system. Kabat-Zinn was also involved in a study that showed that people with the skin disease psoriasis who were receiving ultraviolet light treatments cleared up their skin four times faster if they practiced mindfulness than a group that received only the light treatment.

Most non-Indigenous, Western mindfulness researchers and practitioners who write about mindfulness regard it as having its origins in eastern Buddhist meditation traditions, beginning with the enlightened being known as Buddha who lived more than 2,500 years ago. However, some argue that evidence from cave drawings suggest that ancient yogis in regions of what is now India and Nepal may have been doing meditation and other mind body mindfulness practices a thousand years earlier. In other parts of the world, Indigenous Peoples have been engaged in practices that incorporated mind body meditation and mindfulness principles for thousands of years. By the way, the Buddha ("the enlightened one") was Indigenous. He was a member of Shakya tribe, his clan name was Gautama, and his given name was Siddhartha.

There is a part of mindfulness that most mindfulness scholars and practitioners fail to mention or understand: the "politics of mindfulness," which concerns how colonization activities were instrumental in destroying the mindfulness traditions and practices of Indigenous Peoples. For instance, when colonizers outlawed or ridiculed important ceremonial songs and dance, many Indigenous Peoples' brain circuits of hope, happiness, and purpose that were associated with these practices were undoubtedly reduced, inactivated, and/or deleted. As these brain networks became inactivated, the importance of ceremonial activities would correspondingly lose their importance and appeal. In place of Indigenous ceremonies and practices, colonizers offered Christian religion and beliefs, stressing their importance since they were received directly from THE CREATOR and indispensable because they "saved" Indigenous Peoples from their primitive beliefs, and the Christian Hell, and enabled them to get to the Christian Heaven or Paradise.

F. My Use of Mindfulness as a Neurodecolonization Tool

Every morning I engage in my mindfulness sitting meditation practice for forty-five minutes to an hour. Sometimes I will add an evening practice to my routine. Most times I practice right after I wake up, when I am feeling rested and alert. If I have not slept well and need to shake the kinks out of my brain, I go on my early morning walk-run and practice when I get home.

Many mornings I will add a short ten-minute practice session sitting with my five-year-old daughter, Arundhati (figure 4.3). After three and a half years of formal practice, she can now sit mindfully, with her eyes closed, on her cushion, in her semi-lotus position,

Figure 4.3. Arundhati Yellow Bird, photo from author's collection.

for up to a half hour. Her mother, Erin, often sits with her in the afternoon or evening if she misses her morning practice with me. Our youngest daughter, Solana, who is two and a half, has not quite gotten the flow of practice like her older sister (figure 4.4). Her little monkey mind is clearly in charge. Still, she continues to make small gains sitting quietly; she is a work in progress.

My mindfulness practice is not limited to sitting in meditation. I often include mini-mindfulness practices into my daily life, stopping for two to three minutes every hour to an hour and a half to check in with myself to become as aware as I can in that moment of how I am feeling and behaving, and what I am thinking. When I first added this practice, I used the timer on my wristwatch to sound the alarm for these breaks. Now that I have been doing this practice for some time, I have conditioned myself to use many other cues, sounds, or shifts in activity to remind myself to take my meaningful pauses.

I have included a number of different mindfulness practices in my morning routine throughout the years. My core practices include *breath counting, breath*

Figure 4.4. Solana Yellow Bird, photo from author's collection.

awareness, *body awareness*, awareness of my mind's activities, and a neurodecolonization practice of *releasing my mind* (from emotions and beliefs that inhibit my well-being).

I incorporate three or four of the practices in one sitting. For instance, I will sit for fifteen minutes doing breath counting where I silently count my *in* and *out* breaths (1—on the in breath; 2—on the out breath; 3—on the in breath; and 4—on the out breath). I switch to fifteen minutes of breath awareness, silently saying to myself on the in breath "*I know that I'm breathing in*," and on the out breath, "*I know that I'm breathing out.*" I finish with the mindfulness neurodecolonization exercise, silently saying to myself on the in and out breaths, "I release my mind from this emotion/feeling/problem." And if I want to work on deleting a difficult memory from my brain's neural networks, I silently say, "I release my mind from this memory" on each in and out breath.

I also practice mindfulness when I wash the dishes, take a shower, drive my car, and sweep the floors. During these activities I focus my attention, as fully as I can, on what I am doing and what is

occurring. For instance, I consciously feel the texture and shape of the dishes and utensils and the warmth of the water when I am washing the dishes. When I shower I make a point of seeing how it feels when the water first touches my body and how my feet feel when they are in contact with the shower floor. As I drive I periodically and consciously squeeze the steering wheel to see how my hands and fingers feel touching it and also use it as a reminder to stay aware. I consider my commitment, study, and practice of mindfulness to be one of my most passionate acts of decolonization and my lifeline to well-being.

I began practicing years ago to help myself cope with and overcome the repeated traumas, racism, stress, and hate that I experienced growing up. Throughout much of my life I had witnessed the premature, sad, and violent death of many of my friends and relatives in my reservation community. Much of it was due to alcohol abuse. Also contributing to my stress was the mean-spirited, hateful acts of racism, name-calling, and physical intimidation I encountered off the reservation as a child and a young man. For years and years I would ruminate about, and relive, many of the negative experiences. Sometimes I would find myself "daydreaming" about them, and when I slept I had constant nightmares (I still have notebooks filled with these dreams and my comments about what they meant and where they were coming from). The ones that stayed freshest in my mind were the violent, bloody, painful ones, which constituted a large number over a period of many years.

The disruption of colonization is directly linked to the excessive rates of death in my community. I knew there had been a lot of premature deaths among our people, especially the young men, but did not quite know what the actual rates were until the summer of 2004. I had decided to visit several of the cemeteries in our small community in memory of my many friends and relatives. When I started noticing how young many of the men were, I got a pencil and paper and recorded from their headstones when they had been born and died. I averaged the age of death for the group to discover it was forty-two years. Many of these guys I knew personally; for those that I did not, I asked others about them. What I learned, which was not much of a surprise, was that whatever caused their death (suicide, murder, drowning, freezing to death, or car accidents), a large number of them had been using alcohol.

And then there was the obvious—the large number who had died from cirrhosis and other liver disease due to alcohol use. As I reflected on the excessive death rates, I remembered that many of the men, like me, had experienced the continuous loss of healthy role models and our tribal language, ceremonies, and culture. At the same time, they (we) experienced an abundance of racism, abuse, and control by white authorities and institutions. Most of us had rarely, if ever, experienced the healing power of our own tribal mindfulness practices since they had been "lost" during different periods of colonization.

It was not long before other problems related to the losses and insults of colonialism set in. Physical problems emerged that had not existed before: obesity, diabetes, hypertension, skin disorders, cancers, and heart disease. Mental problems and mood disorders such as depression, anxiety, grief, sadness, and low self-esteem gripped the members of our community. Spiritual disorganization spread among us, and many experienced loss of hope, optimism, purpose, meaning, and sacredness. To cope, many joined Christian religions that promised salvation but centered on a fearful, critical Creator (one that thought Indigenous Peoples needed to be saved by white religious beliefs) and an afterlife of suffering, something that was not central in our spiritual beliefs. Imagine how this change shaped the function and structure of the minds and brains of the people.

Living in this environment created a deep well of anger, rage, depression, violence, anxiety, fear, sadness, and confusion in me. My mind, brain, and nervous system were often engaged in a continuous *fight* or *flight response*, and I was constantly trying to escape the traumatic thoughts and feelings in my mind and flee from the environment that spawned them: the reservation.

I used humor, alcohol, sports, music, and prayer to cope. None of them was long-lasting, especially since none helped me change my relationship with my traumas, memories, feelings, and beliefs. In fact, it was not until much later that I came to understand that I needed to formally engage in mind and brain activities, such as mindfulness, for long, sustained periods of time, and in creative, non-judgmental ways, in order to change my *neurocircuitry*, which had been negatively shaped according to my colonial experiences.

In 1975, when I was an undergraduate student in college, I happened upon Lawrence LeShan's book *How to Meditate*, which helped me understand how meditation practices could aid me in attaining greater levels of calm and help me cope with my traumas. I spent a lot of time practicing sitting meditation in my dorm room, generally in the early morning or late at night. Sometimes when my roommate was studying I would sit in the shower on my pillow, silently doing my breath counting and working on not judging or attaching to my difficult memories. I tried to practice in private since I was unsure of what I was doing and did not want to explain to others what I was trying to achieve.

I read different parts of LeShan's book often and practiced some of the basic types of meditation, paying attention to how he suggested they be done and to any physiological and psychological effects that he said would occur. I worked on the exercises over the next several years, sometimes consistently and at other times sporadically. The exercises were helpful and I did experience feelings of well-being from time to time, but they did not last since my practice was inconsistent. If I would have had a teacher at this time, she or he might have reminded me to stay in the present and observe how my thoughts and experiences changed from moment to moment. A teacher would have taught me that my job is to not judge, fear, or become attached to my thoughts; like everything else, they will pass and be replaced by other thoughts, feelings, and memories.

ACTIVITY:

How often do you judge, fear, or attach to certain thoughts, feelings, or memories? What do your tribal traditions teach about how to treat negative thinking, memories, and feelings? Do you have a teacher, elder, or someone who instructs you on how to train yourself to effectively respond to the negativity in your mind and brain so that you can become a healthier, more optimistic person? What would it take to find such a person? Take time to write some of your responses below.

_____

_____

_____

_____

_____

_____

In 1989 when I was working on my PhD in social welfare, I experienced a major episode of depression. Much of it was centered on the continuing trauma in my reservation community that I experienced firsthand when I visited, and secondhand when I called home and heard the bad news. It did not take much for me to begin experiencing deep emotions of anger, sadness, and grief that I still carried from the past. When I felt the first pangs of the depression set in, I took a break from school and went to visit my parents back on my reservation. Not long after I arrived I begin witnessing some of the everyday tragic situations that had engulfed the lives of different friends and relatives in the community. During the evenings my mind and brain were flooded with the social carnage I had witnessed, and I soon bottomed out and ended up in a psychiatric unit in an off-reservation hospital. In this environment I immediately returned to practicing my meditation in the early mornings and evenings in my room, believing that at some point mental and emotional relief would slowly return.

When I checked out of the unit I returned to my PhD studies. In between my work and mindfulness practices, I began looking for reading materials that would aid in my recovery. I knew that if I did not address the traumas of the past, those of the present would continue to "come on baby light my fire." In my search I began finding articles and books on the topic of "_psychoneuroimmunology_," which integrated psychology, neuroscience, and immunology. Psychology provided an understanding of one's mental state; neuroscience centered on what the brain did with these emotions; and immunology focused on how the immune system responded to what the brain was interpreting in regard to the emotions.

I first encountered this term when I read a book written by Norman Cousins called *Head First: The Biology of Hope and the Healing Power of the Human Spirit*. A number of other health, biological, and medical-related disciplines are now considered part of this field, and they are gaining an understanding of the mind's ability to influence the body's health. *Head First* described Cousins' ten-year quest to find the proof that positive attitudes are actually biochemical factors that combat disease. I enjoyed reading this book and was inspired by the stories and science. I thought that it was such a special book that offered so much hope, I gave it to an Indigenous guy I met while we were both participating in a Sun Dance ceremony; he had been recently diagnosed with cancer and I had only recently purchased the book and had taken it to read during the dance. Like we say, "Someone needed it more than me," and that is why I brought it there.

In 1991 as I continued my healing quest, I discovered a book called *Full Catastrophe Living*, written by Jon Kabat-Zinn (this book is now considered one of the classics of mind body medicine). This work was the first I had read about how mindfulness had been used to help many people cope with and heal from many different medical conditions. I was inspired by Kabat-Zinn's book and I begin using it to help me learn how to do mindfulness practices such as "Sitting with the Breath and Body," "Sitting with Sound," and the "Body Scan." It helped me to understand the connection between stress and illness and how they were connected to my experience, my community, and that of other Indigenous Peoples who had gone through the traumas of colonization. About a year after I read and re-read the book and had talked about it with some

of my PhD student colleagues, I was asked to do a workshop on mindfulness for social workers and other helping professionals who were attending a Native American Child and Family conference. I talked about what Kabat-Zinn had written, especially the activities in his Stress Reduction and Relaxation Program (SRRS). I had the audience do the now famous "Raisin Exercise," and the "Sitting with Breath and Body" exercise.

The Raisin Exercise is where one mindfully and deliberately eats a raisin. First, it is picked up and its shape, color, and wrinkles are carefully examined. Next, it is gently rolled between the thumb and index finger and carefully squeezed to note its texture. At this point, thoughts can be entertained about where it came from, how it was a grape before it got to you, and how the sun slowly dried it to create what you are now holding. It is next brought up to the nose and smelled to note any fragrance. Finally, it is put into the mouth, rolled around by the tongue to feel its shape and texture, and then swallowed. As it makes its way down the throat, any sensations can be noted.

From 1992–1995 I dedicated nearly every morning to forty-five minutes of sitting meditation, where I continually practiced breath awareness, breath counting, visualization, and imagery. I practiced in the quiet of my bedroom when my sons were asleep or in the darkness of the laundry room when they were awake. I had many mental, emotional, and spiritual gains during this time and I began to enter into a state of deep calm, peace, and awareness. In 1993, while I was on the faculty of the School of Social Work at the University of British Columbia (1992–1994), I was invited to visit the Vancouver Aboriginal Friendship Centre on East

> "This research has yielded stunning results, which if replicated will alter forever certain basic scientific assumptions—for example, that systematic training in meditation, when sustained steadily over years, can enhance the human capacity for positive changes in brain activity to an extent undreamed of in modern cognitive science."
> —Daniel Goleman,
> Foreword in *Joy of Living*

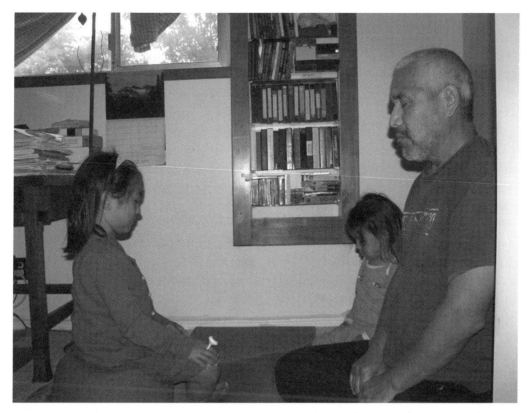

Figure 4.5. Michael, Arundhati, and Solana Yellow Bird meditating. Photo from author's collection.

Hastings Avenue where I spent time teaching Native youth mindfulness exercises from Kabat-Zinn's book.

Even as I practiced mindfulness and had opportunities to teach it, the demons of the past still visited me; but now it was less frequent and intense. From 1995 to 2006 I continued my practice, but it was sketchy, disrupted, distracted, and without purpose. Changes, jobs, moving, and other life circumstances were obstacles to my practice and study. However, due to many stressors and disruptions in my life, this was a time that I should have been practicing even more. Following another visit from the depression demon in 2006, I rededicated myself to my mindfulness practice and have maintained it ever since.

I have spent time with my partner practicing with our two little daughters (figure 4.5) nearly every day, and I share the science of its benefits with my extended family and relatives and tell them about its healing potential. I require the students in my graduate and undergraduate courses to practice mindfulness at the start of each class (I have been doing this since 1992); I write a column for my tribal newspaper on the topic and urge folks to try it; I do presentations in tribal communities, at professional conferences, and sometimes give radio interviews; I have also conducted qualitative research on its effects on a group of Indigenous youth in a tribal school setting.

G. The Neurobiology of Mindfulness (and Decolonization)

Neurodecolonization is built from the studies of mindfulness. The neurobiology of mindfulness concerns the neuroscientific investigation of the neural systems that are utilized to achieve meditative states and to determine the effects of regular mindfulness practice on brain structure and function. In this section I will discuss what neuroplasticity is all about, several regions of the brain that are affected by mindfulness practices, and what these practices imply for decolonization. There are numerous studies of how the brain and its processes are changed by mindfulness. What I include here is only a snapshot of what is being reported in the scientific literature. A complete discussion is well beyond the scope of this chapter. In this section I will review neuroplasticity, brain state and trait effects, and EEG studies of brain waves and meditative states. I also discuss the dorsolateral prefrontal cortex and executive brain function, anterior cingulate cortex, temporal parietal junction, amygdala, insula, and the orbital frontal cortex. It is important to say at this point that neuroplasticity varies greatly among people, and the brain regions I cover have many overlapping, complex functions. The neurobiology of mindfulness is still in its infancy, and what I am providing here is quite simplistic, although it is based on hard science, and only skims the complexity and processes of the human brain.

Neuroplasticity

One of the most important findings of neuroscience investigations is that of *neuroplasticity*, which refers to our brain's lifelong capacity for change according to the experiences we have. *Neuro* refers to the brain's nerve cells (which I discussed earlier) and *plasticity* refers to our brain's ability to change its shape and function (neural networks) to accommodate our learning, thinking, and other active experiences. Recall that if our experiences have been more negative (especially in the case of colonialism), we create neural networks of negativity. If we have more positive experiences, our networks will enable more optimism and well-being in our lives.

Speaking about neuroplasticity, neuroscientist Dr. Richard Rystak, author of the book *The New Brain: How the Modern Age Is Rewiring your Mind*, says that "thoughts, feelings, and actions, rather than mechanical laws, determine the health of our brain. Furthermore, we now know that the brain never loses the power to transform itself on the basis of experience, and this transformation can occur over very short intervals." Sharon Begley, author of *Train Your*

Mind, Change Your Brain, says that studies "suggest that brain changes can be generated by pure mental activity: merely thinking about playing the piano leads to measurable, physical change in the brain's motor cortex, and thinking about thoughts in a certain way can restore mental health." Begley further asserts that "we are not stuck with the brain we were born with but have the capacity to willfully direct which functions will flower and which will wither, which moral capacities emerge and which do not, which emotions flourish and which are stilled." The *Dana Guide to Brain Health*, published in 2006, says the most important trait that the brain brings to adulthood is plasticity. The guide says that "plasticity allows us to learn, to form new habits, to adjust to new circumstances—whether as simple as remembering to make enough morning coffee for two after marriage, or as complicated as learning to use information technology when your employer decides to carve out a place in the 'new economy.'"

An important way to change our brain's negative experiences, beliefs, and memories is to intentionally practice mindfulness. Recall that mindfulness is a powerful strategy in the tool box of neurodecolonization. By engaging in mindfulness we can become intentionally aware of our experiences, thoughts, and feelings as they unfold in our practice. By being aware of what they are and treating them not as fact but as only experiences, we can change our perceptions, relationship, and response to them and become less reactive and more creative in resolving them. This is what Sharon Begley means when she writes "train your mind, change your brain." In his book *Mindsight*, UCLA professor and neuroscientist Daniel J. Siegel, MD refers to our ability to pause before we act on the thoughts that come up in our practice as "response flexibility." He says this response "harnesses the power of the middle prefrontal region to put a temporal space between input and action. This ability to pause before responding is an important part of emotional and social intelligence. It enables us to become fully aware of what is happening—and to restrain our impulses long enough to consider various other options."

The Brain's State and Trait Effects

In the study of mindfulness, researchers focus on two important effects that occur in the brain when it is at rest or doing a task. The first of these are *state effects*, which concern the changes that occur in individuals as they actively meditate—or to put it another way, you might ask what is the state of my brain as I do this activity?

Trait effects are the changes that occur gradually over time as a consequence of continuous meditation practice. Trait effects are regarded as "permanent" or long-lasting and continue to persist even when one is not meditating or stops practicing altogether for long periods of time. Neuroscientist Richard Davidson says that "left prefrontal activation appears to be associated with a constellation of positive attributes, including reduced levels of the stress hormone cortisol, and reductions in other biological and immune parameters that are associated with negative affect." Furthermore, he says that "activation patterns in the right prefrontal cortex, by contrast, are more associated with certain types of negative affect accompanied by increased vigilance to threat-related cues, a symptom that often occurs with certain types of anxiety." Does colonialism produce its own brands of unique anxieties? I believe it does. It is important to remember from the neuroplasticity discussion that the more one uses mindfulness to avoid judging themselves, the negative content of the thoughts that arise in practice, and the more one gently detaches from the negativity—the more activated and permanent the optimistic traits of the left side of the prefrontal cortex become. This is fundamentally what neurodecolonization is all about.

Research shows that our brains exhibit different waves of activity. They give an indication of how the brain is performing as it responds to different tasks and circumstances. *Gamma* band waves are the highest; *Well-being*, or *Beta* band waves are next, followed by *Alpha*; and finally there are *Theta* and *Delta*. Gamma waves are the highest and operate at forty cycles per second. They are involved in higher mental activity and are associated with perception and consciousness.

Well-being waves function between thirteen and thirty cycles per second. Someone operating at this level would be experiencing awakened awareness, extroversion, concentration, logical thinking, and active conversation. A person making a speech or debating, or a teacher or a talk show host would all be in Beta when they are engaged in their work; the higher the engagement, the higher the band wave.

When one is in an Alpha state, brain waves are functioning at seven to thirteen cycles per second, which corresponds to relaxation times, non-arousal, meditation, and hypnosis. The Theta state operates at four to seven cycles per second. In this phase one may be daydreaming, thinking creatively, meditating, or experiencing paranormal phenomena such as out of body experiences or ESP. At Delta, which operates at zero to four cycles, one is undergoing the deepest level of sleep. Some studies say that this state is associated with sleepwalking.

In the *Clinical Handbook of Mindfulness* (edited by Fabrizio Didonna), research suggests that individuals who are long-term meditators appear to have higher levels of Alpha and Theta band activity, which are associated with relaxation and rest. Other studies report that meditation practices that emphasize deep physical relaxation are more likely to produce higher Theta and Delta activity (associated with deep sleep), while practices that focus more on intensive concentration will likely have higher Alpha and well-being power. Gamma brain waves are associated with meditators who have put in the most hours of practice, sometimes tens of thousands of hours over a lifetime. Research shows that meditators who achieve Gamma band brain activity during meditation have the ability to put the brain into a state in which it is maximally sensitive and consumes power at a lower (or even zero) rate. A brain with this sensitivity can achieve high levels of consciousness and perception, and still remain fresh due to the low usage of brain resources. I believe that many Indigenous spiritual leaders who regularly practiced traditional mindfulness meditation in sacred and secular ceremonies very likely achieved a Gamma brain band wave state.

Key Brain Regions

Dorsolateral Prefrontal Cortex and Executive Brain Function. Brain imaging studies reveal that mindfulness meditation activates the dorsolateral prefrontal cortex (DLPFC), an area associated with executive decision-making and attention. The activation means that the DLPFC and the executive brain function more smoothly and effectively. This area, which is located in the front part of the brain, is particularly important since executive brain function is responsible for our working memory, cognitive flexibility, and the ability to delay gratification and distraction. The forefront of the brain image is where the executive function is located (intelligence, judgment, and behavior).

Working memory concerns our ability to recall how to do a particular task, such as adding numbers without using a pencil and paper or calculator; the more digits and mixing of numbers, the more difficult the task and the more we have to call on our working memory. How good is yours? Try adding these numbers in your head: 22 plus 22. Pretty easy, right? Now try adding 563 plus 784. Little more difficult? Well, folks who practice and practice doing such things have a good working memory for doing these kinds of "simple" mathematical operations. Of course the more they practice, the more they develop the neural networks to support their ability to manipulate numbers. Again, we know this from our discussion of neuroplasticity—the brain is always changing to accommodate the experience we have or the task we undertake.

Want to try another exercise? Try saying the alphabet backwards and see how long it takes you. Practice saying it backwards until you get pretty good at it and then have someone test you. Then wait for a week or two without practicing and try it again. How well you do depends on how much you practiced and to what extent your brain made the neural connections to support your performance.

Cognitive flexibility has to do with our capacity to move from one cognitive task to another without too much difficulty. An example I like to use concerns children. Imagine you are a Head Start teacher and your students have been happily playing with toys for much of the morning. Oh, how they love their toys! But, now it is time for another activity that most of them do not like but will tolerate. You have the children put away the toys so you can begin the next activity; some follow your orders but a few do not listen. You ask them again, with no response. You walk over and begin taking the toys to help them put them away. Some of the children are okay with this and begin helping you so that they can quickly fall in line with the first group. However, a few others flip out and begin crying, hitting you, and pounding their heads on the floor. You might have already guessed that those who responded the most quickly probably did so because they have the highest levels of cognitive flexibility, while those who did not are not so good in this area. As times goes by they will get better, you hope.

Finally, housed in the executive brain region is one's ability to put off distractions and the need for immediate gratification. This is an area where many of us need a lot of work. While most of us are easily distracted, distraction has become particularly noticeable since the arrival of cell phones, portable laptop computers, iPads, iPods, and other new technology. Today we see youth, adults, elders, men, and women excessively texting, twittering, gaming, endlessly surfing the Internet, and checking their Facebook and other social networks several times a day. Try having a conversation with these folks.

Delaying gratification is also an issue for most of us who live in this world of fast, easily accessible material things. For instance, let us say that you are wishing for a slice of your mother's famous homemade chocolate cake that you know how to make, but do not want to go through the trouble of making it and then having to clean up the mess. You are not really hungry, but as you think about it your desire for it grows stronger. However, instead of baking that cake from scratch, using your mom's clean, healthy recipe of organic, dark, fair-trade chocolate, you jump in your car, drive down to the market, and pick one up. As you are paying for it you notice the label with numerous chemicals and additives that you have never heard of or that you cannot pronounce.

Instead of mindfully sewing a torn shirt or dress, we can zip to Wal-Mart and buy a cheap, sweatshop replacement; instead of writing a letter to a friend that we have been missing, we send them a short Facebook message and a picture of ourself after losing forty pounds on the Paleolithic diet. In this fast-paced, frenetic, driven world of colonialism, we have been taught "time is money" and "good things do not come to those who wait." Unlike our ancestors who learned the lessons of patience and mindful eating, our inability to delay our gratification for food has resulted in extraordinary levels of obesity. Our inability to be happy with what we have has led us into mindless consumption and compulsive buying; our inability and unwillingness to take a mindful walk to the store or to visit our friends, and instead drive there in our huge SUV, has increased our carbon load on Mother Earth. Engaging in systematic mindfulness practices to improve our brain's executive function is an example of neurodecolonization.

Anterior Cingulate Cortex. Mindfulness practices increase activation in the cingulate cortex, particularly in the anterior subdivision. This area plays a role in the integration of attention, motivation, and motor control. Many studies also show that functions such as error detection, anticipation of tasks, and the variation of emotions take place in this brain region. Research shows that longer-term meditators can sustain longer periods of attention than short-term meditators. This brain region is important in neurodecolonization since many who have been traumatized by colonialism have more difficulty with detecting errors in their thinking and actions, trouble maintaining attention and motivation, and difficulty moving between their emotions. This faulty processing in this brain region will make our relationships and other experiences in our lives more difficult.

Temporal Parietal Junction. The temporal parietal junction is an area that becomes activated during meditation practices. This region of the brain is associated with the ability to perceive the emotional and mental state of others, such as in emotional intelligence (EI). An individual with good EI is able to identify, assess, and respond to the emotions of him/herself and others.

Having healthy levels of EI is important since we interact with different kinds of people in many different situations, and we must act with appropriate behaviors and emotions. Indeed, how we manage ourselves determines how successful we will be in our relationships with others. Studies show that this brain area is more active in meditators than non-meditators, even when they are not meditating. Emotional intelligence is especially important to come to understand our levels of colonization and how much we must engage in neurodecolonization activities to activate this part of our brain.

Amygdala. The amygdala is in part of the area of the brain called the limbic system. It is responsible for processing fear and aggression and our fight and flight response. If we get into an argument or another difficult situation, it is our amygdala that sends the alarm for how to respond. Many studies have focused on this region of the brain since it is a highly volatile area. Among other things, the amygdala plays a role in binge drinking and is associated with various psychological disorders, such as anxiety and obsessive compulsive disorders, and post traumatic stress disorder (PTSD).

The amygdala also plays a role in our fearful reactions. In some studies, individuals who were shown images of frightened faces or people from another race were observed to have increased activation in this region. However, new research shows that when people from one group (say a racial group) develop positive social relations and understanding of another group, social anxiety and racism decreases. Imagine what the world would look like if colonizing societies truly developed good relations and a sincere understanding of the effects of their activities on those whom they have colonized.

Brain imaging of meditators shows that meditation calms and activates many important parts of the optimistic brain; it also quiets the activity of the restless, easily angered, and fearful amygdala. Research shows that long-term practitioners have lower activation in this region, especially when encountering different distressful situations. It is not unreasonable to believe that the amygdala in the brains of individuals who have not fared well under the oppressive conditions of colonialism may have high activation in this part of the brain.

Insula. Neuroscientists credit the insula as being a fountain of social emotions. Things like lust and disgust, pride and humiliation, guilt, and atonement are associated with this brain region. Moral intuition, empathy, and the capacity to respond emotionally to music are all within the function of the insula. Other research has said that the insula is also associated with "interoception," which refers to what happens when one processes the world mainly through feelings and emotions. It can be thought of as the "gut" feelings we have when we experience different situations, and the ability to be aware of and to understand the processes of our internal body state as we experience them. This area of the brain is important because individuals who may have been overwhelmed in the colonial context may have difficulty processing the moment-to-moment changes that they experience and may have difficulty knowing and sharing how they feel. Studies show that regular mindfulness meditation practices activate the insula, which can enable the practitioner to gain a greater understanding of the feelings and sensations that she or he may be going through at any given moment.

Orbital Frontal Cortex. The orbital frontal cortex (OFC), located in the front of the brain just above and behind the eyes, is an especially interesting and important brain region with regard to neurodecolonization. This circuit is thought to provide us with our internal reality check of how we are coming across to others. Jennifer Beers and Brent Hughes from the University of Texas have studied this area and found that it biases us to have an overstated evaluation of our skills, intelligence, personality, and health, mostly because we do not call upon this part of the brain to evaluate our "true" capacities. Instead we view ourselves as better than we are. Beers and Hughes refer to this inflated view as the "above-average effect," which implies that, despite the evidence to the contrary, we think that we are better than we actually are. Beers and Hughes

found that the less activity in this area, the more we are likely to see ourselves through "rose-colored glasses."

When I am discussing neurodecolonization in my presentations, I often refer to this region as being responsible for "colonial brain disorder." What I mean by this is that the OFC is involved in processing reflection, judgment, and how one views the world. However, as Beers and Hughes maintain, this area is not called on much since there is an inflated, inaccurate view of oneself that is not easy to change. To extend their analysis, I argue that when a colonizer (a person of the colonial society) is "brainwashed" to believe that they are the right color, have the right values and beliefs, live in the greatest country on earth, and are from an exceptional class of people, they will have extreme difficulty engaging this brain region— which of course means that they will lack the ability to mindfully and honestly critique their privilege, culture, beliefs and values, and their nation's own failures and weaknesses. In other words, their OFC will be on a long, long vacation. Instead they will see and regard their situation as the standard to achieve, and come to see their colonizing activities as justified. This does not mean that all people who are colonizers do not have a capable, functioning OFC; there are many who do and often ally themselves with Indigenous Peoples in their struggles against the colonial situation.

Neurodecolonization requires that we must understand the OFC of the colonizer and how he arrived at the point of believing in the "over-stated" attributes of colonialism. Neurodecolonization requires that we understand that the colonizer may not be deliberately avoiding an evaluation of colonialism's negative effects on Indigenous Peoples. Rather than just sheer stubbornness, many colonizers are suffering from a brain disorder in the OFC. Knowing this, Indigenous Peoples should understand that using sheer force against a non-Indigenous force that has a disorder in this important part of the brain will be frustrating and unproductive. Instead, neurodecolonization strategies urge Indigenous Peoples to engage in sustained, highly intelligent, creative, original approaches that can be used to help heal this brain disorder of the colonizer, so that the colonist can come to understand the extent and damage of his actions.

There is a caveat here: neurodecolonization calls for us to understand the functioning of our own OFC in order to recognize how it operates in our own world. It is imperative that we ask ourselves if we truly believe that we are better than we are. Are we more important than other humans, races, and forms of life? Do we know how our social behavior affects others? It is important that we understand this part of our brain since "humility" is often regarded as a high order, traditional value among many Indigenous Peoples. If we do not, it should not come as a surprise when others tell us how distasteful and arrogant our social behavior is toward them or other forms of life.

H. An Indigenous Peoples' Neurodecolonization Policy

The first perceptions of the oppressive processes of colonialism happen in our minds, which send signals to the brain of how we should respond. A brain that is healthy and well-balanced can respond in an optimistic, courageous, intelligent, creative, and resilient manner. On the other hand, an unhealthy brain is more likely to respond with fear, frustration, anger, helplessness, and negativity. Research shows that the brain that has been shaped by mindfulness and other positive contemplative practices will respond in a much more optimistic and effective manner.

Neurodecolonization is an emerging science that examines how the human brain functions in a colonial situation and how the use of specific mind and brain activities can change important neural networks to enable one to overcome the myriad effects of colonialism. It recognizes that our brain's plasticity enables our neural networks to rewire and change themselves over our lifetime according to our experiences. It advocates the use of contemplative practices, such as mindfulness, which can profoundly change our brain for the better. It also reminds Indigenous Peoples that they can get the same benefits if they systematically and purposefully engage (in a long-term and sustained manner) in traditional and contemporary secular and sacred contemplative practices that encourage meaning, purpose, positivity, and well-being.

Mindfulness practices are one of the core activities that promote neurodecolonization. Mindfulness practices have been essential to my own healing, creativity, and well-being, and to improving the functioning of the brains of my two little daughters. Mindfulness practices make important changes in our brain band waves and in several important brain regions that are associated with positive feelings, thinking, and actions.

I believe that every Indigenous person, community, leader, teacher, parent, youth, and elder should embrace neurodecolonization and the mindfulness practices that are central to its core. Mindfulness is not a foreign way of life, philosophy, or religion. Since time immemorial Indigenous Peoples have embraced mindfulness before, during, and after many of their secular and sacred ceremonies. When we practice mindfulness as a neurodecolonization activity, we can delete the old ineffective neural networks in our brains and activate new empowering ones. Every time we sit quietly, on purpose, and formally concentrate on our breath as it enters and exits, or we focus and keep our attention on what we are doing, without distraction, we activate key brain circuits that help us improve our awareness and ability to concentrate. Mindfulness will enable us to reduce our negativity and improve our brain's plasticity. It will increase our compassion, patience, creativity, emotional intelligence, and courage. Through these practices we will gain a greater understanding of how our mind and brain work, especially as we confront the stressors of colonialism. In ending this chapter I want to propose a simple neurodecolonization policy that I believe will improve our minds, brains, and overall health.

1. Indigenous Peoples should carry out studies of community members to determine the levels of stress, anxiety, depression, anger, and negativity, as well as the levels of optimism, happiness, gratitude, and well-being.

2. Indigenous Peoples should develop a list that describes unhealthy colonized views, behaviors, attitudes, and thinking, as well as a list of those that are healthy, decolonized, and traditional. Community members can be mindfully and gently

instructed and guided toward those on the second
list.

3. Indigenous Peoples should implement mindfulness practices in Indigenous Peoples' communities,
   schools, organizations, and homes. Mindfulness
   should become a regular activity for all age groups.

4. Indigenous Peoples should conduct research on
   the effects of mindfulness on their communities,
   paying special attention to reductions in stress and
   negativity and increases in well-being.

5. Indigenous Peoples should return to practicing traditional secular and sacred contemplative
   (mind brain) practices that promote optimism,
   health, creativity, courage, resilience, and a sense of
   identity.

6. Indigenous Peoples should develop a curriculum
   that teaches mind and brain science in an accessible, practical, and applied manner.

7. Indigenous Peoples should develop and implement a curriculum that teaches individuals and the
   community to engage in different, evidence-based
   mind brain activities, such as optimistic thinking, creative imagery and visualization, memory
   exercises, and critical thinking.

Our minds and brains have incredible healing
power. However, they can also be the chief contribu-
tor to our oppression. We have more than enough
evidence that contemplative practices such as mindfulness offer powerful antidotes to colonialism. Imagine a world of Indigenous Peoples with balanced,
healthy, creative, intelligent, and courageous minds
and brains—just like our ancestors who were able to
overcome forces many times more potent than colonialism. If we fail to take actions we will not improve
our condition or our control over the oppressions of
colonialism. If we do, we will come to understand
what the Buddha meant when he said that freedom
from suffering was possible in this lifetime. I am a firm
believer in this message, and for me the freedom from
the traumas of colonialism is but one breath away.

I. Resources

Amen, Daniel. *Making a Good Brain Great*. New York: Three
Rivers Press, 2005.

Baer, Ruth A., ed. *Mindfulness-Based Treatment Approaches:
Clinicians Guide to Evidence Base and Application (Practice
Resources for the Mental Health Professional)*. Burlington, MA:
Elsevier, 2006.

Begley, Sharon. *Train Your Mind, Change Your Brain: How a
New Science Reveals an Extraordinary Potential to Transform
Ourselves*. New York: Ballantine Books, 2007.

Bloom, Floyd E., M. Flint Beal, and David J. Kupfer, eds. *The
DANA Guide to Brain Health: A Practical Family Reference
from Medical Experts*. New York: DANA Press, 2006.

Cousins, Norman. *Head First: The Biology of Hope and the
Healing Power of the Human Spirit*. New York: Penguin
Books, 1989.

Davidson, Richard, et al. "Alterations in Brain and Immune
Function Produced by Mindfulness Meditation." *Psychosomatic Medicine* 65, no. 4 (2003): 564–570.

Didonna, Fabrizio, ed. *Clinical Handbook of Mindfulness*. New
York: Springer, 2009.

Doidge, Norman. *The Brain That Changes Itself: Stories of Personal
Triumph from the Frontiers of Brain Science*. New York:
Penguin Books, 2007.

Goleman, Daniel. Foreword. *The Joy of Living: Unlocking the Secret
and Science of Happiness*. Yongey Mingyur Rinpoche. New
York: Three Rivers Press, 2007.

Hanh, Thich N. *Peace Is Every Step: The Path of Mindfulness in
Everyday Life*. New York: Bantam Books, 1991.

Hanson, Rick, and Richard Mendius. *Buddha's Brain: The Practical
Neuroscience of Happiness, Love, and Wisdom*. Oakland, CA:
New Harbinger Publications, 2009.

Kabat-Zinn, Jon. *Full Catastrophe Living: Using the Wisdom of Your
Body and Mind to Face Stress, Pain, and Illness*. New York:
Delacorte Books, 1990.

Kabat-Zinn, Jon, et al. "Influence of a Mindfulness Meditation-
Based Stress Reduction Intervention on Rates of Skin Clearing
in Patients with Moderate to Severe Psoriasis undergoing
Phototherapy (VB) and Photochemotherapy (PUVA)."
Psychosomatic Medicine 65 (1998): 625–632.

LeShan, Lawrence. *How to Meditate: A Guide to Self-Discovery*. New
York: Bantam Books, 1974.

Newberg, Andrew, and Mark R. Waldman, *How God Changes Your
Brain: Breakthrough Findings from a Leading Neuroscientist*.
New York: Ballantine Books, 2009.

Rystak, Richard. *The New Brain: How the Modern Age Is Rewiring Your Mind.* Emmaus, PA: Rodale Press, 2003.

Siegel, Daniel J. *Mindsight: The New Science of Personal Transformation.* New York: Bantam Books, 2010.

Websites

Davidson, Richard. "Understanding Positive and Negative Emotion." http://www.loc.gov/loc/brain/emotion/Davidson.html.

Ken McLeod's Seeing from the Inside. "Awareness Through Breathing." *Natural Awareness.* http://www.naturalawareness.net/anapanasati1.pdf.

Lynch, David. "The Visionary." Interview by Deborah Solomon. *The New York Times Magazine.* November 21, 2008. http://www.nytimes.com/2008/11/23/magazine/23wwln-q4-t.html.

Marano, Hara E. "Why We Love Bad News." *Psychology Today.* http://www.psychologytoday.com/articles/200305/why-we-love-bad-news.

Chapter 5

LIVING IN A LONGER NOW
MOVING BEYOND THE STATE-CENTRIC SYSTEM

Jeff Corntassel

A. Introduction

I will first acknowledge that it is an honor to be welcomed as a visitor to Lekwungen and Wsanec Nation territory, which is where I am currently living with my family. I am writing this chapter as a Tsalagi (Cherokee) who happens to be trained as a political scientist—or maybe I should say that I am currently a "recovering" political scientist! I always believed that the amount of time it took to earn my PhD (eight years) demanded an equal or greater amount of time to decolonize and unlearn some of the *yonega* (white settler) frameworks and ways of thinking that became embedded in my professional and personal life.

As I began writing this chapter, Kitoowhagi, or Kituwah mound—the place where the sacred fire was kept for all Tsalagis—was in danger of being over-run by developers. Duke Energy, an energy corporation with interests and assets in North and Latin America, has proposed building a power substation near the mound. Just as my Tsalagi ancestor A-ga-yv-la ("Ancient One" or "Old Man of Kituwah") gave his life to protect the sacred fire of Kituwah mound from invasion by British troops in 1761, do we not have a similar responsibility to protect our homelands? As Waziyatawin asks in chapter 2, "Do we still envision ourselves as protectors of the land, or have we fallen prey to a belief in our own helplessness?" While our roles and responsibilities as Indigenous Peoples are spoken of with great reverence, what are we doing to renew those relationships with our territories? Have we been reduced to "word warriors" rather than protectors of the land? Have we forgotten who we are and where we come from?

There is a lot of forgetfulness within a colonial context, and this is no accident. According to the late Tsalagi anthropologist Bob Thomas, colonization is the calculated deprivation of experience. By attempting to deprive Indigenous Peoples of our experiences, colonization can sever our relationships with our homelands, families, clan systems, medicines, and all aspects of the natural world. As Blackfoot scholar Leroy Little Bear pointed out at the 2009 Indigenous Leadership Forum, at one time there was no "choice" in terms of whether you wanted to be Indigenous or not. For example, if you were born in a Tsalagi clan town, you lived as a Tsalagi and were identified as a Tsalagi. Now we see folks who are confused about their identities and who even describe themselves using state-created terms, such as "Native American" or "Aboriginal." Additionally, while more and more people proudly proclaim Cherokee ancestry, most have forgotten to renew their relationships with their families, communities, or territories. In some cases, we have forgotten who we are, where we come from, and even what community means.

This is just what states had planned for Indigenous people—to forget who we are and become part of the dominant culture as "Canadian" or "United States" citizens. From this standpoint, colonial powers (such as states, corporations, etc.) are like shape-shifters, constantly inventing new ways to erase Indigenous histories and senses of place. States demand that we replace our Indigenous histories with their fictional colonial histories. For example, when speaking to other state leaders from around the world in 2009, Canadian prime minister Stephen Harper made the infamous statement that "we" in Canada "have no history of colonialism." Does he really think that Indigenous Peoples on Turtle Island have forgotten over five hundred years of colonial invasion and genocide? The ideal state citizen has a short-term memory, and lives in complete denial about our colonial realities today. Unless we reject the state's distorted version of history, the state will continue to be a dominant force in our lives.

Ultimately, we are only as strong as our collective memories. A Tsalagi saying, "Live in a longer 'now'— learn your history and culture and understand it is what you are now," urges us to remember our histories by strengthening and revitalizing our relationships. In this sense, community means a lot more than associating with other people or sharing similar interests. It is about accountability. The Tsalagi term *gadugi* illustrates this accountability to others within a community context. As Tsalagi elder Benny Smith has taught me, gadugi is a "built-in spirit of community camaraderie. This means that whatever issues or concerns arising in collective living have to be addressed in a unitary way and that no one is left alone to climb out of a life endeavor." Gadugi is a community-centered process. Our responsibility to our communities has to be continuously renewed or that system breaks down. For this reason, there is an urgency for Indigenous Peoples to relearn how to live in a longer "now." Remembering is resistance!

Colonialism is all about distorting Indigenous histories and destroying our collective and individual confidence. The late Shuswap grand chief George Manuel and co-author Michael Posluns pointed out, "The colonial system is always a way of gaining control over another people for the sake of what the colonial power has determined to be 'the common good.' People can only be convinced of the common good when their own capacity to imagine ways in which they can govern themselves has been destroyed." The state still tries to define our "common good" by telling us how to elect leaders, when we can fish and hunt, and even how to raise and educate our children. Do we remember how to govern ourselves as Indigenous people?

ACTIVITY:

What does it mean to be Indigenous (e.g., Dakota, Tsalagi, Mohawk)? How are you accountable to people in your community?

_____

_____

_____

_____

As with other Indigenous Peoples, Tsalagis have been provided with things that help them survive and thrive, such as fire, water, stones, rattles, songs, dreams, and plants. What are some things that help you as an Indigenous person? And what are your responsibilities to protect them?

_____

_____

_____

_____

B. Decolonization

What does decolonization actually mean when it is applied to our daily lives? Sahnish/Arikara and Hidatsa First Nations scholar Michael Yellow Bird describes decolonization as both an event and a process. According to Yellow Bird, it means creating and consciously using various strategies to liberate oneself from oppressive conditions; and it means restoring cultural practices, thinking, beliefs, and values that were taken away or abandoned but are still relevant and necessary for survival.

If colonization is about denying our experiences, then decolonization is about reconnecting with our relationships and renewing our roles and responsibilities within our communities. These daily acts of resurgence challenge the colonial status quo. For me, it was not one single event but a series of events that raised my level of awareness about the colonial condition, and much of this occurred when I was in graduate school at the University of Arizona studying world politics and Indigenous policy. Graduate school was a time when I met with several other Tsalagis (relatives, students, professors, etc.) and began reading works by eminent Standing Rock Sioux scholar, Vine Deloria Jr. This training, along with mentoring from fellow Tsalagis, led me to think more deeply about the destructiveness of colonization (both historical and ongoing) on Indigenous nations. This was a series of connections that I made over time and in many places: the classroom, my family territory in Westville, Oklahoma, and ceremony, which, to me, demonstrates the interrelatedness of politics and spirituality.

Cheyenne Sundance Woman and historian Henrietta Mann once told me that "we're not human beings seeking a spiritual path—we're spiritual beings seeking a human path." After all, the only way that I survived school was by participating in ceremonies. Sweats, Green Corn, and other ceremonies kept it "real" for me while I was immersed in an artificial, academic life that values myths of objectivity over experiential knowledge. This is still the case for me. Just as I started this chapter by saying that I am a Tsalagi first, who happens to be trained as a political scientist, I feel the same way about working within a university. I fulfill my responsibilities as a professor so that I have the time and ability to engage in meaningful work with my community. There's no "walking in two worlds" philosophy here. My rootedness as a Tsalagi informs everything that I do.

The danger is when we allow our lives to become compartmentalized. For example, when spirituality is treated as being separate from politics, we lose sight of the bigger picture of our interconnectedness as Indigenous Peoples. We cannot separate our spirituality from any aspect of our lives, such as the links between our Indigenous languages, living histories, clan governance, relationships to our homelands, ceremony, and so forth. This interconnectedness is key to our existence as Indigenous nations, which is why we do not have rights as Indigenous Peoples—we have inherent responsibilities. These responsibilities come from our lived relationships with our homelands and the natural world, while rights are the artificial creations of the state. Oren Lyons, Faithkeeper of the Turtle Clan of the Onondaga Nation, has said on a number of occasions that "Spirituality is the highest form of politics." To this end, Indigenous use of pipe ceremonies as well as other protocols in all aspects of Indigenous diplomacies demonstrates the deep interrelationship between politics and spirituality. This spiritual aspect is crucial to any process of decolonization and our regeneration as Indigenous nations. Our regeneration as Indigenous Peoples calls for spiritual revolution. But how do we begin this process? How many folks have made such critical realizations at some point in their lives but never acted on them? For me the process of decolonization begins with individual accountability and spreads outward to our families, clans, and communities. As long as colonialism exists, decolonization is needed to counter the destructiveness of shape-shifting colonial powers, such as states and corporations.

Ultimately decolonization is about individually and collectively engaging in the activities of recovering,

> **Kanien'kehaka (Mohawk) scholar Taiaiake Alfred writes about the need for a spiritual revolution in order to transcend the clutches of imperialism: "The end goal of our Wasáse—our warrior's dance—must be formulated as a spiritual revolution, a culturally rooted social movement that transforms the whole of society and a political action that seeks to remake the entire landscape of power and relationship to reflect truly a liberated post-imperial vision."**
>
> **—Wasáse: Indigenous Pathways of Action and Freedom**

dreaming, and restoring Indigenous communities through a commitment to action. According to Kanaka Maoli (Native Hawaiian) scholar Poka Laenui, the dreaming phase of decolonization is probably the most important, and "it is during this phase where people colonized are able to explore their own cultures, their own aspirations for their future, considering their own structures of government and social order which encompass and express their hopes."

Decolonization demands action and "leadership by example." Most Indigenous nations regard leadership by example as a necessary quality for generating respect and for identifying leaders whom others will want to follow. As I have been taught, a Tsalagi notion of leadership is no different: a person starts with a vision for the people, then supports that vision by taking action to inspire others, then makes his/her vision understandable to other people through words and actions, and finally offers some direction for other people to take action. Basically, you do not take action until you have lived it. Others witness these actions and are persuaded by the value of your lived experiences. This form of Indigenous leadership is inherently anti-colonial because it demonstrates the importance of our experiential knowledge and community accountability. This is how we represent ourselves on our own terms while rejecting state interference in our lives.

Throughout this chapter, I will discuss Indigenous leadership and decolonization strategies in more detail by exposing some of the myths of the nation-state and the world system. Providing a brief history of the state system enables us to see that the real power for change lies within our own communities. While there are other powerful actors complicit in colonialism against Indigenous Peoples, such as transnational corporations (e.g., ExxonMobil, Enbridge, Monsanto, Coca Cola), intergovernmental organizations (e.g., United Nations, Organization of American States, European Union), and non-governmental organizations (e.g., Doctors Without Borders, Amnesty International), as well as other transnational political networks, states are still key actors in world politics today.

Despite claims that the state system is in decline due to processes of globalization, states appear more resilient and powerful today than ever. To begin this discussion, I will start by offering some working definitions of states, nations, sovereignty, and decolonization that will guide activities designed to promote greater awareness and some realistic steps toward a process of decolonization. As you will see by reading this section, the state system in which we currently live is built on historical, political, legal, economic, and social myths. Once we begin to strip the shape-shifting colonial state of its myths and political and legal fictions of legitimacy, it begins to look vulnerable as an entity that has no meaningful relationship to the earth.

> **When we live in a longer now, we quickly see that states haven't been around that long and that our communities will outlive these artificial entities.**

C. Exposing the State

To begin, states and nations are two entirely different things. There are approximately two hundred recognized states within the world system today and yet there are more than five thousand Indigenous nations. These nations are often trapped within state borders. States are often referred to as nation-states, creating the illusion that the state is one single group of people. However, since its origins in 1648 (Treaty of Westphalia), the state has always been violent and colonial. By definition, a state is *a political/legal*

> According to the *1933 Montevideo Convention on the Rights and Duties of States*, in order to be recognized as a state under international law, a state must have the following four characteristics:
>
> 1. A permanent population
> 2. A defined territory
> 3. A government
> 4. A capacity to enter into relations with other states

creation of borders and a centralized political system that imposes its authority through violence on pre-existing Indigenous Nations and Peoples.

When looking more closely at the 1933 global standards for statehood, it becomes clear that most states apply these criteria arbitrarily. For example, most First Nations in British Columbia have never given up title to their homelands, and are closer to meeting the above criteria than the government of Canada. But the key to these criteria is recognition. If you are recognized as a state by other powerful states, then your authority is unquestioned. Unfortunately for some three hundred and seventy million Indigenous Peoples trapped within seventy states around the world, these four arbitrary requirements for statehood often come at the expense of their relationships to the land, their communities (clans, societies, families, etc.), traditional forms of governance, and forms of political diplomacy. These criteria for state recognition are symptoms of an immature society—a society that prioritizes the accumulation of information and material resources over lived values such as wisdom and respect.

States are thought to have sovereign powers, which means that there is no higher authority than states in the world today. But this is political and legal fiction. Therefore, from an Indigenous perspective, *sovereignty is the state's claim to have the exclusive authority to forcefully intervene in all activities within its borders—whenever necessary it practices violence on peoples residing within its legally recognized borders as they challenge the legitimacy of the state's authority.* Based on the above definition and given the colonial history of states, sovereignty is clearly an inappropriate term to describe the goals and aspirations of Indigenous nations.

In contrast to states, *Indigenous nations are communities of Peoples who identify themselves, based on oral and/or written histories, as descendants of the original inhabitants of their ancestral homelands who are land/water-based cultures disrupted by colonial invasion(s).* It is this place-based existence, along with an awareness of being in struggle against foreign states seeking to strip us of our homelands, that fundamentally distinguishes Indigenous nations from other peoples of the world. When discussing Indigenous nations' resistance to states, the words "self-determination" are often used. According to geographer Bernard Nietschmann, "Because they are occupied parts of states, nations will not be 'given' self-determination. Self-determination is something that is taken, not given; it is achieved by economic, political, and military force, not by the goodwill of state governments." By denying Indigenous self-determination, states are exposed for their inherent violence against Indigenous nations. This shows how acts of state-building are also actions of Indigenous nation-destroying.

ACTIVITY:

What are some ways to represent yourself on your own terms rather than being defined by others?

_____

_____

_____

_____

So if a state is a legally recognized entity and a nation is a community of self-identifying peoples, what is a nation-state? As mentioned earlier, the term nation-state assumes that the nation and state are the same thing. According to this logic, within the state of Canada, there should be only one nation residing within its borders. This is clearly not the case, as there are over six hundred Indigenous nations within Canada. Since more than 95 percent of all states have more than one nation within their borders, it is safe to say that the concept of the nation-state is a myth.

There are other myths created by the state in order to promote its own legitimacy. Terminology is used to justify state actions, but these terms hide larger truths. I have compiled some of these commonly used terms in table 5.1, below, in order to uncover their true meanings.

The listed terms below, which are still commonly used by states, demonstrate that colonialism is an ongoing process. A simple test I use to decode statespeak is how do these terms correspond to words in our own Indigenous languages. For the most part,

terms like reconciliation and economic development do not exist in Indigenous languages. That makes them alien terms rooted in settler values. Since terms like "protest" and "rebels" are framed according to settler values, then how useful are they to Indigenous processes of decolonization and liberation? For example, reconciliation, whether applied to a truth and reconciliation commission or a land claims negotiation, may promise a renewed relationship with the state. However, in practice it has been used to further colonize Indigenous nations and legitimate the presence of states and other shape-shifting colonial actors on Indigenous homelands. As another example, economic development programs are used in a similar way, as a state-based solution to Indigenous "poverty." But is an economic approach really strengthening and enriching Indigenous communities or are Indigenous communities actually putting their energies into strengthening the dominant economic system? In other words, who benefits and how? According to Taiaiake Alfred, "There is in fact not a shred of empirical evidence that increasing the material wealth of Indigenous people,

Table 5.1. State terminology designed to legitimize its occupation of Indigenous nations

State Terminology	Indigenous Translation
State-building	Indigenous nation-destroying
Political integration	Invasion of Indigenous territories
Economic development	Land theft and plunder of Indigenous homelands and resources via extractive industries
Reconciliation	Using a state process to legitimize continuing colonial occupation of Indigenous homelands
Protest	Protecting Indigenous homelands
Assimilation	Genocide
Separatists	A nation that never joined the state
Rebels, militants, and/or terrorists	A group of armed Indigenous people who pose a credible threat to the legitimacy of the state
National security	State military occupation of Indigenous nations

Adapted from Table 13.1 in Bernard Nietschmann's *The Fourth World: Nations Versus States*, 1994.

or increasing the economic development of First Nations communities, in any way improves the mental or physical health or overall well-being of people in First Nations communities." Indigenous Peoples can decode the true motivations behind these terms and find viable strategies to counter the state's "politics of distraction."

Overall, the impacts of these state actions on Indigenous nations and communities are devastating. By decoding these actions, we can see state colonial behavior for what it is. An example of this is "human rights." On the surface this appears to be a positive development. After all, the United Nations Declaration on the Rights of Indigenous Peoples was adopted in 2007 (except for Canada, the United States, Australia, and New Zealand, which voted against it but later changed their positions after a great deal of criticism and pressure) and outlines protections for Indigenous nations. Two things are worth pointing out here. First, the Declaration is merely a guideline and is not legally binding under international law. Second, states that "host" Indigenous nations within their borders are considered the main guarantors of these rights. How can a colonial power be trusted to protect the rights of Indigenous Peoples to self-determination, or to protect Indigenous homelands for that matter? Remember, according to international law, no actions by Indigenous Peoples can be seen as "dismembering or impairing, totally or in part, the territorial integrity or political unity of sovereign and independent States." Finally, where does a state's authority to grant these rights originate? States claim that human rights are gifts from their government to you. And yet the state can take these "gifts" away at any time. Furthermore, as a colonial power, the state has no legitimate authority to even offer us these false gifts. Besides that, Indigenous Peoples do not need them—we already have inherent powers and responsibilities based on our relationships to our land, culture, and community.

Globalization is another buzzword that needs decoding. Through Indigenous eyes, globalization reflects a deepening, hastening, and stretching of an already-existing colonial empire; it is merely the contemporary version of empire-building that brought Europeans to Turtle Island in the first place. According to Zapatista spokesperson Subcomandante Marcos, "In the cabaret of globalization, the state performs a striptease, at the end of which it is left wearing the minimum necessary: its powers of repression. With its material base destroyed, its sovereignty and independence abolished, and its political class eradicated, the nation state increasingly becomes a mere security apparatus in the service of the mega-enterprises which neoliberalism is constructing." It is time to expose the violence of the state while also focusing on revitalizing Indigenous natural laws, land-based practices, and languages. It is time to move from rights-based movements to responsibility-based movements. Pursuing the Western notion of sovereignty will not get us there. We need to decolonize on our own terms.

D. The Peace of Westphalia and Other Common Historical Myths

As Indigenous nations, we existed long before states originated. And the state system did not simply spring up after 1648—it took centuries of deepening trade networks, bureaucratization, empire-building, and competition between political powers to form the states that we know today. In fact, the majority (over 70 percent) of the approximately two hundred states in the world today are less than seventy years old! Some of us have parents who are older than most states in the world today! Unfortunately these immature societies have very short memories about the Indigenous Peoples living within their borders. For these states, decolonization was something that happened only in the 1950s and 1960s and is not relevant today.

According to the United Nations, decolonization is over. There are no more groups that deserve independence. How can this outrageous claim be made? Again, one has to look closely at how the states maintain the status quo. Decolonization that occurred during the 1950s and 1960s (predominantly in Africa and Asia) was highly regulated by colonial powers in order to ensure that existing countries stayed intact: "Any attempt aimed at the partial or total disruption of the national unity and the territorial integrity of a country is incompatible with the purposes and principles of the Charter of the United Nations" (1960 UN General Assembly Resolution 1514). That same year, the United Nations (UN) set further conditions on which territories could decolonize: "There is an obligation to transmit information with respect to a territory that is geographically separate and is distinct ethnically and/or culturally from the country administering it on decolonization" (1960 UN General Assembly Resolution 1541). Basically, if you were not separated from your colonizer by a body of water, you could not decolonize.

Where did that leave Indigenous Peoples who were not geographically separated from their colonizers? Ironically, Indigenous Peoples became re-colonized by newly decolonized states! This uncovers yet another myth: the myth of decolonization and the false perception that the decolonization process has ended. Indigenous Peoples have become trapped within states as internal colonies.

Another myth that is prevalent in the world system today is the right of self-determination. According to the United Nations Charter: "All peoples have the right of self-determination. By virtue of that right they freely determine their political status and freely pursue their economic, social and cultural development."

The right of self-determination is considered a universal human right, but how can true self-determination

> In what became known as the "Salt Water Thesis," only those territories separated by water or that were geographically separate from the colonizing power could decolonize and become independent states.

occur for Indigenous Peoples as long as we are trapped within a colonial state system? Decolonization must occur in order for meaningful self-determination to take place. According to Alfred, "It is still true that the first part of self-determination is the self. In our minds and in our souls, we need to reject the colonists' control and authority, their definition of who we are and what our rights are, their definition of what is worthwhile and how one should live, their hypocritical and pacifying moralities. We need to rebel against what they want us to become, start remembering the qualities of our ancestors and act on those remembrances." A Mayan proverb also demonstrates the urgency of remembering: "There's nothing new under the sun, only what we forget—more or less."

As Indigenous Peoples, we need to avoid directing our energies to state-centered forums and processes (like the United Nations) regarding how to define self-determination. This only distracts us from our real priorities. After all, self-determination is asserted, not negotiated. For Tsalagis, we need to remember our traditions of gadugi, and act on them. As Deskaheh (1872–1925), Cayuga Chief and Speaker of the Six Nations Council, put it, "We are determined to live the free people that we were born." This is how spiritual revolutions begin.

ACTIVITY:

Drawing on your own Indigenous language, do you know of a word or words that relate to freedom, governance or leadership? (If you do not know, call a relative or language speaker who does and make sure you provide a gift for his/her time.) Describe the meanings of this word in as much detail as possible.

How does the meaning of this Indigenous word go beyond the limits of phrases like "self-determination"?

_____

_____

_____

_____

_____

Can you envision Indigenous nationhood without the existence of the state? What are you doing to prepare yourself for a life without the existence of the state?

_____

_____

_____

_____

The late Seneca scholar John Mohawk stated, "The main elements about our colonization —and let us not ever forget our colonization—was that we were to be rendered as children, unable to take care of ourselves. Self-sufficiency doesn't only mean that you raise your own food, and heat, and housing. Self-sufficiency means that you have the capacity, the intellectual cultural capacity, to meet all your needs, to meet your economic needs, to meet your political needs, to meet your social needs."

—quoted in *Paradigm Wars: Indigenous Peoples' Resistance to Economic Globalization*

Indigenous pathways to freedom start with Indigenous people confronting colonialism both individually and collectively—these decolonizing practices eventually expand from the self to family, clan/society, community, and into all of the broader relationships that form an Indigenous existence. However, our decolonization needs to encompass all aspects of our health and well-being as Indigenous Peoples. Alfred writes, "If we are sick, if we are weak as physical beings, if we burden our children and grandchildren with our ailments and do not teach them how to live in a healthy way, we will eventually fail to carry out our responsibilities, spiritually, politically, and

culturally." In other words, we have to decolonize our bodies and diets, which means regenerating our hunting and fishing practices, eating traditional foods, and strengthening ourselves physically as well as spiritually and intellectually.

There is no easy or neat model for Indigenous self-determination. Nor are there clear and definite steps that we can list for people to check off as milestones on their march to freedom. But there are identifiable directions of movement, patterns of thought, and action that reflect a shift to an Indigenous reality from the colonized places we inhabit today in our minds, bodies, and souls.

ACTIVITY:

What are some everyday actions you can take to ensure the survival of your Indigenous nation? What would you tell future generations to do in order to secure the survival of your Indigenous nation?

_____

_____

_____

_____

How can your ancestors recognize you as Indigenous? How will future generations recognize you as Indigenous?

_____

_____

_____

_____

In closing, it is important to remember that change often happens in small increments: "one warrior at a time"—the movement toward decolonization and regeneration will come from transformations achieved through experiences in small, personal groups and one-on-one mentoring. As educators, it is our role to make settlers feel uncomfortable on the Indigenous homelands they are occupying.

We need to remind settlers whose territories they're visiting, as my relative Kai-yah-the-hee, or "First to kill" (aka Old Tassel), did in 1777 with US treaty negotiators:

"Again, were we to enquire by what law or authority you set up a claim; I answer, none! Your laws extend not into our country, nor ever did; you talk of the law of nature and the law of nations, and they are both against you. Indeed much has been advanced on the want of, what you term, civilization among the Indians; and many proposals have been made to us to adopt your laws, your religion, your manners, and your customs. But, we confess, we do not yet see the propriety or practicability of such a reformation; and should be better pleased with beholding the good effects of these doctrines on your own practice, than with hearing you talk about them, or reading your papers to us upon such subjects.... You say, 'Why do not the Indians till the ground, and live as we do?' May we not, with equal propriety, ask why the white people do not hunt and live as we do?"

Kai-yah-the-hee's words about defending our homelands and Indigenous values are just as relevant today as they were over two centuries ago. Yet Kai-yah-the-hee's words are only as strong as the actions behind them. How many of us are defending our homelands today? When we expose the myths of the nation-state, it is clear that the state system is vulnerable. The state can operate only if its citizens live with fear, complacency, and short-term memories. As a by-product of centuries of political and legal fiction, the state ultimately depends on its citizens to protect and police its artificial borders and sovereign "authority." The legitimacy of the state is only as strong as peoples' inability to imagine life without it. Do you really believe that there are no viable alternatives to the state system? The existence of some five thousand Indigenous nations throughout the world today tells us that there are at least five thousand viable alternatives to state rule.

Once you strip away the veneer of legitimacy, as Marcos pointed out, all the state has left are its powers of repression. When Alfred states "May a thousand Okas bloom!" he is highlighting the vulnerabilities of the state. According to Nietschmann, Indigenous resistance can economically bleed the state with three interconnected actions:

1. Continue small ambushes and sabotages that force the state to keep a large and expensive military in the field

2. Destroy or disrupt all state economic exploitation of national resources

3. Through external political and environmental activism, block state receipt of "development" (occupation) funds from international donors, such as non-governmental organizations, corporations, global forums, and states.

The state cannot survive over time unless it has legitimacy and support from the people within its borders. Rather than focus on the state, our focus can shift to resurgence by strengthening our relationships with other Indigenous nations. By engaging in inter-Indigenous treaty-making and alliances to promote new forms of Indigenous unity (revitalizing old trade networks, offering protection for border crossing, protecting of homelands, etc.), strong confederations of Indigenous families and communities emerge as potential challenges to state authority. Since self-determination is something that is taken, and not negotiated, this is about Indigenous Peoples re-asserting our responsibilities, not rights. Then we can once again say that we are defenders of our homelands.

Indigenous Peoples are persistent and resilient—we are nations that existed well before states were created, and our nations will outlast them. Unlike artificial state power, which arises from force and coercion, our power arises from responsibilities and relationships to our territories and families. Ultimately, only Indigenous laws can flourish on Indigenous homelands. That is what living in a longer "now" is all about. As Euchee scholar Dan Wildcat observes, "The most fundamental of these questions is, 'How shall we live?' and this question is at its core a moral question, encompassing power, place, personality, and ultimately, self-determination."

* * *

Wado (thank you) to Taiaiake Alfred and Indigenous Governance MA students from the graduate seminars on "Indigenous Self-Determination" (2010), and "Indigenous Peoples Confront Globalization" (2010) held at the University of Victoria for their comments and insights on earlier versions of this chapter.

E. Resources

Alfred, Taiaiake. "Colonialism and State Dependency." *Journal of Aboriginal Health* 5 (2009): 42–60.

———. *Peace, Power, Righteousness: An Indigenous Manifesto,* 2nd Edition. Oxford: Oxford University Press, 2009.

———. *Wasáse: Indigenous Pathways of Action and Freedom.* Broadview/UTP, 2005.

Corntassel, Jeff. "Toward Sustainable Self-Determination: Rethinking the Contemporary Indigenous-Rights Discourse." *Alternatives* 33 (2008): 105–132.

Deloria, Vine, Jr., and Daniel Wildcat. *Power and Place: Indian Education in America.* Boulder: Fulcrum Resources, 2001.

INCITE! Women of Color Against Violence, ed. *The Revolution Will Not Be Funded: Beyond the Non-Profit Industrial Complex.* Cambridge, MA: South End Press, 2007.

Klein, Naomi. *The Shock Doctrine: The Rise of Disaster Capitalism.* New York: Metropolitan Books, 2007.

LaDuke, Winona. *Recovering the Sacred: The Power of Naming and Claiming.* Cambridge, MA: South End Press, 2005.

Laenui, Poka. "Process of Decolonization." In *Reclaiming Indigenous Voice and Vision.* Ed. Marie Battiste, 150–160. Vancouver: UBC Press, 2000.

Mander, Jerry and Victoria Tauli-Corpuz, eds. *Paradigm Wars: Indigenous Peoples' Resistance to Economic Globalization.* San Francisco: Sierra Club Books, 2006.

Manuel, George, and Michael Posluns. *The Fourth World: An Indian Reality.* Toronto: Collier Macmillan Canada, Ltd., 1974.

Marcos, Subcomandante. *Our Word Is Our Weapon: Selected Writings.* New York: Seven Stories Press, 2002.

Nietschmann, Bernard. "The Fourth World: Nations Versus States." *Reordering the World: Geopolitical Perspectives on the 21st Century.* Ed. George Demko and William Wood, 225–242. Boulder: Westview Press, 1994.

Regan, Paulette. *Unsettling the Settler Within: Indian Residential Schools, Truth Telling, and Reconciliation in Canada.* Vancouver: UBC Press, 2010.

Shiva, Vandana. *Earth Democracy: Justice, Sustainability and Peace.* Cambridge, MA: South End Press, 2005.

Simpson, Leanne, ed. *Lighting the Eighth Fire: The Liberation, Resurgence, and Protection of Indigenous Nations.* Winnepeg: Arbeiter Ring, 2008.

Smith, Andrea. *Conquest: Sexual Violence and American Indian Genocide.* Boston: South End Press, 2005.

Speed, Shannon. *Rights in Rebellion: Indigenous Struggle and Human Rights in Chiapas.* Palo Alto: Stanford University Press, 2007.

Turner, Nancy J. *The Earth's Blanket: Traditional Teachings for Sustainable Living.* Vancouver: Douglas & McIntyre, 2005.

Waziyatawin. *What Does Justice Look Like? The Struggle for Liberation in Dakota Homeland.* St. Paul: Living Justice Press, 2008.

Websites

Captain Hook Awards for Biopiracy. Cog Awards for Resisting Biopiracy. http://www.captainhookawards.org/winners/cog_2008.

First Voices. First Voices Indigenous Language Archives. http://www.firstvoices.com/en/home.

Historic Waikiki. Decolonizing Waikiki. http://www.downwindproductions.com/.

Indigenous Food Systems Network (http://www.indigenousfoodsystems.org/).

Jeff Corntassel's website: www.corntassel.net.

Chapter 6

COLONIZATION IS ALWAYS WAR

Scott DeMuth

A. Dakota People and Minnesota's Sesquicentennial

My first experience of Indigenous liberation was in the Summer of 2006, supporting the Six Nations Haudenosaunee in a land reclamation outside of Caledonia, Ontario. I had heard about the reclamation from a few friends, who invited me to do support work, and quickly found myself on the land. After a twenty-four-hour bus ride from Minneapolis, Minnesota, to Hamilton, Ontario, and no sleep, I was thrown onto the frontline checkpoint on the site. It was here where I experienced firsthand the spirit and culture of resistance to colonialism. I listened to elders telling of struggles ranging from Wounded Knee to Ganienkeh to Oka to Chiapas and beyond. I witnessed the low-intensity warfare waged at that site. I spent countless sleepless nights on patrol, sitting at posts, cooking meals, and doing lots and lots of dishes. I left the site for the last time in the winter of 2007 with the instructions to return to my own community, inspired by the possibility of taking back and holding land.

I returned home to begin working with other people in Dakota communities organizing to challenge the State of Minnesota's sesquicentennial celebrations of statehood. Missing among the Sesquicentennial was even an acknowledgment of the state's genocidal history, including the 150-mile forced march of more than seventeen hundred Dakotas; three hundred Dakota people murdered in concentration camps; and state-sanctioned ethnic cleansing through military expeditions, bounties, and forced removals.

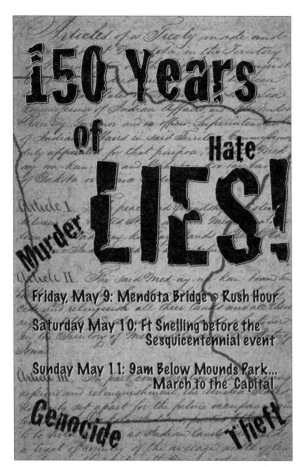

Figure 6.1. 150 Years of Lies poster. Courtesy of protest
organizers Scott DeMuth and Waziyatawin.

Figure 6.2. Minnesota Sesquicentennial Wagon Train reenactors, Fort
Snelling, May 10, 2008. Video still courtesy of Craig Marsden.

A group of Dakota scholars and educators had
met earlier with the Minnesota Sesquicentennial Commission to offer a Dakota perspective on Minnesota
statehood. They suggested that the sesquicentennial
could be an opportunity to reflect on the atrocities, to
begin truth telling, and to pursue a vision of justice.
The Commission declined, choosing instead to ignore
the state's shameful history, and proceeded to celebrate
a distorted vision of its past.

May 11, 2008 was the kickoff for the Minnesota Sesquicentennial at the State Capitol. With
truth telling and a Dakota perspective ignored in the
celebrations, a small group of Indigenous people began
preparing other ways for a critical voice to be heard.
Stickers and posters were already showing up around

town in the weeks before the kickoff stating: "150
Years of Lies!" (figure 6.1) over a silhouette of the state.

The day before the kickoff celebrations, a wagon
train made its way through Minnesota with its last
stop at Fort Snelling before finally heading to the state
capitol (figure 6.2). The wagon train and fort are both
powerful symbols, representing Manifest Destiny, colonization, and the historic injustices Indigenous people
have faced. For Dakota people in particular, Fort
Snelling is where seventeen hundred women, children,
and elders were imprisoned in a concentration camp
and more than three hundred were murdered. This was
a slap in the face to Indigenous Peoples, and we chose
this as an important event to be stopped.

The wagon train was escorted to the fort with at
least eleven law enforcement units, including sheriff's
departments, airport police, numerous unmarked
cars, and a horseback patrol. We filled in the narrow
roadway that led into the fort, and the wagon train
came to a halt parallel to its police escort. For an hour
and a half, we blockaded the wagon train. Mounted
police forced frightened horses through the group.
Some scattered to the sidewalks while two young men
pushed the horses away from a group of children. A
police unit slowly led the wagons through the crowded
street. Two teenagers sat in the road with signs that

Figure 6.3. Chris Mato Nunpa speaking during the Sesquicentennial Protest at the Minnesota State Capitol, May 2008. Photo courtesy of Mona Smith, Allies: media/art.

asked: "If we get in your way, will you kill us again?" Seven people were arrested, including the two teenagers, before police began pushing us out of the street with truncheons. The Sesquicentennial Commission attempted another celebration of Statehood Week for the following weekend. Indigenous people were in attendance and, once again, we were not celebrating (figure 6.3).

During nonviolent protests, arrests increased and police threats of violence intensified against Dakota people and our Anishinaabeg supporters. Law enforcement drove horses at our crowds. They arrested young people and anyone else who spoke out. They wore body armor, carried shotguns, and were backed by sniper teams.

We succeeded in what we sought to do. We

let it be known that Dakota people would not stand silent as the state attempts to rewrite and whitewash accounts of the past. But success does not come without need for improvement. Our actions were largely reactionary and limited to the events that the Sesquicentennial Commission had been planning. We did not take the initiative to provide well-planned counter-events with which both Minnesotans and other Indigenous people could engage.

Arguably the most important outcome is that the sesquicentennial protests brought together a group of Dakota people dedicated to the liberation of the Dakota Nation and the homeland of Minisota Makoce (Land Where the Waters Reflect the Skies). Relationships were formed. Alliances were built. And new organizers emerged, willing to challenge historical and present injustices.

The following September we began efforts to reclaim the sacred spring of Mini Owe Sni (Coldwater Spring) and the surrounding land of Bdote (the Bdewakantunwan Dakota site of genesis and genocide). These efforts began with occupying the site for four days of ceremonies to celebrate the transition from summer to fall. While we did not ask for a permit for the four days, one was issued by the property manager of the abandoned federal property. Despite our permit and the ceremonies we were holding on site, we experienced heavy surveillance by Homeland Security, county sheriffs, and riot police from various police agencies. While we announced that we would depart on the last day of ceremonies, warriors at the site made a pledge to return.

B. Colonization Is Always War

In *Colonization and Decolonization: A Manual for Indigenous Liberation in the 21st Century*, colonization is defined as a war for territory and resources. It also includes the religious, political, and economic conversion of Indigenous Peoples and the boarding schools in which the children were institutionalized. In addition, colonization is psychological warfare with the goal of dampening both Indigenous resistance to the exploitation of the land and the source of that resistance—Indigenous culture.

If colonization continues today, then it follows that war continues to be waged against Indigenous Peoples and territories. This statement should be obvious to anyone who has observed the historical and current effects of colonialism within Indigenous homelands. As the United States government overcame military resistance in their invasion of Indigenous territories, it then used political, economic, and cultural force, with the backing of the threat of violence, to maintain control. These tactics are much harder to observe and identify than open military force.

The colonizer must strike a balance between military, cultural, and psychological warfare. Open repression or threat of violence creates more resentment among the Indigenous population, but too little repression can make resistance easier. **Assimilation** tactics and psychological warfare—previously through residential schools and more currently through public education, mainstream media, and even tribal political institutions—help to temper resistance and control the Indigenous population. All of these tactics serve to obscure the full nature of this war.

Just as in military warfare, there are casualties. Louis Karonhiaktajeh Hall, who participated in the re-occupation at Ganienkeh and who wrote the *Warrior's Handbook*, stated that the casualties are evidenced in suicide, alcohol, drugs, and gangs and the fact that our populations face the additional problems of high rates of infant mortality and imprisonment, low life expectancy, and major health crises. Boarding schools claimed thousands of lives, and the abuses perpetrated in these institutions have had intergenerational consequences. These are the new casualties of the modern era. These are the new casualties of this continued war.

Assimilation:

This is the process of dismantling and erasing Indigenous society and culture, and replacing it through religious, political, and economic conversion. This is a form of psychological warfare institutionalized within the colonial state through boarding schools. It should be noted that this is not true assimilation, as the goal is not to incorporate Indigenous populations into colonial society, but instead to control and gain access to territory and resources—including humans.

We direct our anger and violence in our communities at one another and at ourselves. It becomes easier to join a gang, whether deemed criminal or legal (such as the military, police, or corporations), or to strike against those who are in our communities than to identify and strike against an obscure enemy. It becomes easier to assimilate or to become apathetic than to risk action. If we are unable to comprehend colonization or the conditions of war, then we are unable to identify the means of oppression or our position in the context of history. Ultimately, if we are unable to identify our enemies, we are unable to develop effective strategies to combat them.

We can gain an understanding of our position only through an understanding of colonization. Through education and the development of a critical consciousness, we can identify the colonial system as an enemy of our Indigenous nations. We can acknowledge the current reality of colonialism and threat of military force within our communities. We need to understand our histories of resistance to colonialism, the use of military and state repression against us historically, and how that repression continues against our fiercest resistors to colonialism today. There are some who would believe that military force and state violence are not a present reality for Indigenous people. While military campaigns have been replaced with campaigns of psychological warfare, to say that state violence is absent is far from the truth. The threat of military violence continues today and becomes especially apparent when exercised against resistance movements.

Within the last forty years, the United States and Canada alone provide numerous examples of

1973 At the Takeover of Wounded Knee, South Dakota, hundreds of police, FBI, and paramilitary units held siege to the encampment, using military assistance, vehicles, weapons, and ammunition. Two warriors were killed.

1974 At the Mohawk re-occupation of Ganienkeh in New York State, hundreds of state police were deployed. Re-occupation ended in negotiation for a parcel of land still occupied today.

1975 Two FBI agents and one warrior were killed during a botched FBI raid of an American Indian Movement (AIM) camp near Oglala, South Dakota. Hundreds of FBI agents and state police were deployed to Pine Ridge in a manhunt for AIM members.

1979 Over seventy AIM members and Lakota traditionalists at Pine Ridge, South Dakota, were killed by federal and FBI-trained and supported paramilitary forces.

1981 In Restigouche, New Brunswick, over 500 Quebec police raided the Mi'kmaq community because of "illegal" fishing.

1990 At standoffs at Mohawk communities Kanehsatake (Oka) and Kahnawake, near Montreal, Quebec, over fifteen hundred police and four thousand Canadian soldiers were deployed. A raid by heavily armed tactical police units resulted in one police officer killed. One Mohawk man was killed from tear gas poisoning during the raid, and another died of heart failure following an attack from a settler mob.

1995 At a standoff at Ts'Peten near Gustafsen Lake, British Columbia, heavily-armed Royal Canadian Mounted Police (RCMP) were deployed, using armored personnel carriers (APCs) from the Canadian military. Explosives and APCs were used to disable a vehicle transporting water. More than twenty thousand rounds were fired by police in a subsequent firefight. One defender was wounded.

1995 At a re-occupation of Ipperwash Provincial Park, Ontario, tactical police squads were deployed. Police killed one unarmed protester, Dudley George. A fifteen-year-old youth was shot and injured by police.

2001 At Burnt Church, NB, heavily armed police were deployed against Mi'kmaq lobster fishers. West Coast Warrior Society members were present to provide security from white vigilantes who destroyed lobster traps.

2001 At Sutikalh re-occupation camp near Mt. Currie, BC, heavily armed tactical police units and a helicopter were used to dismantle a roadblock and arrest seven people.

2002 RCMP and an anti-terrorist unit raided the homes of West Coast Warrior Society members on Vancouver Island, BC.

2003 RCMP police, with tactical units and a helicopter, raided Native Youth Movement (NYM) member homes in Bella Coola and Neskonlith, BC, seizing computers, discs, address books, and printed materials.

2005 More than thirty Vancouver police and RCMP, including tactical and anti-terrorist units, arrested two members of the West Coast Warrior Society in Vancouver. Ten legally purchased rifles were confiscated. No charges were pressed, and weapons were kept as part of an ongoing investigation.

2006 At reclamation of a housing development in Caledonia, ON, near the Six Nations Reserve, hundreds of Ontario Provincial Police were deployed. Police attempted to remove blockades while using batons and pepper spray, but they were fought back by community members.

2008 At a blockade of Longview hog farm on tribal lands near the Yankton reservation in South Dakota, over a hundred officers and sniper teams were deployed despite tribal members using nonviolent tactics.

military force and repression being deployed against Indigenous people (see p. 103).

Even in the last few years of organizing in Dakota communities, I have already seen firsthand evidence of state repression. Police snipers, or what they call "lethal over-watch," have been present at each of our nonviolent, truth-telling protests during the State of Minnesota's sesquicentennial celebrations. Despite being on an oxygen tank for recent lung ailments, Anishinaabe elder Steven Blake was singled out and attacked by police while drumming and singing an honor song for the thirty-eight Dakota men hanged at Mankato. Blake was hospitalized after the incident and never fully recovered from resulting complications. At nonviolent protests during a "histor-ical" reenactment at the Yellow Medicine Agency, state police wore body armor and openly brandished shotguns. During the occupation of one of our sacred springs for four days of fall ceremonies, we were subjected to intimidation by low-flying helicopters and squads of riot police.

Throughout the above-mentioned incidents, the threat and application of military force is clear. Thousands of soldiers and police, using military weapons, vehicles, equipment, and tactics, continue to be deployed against Indigenous resistance movements. At protests, roadblocks, and re-occupation camps in defense of land and resources, Indigenous people are faced with heavily armed police, surveillance, and lethal over-watch. As a result, hundreds of Indigenous people have been assaulted, arrested, and jailed. At least six Indigenous people have been killed directly by police or military forces in these conflicts. Additionally, from 1973–1979, on the Pine Ridge Reservation, over seventy AIM members and traditionalists were killed by federal and FBI-trained and -supported paramilitary forces.

The threat of military force and the use of violence and intimidation by state police is a present reality. While Indigenous people are not faced day to day with military campaigns, the state is quick to direct these forces against those who are involved in protest and resistance activity. The colonial state must use military force and military tactics to maintain its control over colonized populations and resources. The attacks on Indigenous sovereignty and the underlying threats of military force speak to the current state of war. As economic and environmental conditions decline, as they are doing now, the potential for conflict between the colonizer and the colonized will increase, especially around issues such as mining and tar sands extraction. This is only a potential conflict, as there is the option that communities may choose to remain complacent because of promises of monetary rewards or out of fear of military violence and state repression. But if Indigenous people are serious about defending their communities and liberating territories, this conflict is inevitable.

> **As stated by the Native Youth Movement:**
> **"Colonization is always war." Decolonization requires a proper response.**

Colonization is a war, and it is a war in which Indigenous people are primarily losing, whether it is a loss of land, resources, or people. Indigenous groups serious about defending their communities, land, and resources will need to increase the fighting spirit of our nations, build a culture of resistance within our communities, as well as organize and train warrior societies.

C. Decolonization Is Self-Defense

Just as we need to recognize the true nature of colonialism and the conditions of war in order to understand the roots of our oppression, we also need to understand the true nature of decolonization and what it requires. In Dakota, the process of **decolonization** is *ki wasicu etanhan ihduhdayapi*—to tear yourself away from the *wasicu* (white/Western/colonizer) way. This does not suggest that we buy our way out of colonization. We do not wait our way out of colonization. We do not just educate ourselves out of colonization.

This definition suggests that decolonization is a violent process, and we must tear ourselves away from colonization. We disengage from the ways of the colonial system. We re-learn our family relations, our culture, our language, our songs, and our ceremonies. We relearn our lifeways within our territories. We relearn these things, and we live them. We must live these things, and we must defend them.

Decolonization is the ending of colonialism and the liberation of the colonized. The process of colonization must be reversed, beginning with the psychological aspects and moving toward the physical. Decolonization can start as an act of cultural revitalization, and focusing on revitalizing culture can create the conditions for liberation. However, a sole focus on cultural identity will not lead to the liberation of land or people. Liberation requires the dismantling of the colonial government and the source of control and exploitation in our territories. Therefore, this is a revolutionary struggle that seeks to dismantle power at the national and state levels while building power at local and traditional levels. Decolonization is a struggle that has historically ranged from peaceful negotiations and nonviolent action to armed struggle by the Indigenous population. Even the United Nations—in no way an ideal body for affirming the rights of Indigenous nations—has stated that these are legally justified actions, and that in the process of decolonization there is no alternative to the principle of self-determination.

If our goal is the dismantling of the colonial state and the liberation of Indigenous Peoples and territories, decolonization can be seen as the process of getting there. In order for any decolonization movement to succeed, the following elements are crucial: resistance movements and an understanding of these movements; an understanding of state repression; a diversity of tactics; a culture of resistance and security; and an effective strategy. While effective strategies will differ according to the Peoples, communities, and movements engaging in resistance, it is important to strike where the enemy is weak and where you are strong.

> **Adapting the slogan of the Gaelic revival and Irish independence movement may add some clarity and offer a useful example for decolonization:**
> **Not merely free, but Irish as well;**
> **not merely Irish, but free as well.**

ACTIVITY:

In what ways did your nation resist colonization historically?

_____

_____

_____

_____

_____

Who were the patriots in that struggle? How are they celebrated today?

_____

_____

_____

_____

_____

_____

What are your nation's current and historic land struggles? How are they being fought?

_____

_____

_____

_____

_____

_____

D. Building a Resistance Movement

A key part of building a **resistance movement** is to know the history, lessons, and mistakes of past examples. As Indigenous Peoples, we need to know our own stories of resistance to colonialism. We need to know how the colonizer has responded to our resistance, the resistance of other Indigenous Peoples, and other resistance movements more broadly. In addition, we need to understand how resistance movements form, how the state suppresses movements, and how we can effectively liberate our territories.

In *The New State Repression*, author Ken Lawrence

Resistance Movement:
A group, or collection of groups, dedicated to fighting an invader in an occupied country through the use of physical force, using both nonviolent and militant tactics. The term *resistance* is generally used to designate movements considered illegitimate by the occupying forces.

discusses how political repression has changed—not only on the level of technology, but more significantly on the level of strategy. In the past, the ruling class and its security forces often viewed insurgencies and rebellions as occasional and erratic disturbances from the normal operations of society. Today's political repression operates from the assumption that insurgency is a permanent and constant fixture, which calls for a strategy of permanent repressions. Tactics developed and tested in the colonies and occupied territories are later deployed against the colonizer's own citizens. This can be seen in the United States with the use of drone spy planes developed for and deployed in the so-called War on Terror and now used domestically to aid in the arrest of US citizens and to kill them in other countries. In Canada, spy planes were a staple of surveillance at the Gustafsen Lake standoff.

Frank Kitson, a British commander with experience combating resistance movements in Northern Ireland, developed many of the basic tactics of counterinsurgency used today. While his book *Low Intensity Operations: Subversion, Insurgency, and Peace-Keeping* was developed to disrupt resistance movements, it provides an understanding of the development of resistance movements, and how they are suppressed, in each of its three phases: (1) the preparatory phase, (2) the nonviolent phase, and (3) insurgency.

During the preparatory phase, the movement begins by mobilizing the population and building support for its cause. While this appears to be a time of calm, action is required on the part of security forces. The state will avoid the use of force as much as possible and instead focus on gathering intelligence. They will attempt to undermine movement support and promote the state by building sympathy with the civilian population. However, intelligence is the most crucial element for the state as the early stages may be the only opportunity to identify movement members and infiltrate organizations. During this stage, movement members are often ignorant of surveillance techniques and lax about precautions to counter surveillance. The state security forces will exploit this situation by limiting overt surveillance and repression, and will instead gather intelligence through covert surveillance, wiretaps, informants, and infiltrators. This phase can be seen in many Indigenous communities, where the state actively solicits informants, particularly people who have been arrested and are facing drug and criminal charges. State tactics can be limited by the movement's adoption of a *security culture* early on.

The nonviolent phase is when the movement begins to mobilize members of the population and begins using many of the visible tactics associated with social movements, such as marches, protests, and civil disobedience, escalating to occupations, sabotage, and other forms of direct action. These have been common features in many Indigenous communities, particularly those that have resisted the exploitation of their land base and natural resources. As the colonizer's resources decline, we will see an increase in conflict around these areas, such as the current resistance to tar sands extraction in Canada, the Keystone XL pipeline, as well as exploratory mining. While the previous objective of the state security forces was to collect intelligence, they must now attempt to disrupt movement activity, undermine public support, and neutralize organizers.

Security forces will often use arrests to disrupt, criminalize, and discredit the movement. This is

COINTELPRO:

Counter Intelligence Program. A series of covert, and often illegal, operations conducted by the United States Federal Bureau of Investigation (FBI) aimed at infiltrating, disrupting, marginalizing, and/or neutralizing social movements. Tactics include infiltration, surveillance, psychological warfare, legal harassment, vandalism, break-ins, assaults, beatings, and assassinations.

evidenced in the state's response to re-occupation efforts by Indigenous people. At the standoff at Ts'Peten in 1995, the state and the media attempted to label warriors as thugs, criminals, and terrorists. This can also be seen in the raids and arrests of Native Youth Movement and West Coast Warrior members in British Columbia by police and anti-terrorist units. Other tactics such as intimidation, harassment, violent assaults, and even lethal force may be used. Examples can be seen from the civil rights and liberation struggles in the United States throughout the 1960s and 1970s. The FBI and various police and state agencies used COIN-TELPRO (Counter Intelligence Program) tactics against the Black Civil Rights Movement, the Black Panther Party, the Puerto Rican independence movement, the anti-war movement, and the American Indian Movement. Surveillance, informants, and infiltrators were used against these organizations. Homes and offices were broken into, and organizational materials were seized or destroyed. Infiltrators exploited imbalanced power dynamics and debates surrounding tactics to divide movements. Key organizers were arrested, jailed, and in some instances, executed. Because of these latter tactics, more militant organizers went underground.

Kitson suggests that it may be disadvantageous to use brute force against a nonviolent movement as it may force movement members into organizing clandestinely, making it difficult to identify organizers. Nonviolent movements are much easier to infiltrate, and therefore he recommends that the state disrupt the movement through undermining public support and neutralizing the movement organizers. The *Counterinsurgency Field Manual 3-24* states: "Some of the best weapons for counterinsurgents do not shoot." In addition to propaganda and criminalizing the movement,

> **Insurgency:**
> An organized movement aimed at the overthrow of a constituted government through the use of subversion and armed conflict. It is an organized, protracted politico-military struggle designed to weaken the control and legitimacy of an established government, occupying power, or other political authority while increasing insurgent control.
> —*Counterinsurgency Field Manual 3-24*

the state may offer concessions to regain support from the population, discover and neutralize the subversive elements and leadership, and associate prominent organizers with the government, "especially those who have engaged in non-violent action." This is called co-optation, and Kitson describes this tactic as "drowning the revolution in baby's milk." Co-optation often occurs through revising minor laws, addressing minor grievances through truth commissions, or monetary settlements for land claims. This could also include a number of formerly militant organizers or organizations that are now incorporated, receive government funds, and sponsor government programs.

Again, the state takes advantage of lax security measures and internal divisions. Thus, all organizations involved in resistance movements, regardless of tactics, should take security concerns seriously and should adopt a level of security that is congruent with the risk of their resistance. For example, a group involved in organizing a mass demonstration may need to organize openly and publicize their activities to mobilize people for the action. However, a group involved in illegal acts of sabotage would need to organize secretly in a closed group of trusted comrades. Because the state will target nonviolent organizations and leaders for co-optation, it is essential that a resistance movement, especially those espousing non-violent tactics, embrace and build cohesion between different tactics.

The next stage is when the resistance movement erupts into an **insurgency**. While all three phases are regarded as part of an insurgency, this is the most visible and recognizable revolt against the occupying force. Although insurgency involves combat forces (usually guerillas), it also requires the population to provide support to the resistance movement and disrupt the operations of the state. It is in the stages of armed conflict that much of the resistance movement will need to practice clandestine organizing, often referred to as operating **underground**. All security and counter surveillance measures are practiced to the fullest extent, thus restricting the state's ability to gather intelligence. The state security forces will rely on integrating police and military efforts as evidenced in the *Counterinsurgency Field Manual 3-24*. This can also be seen in the above examples of state repression where the state police use military equipment, training, and tactics, where the military engages in policing operations, and where the state police and military conduct joint operations. During this phase of the conflict, the *Counterinsurgency Field Manual 3-24* suggests that a troop density of twenty to twenty-five counterinsurgents is necessary for every thousand residents. The operations in Pine Ridge during Wounded Knee and the Reign of Terror and at Kahnawake and Oka in Quebec in 1990 reflect many of these counterinsurgency principles.

> **Underground:**
>
> A movement, organization, cell, or individuals who operate secretly and covertly in order to evade state repression and engage effectively in resistance.

While not necessarily an insurgency or a guerilla war, armed occupations and standoffs have been a prominent feature of Indigenous resistance in the past couple of decades. Kitson summarizes the primary objective and difficulty of the state during this phase: "The problem of destroying enemy armed groups and their supporters therefore consists very largely of finding them." While armed land occupations and standoffs can be symbolically and culturally meaningful and politically powerful, and have sometimes led to successes for some communities, they are inherently vulnerable to state attacks. Veterans of these conflicts have suggested that unless armed re-occupations are ready to defend themselves militarily, it may be more advantageous to use nonviolent tactics or unarmed defenses. However, contrasting the re-occupations of Gustafsen Lake (Ts'Peten) and Ipperwash Provincial Park in 1995, the former was an armed standoff with no casualties while the latter, a nonviolent re-occupation,

resulted in the killing of George Dudley and the wounding of another young man.

Kitson's analysis of this stage is primarily in response to a widespread, armed insurrection or guerilla war. The *Counterinsurgency Field Manual 3-24* suggests that "a small number of highly motivated insurgents with simple weapons, good operations security, and even limited mobility can undermine security over a large area." In *Peace-keeping in a Democratic Society: The Lessons of Northern Ireland*, Robin Evelegh responds to the problem of finding movement members who have gone underground. While the state will often take advantage of lax security to track and disrupt clandestine groups, it can also encourage defection and informants by offering monetary and legal incentives such as reduced criminal charges.

While informants can often be difficult to detect, the damaging effects of informants can be mitigated through heightened methods of security and ensuring that firewalls exist between clandestine cells and with wider, aboveground movement. However, increased security and clandestine operations severely limit the recruitment of new members. Militant groups in North America, such as the Black Liberation Army, were unable to continue operations because they were unable to recruit new members to replace those who had been imprisoned or killed. This is why it is crucial to have community support and to build a culture of resistance within that community early in the movement.

E. Diversity of Tactics

As in nature and social movements, diversity can be a strength, not a weakness. The more diverse the tactics are in a movement, the more accessible it is for people to become involved. One of the greatest threats to resistance movements, excluding the colonial system of course, is the divide between militancy and nonviolence. As demonstrated above, this divide is often exploited to undermine and co-opt social movements.

Three things that help widen this split are myths of pacifism, a simplistic view of violence, and the conflation of tactics and strategy.

Resources are listed at the end of this chapter that will deepen a discussion about a diverse tactics. It should be understood, however, that all violence is not equal, especially in the context of self-defense against colonization. Not only do we have a right to liberate our people and defend our territories by whatever means and tactics are at our disposal, but some believe that we have an obligation to do so.

It should also be understood that nonviolence and militancy are not goals, and they are not strategies. They are tactics. The goals of decolonization have been stated above: liberation of people and territory. Our strategy is a plan or series of plans of how we will accomplish our goals: revitalizing Indigenous culture, neutralizing the destruction of our land base, and reclaiming traditional territory. Tactics are the conduct and actions that fulfill a strategy: teaching language classes and participating in ceremony; a nonviolent blockade of a tar sands operation or sabotaging mining equipment; and occupying a specific site or land base, with or without the use of an armed defense.

Finally, nonviolence should not be confused with pacifism, nor should it be confused with complacency. It is not about trying to educate or convert those in power. It is a tactic used to confront and directly stop oppressive power. Gene Sharp, whose ideas have been used in a number of liberation struggles, wrote in *The Politics of Nonviolent Action* that power does not come from the state; instead the power held by the state is derived from its subjects' obedience. If subjects withdraw their consent, if they do not obey or if they disrupt the rule of order, political leaders are left with nothing. This occurs through both acts of omission—withdrawing from the system (e.g., boycotts, strikes, and nonparticipation) and commission—disrupting the system (e.g., sit-ins, blockades, sabotage, and occupations).

Additionally, to engage in a resistance movement requires us to be brutally honest about our capacities, our strengths and weaknesses, and our limits. We need to come to terms with what we can and cannot do, but also with what may be required of us.

We have already established that the conditions of colonization and the evidence of this violence abound. This includes the genocide of Indigenous people, the theft of Indigenous homelands, and the continued destruction of these lands. Whatever choice we make, whether to take action or remain complacent, there is already violence. *To remain complacent is not a nonviolent choice; complacency is only an acceptance of violence.* Therefore, we should conceive of a divide not between violence and nonviolence but between action and inaction, resistance and complacency. Different tactics and even strategies are necessary in a revolutionary struggle and should be seen as parts of a mutually beneficial whole. This is why I embrace a diversity of tactics as part of an effective strategy.

Honoring a diversity of tactics means refraining from attacking allies who have chosen a different approach, and instead providing any missing elements to make their efforts effective. Strategy and

In *What We Leave Behind*, Derrick Jensen and Aric McBay say:

"A culture of resistance is, collectively, that group of people with an understanding of the root cause of their predicament, and a willingness to work together in opposition to authority to address those causes.

"A culture of resistance is not the same as an organized resistance movement, but is necessary for the success and growth of such a movement. In every country where a successful revolution has taken place, there has been a culture of resistance. In every occupied nation with an ongoing resistance movement, there is a culture of resistance. If a resistance movement is a sturdy tree, a culture of resistance is the soil from which it grows, a soil itself enriched by the growth of the tree."

participation is reframed in terms of personal responsibility: the question is not what somebody else should be doing (as long as they are doing something) but what you can do.

F. Keeping Our People Strong—Building a Culture of Resistance

A culture of resistance in a community includes the norms, behaviors, and common understandings that are necessary to support a resistance movement. In order for a resistance movement to flourish, two essential requirements are loyalty and material support. A culture of resistance can help provide these.

If we were to measure community loyalty on a continuum, there would be a range from active supporters to active collaborators (see activity below). Within this range there would be passive supporters, neutral/apathetic observers, passive antagonists, unwitting collaborators, and active collaborators. Active collaborators are people whose loyalties are with the colonial system and whose activities directly disrupt a resistance movement. This can include perpetrators of **neo-colonialism**, such as tribal leaders or tribal paramilitary forces who enforce the colonial state against their own people. It could also include persons in the community who have been wooed by the capitalist system and accrue benefits to allow resource extraction or who provide information to state police. Infiltrators are both state and non-state agents who actively join resistance movements in order to disrupt movement activity or to obtain intelligence for the enemy.

Informants are primarily non-state actors who supply intelligence to the enemy. Informants may be passive antagonists, such as "canary birds" who are not a part of resistance activities but report on community activity. They may also be unwitting collaborators, such as members of the resistance movement who do not consciously supply intelligence but do so through improper conduct, including but not limited to practicing lax security, spreading gossip or rumors, engaging in divisive behaviors, conducting poor counter surveillance, or even unknowingly operating with informants, and thus supplying information. Movement members who are captured or confronted by state agents may become active collaborators by supplying information or becoming informants out of fear, for financial awards, or reduced prison sentences.

ACTIVITY:

Active Supporter—Passive Supporter—Neutral Observer—Passive Antagonist—Collaborator

Where are you on this continuum?

_____

_____

_____

_____

Where do you see the majority of your community on this continuum?

_____

_____

How did your nation historically deal with collaborators?

_____

_____

_____

_____

_____

_____

What strategies could you use to shift your community into a culture of resistance?

_____

_____

_____

_____

_____

_____

A primary goal of a culture of resistance is to shift community loyalty in favor of the movement. Historically, active collaborators were neutralized through community isolation or reprisals, which can be severe depending on the severity of the collaboration. During the Dakota War of 1862, for example, Dakota patriots targeted collaborators, often burning their homes or fields. The actions of passive antagonists and unwitting informers can be neutralized or turned to support through the actions of the resistance movement, community norms supporting the movement, and practicing good security. The goal should also be to shift passive supporters into active supporters, and active supporters into movement actors.

Groups that have developed successful tactics in dealing with collaborators include the Irish Republican Army (IRA), the Basque Separatists (ETA), and the French Resistance to Nazi-occupation (Marquis). Gestapo records show that less than five percent of detained Marquis were "cooperative," even under "enhanced interrogation techniques." The ETA was structured around kinship and community relationships, and the Basque communities developed a strong culture of resistance based on common experiences of repression from the Spanish state and the deep connections within their community. Neighbors, co-workers, and friends would all react negatively to collaborators. Community shame and reprisals were severe enough that collaborators would have to relocate.

The American Indian Movement (AIM) provides another interesting example. AIM experienced brutal repression by the federal government, along with a high number of informants and collaborators who worked to infiltrate or undermine the group. This created an environment of snitch-jacketing, naming movement members as informants without actual evidence, and considerable infighting among movement members. However, the latter trends were largely confined to the urban chapters. The rural, more traditional, and family-based chapters from the reservations, while fiercely targeted by the federal government, were much more difficult for federal agents to infiltrate. If anything discourages people from informing on one another, it is blood ties and a healthy community. The stronger the ties and benefits that bind an individual to a community, the less likely they will turn against it. Healthy relationships are the backbone of strong communities and communities of resistance. Unaddressed conflicts, unbalanced power dynamics, oppressive relationships, and lack of trust in communities are all exploited by those who seek to dominate or destroy us. One needs only to look at any of the North American protest movements of the 1960s and 1970s to see clear evidence of this.

One movement that had been successful in deterring members from collaboration, even while heavily infiltrated by undercover police, was the Irish Republican Army (IRA). A culture of resistance was entrenched within the Irish movement, as is evident by the vast number of songs praising the members, actions, and even weapons of the IRA, known and sung regularly by pub patrons. However, a defining element of the Irish struggle is the high level of energy and resources put into prisoner support and the recognition of IRA prisoners as prisoners of war (POW). This included building a consciousness of political prisoners, the glorification of political prisoners through art and song, and giving ex-prisoners the status of veterans. Nearly a third of all funds raised by the IRA went into prisoner support. This included the ongoing support and organizing of comrades in jail, but also supporting the families of those imprisoned. If one thing can be learned from the IRA, it is how they were able to successfully reduce the punitive nature of incarceration, neutralize government incentives to collaborate, and even make the status of political prisoner one of honor and privilege.

If we want to build communities of resistance that will one day win, we must think of ways to strengthen our communities and build sustainable resistance. Prisoner support is crucial because it removes part of the threat that the state holds over our people, a threat that inhibits many of us from action. Those taking action have less to worry about, knowing they will be supported and cared for if captured, and those captured and imprisoned have fewer reasons to abandon their principles and betray their communities. The same is true of resistance fighters who require moral and material support.

This material support is the other primary task of a culture of resistance. Only a very small percentage of a resistance movement is actually involved in confrontations—the majority of people are involved in support work. The main support roles include logistics and infrastructural support, recruiting and training new members, communications and propaganda, obtaining and moving materials, medical support, feeding troops, prisoner support, and establishing safe houses. This mostly describes the work done by movement members and active supporters within a culture of resistance.

Passive supporters will be involved in less overt means of support. It may also include vocal support and promotion within the family or community. Or it may include a sporadic participation or willingness to participate in low-risk movement activity, such as communications, propaganda, acquiring materials, vocal promotion of militants and militancy, and even providing safe houses. While they may not be actively engaged or organized in movement activity, passive supporters are at least ideologically aligned with the resistance movement. A successful resistance movement does not need active support from every person; it only needs the majority to not work against it.

A culture of resistance creates a willingness to withdraw support from colonial authority and a willingness to work with those in opposition to colonial authority. It means knowing your legal rights and exercising them. It means not collaborating directly with colonial agencies through informing or providing intelligence, and it means not collaborating indirectly,

> "There is a tendency to bring conflicts up to date and to modernize the kinds of struggle which the stories evoke, together with the names of heroes and the types of weapons…. The formula 'This all happened a long time ago' is substituted by that of 'What we are going to speak of happened somewhere else, but it might well have happened here today, and it might happen tomorrow.'"
>
> —Frantz Fanon,
> *Wretched of the Earth*

which is achieved by practicing good security culture, encouraging movement solidarity, and promoting healthy community relationships. It means supporting a broad diversity of tactics, a diversity of struggles, and a diversity of involvement, all working toward the same goal: the dismantling of the colonial state and the liberation of Indigenous land and People.

For Indigenous Peoples, a culture of resistance can revitalize culture and life ways. Conversely, traditional culture can become both a means of resistance and also an inspiration for resistance and further action. In *Wretched of the Earth*, Frantz Fanon says of the place of resistance in cultural revival: "It is the fight for national existence which sets culture moving and opens to it the doors of creation." What Fanon describes is the use of literature, oral tradition, ceremonies, and arts as "a literature of combat, in the sense that it calls on the whole people to fight for their existence as a nation." This can include oral traditions, traditional stories or songs, and histories of resistance to colonialism.

This can also include our songs and ceremonies. Veteran songs, formerly sung for those who fought in the colonial army, might be sung for those who defend our people and land. Alongside round dance songs, love songs, and 49ers, our social dances will include songs of our warriors and their actions. And as our resistance movements begin to draw more strength from our ceremonies, our fire-keepers will resume their role of defending the participants of a ceremony from state repression.

ACTIVITY:

Using the discussion of traditional culture as a means of culture of resistance, what aspects of your culture (e.g., stories, songs, roles, and phrases) provide a basis for a decolonization struggle?

For example, in Dakota culture, we can think about building a culture of resistance by focusing on the following traditional practices:

Iya the Eater	Story of gluttonous monster, comes to represent colonization
Veteran Songs	Formerly sung for colonial army, now sung for land defenders
Firekeeper	Resumes the role of protecting ceremony and its participants
Toksta	Common farewell phrase for "Indeed I will see you again" takes on new meaning in the phrase "*Toksta nikci mat'e kte*"— "Indeed I will die with you" —famous quote by Dakota patriot Taoyateduta or "*Toksta oyate nipi kte*" — "Indeed the people will live."

_____   _____

_____   _____

_____   _____

_____   _____

_____   _____

G. Keeping Our People Safe—Security Culture

As has been evidenced throughout this chapter, resistance movements have faced state repression for years. In a post-9/11 world, targeting of political dissent has only increased. If we are to organize successful resistance movements, it is important that we develop strategies to combat surveillance, counterinsurgency tactics, and state repression. A first basic step is to adopt an active use of a collective security culture.

On a very basic level, this includes community norms and practices that are widely adopted, such as refraining from gossip, discussing your or someone else's involvement with an underground group or an illegal action. Generally, it is a bad idea to talk about people, groups, places, times, targets, or events in relation to illegal actions, even if it is a joke, gossip, or speculation. The only exceptions would be planning an action with trusted members in a secure fashion or if someone has been arrested and convicted of an action and discussing the action would not implicate others. However, this is different from speaking about resistance or illegal activities in abstract or general terms. It is perfectly acceptable and desirable to speak out in support of all forms of resistance.

People breach security culture in a number of different ways and for different reasons: gossip or speculation, asking inappropriate questions, lying or bragging to gain credibility, addictions to drugs or alcohol, starting or spreading rumors, or being informers or infiltrators. When people violate security culture, their actions should be quickly addressed. The person should be educated about why their actions violate security culture, and violations should not be allowed to become habit. Chronic violators can act as unwitting informers and should be told to leave the group or organizing space.

The state has often exploited individuals' addictions and resulting criminal prosecutions from drug and alcohol abuse. The indictment and convictions from Operation Backfire against members of the Earth Liberation Front (ELF) were the result of an informant who was a heroin addict who cooperated with the state to reduce criminal charges. If for no other reason than this, refraining from drug and alcohol abuse should be considered a best practice. This has been adopted in the code of conduct of the Native Youth Movement.

Security culture also includes familiarizing and

> **Security culture** as defined by *Security Culture: A Handbook for Activists*, is: "A culture where people know their rights and, more importantly, assert them. Those who belong to a security culture also know what behavior compromises security and they are quick to educate those people who, out of ignorance, forgetfulness, or personal weakness, partake in insecure behavior. This security consciousness becomes a culture when the group as a whole makes security violations socially unacceptable in the group."

adopting a number of counter surveillance techniques. It is generally a best practice to use encryption software for electronic data. Even if an organizer is not engaged in underground or illegal activities, the state will use any evidence at its disposal to manufacture criminal charges, as has been demonstrated in the numerous conspiracy charges against activists in the United States. For groups engaging in illegal actions or operating clandestinely, security culture will include security procedures such as firewalls between different affinity groups or cells and also between underground and aboveground organizations.

H. Developing Warrior Societies

One of the most effective and proactive measures that can be taken in almost any community is the development of warrior societies and the revitalization of warrior traditions. In addition to building a culture of resistance, fostering a fighting spirit, and defending territory and people, **warrior societies** may help curb many of the social problems in our communities as well as revitalize language and culture.

Historically, societies were organized differently according to traditions within each respective nation. Traditionally for the Dakota, the *zuya wicasta* were responsible for the armed defense of our people, resources, and territories. They also conducted guerilla raids on enemy camps and captured weapons and supplies. The *akicita* provided security for villages and, when the need arose, the punishment for serious anti-social behavior. Any society might be required to fulfill one or both of these roles. Societies also served a social function in initiating young people, and hosting hunting parties, dances, feasts, and giveaways. Another function was ceremonial, giving spiritual strength and guidance. There were also veteran societies, made of war chiefs no longer engaged in warfare, who would often serve as an advisory council to other societies.

A warrior society is a group of people organized, trained, and ready to defend their people, territory, and way of life.

The warrior traditions of the Dakota were traditionally ritualistic with a complex system of honors, the highest of which was touching an opponent, often with the hand, staff, or lance. Warrior traditions adapted as American forces invaded. The rifle was adopted through trade and an alliance with the British during the Revolutionary War and the War of 1812. During the Dakota War of 1862, warfare strategies were adapted after learning from both victories and losses. In the subsequent wars against settler encroachment in the Dakota Territory and the Plains Wars, guerilla warfare strategies culminated in overwhelming victories. Dakota warriors made use of new strategies and available military technology, incorporating these into traditional forms of weaponry and tactics.

ACTIVITY:

What is your nation's word(s) for warrior? What does this mean?

_____

_____

_____

What is your nation's warrior tradition? What types of weapons and tactics were traditionally employed? What songs or ceremonies existed?

_____

_____

_____

_____

How were warrior societies structured? What were their roles or functions?

_____

_____

_____

_____

Today, military force is not often used by Indigenous people unless it is to fight in the service of the colonizers. This is because of an unwillingness to engage on that level, but also because most communities are simply unprepared for that level of conflict. When Indigenous people have engaged in military conflict, it is often defensive, such as in land re-occupations or standoffs with military or police forces. But even defensive actions include the possibility for armed conflict, as the colonial state has been more than willing to demonstrate in the past forty years.

As discussed earlier, colonization does not rely solely on military warfare, but also the use of political, economic, and psychological warfare. A decolonization effort must not rely solely on one form either. Warrior training must entail more than just military training; it should also involve culture, language, ceremonies, and traditional skills. These are essential to creating strong communities and fostering a culture of resistance. The connection between resistance, culture, and language has been discussed earlier as a literature of combat. Ceremonies can create solidarity between warriors, their culture, people, and homeland, as well as with the spirit world and the long line of ancestors who came before them. Traditional skills include hunting, gathering wild foods, and relearning life ways. These help to reinforce traditional culture and values, as well as engaging in active observation and familiarity with the land base. Given the inevitability of resource

decline, these skills will become vital in providing for future generations.

Colonization, however, was perpetuated through military force, and it is this monopoly on force and the threat of violence that allows the colonial system to maintain control of territory, exploit resources, and impose its own will against the wishes and sovereignty of Indigenous Peoples. Louis Karonhiaktajeh Hall writes in _What Is the Warrior Society_, "In any international dispute, no nation has a chance to prevail in the negotiations if it hasn't got defense and protection. It would be negotiating from a position of weakness." Without this bargaining power, the nation will "be forced to make concessions and back down on their demands. The government may even refuse to negotiate."

The greatest obstacle we face in organizing a resistance movement is fear. It is the fear of the state's violence and repression that hinders many from acting to defend territory. This is a fear of potential casualties. While these are reasonable fears given the state's use of violence against social movements, even nonviolent ones, we must remember that colonization is violent by its very nature. Regardless of what actions we take, there are already real casualties occurring on the streets, reserves, and reservations.

In addition to defending land and territory, warrior societies, coupled with culture, language, and ceremony, can give purpose and strength to young people who might otherwise be lost to gangs, prison, the military, drugs, or suicide. Without the means to confront colonization, many of our people lack a will to resist, and even a will to live. A recent study was done by psychologists of Aboriginal suicides among First Nations communities in British Columbia. They showed that when self-government (defined as the community's ability to litigate for Aboriginal title of traditional lands) is present in a community, the suicide rate is dramatically lowered. Further findings suggest that there is a significant relationship between lower youth suicide rates and a community's withdrawal from the BC treaty process and the community's refusal to take monetary payment to settle land claims. It is simply an empirical fact that native communities in British Columbia who fight for their land have lower youth suicide rates or none at all. Would not it be wise for us to simply urge the same actions in our own communities?

The other challenge that we face in organizing warrior societies is the feeling that "now is not the right time to resist." People cite any number of reasons for this sentiment, whether it is because we do not have enough numbers or our enemy is far superior in numbers, armaments, or training. This feeling that "now is not the right time" is accurate, but for reasons different than most espouse.

The right time was not when the first fort was built in Minisota Makoce. It was not when Tecumseh led a coalition to keep settlers east of the Ohio River Valley. It was not when British pilgrims landed in Nauset territory. It was not when Cortez led his invasion through Central America. The right time to resist colonization was when a lost Italian sailing from Spain landed over five hundred years ago.

The "right time" has long passed, but opportunities to organize and defend land and People are continually present. These opportunities will increase as resources decline, and the burden is on us to take on these opportunities, create, and expand them.

The nature of this struggle is ironically best summarized by US general Petraeus, co-author of the *Counterinsurgency Field Manual 3-24*: "You have to recognize also that I don't think you win this war. I think you keep fighting.… You have to stay after it. This is the kind of fight we're in for the rest of our lives and probably our kids' lives."

ACTIVITY:

What skills/materials/knowledge do I currently have?

_____

_____

_____

_____

_____

_____

What skills/materials/knowledge do I need to acquire?

_____

_____

_____

_____

_____

_____

If I do not act, who will?

_____

_____

_____

_____

_____

_____

List the five most important aspects of creating a functioning community:

1. _____

2. _____

3. _____

4. _____

5. _____

List the five most important activities of a culture of resistance:

1. _____

2. _____

3. _____

4. _____

5. _____

List the five most important actions to defend your land base:

1. _____

2. _____

3. _____

4. _____

5. _____

I. Resources

Colonization Is War

Fanon, F. *Wretched of the Earth*. New York: Grove Press, 1963.

Memmi, Albert. *The Colonizer and the Colonized*. New York: Orion Press, 1965.

Zig-Zag. *Colonization: A War for Territory*. British Columbia: Warrior Publications, 2012.

Building a Resistance Movement

Evelegh, Robin. *Peace-keeping in a Democratic Society: The Lessons of Northern Ireland*. Montreal: McGill-Queen's University Press, 1978.

Kitson, Frank. *Low Intensity Operations: Subversion, Insurgency, and Peace-Keeping*. London: Faber and Faber, 1991.

McBay, Aric, Lierre Keith, and Derrick Jensen. *Deep Green Resistance*. New York: Seven Stories Press, 2011.

US Army. *Counterinsurgency Field Manual 3-24*. Washington, DC: Headquarters, Department of the Army, 2006.

Diversity of Tactics

Churchill, Ward, and Mike Ryan. *Pacifism as Pathology: Reflections on the Role of Armed Struggle in North America*. Oakland, CA: AK Press, 2007.

Gelderloos, Peter. *How Nonviolence Protects the State*. Cambridge, MA: South End Press, 2007.

Schock, Kurt. *Unarmed Insurrections: People Power Movements in Nondemocracies*. Minneapolis, MN: University of Minnesota Press, 2004.

Sharp, Gene. *The Politics of Nonviolent Action Part I-III*. Boston, MA: Porter Sargent Publishers, 1985.

Security Culture

Churchill, Ward, and Jim Vander Wall. *Agents of Repression: The FBI's Secret Wars Against the Black Panther Party and the American Indian Movement*. Cambridge, MA: South End Press, 2001.

Lawrence, Ken. *The New State Repression*. Portland, OR: Tarantula Press, 2006.

Resist!CA. *Security Culture: A Handbook for Activists*. Vancouver: Resist! Collective, 2001. http://security.resist.ca/personal/securebooklet.pdf.

Developing Warrior Societies

Chandler, M., and C. Lalonde. "Transferring Whose Knowledge? Exchanging Whose Best Practices?: On Knowing About Indigenous Knowledge and Aboriginal Suicide." *Aboriginal Policy Research*. Ed. D. Beavan and J. White. London, ON: Althouse Press, 2004.

Goodleaf, Donna. *Entering the Warzone: A Mohawk Perspective on Resisting Invasion*. Penticton, BC: Theytus Books, 1995.

Hardt, Michael, and Antonio Negri. *Multitude: War and Democracy in the Age of Empire*. New York: Penguin, 2005.

Karonhiaktajeh Hall, Louis. *Warrior's Handbook*. Self-published, 1979.

Ramirez, Gloria Munoz. *The Fire and the Word: A History of the Zapatista Movement*. San Francisco: City Lights Books, 2008.

York, Geoffrey, and Loreen Pindera. *People of the Pines: The Warriors and the Legacy of Oka*. Toronto: Little, Brown Company, 1992.

Zig-Zag. *Colonization and Decolonization: A Manual for Indigenous Liberation in the 21ˢᵗ Century*. British Columbia: Warrior Publications, 2006.

Chapter 7

ZUYA WICASTA NAKA ICAHWICAYAPI (RAISING NEW WARRIORS)

Waziyatawin

A. De-Problematizing Indigenous Youth

In March 2010, Valerie Taliman published an article in *Indian Country Today* entitled "Stop the Racist Attacks on Our Children." She was responding to the website UsedWinnipeg.com, which ran an advertisement the previous week with the headline "Native Extraction Service" and a photograph of three young Indigenous boys. Taliman reported, "The service offered to round up and remove First Nations youth like wild animals, and 'relocate them to their habitat.' The text of the ad read: 'Have you ever had the experience of getting home to find those pesky little buggers hanging outside your home, in the back alley or on the corner??? Well fear no more, with my service I will simply do a harmless relocation. With one phone call I will arrive and net the pest, load them in the containment unit (pickup truck) and then relocate them to their habitat.'"

Although we live in the twenty-first century, such ads remind us that colonizer society today very much views our youth in the same manner they did in the nineteenth and twentieth centuries when our children were routinely rounded up like stray, barely-domesticated animals. Colonial governments and societies across the globe have frequently targeted Indigenous youth for "civilizing" campaigns, abducting them, and sending them to boarding schools, residential schools, sanatoriums, and white homes because they viewed them as part of a "problem" population. The only difference in the ad quoted above, is that the "civilizing" campaign has been abandoned in favor of a simple removal or relocation of the "problem." It was hateful in the nineteenth and twentieth centuries, and it is hateful today.

Ironically, the three youth indicated as "pests" in the photo on the website are accomplished, award-winning, young documentary filmmakers from the Seattle area, and the photo was stolen from Longhouse Media. When settler society views our youth, however, all they see is the "problem."

How does settler society justify the "problematizing" of our youth?

B. Understanding the State of Crisis

It is no secret that our populations are suffering. We know that the social problems in our communities ballooned in the reserve/reservation era and have continued to flourish under colonial rule. This is marked today by a host of statistics that reveal the extent to which our young people have difficulty negotiating colonial institutions and the hardships they suffer as a consequence.

For example, in January 2010, researchers Susan Faircloth and John Tippeconnic released their revealing report "The Dropout/Graduation Rate Crisis among American Indian and Alaska Native Students: Failure to Respond Places the Future of Native People at Risk," which relayed stark statistics regarding Indigenous graduation levels. Using data from the National Center for Education Statistics (NCES) and the 2000 Census, they focused on 2005 data "from the seven states with the highest percentage of American Indian and Alaska Native (AI/AN) students as well as five states in the Pacific and Northwestern regions of the United States. Findings indicate that the number of American Indians and Alaska Natives who graduate continues to be a matter of urgent concern. On average, less than 50 percent of Native students in these twelve states graduate each year."

The low graduation figures certainly can be viewed as an example of our young people rebelling against society and rejecting the institutional brainwashing of the colonizers. In fact, many might speak about the uselessness of the educational system, or the racism within the system, both of which would reveal their understanding that the educational system does not serve their interests, but serves the interests of the colonizers. The anger and frustration our young people feel toward the educational system are entirely justifiable. But, even if young people view their decision as a form of rebellion, it does not mean that their dropping out helps anyone but the colonizers. For it to be a decolonizing act, a rejection of Western education must be a conscious form of resistance that also embraces an Indigenous education, or a means of supporting indigeneity.

Statistics according to The Dropout/Graduation Rate Crisis Among American Indian and Alaska Native Students:

- On average, the report found that graduation rates for American Indians and Alaska Natives (46.6 percent) were lower than the graduation rates for all other racial/ethnic groups including whites (69.8 percent), Asians (77.9 percent), Blacks (54.7 percent), and Hispanics (50.8 percent).

- The lowest graduation rate for American Indian/Alaska Native males was found in South Dakota where 28.2 percent of American Indian/Alaska Native males graduated compared to 71.4 percent of all male students.

- The lowest number of American Indian/Alaska Native female students graduated in South Dakota where 31 percent of American Indian/Alaska Native students graduated compared to 77.2 percent of all female students.

> **According to the UN:**
>
> "Fundamentally, poverty is a denial of choices and opportunities, a violation of human dignity. It means lack of basic capacity to participate effectively in society. It means not having enough to feed and clothe a family, not having a school or clinic to go to, not having the land on which to grow one's food or a job to earn one's living, not having access to credit. It means insecurity, powerlessness and exclusion of individuals, households and communities. It means susceptibility to violence, and it often implies living on marginal or fragile environments, without access to clean water or sanitation."

For example, Paulo Freire in *Pedagogy of Freedom: Ethics, Democracy, and Civil Courage* tells us, "One of the basic questions we need to look at is how to convert merely rebellious attitudes into revolutionary ones in the process of the radical transformation of society. Merely rebellious attitudes or actions are insufficient, although they are an indispensable response to legitimate anger. It is necessary to go beyond rebellious attitudes to a more radically critical and revolutionary position, which is in fact a position not simply of denouncing injustice but of announcing a new utopia." Thus, in rejecting Western education without replacing it with an anti-colonial, Indigenous alternative, our young people risk placing themselves at further risk of exploitation and subjugation.

In fact, dropping out of high school tends to detrimentally affect people the rest of their lives. In some cases this might mean an increased likelihood of ending up in the criminal (in)justice system. But there are other factors, as well. Within this society, less education typically means less earned income. As I will discuss later, this too is not a bad thing at all if it is part of a conscious choice to reject the capitalist

system, and to live simply, close to the land. Generally, however, poverty in the twenty-first century, especially among urban populations, means something quite negative. Faircloth and Tippeconnic report that the "inability to earn competitive wages results in American Indians and Alaska Natives living in poverty at more than twice the rate of their non-Native peers— 26% of American Indians and Alaska Natives compared to 12% of non-Natives." Poverty for Indigenous people today does not indicate an anti-material and anti-consumerist lifestyle choice, but instead reveals a lifestyle that is detrimental to health and well-being while also being fraught with a host of other problems. Most seriously, it means the inability of an individual or family to meet their basic needs.

Why do our young people continue to drop out at such alarming rates? The report cites research indicating that a "lack of student engagement is a primary attributing factor to the dropout crisis." At the school level, they report such factors as "large schools, a perceived lack of empathy among teachers, passive teaching methods, inappropriate testing and lack of parent involvement." In terms of student level factors, they cite such reasons as students "feeling 'pushed out' of schools, poor quality of student-teacher relationships, lack of parental support, peer pressure, distance from school, difficulty with classes, poor attendance, legal problems and language barriers, among other factors." While we are not always aware of the extent of the problems on a national level, Indigenous people are generally not surprised by the difficulties our young people have in completing a high school education. These have been issues for generations of our Peoples.

Unfortunately, dropout rates are not the only concerns within our communities. According to Terry Cross, the founder and director of the National Indian Child Welfare Association, of the two million American Indian and Alaska Native young people under the age of nineteen, "twenty percent (800,000) are at risk, while 60,000 suffer abuse or neglect each year." Furthermore, citing the *Youth Violence Research Bulletin*, Cross states, "the suicide rate for American Indian juveniles (57 per 1 million) was almost twice the rate for white juveniles and the highest for any race. In addition, 200,000 are believed to suffer from serious emotional disturbances." Moreover, like the adult Indigenous population, Indigenous youth are greatly disproportionately represented in both state and federal criminal (in)justice institutions. Cross states, "Incarcerated Indian youth are much more likely to be subjected to the harshest treatment in the most restrictive environments and less likely to have received the help they need from other systems. AI/AN youth are 50% more likely than whites to receive the most punitive measures. Pepper spray, restraint and isolation appear to be grossly and disproportionately applied to Indian youth, who have no recourse, no alternatives and few advocates."

Our youth are not the problem, however. Settler society is. In fact, settler society is still waging a war against our youth. Once our children enter the educational and criminal (in)justice systems, they will be targeted and labeled as problems because of who they are, not because they are inherently bad.

While we certainly have issues of major concern in our communities regarding our youth, colonizing society uses approaches that serve to blame the youth, parents, communities, or Indigenous nations rather than identifying these issues as a direct consequence of the ongoing colonization of our people. We cannot solve these social circumstances while the root causes—all the systems and institutions of colonialism—remain in place. Everything about the current structure is designed to support settlers and their way of life, and to eradicate our ways of life so that we will forget who we are, and forget our relationship to our homelands. Once our memory is erased, we will no longer remember to fight for our land bases and to protect them from harm. Rather than thinking about how our children might function better within an oppressive society, we need to think about how we can restore in our youth the skills they will need to function sustainably in our territories according to the original directions provided to us. Then we need to think about how we can more effectively challenge settler society, so that we can live freely as our Peoples were meant to live.

ACTIVITY:

Delving deep into your People's oral tradition, what were your Original Instructions about how you are to live? If you do not know these teachings, ask elders or other knowledgeable people in your family, community, or nation if they can help teach you.

_____

_____

_____

_____

_____

What are the core values central to your People's way of life?

_____

_____

_____

_____

Which of those values do you still adhere to in your everyday life? Which ones do you no longer follow on a daily basis? Which ones are impossible to follow while living in this society?

_____

_____

_____

_____

C. Our Current Needs

So how do we begin to think about addressing the root cause—the colonization of our Peoples and lands—so that our future generations might be freed from the shackles endured by previous generations and they can begin to live as Indigenous Peoples within our homelands once again? We must teach them that they are the beloved children of the land (and water) and prepare them to take back their inheritance. As Freire stated, we need to help our young people "convert merely rebellious attitudes into revolutionary ones in the process of the radical transformation of society."

As already discussed in my previous chapter in this collection, we are in the midst of a series of crises including global warming and climate change, the end of oil, the collapse of the American economy, and most recently, the very real threat of possible global pandemics. For Indigenous Peoples, we face an additional crisis that cuts to the very core of our status as Indigenous Peoples. In the most basic terms, we are forgetting who we are and we are forgetting our obligations to our homelands. This is not something we need to feel hopeless about, however. This is an area where we can take personal responsibility for our decolonization and engage in the hard work necessary for our Peoples' survival.

How do we determine who we are? How do we maintain our identities? At one time these questions could be answered simply. We would continue the language and way of life passed down to us from our parents, grandparents, and great-grandparents. Furthermore, we would do so on land bases that we had occupied for millennia. What was once taken for granted has been interrupted by our disconnection from our homelands, our disconnection from our ancestors, and the attempts by colonizing society to systematically eradicate our identities as Indigenous Peoples.

Consequently, our language is in a state of crisis. We need to think about raising a new generation of Indigenous people, prepared to re-learn Indigenous languages, cultures, and relationships with the land, while also considering how to survive in a rapidly changing world. We need to think about re-instilling in our young people a sense of obligation to protect our homelands. One way to address this issue is by focusing our attention on young adults.

I began to think about the idea of developing an intensive cultural immersion camp for young adults as a way to combat the problems with crystal meth within Dakota communities. This was an extraordinary problem in my community during the first decade of the twenty-first century. I believed that if we could work on restoring our identities as Dakota people and reaffirm our connections and responsibilities to our ancestors and homelands, it would allow a whole generation of our young people to experience a newfound sense of purpose, sense of unity, and sense of self-worth that would allow them to reject drugs as the undesirable toxins they are. Further, the hope was that we would work to create a new generation of warriors committed to once again defending our lands and way of life. While the brief plan I developed was never implemented within my community by our tribal leaders, the nonprofit Oyate Nipi Kte (The People Shall Live) with which I work, is hoping to advance this idea for Dakota people. This chapter is intended to provide a glimpse into how a camp for young adults might be conceptualized, as well as suggest decolonizing activities for people interested in transforming our colonized selves.

D. What Would This Cultural Immersion Camp Look Like?

When considering how to structure such a program, I was particularly concerned with how the values of settler society continue to be uncritically embraced and accepted within our communities. For example, I was interested in why our young men and women continue to join the US military in service to the very government that continues to keep us oppressed and colonized. Why would they work in service of imperialist aims and risk their lives so that the United States can maintain access to oil and other resources around the globe? Why would they fight against other dark-skinned people, many of whom simply seek to defend their own lands? Or, equally as detrimental, why would they choose life as a gang member?

I was interested in why we seemed to be no longer resisting the negative influences of settler society and were instead embracing the food, consumer-culture, and relentless exploitation of the environment. Why were we not at war when this society is still at war against us and our beloved homelands? What seems to have replaced the Indigenous spirit of resistance is a spirit of complacency and complicity. Rather than fighting the persistent destruction of our beautiful ways of life and desecration to our homelands, most of us have been joining right in. While I understood that these are clearly the results of generations of colonization, I kept wondering where our resisters were. Where were our Little Crows, our Crazy Horses, our Geronimos, our Tecumsehs? Thus, I became particularly interested in how we revalue our ancestors' ways of being and revive that spirit of resistance. Our young people need to be groomed for, and encouraged, to take up these warrior roles.

In conceptualizing a training program for our young adults, I envision a live-in, communal facility that would house the youth and mentors twenty-four hours a day. The youth would be taught physical strengthening and discipline; traditional Indigenous ways including language, culture, spirituality; loyalty to their Indigenous nation; strong critical thinking skills; training in decolonization; healthy eating through gardening, harvesting, and hunting; self-sufficiency; self-defense, weapons, and military tactical training; and how to nurture supportive relationships. I have detailed these further in the accompanying table 7.1, Zuya Naka program for young adults, which is in part based on the "Model of the Effects of Colonialism" developed by Dr. Michael Yellow Bird. The table highlights the positive actions we could initiate in seven areas of personal development.

Since one of the problems with the way alcohol and other drugs have infiltrated our community is not just how to get people to stop using the drugs, but also how to build a community where there is constant reinforcement for not using drugs, a program like this would specifically be designed to create a community of support for healthy living. Eventually we would have an entire generation of young people able to support one another in making personal choices that would, in the long run, benefit the entire nation.

Table 7.1. Zuya Naka program for young adults

Area of Development	Strategies for Development
Physical	Strong daily physical training regiment, self-defense or martial arts lessons, traditional weapons practice (bows, lances, war clubs), healthy eating of natural, whole foods through emphasis on a traditional Indigenous diet, stress reduction techniques, and physical labor as part of community service obligation.
Spiritual	Introduction to and practice of Indigenous spirituality, access to traditional ceremonies, training in spiritual values, male/female/two-spirit gender roles, accessing and understanding sacred sites, developing ecological awareness and daily connection with the land, and strengthening relationships with ancestral spirits through participation in or support of cultural events.
Intellectual	Develop critical thinking about the status of Indigenous Peoples in the United States, Canada, and around the globe, learn to critically interrogate dominant society's master narratives/ideologies, understand how historical events have shaped our present, deconstruct racism and colonialism, learn how individual behavior resists or supports systems of oppression, conceptualize and practice meaningful resistance strategies, and develop mindfulness skills.
Psychological	Train to recognize psychological oppression, teach how Indigenous Peoples have internalized colonialism regarding our status as human beings, address previous abuses, develop individual self-worth by encouraging personal and group accomplishments, challenge course activities to develop trust in oneself and one another, develop pride in Indigenous identity by revaluing and encouraging the best of Indigenous characteristics, and teach peaceful conflict resolution.
Social	Learn to live in a healthy communal setting, develop trust in oneself and others, learn cooperation in work and play, understand interconnectedness of all group members as well as all of creation, restore kinship terms, develop sense of responsibility to community through service work, develop self and group discipline through daily routines and constant accountability, and emphasize revaluing of group harmony and balance over competition and individual success.
Economic	Teach about various economic systems to understand the negative role of capitalism and materialism in the world, teach and practice self-sufficiency and living simply, learn cooperative economic strategies, and value sustainability over exploitation.
Political	Teach historic and contemporary models of leadership, teach consensus building, develop Indigenous nationalism, require oath to Indigenous nation, provide meaningful service to the community elders and those in need, create a New Warrior society dedicated to serving the nation, and work toward Indigenous liberation.

Ideally, the physical setting for the program would include a facility that could house about twenty to thirty young people at any given time, plus room for staff, quarters for communal eating, living, and recreation, a library/work area, a large kitchen, and multiple showers and bathrooms. It would also require some acreage that could be used for gardening, planting Indigenous flora, harvesting a variety of food and medicinal plants, perhaps raising livestock, and hunting or fishing grounds.

I initially thought about this as a two-year program for young adults (18–20 years of age) that could be implemented immediately in any of our Minnesota Dakota communities given the current disbursement of enrollment benefits, or with some fund-raising and planning in other Dakota communities. It was designed to produce strong women and men committed to the Dakota Oyate, Dakota homeland, and Dakota traditions.

Such a program could be extraordinarily strengthening to young people suffering from trauma or addictions. If all young people were required to participate, there would be no stigma placed on those young people who were having drug and alcohol problems or who were in the juvenile justice system. Instead, all young people would be participating for the betterment of themselves and the community. Furthermore, full membership benefits would be a strong incentive for them to successfully complete their service obligation.

For the communities with per capita payments provided to community members as shareholders in gaming or other economic enterprises, the program could be a mandatory service requirement for all young people seeking adult membership benefits. However, even without benefits (such as per capita payments from tribal economic ventures), mandatory service requirements could become part of cultural and social expectations and norms if a collective agreement about this was achieved within a community. A life lived close to the land does not have to be a well-funded venture, as long as there is access to an abundant land base from which adults and youth can feed themselves and create shelter from materials on the land.

It does require, however, that all involved are either already disconnected from the capitalist system, or do not mind being disconnected more permanently from it. The capitalist system is designed to draw our youth in when they are very young. As soon as they get a car loan, need car insurance, are committed to a cell-phone contract, or get caught in a debt cycle because of their investment in consumer culture, they become entrapped in what often becomes a lifelong cycle. As young adults are solicited by credit card companies, what initially appears as a form of financial freedom quickly turns into financial servitude.

Given the loyalty and sense of duty that is fostered by settler society for participation in the armed services, Indigenous communities ought to be able to foster that sense of loyalty and duty within our tribal nations. It is not unreasonable for us to expect our young people to be of service to our own communities. The problem, however, is that we do not currently provide the expectation or the meaningful opportunity for our young people to be of service.

ACTIVITY:

Does your community currently provide a meaningful service opportunity for your young adults? If so, what form does that take? If not, what structures are in place that would allow you to think about establishing a service opportunity (i.e., facilities, economic support, promise of membership benefits, etc.)?

_____

_____

_____

_____

What might be gained by such an opportunity within your community?

_____

_____

_____

_____

Certainly the idea of being of service to one's People is an Indigenous one. It is only in recent generations that Indigenous people have bought into the sense of individualism pervading settler society that teaches each of us to be concerned only with our own happiness and needs. Our children are often taught to pursue professions that satisfy their own desires or some colonial notion of success, rather than how to live in a way that best serves our nations and territories. It is through our experience under colonization that our people have become increasingly more selfish. The drive for economic success, and having more and more money, is an expression of our increasingly individualistic and materialistic tendencies.

Traditionally (meaning prior to colonization), all members of our nations were expected to contribute to the greater whole. Everyone helped procure food in some way. Everyone worked toward the well-being of the community. And when the People were under attack, everyone did whatever they could to help with the community's defense. It is much harder to keep a united population subjugated, which is why the colonizers worked so relentlessly to divide our populations and instill selfish behaviors. This is not to suggest that there was no sense of individual freedom within our societies, but our communities could not be maintained if people valued self-interest over community interest. The latter helped ensure that everyone's needs could be met. Severe repercussions often existed for those who violated this communal ethic.

Under colonization, we have come to expect so little from one another in terms of the contributions to the community. Even our leaders are on a payroll now. Part of decolonization necessarily means thinking critically about how our sense of duty to our nations has shifted and restoring our obligations to our communities. This may begin with our young people.

While youth might initially dislike the idea of mandatory participation, through time this kind of intensive experience would allow for the development of a close-knit, highly cohesive group of capable and strong young people dedicated to the empowerment and self-determination of Indigenous Peoples. It would be similar to the sense of unity experienced by soldiers serving in combat together or sundancers who sacrifice together. This program would be dedicated to teaching Indigenous ways of thinking and being to counter much of what has been forced upon us by the dominant society. Ideally, Indigenous culture (including values, cosmology, and language) would underpin all aspects of what we might call New Warrior training. Yet, at the same time, because our ancestors did not experience precisely the same circumstances we have today, we must also be willing and open to learning skills and engaging in actions that might not be deemed traditional but will assist us in regenerating our core values and teachings. Because we face a desperate situation with increasing pressures from a variety of circumstances, I believe these kinds of positive, radical measures are needed.

The success of such a program would also be dependent upon community support and encouragement. If a group of New Warriors (*Zuya Naka* in Dakota) were honored and celebrated at Dakota functions, there would be less incentive for our young people to join the US military or seek success according to standards set by the outside world. If they were valued for their dedication to our communities, they would want to continue to work for our Peoples. Furthermore, if one of them began to experience difficulties after leaving the program, they would have a group of program graduates who were specifically trained to help lift them up again. We would prepare a generation of strong, competent Indigenous warriors prepared to handle whatever challenges the changing world will bring.

E. The Physical

Like other warrior training programs around the world, within Indigenous communities we need to revive intensive physical training regimes for our young people. While some communities may still practice these regimes, particularly for boys, within many of our communities these practices have been abandoned. Nonetheless, even if they are not practiced, many of our people remember stories about traditional training

exercises for warriors. For example, within Dakota society, the warrior training for boys was usually conducted by their mothers' brothers, or the uncles on their mother's side. In addition to waking up before dawn for early morning swims (even in winter), the boys spent hours running long distances, practicing with their bows and spears, wrestling, and learning how to withstand hardship. These are all practices our people can resume and expand to include both young men and women. Additionally, we can incorporate the practice of beneficial workout routines from other traditions or twenty-first century contexts with a proven capacity to build strength, endurance, speed, flexibility, balance, and coordination. These might include programs of weight training, martial arts, yoga, kickboxing, and various sports. New Warrior training would require a rigorous physical workout regime.

As I discussed in the first *Decolonization Handbook, For Indigenous Eyes Only*, physical health is dependent not just upon exercise, it is also dependent upon our eating habits. Our ancestors did not have to concern themselves with making good food choices since everything they ate was a natural, whole food. Today, however, we have to consciously reject unnatural, processed foods in favor of those foods that are far more nutritious. If possible, the most practical and relevant means to ensure a healthy diet is to return to the traditional food sources that sustained our ancestors within our particular ecosystem. If it is not yet completely possible to return to a traditional diet, the next best thing would be to directly grow, harvest, hunt, and forage for our foods and eliminate trips to the supermarket as much as possible. Thus, a significant component of the warrior program would necessarily involve developing healthy food practices (as well as food independence and security) by growing, harvesting, gathering, hunting, and fishing both traditional and non-traditional foods. Our bodies would benefit by not only eating these whole foods, but also by engaging in the physical activity necessary to obtain them.

Unlike our ancestors, however, the well-being of our people today is hampered by the trauma that affects all of us. The trauma stems from historical experiences such as war, genocide, loss of homeland, and boarding and residential schools, as well as contemporary harms from ongoing colonization—assaults from settler society and the effects of dysfunction within our families and communities. Few Indigenous individuals and families are untouched by the effects of historical and contemporary colonization. Just as this trauma affects our emotional, psychological, and spiritual selves, it also affects our physical selves. A physical regiment must also address this trauma. Stress reduction and body calming techniques would, ideally, also be included in New Warrior training.

In addition, given the coming changes, we all could benefit from more physical labor: constructing, building, hauling, planting, pulling, and pounding. New Warriors could develop their skills and their muscles by laboring for the Warrior camp and for elders and others in the community. Not only will they set good examples for other youth, they will also ingratiate themselves to the rest of the community by fulfilling service duties.

ACTIVITY:

How has the physical health of people in your community been impacted by colonization?

_____

_____

_____

_____

What kind of physical training would be useful for New Warriors in your community?

_____

_____

_____

_____

F. The Spiritual

Many of our people raised within Christian religious traditions have accepted the inevitability or normality of Christianity, as though it is part of a natural progression away from paganism. The reality is that the governments of both the United States and Canada worked hand-in-hand with church leaders, missionaries, teachers, and other government employees and settlers to systematically attack and eradicate Indigenous spiritual traditions. It is no accident that our populations are heavily Christianized today, nor is it a result of our people accepting Christianity because of a voluntary attraction to the Christian religions. Exactly the opposite is true. From the first invasions, Europeans arrived with the sword and the cross and few Indigenous people have come to Christianity by free will. Indigenous spirituality was outlawed through government rules such as the 1883 "Indian Religious Crimes Code" in the United States that prohibited ceremonies like sundances and potlatches. Similarly, in Canada bans were implemented on Indigenous potlatches in 1884 and sundances in 1895, with increased prohibitions against appearing in "aboriginal garb" and performing traditional dances in 1914.

Much of the Christian intolerance of Indigenous spirituality stems from the Christian teaching expressed in John 14:6, "I am the way, the truth, and the life. No man cometh unto the Father but by me."

This tenet allows for only one God to exist—the one known to Christians—and the eradication of all the others. For example, the 1492 papal bull Romanus Pontifex required Christians to declare war against all non-Christians throughout the world and allowed for the conquest, colonization, and exploitation of Indigenous nations and our territories. This, combined with the Inter Cetera papal bull issued in 1493 granting Spain the right to conquer the lands "discovered" by Columbus or any others exploring for Spain, meant that Western Christendom set the trajectory for violent confrontations with Indigenous populations throughout the Western Hemisphere. Scholar Steve Newcomb has written about how the Christian Doctrine of Discovery was then adopted into US law through the 1823 Supreme Court case *Johnson v. McIntosh* in which Chief Justice John Marshall asserted that European nations achieved "ultimate dominion" over the lands in America through this discovery, and that Indigenous Peoples only subsequently retained a right of occupancy, having lost our complete sovereignty as independent nations. This essentially legalized US theft of Indigenous lands based on the Doctrine of Discovery.

Such Christian thinking formed the basis of Manifest Destiny ideology in the United States. It was rooted in a belief in the righteousness of American people and values, the responsibility to spread the

---

Even as late as 1921 in the United States, the Indian commissioner Charles H. Burke specified the prohibition of Indian "offenses," many of which were closely associated with Indigenous spiritual practices. They included "acts of self-torture, immoral relations between the sexes, the sacrificial destruction of clothing or other useful articles, the reckless giving away of property, the use of injurious drugs or intoxicants, and frequent or prolonged periods of celebration which bring the Indians together from remote points to the neglect of their crops, livestock, and home interest."

See Francis Paul Prucha, *The Great Father: The United States Government and the American Indians* (Lincoln: University of Nebraska Press, 1984).

American way of life to other lands and Peoples, and the divine sanctioning of these actions by God. Indigenous Peoples consequently suffered the invasion, occupation, and theft of our homelands.

Unfortunately, the imperialistic nature of Christianity meant that the invading Christians could not allow Indigenous Peoples to maintain our spiritualities and cosmologies. Various church denominations sent missionaries to convert our populations to Christianity and they used all methods to achieve their goals. For example, among Dakota people, early missionaries worked with government agents to bribe, coerce, threaten, and shame Dakota people into attending church services and committing to Christianity. When the government imprisoned, force-marched, placed in concentration camps, and sent our People into exile, missionaries were there every step of the way to coerce conversions when our ancestors were most vulnerable. As Dakota elder Clifford Canku has recently discovered in his work translating letters from Dakota prisoners condemned to execution by hanging in 1862, at least some Dakota men converted to Christianity because they thought "being saved" meant they would be physically saved from the gallows. Instead, when missionaries told them they would be saved if they accepted Christianity, they sought to save their souls in the next life. In this life, the missionaries were participants in some of the most heinous crimes imaginable.

Furthermore, colonial governments around the world worked together with churches to target Indigenous children for the most aggressive and reprehensible policies of ethnocide, policies that ruthlessly attacked Indigenous spiritualities and cultures. After agents of the government hauled Indigenous children away from our communities and families, the children were tortured and abused for practicing Indigenous spirituality and were indoctrinated with the belief that Indigenous ways were devilish ways. The self-hatred and shame regarding everything Indigenous continues to flourish in our communities as a direct consequence of church attempts to crush our spiritual traditions. For example, in January 2011, Indigenous people across Turtle Island were stunned and saddened when the Ouje-Bougoumou Cree Nation banned the sweat lodge and other traditional spiritual practices in their own community. Prior to contact, our people would not have fought over religion. This only demonstrates that the larger context of Indigenous conversion is rooted in colonization and continues to be violent.

This does not mean that many of our populations do not vigorously and zealously practice and defend Christianity. Many of our people today gain spiritual strength, healing, and happiness from these practices. But, given

> The Christian teaching regarding [hu]man's relationship with the rest of creation is explicitly stated in Genesis 1:26 of The Bible: "Then God said, 'Let us make man in our image, in our likeness, and let them rule over the fish of the sea and the birds of the air, over the livestock, over the earth, and over all the creatures that move along the ground.'"

some of the foundational teachings of Christianity such as the hierarchy of creation (stated in Genesis and repeated in the Books of Psalms, Jeremiah, and Daniel) and the belief that the Christian way is the only way, it is hard to argue that Christianity can help our people recover a sense of balance, respect, and reciprocity with the rest of creation.

Given that the New Warrior training would attempt a radical (but actually ancient) Indigenous way of living on the planet in a good way, this training would need to offer Indigenous young people the teachings, ceremonies, rituals, and prayers that would allow us to restore our relationships with the beings in our home territories. We cannot interact in a good way with our relatives from animal nations, for example, if we view ourselves as superior to them or as having dominion over them. Nations do not respond well to subjugation or view favorably those who seek to subdue them. As beings on this earth, we can no longer afford to so callously and arrogantly dismiss the importance and value of all forms of life. We can no longer afford to believe human lives are the only lives that matter. Given that our spirituality is most fundamentally about restoring, maintaining, and renewing good relations with all spiritual beings, we must work to teach and practice these respectful ways of being, thinking, and praying with the next generations. Christianity simply does not suffice in meeting those goals.

The spiritual relationships with the land, animals, insects, birds, waters, and other spirit beings in creation will all be fostered not only through the restoration of Indigenous ceremonies and prayers, but also through daily connection to the land. Anyone who spends hours each day working with the soil, plants, and animals, or in hunting, fishing, and foraging, will develop a deeper, more respectful relationship with other beings and understand the interconnectedness and interdependency we all share. Life in the New Warrior camp would facilitate the growth and development of these relationships.

ACTIVITY:

What are your People's teachings about the kind of relationship you should have with the rest of creation? How are these values practiced in your culture?

_____

_____

_____

_____

What kinds of ceremonies or spiritual practices would you like to see regenerated in your community? In what other ways can spiritual teachings be practiced?

_____

_____

_____

_____

> **"Get rid of the belief, I mean really get rid of it, that we are somehow inferior."**
> **—Manulani Aluli Meyer,** *Ho'oulu: Our Time of Becoming, Hawaiian Epistemology and Early Writings*

G. The Intellectual

As we stated at the beginning of this volume, crucially important to our work in decolonization is the decolonization of our minds. As in any endeavor, we have to think something before we can act on it. Thought is the first step in action. The colonizers knew this. Thus, they worked endlessly to eradicate our traditional thought practices, particularly through the attacks on our languages and spirituality. Separating us from these elements that shaped our consciousness was one of the first steps in colonizing our minds.

The "cultural bomb" described by Ngugi wa Thiong'o in *Decolonising the Mind: The Politics of Language in African Literature* is precisely what has made the colonization of Indigenous Peoples so successful. Rather than viewing ourselves through our own cultural lenses, we have learned to use the lens of the colonizers. Through their lens we began to see wretchedness in everything Indigenous. Decolonizing ourselves intellectually means we no longer uncritically accept those perverted images, but instead seek to restore the lenses of our Peoples. For us to attempt to challenge the effects of the "cultural bomb," we must first recognize how colonization has affected how we see ourselves both individually and collectively, how we view our ancestors, and how we view our options for the future.

> **"As long as the oppressed remain unaware of the causes of their condition, they fatalistically 'accept' their exploitation."**
> **—Paulo Freire,** *Pedagogy of the Oppressed*

How would we do that? We would teach our own histories from our own oral traditions. We would examine how stories from settler society are constructed to justify and sanction crimes against our people (such as genocide, land theft, destruction of our homelands). We would teach how whole systems of power are supported by institutions that benefit an elite group while devastating the majority. We would illustrate how and why colonization is maintained. When we understand how colonization has negatively impacted our lives, it is much easier to understand the need to resist it. New Warrior training would provide youth with the skills to recognize how our individual and collective behaviors either resist or support colonial systems and structures of power. Although colonizing society seeks to make these systems and structures normal and invisible so that we do not even recognize that there is something to resist, we can work with our young people to develop and implement strategies of resistance.

ACTIVITY:

How has the "cultural bomb" impacted you intellectually?

_____

_____

How might you begin to undo the damage of the "cultural bomb"?

_____

_____

_____

_____

_____

H. The Psychological

Perhaps the greatest effect on our psychological being through colonization has been an accepted belief in our own inferiority. This is not to say that Indigenous people across the board believe everything Indigenous is inferior or that this perspective pervades all aspects of the way we view Indigenous Peoples or ways. I believe the acceptance of inferiority often manifests itself in much more subtle ways. We are comfortable celebrating aspects of our culture such as food, music, and dance. Colonizing society has indicated to us that these are positive or at least tolerable aspects of our cultures. That is, they are non-threatening to the colonial structure and therefore acceptable to practice within a colonial context. But, for the colonizers to justify the genocide and ethnocide perpetrated against us, it was essential for them to convince themselves and make us believe in the superiority of their ways. Thus, we have been indoctrinated with the belief that the societies of our ancestors represented a state of savagery, and that journeying on a natural evolutionary path meant abandoning hunting and gathering ways (in this

narrative it makes no difference that many Indigenous nations were successful agriculturalists prior to invasion), embracing agriculture and urban living, and eventually advancing to the level of modern, industrial civilization. Many of our people have, consequently, embraced a belief in the unstoppable march of progress, and thus the absolute need of our people to shed the values, beliefs, and practices that are not perceived as compatible with the modern world.

In her book _Conquest: Sexual Violence and American Indian Genocide_, scholar Andrea Smith documented how, in the context of colonialism, specific Peoples and lands become marked as inherently "rapable" and that this opens the way for colonizers to repeatedly and violently violate the colonized. We (both our lands and Peoples) have clearly suffered these repeated assaults for centuries. Always, the underlying message in marking another as rapable is that s/he somehow deserves such treatment.

This means that although we might have experienced centuries of violent crimes perpetrated against us as physical crimes, we also experience the accompanying psychological harm resulting from a constant colonizer finger-pointing in our direction suggesting we are to blame. This sentiment has become absolutely normalized within settler society, and some of us have come to believe we actually deserve violent treatment because of our backwardness or savagery. If we just accepted reality, moved on from the past, pulled ourselves up by our bootstraps, got an education, and made more money, we would not have our existing problems. In other words, if we completely accepted the loss of our lands and freedom, ignored the ongoing assaults to our Peoples and territories, all the while embracing the materialistic values and ways of settler society, we would be just fine. If we do not accept those things, or actually resist them, then we are marked again as rapable, and any means necessary are used to ensure our obedience to the state (and corporations). While many of us feel the wrongness of this situation, we have come to accept the violence against us as normal or inevitable. The main indication of this is that we have largely been subjugated into submission; we seem to have lost our collective capacity and will to challenge racism and colonialism. When we do fight back, we often attack one another rather than the colonizers.

A fundamental way to challenge this complacency in the face of violence is to recognize the validity of what Native Hawaiian scholar Haunani-Kay Trask calls "righteous anger," which she defines in her book *From a Native Daughter* as "the emotional/psychological response of victims of racism/discrimination to the system of power that dominates/exploits/oppresses them." In overcoming the negative psychological effects of colonization, we can begin to identify and recognize the assaults when they come and understand how they are used in the context of colonization to keep us immobilized or fighting one another. We can direct our justifiable anger where it should be directed.

We can then work on building ourselves back up.

> "Lateral violence among Native people is about our anti-colonial rage working itself out in an expression of hate for one another."
> —Lee Maracle, *I Am Woman: A Native Perspective on Sociology and Feminism*

A New Warrior training camp would need to facilitate the healing from past harms and abuses, practicing acknowledgment, restitution where possible, and focusing on empowerment to prevent future harms. The camp would work on developing trust in one another while also practicing peaceful conflict resolution and accountability to one another. Because the training would involve developing individual and collective competency, each young warrior would rightly recognize his or her own importance to the well-being and survival of our nations.

Finally, a New Warrior camp would work on restoring pride in indigeneity. Not pride based on the acceptable expressions of culture dictated by settler society, but on the aspects of our cultures, histories, values, and beliefs that will help our nations survive the coming changes and flourish in the future. If we want to begin to transform our mental states and processes and ultimately affect our behavior, we must not only consciously and critically examine the psychological harm caused to our people, we must also engage in activities that will actively rebuild and uplift our psychological selves.

I. The Social

As with the other aspects of harms caused by colonization, we must recognize that the social effects of colonization are a direct result of systematic attacks on our families and communities by government agents, missionaries, and settlers. It is no accident that the social fabric of our communities has been devastated. We are all witness to the political infighting, the lateral violence we perpetrate against one another, the jealousy, mistrust, dysfunction, and divisions. Some of this has to do with the fact that some of our people collaborate with the colonizers and some still resist, with hundreds of degrees in between. Even in the earliest stages of colonization, our people had to determine how they would respond to the invasion or theft of our lands, to missionary influences, and to the pressures to assimilate. The various courses of action taken by our people (which usually boil down to fight, flight, or capitulate) served to divide our populations historically. Many of those divisions still exist within our communities, with the same lineages often following the same courses of action as their ancestors. But, some of the unhealthy practices we have in our communities today also stem from the wide-ranging values and beliefs that can now be found within every community and almost every family. This, too, stems from the divide-and-conquer strategies of the colonizers.

When I work with settler-allies, I often tell them that they can find an Indigenous person to validate whatever position they want validated, so disparate are the values among our people. If colonizers want an Indigenous person to endorse the depositing of nuclear waste on their territory, they can find one. If colonizers want to find an Indigenous person to justify blowing up an oil rig, they can find one. This is indicative of a heterogeneity that would have been foreign to the experiences of our ancestors. At one time in our People's history, everyone would have seen the dangers of engaging in actions destructive to our territories. Unfortunately, that is no longer the case.

Much of the work in decolonization cannot be centered on supporting individualistic ambitions, but instead must focus on developing unity of vision and action. Rather than fostering individual goals within the framework of settler society, we need to focus on larger goals for our nations to which we can individually contribute. We must develop national visions that extend beyond a five-year plan for economic development. Given the dire environmental crises we currently face, we essentially must decide how we are going to take up our responsibilities to our homelands (it is assumed that one who has abandoned the obligation to our homeland would not be interested in decolonization and restoring Indigenous ways of being anyway) and then learn to act in concert. Our capacity for united action will be hindered initially as we struggle to formulate visions we can collectively embrace, but the sense of unity will continue to build and grow and the visions will gain clarity as we take

actions in support of the well-being of our nations and homelands.

Given that we have so much work to do to rebuild trusting, healthy relationships, everything in a New Warrior camp would need to contribute toward this end. We would be pressed to put into practice the ancient teaching that "We Are All Related," restoring our sense of kinship with one another and with all of creation. While this can happen spiritually in a ceremonial context, it can also happen through very practical daily experiences, as well. Living communally, engaging in activities requiring mutual trust, and developing individual and collective competency in various areas can all facilitate this rebuilding of relationships. Further, through tight regimentation and constant accountability, we would learn to expect more of ourselves in terms of our responsibility to our nations, and more from one another. We would consciously engage in activities reliant upon group coordination and success, rather than individual competition. An accomplishment of one would be the accomplishment of all.

J. The Economic

Few of us raised in the United States, Canada, or Aotearoa today have experience living under anything other than a capitalist system. Like most people from settler society, people within our communities have a hard time imagining anything different. Yet we know our ancestors lived thousands of years within a different economic system, one that valued life and relationships over exploitation and profits.

Historically, other than diseases that were usually the first wave of European influence pummeling Indigenous populations, the pull of a market economy was one of the first effects felt by our ancestors in the earliest years of contact with the invaders. Back in Dakota territory, the French, British, and later Americans sought to gain Dakota assistance in exploiting the animals in our region for profit. With the lure of European products (especially guns to protect ourselves against European and European-armed enemies) and a lack of understanding about the monumental and long-term effects of our participation in the fur trade, our relationship with our fur-bearing relatives

> "Studies show that as individual levels of consumption and material accumulation increase well beyond an approximate level of satisfactory comfort and security, a sense of happiness and well-being does not steadily advance at the same rate. As material standards continue to increase, the personal sense of well-being and contentment tends to actually diminish, because of emotional sacrifices required for such acquisitions, and the time and behaviors required for their achievement."
>
> —Jerry Mander, *Manifesto on Global Economic Transitions*

began to shift. While Indigenous Peoples maintained extensive trade networks in which surplus goods might be traded for regional goods from elsewhere, the dependency fostered in the fur trade (actually intended to indebt Indigenous populations to white traders) was of a different nature. Slowly, the notion of animals or nature as a resource from which we could make money began to infiltrate our societies. Then, as our means of subsistence was stripped from us by invaders pushing us out of our homelands and exterminating people, animals, and ecosystems, we were drawn into the low-wage economy to feed our families. Aside from the few communities whose entrepreneurial skills have made them unusually wealthy, since colonization most of our populations have held an economic position within society that may be considered marginal, at best.

In the twenty-first century, while our people are generally considered poor by US economic standards, many of our houses are still equipped with televisions and DVD players, microwave ovens, and other markers of the North American technological and consumerist society. We are taught that we need money to buy things that will make us happy and that money will solve our social problems. Because our people generally do not have as much money as our white neighbors, or as many material goods as our white neighbors, we often seek to have more and more material goods. Yet, our ancestors who possessed none of these material things, who lived much more simply than most of us do today, did not consider themselves poor or lacking in quality of life. Everything our people needed we could obtain from the land and water. That is no longer

> "We all face choices. We can have ice caps and polar bears, or we can have automobiles. We can have dams, or we can have salmon. We can have irrigated wine from Mendocino and Sonoma counties, or we can have the Russian and Eel Rivers. We can have oil from beneath the oceans, or we can have whales. We can have cardboard boxes, or we can have living forests. We can have computers and cancer clusters from the manufacture of those computers, or we can have neither. We can have electricity and a world devastated by mining, or we can have neither.... We can have cities and all they imply, or we can have a livable planet. We can have 'progress' and history, or we can have sustainability.... We can't have it all. The belief that we can is one of the things that has driven us to this awful place."
>
> —Derrick Jensen, *Endgame*

the case, and that is why poverty today is so damaging. Most of us cannot provide for ourselves from the land to meet our basic needs. This is true poverty. Very simply, this is a major reason why all our energy now should be invested in maintaining the integrity of the land and water, and destroying anything that threatens the land and water. Our future survival and happiness depend on it.

Like the rest of the people from mainstream society, however, we have learned to equate money, high-tech gadgets, and material goods with happiness. Yet, as Jerry Mander and other scholars have pointed out, beyond our basic needs, material goods will not make us any happier, and instead are far more likely to actually diminish our sense of happiness. More importantly, if we do not protect that which provides our real needs, we cannot possibly survive at all.

Furthermore, we are now witnessing the failure of the capitalist system and the American economy is on the verge of collapse. As the existing system self-destructs, it is imperative that everyone begins to seek alternative ways to produce, consume, and exchange products and services.

As Indigenous Peoples, it is in our best interest to recognize sooner rather than later that we have much to gain from returning to the material simplicity of our ancestors' ways of life. A New Warrior camp would be designed to teach a critique of the economic system brought by the colonizers and to seek the development of alternative means of exchange and subsistence. A camp would emphasize the systems of exchange based on maintaining good relationships, as well as cooperation and trade. Rather than focusing on the accumulation of more and more things, emphasis would be placed on practicing self-sufficiency, simple living, and long-term sustainability.

ACTIVITY:

In what ways can you begin to meet your basic needs without the use of money? For example, are there services you can trade for goods you need, or are there things you can make, grow, or harvest for barter or exchange?

_____

_____

_____

From what activities do you derive pleasure and meaning today that are not high-tech or reliant upon money and non-renewable energy? These may be a constant source of happiness for you as we necessarily shift away from participation in the capitalist economy and prepare to survive in a post-oil world. Invest in these.

_____

_____

K. The Political

The dismantling of Indigenous political systems and community cohesiveness was evident in the earliest stages of colonization. When colonizers seek to subjugate a population, the leadership of the population is executed, undermined, or otherwise rendered helpless. Colonizers then seek to replace the former leadership and governance structure with ones designed to serve the invading and occupying government. Whole populations thus become subordinated to colonizer interests.

For example, early on in the colonization of Dakota people, US government agents actively worked to undermine the influence of our chiefs. The government used treaty rations to manipulate our leaders, withholding them at various times so their will would bend to that of the colonizers. When that did not work, our leaders were separated from the people and imprisoned. At other times, the colonizers criminalized defensive actions of Dakota leaders and conscripted other Dakota people to hunt them down and kill them. They undermined our chiefs in other ways, as well. Though our chiefs would at one time have held the responsibility of distributing communal goods to the people, the government agent took control of the distribution of rations, dispersing them to male heads of household and setting the government up as the provider to the people. The agents and traders also worked to facilitate Dakota debt, prompting economic dependency and paving the way for land cessions (from which the traders were paid huge percentages of treaty monies). Furthermore, our populations became

permanently factionalized when pliable people collaborating with colonials were pitted against leaders who refused to acquiesce to the colonizer ways. All these actions served to crush our traditional forms of governance.

In acknowledging the permanency of our factionalized state, I want to be clear that our goal for our Peoples must be unity and cohesiveness, but only among those people who are committed to their indigeneity and who are interested in carrying Indigenous cosmologies and sustainable ways of being into the future. Many of our people may possess Indigenous blood but have long ago abandoned any desire to live as Indigenous People connected to our land. Instead, they have cast their lot with the colonizers, choosing values and a way of life antithetical to Indigenous ways of being. Few of them will ever be persuaded to rejoin the People. Thus, our factionalized state will end only when those who reject Indigenous ways die or no longer claim their Indigenous blood. With the coming crises, much of this will get sorted out.

The antidote to the destruction of our traditional political structure and leadership, like other aspects of decolonization, lies in recognizing how colonization has impacted our leadership and governance. In examining both historic and contemporary kinds of leadership we can then begin to both actively reject colonizer-imposed forms of governance and remake a political system rooted in our ancient value systems that will serve our current needs. It is unlikely that we can simply resurrect traditional forms of governance as they may not meet the needs of our current situation. Our traditional structures were not born in the midst of an anti-colonial struggle, nor were they born in a period of unprecedented global strife caused from destructive human actions. We are in a unique and difficult age in which we must summon our collective strength, spirit, and intellect to forge a new political pathway into our liberated future. Our youth will be the ones to lead this struggle and we need to prepare them the best that we can. If our Peoples are to survive, we must teach our young people to live the mantra "For the People! For the Land!"

L. Final Comments

The most compelling aspect of working toward the goal of training New Warriors is that much of the decolonizing work may be undertaken on our own, without permission, sanctioning, or oversight from colonizing society. While this chapter was intended to explore how to raise a new generation of young people dedicated to our Peoples and lands, we can make a personal commitment to implement decolonizing practices in our daily lives, whether or not we are ever part of a young warriors' camp. Those of us with children can begin these practices now. We do not need to wait to take action. We can begin this moment. But, as communities, given the challenges and crises that our younger generations will face in the coming decades, we need to collectively strategize about how we can support our young people in carrying our nations into the future. We can help them return to our core teachings and resume a close relationship with our homelands. They will need tools and support to strengthen their hearts, bodies, and minds. There is already a growing sense among young people that change is coming. *Zuya Wicasta Naka Nazinpi!* New Warriors Are Rising! Let us help them.

M. Resources

Cross, Terry L. "Native Americans and Juvenile Justice: A Hidden Tragedy. Native Americans and Alaska Natives: The Forgotten Minority." *Poverty and Race: Poverty & Race Research Action Council,* November/December 2008.

Faircloth, Susan C., and John W. Tippeconnic, III. *The Dropout/Graduation Rate Crisis Among American Indian and Alaska Native Students: Failure to Respond Places the Future of Native Peoples at Risk.* Los Angeles, CA: The Civil Rights Project/Proyecto Derechos Civiles at UCLA, 2010. http://www.civilrightsproject.ucla.edu.

Freire, Paulo. *Pedagogy of Freedom: Ethics, Democracy, and Civil Courage.* Lanham, MD: Rowman & Littlefied Publishers, Inc., 1998.

Jensen, Derrick. *Endgame: The Problem of Civilization.* New York: Seven Stories Press, 2006.

Mander, Jerry, ed. *Manifesto on Global Economic Transitions: Powering-Down for the Future Toward a Global Movement for Systemic Change: Economies of Ecological Sustainability, Equity, Sufficiency and Peace.* A Project of the International Forum on Globalization, The Institute for Policy Studies, and Global Project on Economic Transitions. San Francisco; Washington, DC: International Forum on Globalization; Institute for Policy Studies, 2007.

Maracle, Lee. *I Am Woman: A Native Perspective on Sociology and Feminism.* Vancouver: Press Gang, 1996.

Newcomb, Steven T. *Pagans in the Promised: Decoding the Doctrine of Christian Discovery.* Golden, CO: Fulcrum, 2008.

Ngugi wa Thiong'o. *Decolonising the Mind: The Politics of Language in African Literature.* Oxford: James Curry, 1986.

Trask, Haunani-Kay. *From a Native Daughter: Colonialism and Sovereignty in Hawai'i.* Honolulu: University of Hawaii Press, 1999.

Chapter 8

DECOLONIZING INDIGENOUS EDUCATION IN A TWENTY-FIRST CENTURY WORLD

Gregory A. Cajete

A. Thoughts on American Indian Education

The purpose of contemporary American Indian education is to ensure that Indigenous people learn the skills necessary to be productive—or at least survive—in post-industrial American society. The educational system teaches Indigenous people to be consumers in the tradition of the "American dream" and all that it entails. We have been encouraged to use modern education to "progress" by being participants in the "system." We have been conditioned to seek the rewards and benefits that success in the world of modern education purportedly provides. We are enticed from every direction to pursue careers in law, medicine, business, and the sciences, which form the pillars of Western thought and conditioning. Although many Indigenous people have succeeded in Western society by embracing this educational system, many have not been very successful or have dropped out entirely. In reality, many students—particularly minorities—have educational experiences that differ dramatically from the ideal. Their experience is wrought with contradictions, prejudice, hypocrisy, narcissism, and unethical predispositions at all levels including the schools. As a result, there have been educational conflicts, frustration, and varying levels of alienation experienced by many Indigenous people following their encounters with mainstream education.

This is the reality of modern education for Indigenous people. As we examine the purpose of modern education, Indigenous people must analyze the effects it has had on our collective cultural, psychological, and ecological viability.

As Nicholas Peroff has explained, Indigenous people have been forced to adapt to an educational process that is essentially not of their own making. Historically, the views guiding the evolution of modern American Indian education have been based on assumptions that are anything but representative of Indigenous cultural mind-sets. In spite of this, traditional educational processes have continued to take place within the context of many Indian families and communities, and while there has been progress in the last thirty years, the integration of modern and traditional approaches to education has been practically non-existent.

Much of contemporary American Indian education is based on teaching academic skills and content, in order to prepare students to compete in the American mainstream workforce that represents the vested political, social, and economic interests of society. Furthermore, it is an educational system devoid of ethical or moral considerations regarding the means that are used to achieve its ends.

B. Reclaiming Our Heritage of Education

The alienation of Indigenous students from education makes it less likely that they will be able to serve their communities to their fullest potential as adults. But this situation need not continue if Indigenous people revitalize and reclaim our own deep heritage of education. Indigenous approaches to education can work if we are open to their creative message and find creative ways to revitalize and reintroduce our inherently universal processes of teaching and learning. These principles are relevant whether one is learning leadership skills through community service, learning about one's cultural roots through creating a photographic exhibit, or learning from Nature by exploring its concentric rings of ecological relationships.

Every community is unique in its experiences and needs, and ultimately it is up to each community of Indigenous people—whether they live in an urban setting or on a reservation—to decide how education can help sustain or revitalize their culture. Each community must find ways to integrate the learning that occurs through modern education with the Indigenous knowledge and values that are essential for perpetuating a community and its way of life; a balanced integration must be created. Over time, the emphasis on only modern educational methods and Western-oriented curricula, by their nature, will erode an Indigenous way of life. Indigenous educators and tribal leaders must understand that when people embrace modern education they are conditioned away from their cultural roots, not toward them. While modern education provides tools that are essential to the survival of Indigenous people and communities, education must also reflect and support Indigenous culture. Indian educators and tribal leaders need to advocate for culturally based education as a foundation of self-determination, self-governance, and tribal sovereignty. Indigenous education offers a highly creative vehicle for thinking about the evolving expressions of Indigenous cultures as they develop in the twenty-first century.

The key questions we must collectively ask ourselves are:

- What has been lost and what has been gained by participating in a system of education that does not stem from, or really honor, our unique Indigenous perspectives?
- How far can we go in adapting to such a system before that system literally educates us out of cultural existence?
- Have we reached the limits of what we can do with mainstream education?
- How can we re-envision and re-establish the "ecology of Indigenous education"—the web of reciprocal relationships, understandings, and responsibilities that guided and sustained our tribal societies?

ACTIVITY:

Based on your experience, in what ways does the current educational system honor Indigenous perspectives?

_____

_____

_____

_____

In what ways does it not honor Indigenous perspectives?

_____

_____

_____

_____

C. "Coming Back to Our Power"

The goal of revitalizing Indigenous education is really about "*coming back to our power.*" In contemporary terms this is often referred to as "empowerment," but "coming back to our power" is a phrase that I believe better describes the multi-faceted process of transforming Indigenous education that is taking place in the Indigenous world.

A primary goal of Indigenous education must be empowerment, which for Indigenous people and communities must begin with an inward transformation, a kind of "in-powerment" that emphasizes the internal work that each of us must do to "come back to our power." This type of empowerment leads to greater

personal, interpersonal, communal, and political power and enables Indigenous people and communities to transform oppressive situations into actions of healing and revitalization.

The colonial history of America is rife with detrimental and devastating effects on every facet of Indigenous Peoples' lives, including physical, political, economic, and social domination; oppression, exploitation, and control; physical and cultural genocide; and cultural assimilation through the various social institutions of religion, education, government, law, and economics. We need to analyze these historical and present-day injustices, acknowledging that this history is rooted in the internalized belief that American

Long-term effects of colonization on Indigenous people include a host of collective and individual ills. Some of the most pronounced are:

- Loss of traditional homelands
- Loss of personal and communal self-sufficiency and traditional sustaining practices
- Disintegration of traditional communities, economies, and languages
- Significant reduction in Indigenous populations
- Consistent disruption of personal freedom and family life
- Loss of personal self-respect, honor, identity, and economic independence

All of these conditions have been described under terms such as "historical trauma," "internalized colonization," and "ethno-stress."

Based on abundant scholarly research on the myriad effects of colonialism throughout its history, some Indigenous scholars and educators are calling for a contemporary expression of Indigenous education to revitalize Indigenous ways of knowing, to facilitate a "coming back to your collective Indigenous power."

colonialism—and the Eurocentric culture and racism it is based on—is superior to Indigenous culture.

In order to begin the process of "coming back to our power" through education, we must especially understand the ways in which colonialism continues to function in hidden forms in educational, institutional, economic, and political structures, and in the psychology of both Native Peoples and non-Native alike. The nature of prejudice and discrimination, and the inherent dehumanization of colonialism, must be understood in historic and present contexts. We must also confront the modern denial of colonialism with its accompanying tendency to blame the victims for their own victimization. Likewise, we must challenge the instances when victims blame themselves and, as a result, act out various forms of self-abuse. The internalized shame and negative self-image that some Indigenous people feel must be understood in their various expressions. Finally, the effects of internalized colonization—manifested most profoundly as hopelessness and powerlessness—must be understood and remedied.

ACTIVITY:

Do you think you have been harmed by being educated in a Western form of education?

_____

_____

_____

_____

What insights have you gained by your experiences with Western education?

_____

_____

_____

_____

D. American Education from an Indigenous Perspective

Throughout history, human societies have attempted to guide, facilitate, and even coerce the human instinct propensity for learning in order to achieve socially defined ends. A variety of educational methods and approaches have evolved to achieve these goals, ensuring the society's survival and expressing its unique *cultural mythos*—a culture's story of itself and its perceived relationship to the world, which forms the foundation for each culture's "guiding vision." This vision sets forth the culture's ideals that create the learning processes contained within the educational system. In turn, these ideals reflect what that culture values as the most important qualities, behaviors, and morals to instill in

> Learning is always a creative act. Through the unique processes of learning, we are continuously engaged in the art of creating our world and creating meaning from our world. For humans, learning is instinctual, continuous, and at the same time the most complex of our natural traits. Learning is also key to our ability to survive in the environments that we create and that create us.

its members, and which are central to the culture's survival.

ACTIVITY:

What ideals are central to the survival of your nation?

_____

_____

_____

_____

These ideals may be considered your guiding vision or *cultural mythos*.

The problems faced in Indian education reflect the critical dilemma of American education. While the legacy of American education is one of spectacular scientific and technological achievement resulting in abundant material prosperity, the cost has been inexorably high. American prosperity has come at the expense of the environment and has resulted in unprecedented exploitation of human and material resources worldwide. As America faces significant challenges while the global community struggles with profound social, economic, and cultural change, the education system must find new ways to help Americans learn and adapt in a multi-cultural, twenty-first century world. It must come to terms with the conditioning inherent in its educational system that contributes to the loss of a shared integrative metaphor of *Life*. The loss of such a metaphor, which may ultimately lead to a social, cultural, and ecological catastrophe, should be of primary concern to every American.

What underlies the crisis of American education is the crisis of modern man's identity and his collective cosmological disconnection from the natural world. Those who identify most with the "bottom line" more often than not suffer from a life of image without substance, technique without soul, and knowledge without context. The cumulative psychological results of this condition are usually unabridged alienation, loss of community, and a deep sense of incompleteness.

E. Indigenous Education as a Sustaining Life Process

In contrast to Western education, traditional Indigenous education historically occurred in a holistic social context that developed a sense that each individual was an important contributing member of the group. Essentially, tribal education worked at sustaining a life process that unfolded through reciprocal relationships between one's social group and the natural world. This relationship involved all dimensions of one's being, while providing both personal development and technical skills through *participation* in every area of community life. It was essentially an environmental education.

Understanding the depth of relationships and the significance of participating in all aspects of life are the keys to traditional Indigenous education. *Mitakuye Oyasin* (we are all related) is a Lakota phrase that captures one of the essences of tribal education because it reflects the understanding that our lives are truly and profoundly connected to other people and the physical world. Likewise, in tribal education, knowledge is gained from firsthand experience in the world and then transmitted or explored through ritual, ceremony, art, and appropriate technology. Knowledge gained through these vehicles is then used in the context of everyday living. Education, in this context, becomes education for "life's sake." Education is, at its very essence, learning about life through participation and relationship to community, including not only people, but plants, animals, and the whole of Nature.

ACTIVITY:

What do you remember learning about your tribal history or tribal ways outside of school, and how you interacted with family, friends, and your community?

_____

_____

_____

How did this learning make you feel? Both good and bad experiences should be listed. Ask friends and relatives about what they remember and how they felt.

_____

_____

_____

F. Education for Life's Sake

The Indigenous ideal of education directly contrasts with the orientation of American education that continues to emphasize "objective" content and experience that is detached from real life and community. This conditioning for being a marginal participant and perpetual observer involved with only objective content is the basis of the crisis of American education and the alienation of modern man from his own being and the natural world.

In response to such a monumental crisis, American education must forge approaches that are truly for "life's sake" and that honor the Native roots of America. A transition from today's American educational orientation to a more sustainable and connected one requires a close look at other cultural, life-enhancing, and environmentally oriented types of education. Traditional Indigenous forms of education are wellsprings for such "new" ways of thinking about education, providing a model of education "for life's sake" in the twenty-first century

G. Stages in a Traditional Education

The goals of wholeness, self-knowledge, and wisdom are held in common by all traditional educational philosophies around the world. Indeed, even through medieval times all forms of European education were tied to some sort of spiritual training. Education was considered important in inducing or otherwise facilitating harmony between a person and the world. The goal was to produce a person with a well-integrated relationship between thought and

action. This idealized outcome was expected to follow naturally from the "right education," which consists of the following guiding principles:

1. The process begins with a deep and abiding respect for the spirit of each child from before the moment of birth. The first stage of Indigenous education therefore revolves around learning within the family, learning the first aspects of culture, and learning how to adapt and integrate one's unique personality in a family context. The first stage ends when one is oriented to place.

2. Education in the second stage revolves around social learning, being introduced to tribal society, and learning how to live in the natural environment. The second stage ends when one has acquired a sense of tribal history and understands how to apply tribal knowledge to daily life.

3. The third stage revolves around melding individual needs with group needs through the processes of initiation, the learning of guiding myths, and participation in ritual and ceremony. This stage ends with the development of a profound and deep connection to tradition.

4. The fourth stage is a midpoint in which the individual achieves a high level of integration with the culture and attains a certain degree of peace of mind. It brings the individual a certain level of empowerment, personal vitality, and maturity, but it is only the middle place of life.

5. The fifth stage is a period of searching for a life vision, a time of pronounced individual learning

and the development of "mythical" thinking. This stage concludes with the development of a deep understanding of relationship and diversity.

6. The sixth stage ushers in a period of major transformation characterized by deep learning about the unconscious. It is also a time of great travail, disintegration, wounding, and pain, paving the way for an equally great reintegration and healing process to begin in the final stage. The pain, wounds, and conflict act as a bridge to the seventh stage.

7. In the seventh stage deep healing occurs in which the self "mutualizes" with body, mind, and spirit. In this stage deep understanding, enlightenment, and wisdom are gained. This stage ends with the attainment of a high level of spiritual understanding that acts as a bridge to finding one's true Center and the transformation to "being a complete man or woman in that place that Indian people talk about."

These stages of inter-relationship form a kind of creative continuum or "life way," which helps us become more fully human as we move through the stages of our life. Indigenous education traditionally recognized each of the most important inter-relationships through formal and informal learning situations, rites of passage, and initiations.

Since the highest goal of Indigenous education was to help each person to "find life" and thereby realize a level of completeness in their life, the exploration of many different vehicles and approaches to learning was encouraged. This was done with the understanding that individuals would find their own best approach in their own time. But "finding oneself and achieving inner peace" was not the goal or central focus of Indigenous education. Seeking peace and finding self was considered a *by-product* of following a path of life, which presented significant personal and environmental challenges, obstacles, and tests at every turn.

This kind of personal development should also not be confused with "individualism," which is so highly prized in American society today. Rather, this is the developmental process of "individuation," as Jung called it. It is a mature stage of human "being" that

Inherent in Indigenous education is the recognition that there is a knowing Center in all human beings that reflects the knowing Center of the Earth and other living things. Indian elders knew that coming into contact with one's inner Center was not always a pleasant or easily attainable experience. This recognition led to the development of a variety of ceremonies, rituals, songs, dances, works of art, stories, and traditions to assist individuals in accessing and utilizing the potential healing and whole-making power in each person. Connecting to that knowing Center was choreographed through specific ritual preparation to help each individual on their journey to their own source of knowledge. Through this process, the potential for learning that is inherent in the major stages of a person's life was engaged in the task of connecting to one's knowing Center. This was the essential reason for the various rites of passage associated with Indian tribes and societies within each tribe.

does not come easily. It has to be earned every step of the way. But in the process of earning it, one learns to put forward the best that one has, learning the nature of humility, self-sacrifice, courage, service, and determination. Indian people understood that the path to individuation is riddled with doubt and many trials. They understood that it was a path of evolution and transformation.

ACTIVITY:

Have a discussion with a few friends or relatives about what our collective history of Indigenous education has to teach us today. What do these traditions and core values of Indigenous education have to teach mainstream society?

_____

_____

_____

_____

H. Ten Essential Characteristics of Indigenous Education

There are basic characteristics that exemplify the transformational nature of Indigenous education. The following are a few of the most important, which may provide guidance for educational goals and content.

First, *learning happens of its own accord if the individual has learned how to relate to his or her inner Center and the natural world.* Coming to learn about one's own nature, and acting in accordance with that understanding, is necessary to prepare the individual for deep learning.

Second, *accept that at times experiences of significant hardship are a necessary part of an individual's education* and that such circumstances provide ideal moments for creative teaching. A "wounding" or memory of a traumatic event, and the learning associated with such events, provide a constant source for renewal and transformation, enlarging one's consciousness if individuals are helped to understand the meaning of such events in our lives.

Third, *empathy and affection are key elements in learning.* In addition, direct subjective experience, combined with reflection, is an essential element of "right" education. Therefore mirroring behavior back to learners helps them understand their own behavior, and how to use direct experiences to their best advantage.

Fourth, *there is an innate respect for the individual uniqueness of each person.* This idea gives rise to the understanding that ultimately each person is his or her own teacher in understanding and realizing their process of individuation. Indigenous education integrates the notion that there are many ways to learn, many ways to educate, many kinds of learners, and many kinds of teachers, each of which has to be honored for their uniqueness and their contribution to education.

Fifth, *each learning situation is unique and innately tied to the creative capacity of the learner.* When this connection to creative learning and illumination is thwarted, frustration and rigidity follow. Learning therefore must be connected to the life process of each individual. The idea of lifelong learning, therefore, is a natural assumption.

Sixth, *teaching and learning are a collaborative, cooperative contract between the "teacher" and learner.* In this sense the teacher is not always human but could be an animal, plant, or other natural entity or force. Based on this perception, a "teachable moment" could be recognized at any time. Distractions and analogies could also be used creatively to define the context for an important lesson. The tactic of *distract-to-attract-to-react* is a common strategy of Indigenous teachers.

Seventh, *learners need to see, feel, and visualize a*

teaching through their own and other people's perspectives. Therefore, telling and retelling a story from various perspectives and at various stages of life enriches learning, emphasizes key thoughts, and mirrors ideas, attitudes, or perspectives back to learners. Re-teaching and re-learning are integral parts of complete learning. Hence the saying, "every story is retold in a new day's light."

Eighth, *there are basic developmental orientations involved with learning* through which we must pass to reach a more complete understanding. Learning through each orientation involves finding personal meaning through direct experience. The meaning that each of us finds is always subjective and interpretive based on our relative level of maturity, self-knowledge, wisdom, and perspective.

Ninth, *life itself is the greatest teacher, and each person must accept the hard realities of life along with those that are joyous and pleasing.* Living and learning through the trials and pains of life are equally important as learning through good times. Indeed, life is never understood fully until it is seen through difficulty and hardship. It is only through experiencing and learning through all of life's conditions that one begins to understand how all that we do is connected and all the lessons that we must learn are related.

Tenth, *learning through reflection and sharing of experience in community allows us to understand our learning in the context of greater wholes.* In a group there are as many ways of seeing, hearing, feeling, and understanding as there are members. In a group we come to understand that we can learn from another's experience and perspective. We also become aware of our own and others' bias and lack of understanding through the process of the group. We see that sometimes people do not know how to take or use real innovation and that many times people do not know how to recognize the real teachers or the real lessons. We see that a community can reinforce an important teaching or pose obstacles to realizing its true message. It is not until, as the Tohono O'odham phrase it, "*when all the people see the light shining at the same time and in the same way*" that a group can truly progress on the path of knowledge.

ACTIVITY:

How can Indigenous people today apply some of the principles of Indigenous education to the issues we face as individuals, families, and communities?

_____

_____

_____

_____

I. Creating a New Circle of Indigenous Education

For Indigenous people, a new "Circle" of education must be founded on the roots of tribal education and reflect the needs, values, and sociopolitical issues as Indigenous people themselves perceive them. A new Circle must encompass the importance Indigenous people place on the continuance of their ancestral traditions. It must emphasize a respect for individual uniqueness in expressing spirituality. It must facilitate a clear understanding of history and culture in the context of life today. As Eber Hampton points out, it must develop a strong sense of place and service to community, and forge a commitment to educational and social transformation that recognizes and further empowers the inherent strength of Indigenous Peoples and our respective cultures.

To accomplish this, Indigenous people must begin to exploit all avenues of communication open to us and establish a dialogue about a contemporary theory for Indian education that evolves from *us* and *our* collective experience. In the past, Indian education has been defined largely by non-Indian educators, politicians, and institutions through a huge volume of legislative acts at the state and federal levels, which for decades have entangled Indigenous leaders, educators, and whole communities in the morass of the federal government's sociopolitical bureaucracy.

In fact, no contemporary theory of Indian education exists that can guide the implementation or direction of curriculum development. Instead what is called "Indian education" today is really what Vine Deloria Jr. called a "compendium of models, methodologies and techniques gleaned from various sources in mainstream American education and adapted to Indigenous circumstances, usually with the underlying aim of cultural assimilation."

It is time for Indigenous people to define our education in our own voice and in our own terms. It is time for Indigenous people to allow ourselves to explore and express the richness of our collective history in education. Among Indigenous Peoples, education has always included a visionary expression of life. Education has been, and continues to be, a grand story, a search for meaning, and an essential food for the soul.

J. Education as Social and Political Struggle

From this perspective, education is a social and political struggle as we try to find ways for it to embody the very "soul" of Indigenous Peoples. These efforts also illuminate the extent to which we have been conditioned by modern educational processes, and how this conditioning has seeped into the deepest levels of our consciousness. We become critical observers of the modern education to which we have had to adapt—an adaptation that demands conformity to a certain way of education that more often than not has been manipulated to serve only certain "vested interests" of American society. Through the exploration of Indigenous education we learn how to demystify the techniques and orientations of modern education. This understanding allows us to use modern education in accord with our needs, and combine the best it has to offer with that of Indigenous orientations and knowledge. We cease to be merely recipients of modern education and instead become active participants and creators of our own education.

On a personal level, Indigenous education liberates both the Indigenous learner and educator to participate in a creative and transforming dialogue that is inherently based on equality and reciprocity. It is a way of learning, communicating, and developing relationships that mirror those ways found in Nature. It also de-stigmatizes the Indigenous learner as being "disadvantaged" with the educator in the position of "provider of aid." Rather, it allows both the learner and educator to co-create a learning experience and together undertake a pilgrimage to a new level of self-knowledge. The educator enters the "cultural universe" of the learner and no longer remains an outside

> **An Ecology of Indigenous Education**
>
> **Indigenous people must forge a new kind of educational consciousness—an "ecology of Indigenous education"—to explore and express their collective heritage in education, and contribute their deep ecological orientation to global educational practices. Exploring traditional Indigenous education and applying it in a contemporary context will illuminate how human learning is integrated with all life, and how it liberates the experience of being human.**

authority. By co-creating a learning experience, everyone involved generates a kind of critical consciousness and enters into a process of empowering one another. With such empowerment, Indian people are able to alter the negative relationship with their current learning process. Ultimately, by reasserting Indigenous values and practices, integrating a contemporary context, and implementing Indigenous processes at all levels of Indian education, Indian people may truly take control of their own history by becoming the transforming agents of their own social reality.

In the final analysis, Indigenous people must determine the future of Indigenous education. That future must be rooted in revitalizing and transforming our own expressions of education. As we collectively "Look to the Mountain" we must truly think of that seventh generation of Indigenous children, for it is they who will judge whether we were as true to our responsibility to them as our relatives were for us seven generations before. It is time for an authentic dialogue to begin to collectively explore where we have been, where we are now, and where we need to go as we embark together on our continuing journey "to that place that Indian People talk about."

ACTIVITY:

In what ways can you apply Indigenous perspectives to your own self-education and the education of those around you?

_____

_____

_____

_____

In doing this activity with dedication you are well on the way toward decolonizing yourself and those around you toward a brighter future for all Indigenous people.

K. Resources

Cajete, Gregory A. *Look to the Mountain: An Ecology of Indigenous Education.* Skyland, NC: Kivaki Press, 1994.

Deloria, Vine. "The Perpetual Indian Message." *Winds of Change* 7, no. 1 (1992).

Hampton, Eber. *Toward a Redefinition of American Indian/Alaska Native Education.* Doctoral dissertation, Harvard University, 1988.

Peroff, Nicholas C. "Policy Research in Indian Affairs: Old Problems and a New Perspective." *Native Americans and Public Policy.* Ed. Fremont J. Lyden and Lyman H. Legters, 265–284. Pittsburgh: University of Pittsburgh Press, 1992.

Sachs, Stephen, and Phyllis M. Gagnier. "Current Development on the Path of an Indigenous Education." *Re-creating the Circle: The Renewal of American Indian Self-Determination.* Ed. Ladonna Harris, Steven Sachs, and Barbara Morris, 344–378. Albuquerque: University of New Mexico Press, 2011.

Sanford, Donald. *Healing and Wholeness.* Mahwah, NJ: Paulist Press, 1977.

Chapter 9

A BROWN PAPER ON THE IRAQ WAR AND THE RESURRECTION OF TRADITIONAL PRINCIPLES OF JUST WAR

Michael Yellow Bird

A. BROWN PAPER on the Iraq War

B. Background

C. Indigenous Peoples and Foreign Wars

D. The Illegality of the Iraq War

E. What Does the Iraq War Mean for Indigenous Nations?

F. The Effect of the War on Iraqis

G. The Effect of the War on Global Safety

H. Lack of Support for the War

I. Ending Indigenous Peoples' Participation in Unjust Wars

J. Solutions

K. The Roles That Indigenous Citizens Can Assume

L. Resources

A. BROWN PAPER on the Iraq War

This chapter is written in the format of a BROWN PAPER, a report intended to solicit discussion from Indigenous, Native, Tribal, and Aboriginal communities on a major public policy issue. In this case the issue is the participation of Indigenous soldiers (Native Americans) in the illegal US-led war against Iraq that began on March 19, 2003. The Indigenous authorship of a BROWN PAPER distinguishes it from a White Paper or Green Paper, which are reports sponsored by colonial parties that often have interests and worldviews divergent from those of Indigenous Peoples. I have purposely refrained from using the language "Red Paper" given the baggage associated with pejorative "Red" terms such as "Redskins," "Redman," and "Red Indians."

Responses to the BROWN PAPER will enable Indigenous Peoples to examine the diverse comments by all interested parties. Those invested in the process can then use the responses to affirm, refine, or establish a position on the issue.

Although this BROWN PAPER is written chiefly with Indigenous Peoples of the United States of America in mind, it is hoped that much of it will be relevant to Indigenous Peoples throughout the world who find themselves conscripted or voluntarily participating in the armed forces of the colonial governments that occupy their territories.

B. Background

On March 19, 2010 the United States of America reached the seventh year of its illegal war against the sovereign nation of Iraq. In commemoration, thousands of people gathered in several US cities to protest the continuing American occupation of Iraq; many criticized the current war policies of the Obama administration and called for the immediate withdrawal of American troops from Iraq and Afghanistan. In Los Angeles, hundreds of protesters marched and shouted anti-war slogans while carrying mock tombstones. In Chicago, anti-war activists poured a "synthetic, non-toxic blood-colored dye" into the Chicago River "to commemorate and protest the seventh anniversary of the beginning of the Iraq War."[1] In a particularly noteworthy speech in the nation's capitol, long-time activist Ralph Nader told protesters in Washington, DC, that there had been little change in American foreign policy since Barack Obama had been elected President. Obama had essentially kept up the policies of the previous Bush administration, Nader said. "He's kept Guantanamo open, he's continued to use indefinite detention." The only real difference is that "Obama's speeches are better."[2]

The numbers of war protesters had dwindled over time and on this anniversary were noticeably much smaller than in previous years. Some of the individuals who were interviewed about the protests that year shared their disappointment at the low turnouts. An Associated Press (AP) news story that covered the seventh anniversary suggested that the commemoration "went largely unnoticed," assuming that many Americans were no longer focused on this war due to the struggling US economy, the war in Afghanistan, the increasing national debt, record high unemployment, and a contentious national health care reform debate.[3]

On August 19, 2010, seven and a half years after invading Iraq, the last US combat brigade (4th Stryker Brigade, 2nd Infantry Division) exited from Iraq, meeting a deadline set by President Barack Obama for US withdrawal from the country. Despite this major exit, the war was not over. The United States continued to keep 50,000 combat troops in Iraq until the end of 2011. These remaining soldiers were to serve in an assist and training role, but in fact they continued to carry out combat operations and "counter-terrorist" missions that included capturing, killing, and torturing suspected terrorists. Most sources agreed that keeping these forces in Iraq would cost more than twelve billion dollars. How many Iraqi and American lives would be lost was anyone's guess.

Over the years the face of the war changed from an all-out US military assault against the Iraqi people to one of cautious cooperation between the major political parties in the two nations in order to establish a fully functioning, independent, post-Saddam Hussein, "democratic" Iraqi government. To be clear, Iraq never invited the United States to invade it in order to establish a democracy; this act was solely the invention and decision of the United States.

There are generally two competing American narratives of this war. One concerns the failures and costs of the war. The war destroyed a great deal of Iraq's services and infrastructure for water, electricity, sewage systems, homes, schools, businesses, and hospitals; much of it was in poor, deteriorating condition before the US-led invasion. Without question, the war has created considerable and widespread physical and mental suffering, violence, displacement, and loss of life among the population—especially the most disenfranchised. The monetary cost of the invasion has been monumental for the United States and has been a major contributing factor to the near collapse of the economy. For instance, the United States has had to pony up about nine hundred billion US taxpayer dollars to pay for the war (through September

> **A BROWN PAPER includes:**
>
> - a discussion of how the main issues intersect with the interests of Indigenous Peoples;
> - background of some of the key issues;
> - proposed solutions, including what can be done by those affected by the issue; and
> - possible benefits of the proposed solutions.

2010). Some sources estimate that the *real* costs will be more likely in the trillions—interest payments on borrowed funds for the war are calculated to cost eight hundred billion; to restore equipment and troop levels to pre-Iraq invasion levels will cost six hundred billion; and long-term care of wounded and disabled veterans may total six hundred billion dollars.[4]

In the second narrative, there are not many everyday folks or policy experts that can rattle off a long list of benefits resulting from the Iraq War. Even the most ardent supporters have a very short and dubious list of "accomplishments." Still, there are those who argue that the war was worthwhile because it removed a brutal dictator (Saddam Hussein) and the world is better off without him. Some say that the war ended the possibility of a nuclear Iraq. Some say the war helped bring about democratic elections in Iraq and has planted the seed of democracy in the Middle East, which is important to the US interests in this part of the world.

It may be some time before the citizens of the United States, as a nation, may say whether one narrative prevails over the other. Indeed, we must all ask ourselves if the economic, political, human, and moral costs of the Iraq War were worth it. Answering such questions requires serious reflection and accepting responsibility for mistakes, neither of which the United States is well versed in. Because the United States is the world's greatest military superpower, no matter what it does no one can require it to reflect on whether the behavior it engages in is right or wrong; much of the rest of the world says, "America is a nation that has developed a tradition of being oblivious to self-reflection."[5] Despite this national character flaw, there are opportunities to examine the merits of competing national narratives, especially since the US involvement in Iraq has ended. Whether this self-examination occurs remains to be seen. In any case, before the United States decides to invade another country to establish its version of democracy or to stem what it regards as "terrorism," it is important that Indigenous Peoples critically discuss and act upon the many lessons that have been learned from this war.

C. Indigenous Peoples and Foreign Wars

The war in Iraq, and any future wars that are initiated by the United States of America or any other colonial power that makes use of Indigenous soldiers and resources, should be a major public policy issue for all Indigenous Peoples. War is a very serious and grave event and can be defined as an "*open and declared armed hostile conflict between states or nations.*"[6] (The questions What is war? What are the stages of war? and What is a just war? are explored more fully at the end of the Solutions section.) This definition, however, cannot fully convey the horrors of war, the reasons we fight, or the diverse views that humans hold about war. While some glorify and speak of it as normal or necessary for peace, others lament its destructive, violent, and inhumane nature and consequences. Chris Hedges, a veteran war correspondent and author of the book *War Is a Force That Gives Us Meaning*, said war is "organized murder" that promotes the agenda of "killers" and "racists;" it is a time when people sink to the lowest depths in their treatment of others. The film *War Photographer*, by Christian Frei, features James Natchwey, who states that war is a time when all rules of human decency are suspended. Author James Hillman, the author of *A Terrible Love of War*, maintains that war is "the first of all psychological tasks since it threatens your life and mine directly, and the existence of all living things."

For some, war can be a defensive maneuver against the tyranny of others. For some it is waged due to territorial needs and wants, beliefs in superiority of religion, politics, and race, or because of incompetent, uncompromising leadership. War is an important moral, social, economic, and spiritual matter that must be approached in the most principled and serious manner due to its long-lasting, devastating effects. The US-led war against Iraq is no exception.

War is particularly important to Indigenous Peoples since they have the ability to start or stop war according to their powers of self-government (or sovereignty), which reside in the tribal membership according to long-established social, political, and economic practices and beliefs. Self-government also enables

Indigenous Peoples to legislatively determine whether they should or should not participate in a war that is or is not of their making. The power and right of Indigenous Peoples' self-governance has existed "from time immemorial" and enables Indigenous communities to form their own governments, determine their membership, regulate tribal and individual property, impose taxes, maintain law and order, exercise jurisdiction over all within their borders, and regulate domestic and international relations, trade, and commerce.

Two of the most ancient and fundamentally inherent powers are (1) to formally deliberate the costs and realities of war and (2) to determine and execute declarations of war and peacemaking.

Unfortunately, the imposition of colonial government laws have divested most Indigenous Peoples of these two indispensable practices, leaving them with an inability to approach war and peacemaking as a thoughtful deliberation and act that is independent from that of the colonial powers. Most Indigenous Peoples now surrender (willingly or reluctantly) their war decision-making powers to the colonizers, leaving the oppressor to decide which nations and races of people are enemies or allies and when, where, and how war will be waged. The exercise of such unmitigated power over Indigenous Peoples constitutes an egregious violation of Indigenous sovereignty and the ancient, traditional tribal decision-making processes from which the inherent powers of self-government originated.

Today a majority of Indigenous communities and governments no longer possess functioning "traditional" war or peace-making councils or leaders, which in the past were central to creating peace, preventing war, and/or promoting "just war" behavior. Stripped of this critical aspect of governance, a majority of Indigenous nations no longer possess formal systems for teaching their membership about the various crucial aspects of war and peace. Most no longer make use of the traditional, Indigenous principles of just war that served as criteria to determine (a) whether their Indigenous community or nation should enter a war, (b) how it should be waged, (c) how it can be ended, (d) what can be done to keep peace, and (e) how to

constructively reconcile with the former "enemy."

Despite the fact that overwhelming numbers of people and governments around the world considered the Iraq War to be unjust, a majority of Indigenous leaders in the United States did not hold formal, open, critical community-wide discussions to assess the legitimacy of this war and its consequences for its citizens, the Iraqi people, and Mother Earth. In essence, it is not clear what agreement or disagreement exists regarding whether Indigenous soldiers should or should not have participated in the US war against Iraq. Few Indigenous communities formally declared through tribal governmental resolution whether they supported or condemned the numerous actions that the US government took to prolong or end this war. Many positions are still unclear, including:

- how Indigenous nations viewed US congressional appropriations to continue funding the war and occupation effort, which in the end cost trillions of dollars;

- if they supported the Bush administration's 2007 "surge" of 30,000 troops into Iraq to stabilize the situation or the Obama administration's call to withdraw all American troops by the end of 2011;

- how they viewed the Pentagon's 2007 move to extend the time of service for active-duty army soldiers in Iraq and Afghanistan by three months (from twelve to fifteen months), putting soldiers in harm's way for a longer period of time; and

- how they viewed the testimony of General David Petraeus and the ambassador to Iraq, Ryan Clark Crocker, who on April 8, 2008 testified before the US Senate Armed Services Committee that there has been "significant but uneven progress in Iraq…" and "the situation in Iraq remains exceedingly complex and challenging."[7]

Furthermore, how might Indigenous communities view a war against the sovereign nation of Iran—a war that seems to be in the making—given all that's happened in Iraq? On April 29, 2008 David Martin of CBS News reported that the Pentagon has ordered military commanders to develop options for attacking

Iran (http://www.cbsnews.com/sections/i_video/
main500251.shtml?id=4057250n).

Formal positions on the above issues are critical since they are in line with the actions of sovereign
Indigenous self-governance and because Indigenous
Peoples have consistently put a disproportionate number of their citizens in harm's way to fight in US-led
wars.

D. The Illegality of the Iraq War

Indigenous soldiers who have served or are
serving in Iraq have participated in one of the most
unpopular, illegal, misleading, mismanaged, condemned, and unjust wars in the recent history of the
United States. The international legal community
has described the Iraq War as an illegal act of aggression against a sovereign nation.[8] Specifically, the Bush
administration's goal of "regime change" (removing
Saddam Hussein) violates Article 2, Section 4 of the
UN Charter.[9] The United States instigated the war
because the Bush administration claimed that Iraq
had weapons of mass destruction; it did not. Iraq was
also accused of having ties with Osama bin Laden; it
did not. One only need watch former US president
George W. Bush on a YouTube video to hear these
admissions ("Bush Admits that Iraq Had Nothing To Do
With 9–11"). His comments can be viewed at http://
youtube.com/watch?v=f_A77N5WKWM.

The US-led war against Iraq was never endorsed
by the United Nations Council or the majority of
the world community. An overwhelming number of
international governments wanted UN-sanctioned
inspections for weapons of mass destruction (WMD)
to continue until there was clear, compelling evidence
that WMDs did or did not exist. But the UN mandate
was not completed because the United States, against
the will of the world community and international law,
invaded Iraq before the inspections were concluded.
Prior to the US-led invasion, former UN weapons
inspector Scott Ritter stated in an interview on July
17, 2002 that 90 to 95 percent of Iraq's weapons of
mass destruction capacity had been eliminated by
December 1998. What remained were only bits and
pieces of that program, which constituted no threat to
the United States.[10] To date there is no evidence to the
contrary. None.

E. What Does the Iraq War Mean for Indigenous Nations?

Although Indigenous nations are not presently
regarded as sovereign states by the United Nations,
they do constitute an integral part of the global community. For instance, on September 13, 2007 the UN
General Assembly adopted the United Nations Declaration on the Rights of Indigenous Peoples, which
emphasizes the right of these groups to maintain and
strengthen their own institutions, cultures, and traditions and to pursue their development in accordance
with their aspirations and needs. The Declaration
also recognizes Indigenous Peoples' rights to self-
determination, land, territories, resources, and cultural
integrity, and that existing treaty rights must be
respected. The Declaration was passed due to a long
history of violations of the sovereignty and rights of
Indigenous Peoples by colonizing powers that routinely invaded their territories to commit acts of genocide, deny their cultural rights, and appropriate, often
by force, the lands and resources of these groups.

Prior to the Declaration there were few places
that Indigenous Peoples could go to seek justice since
these and other concerns had been "submerged by
the dominant colonial societies which have controlled
access to domestic and international legal fora."[11]
Despite its passage, the UN Declaration on the Rights
of Indigenous Peoples is not legally binding under
international law, and some of the most powerful
colonial powers have opposed it. When the United
Nations voted on the Declaration, 143 nations voted
in favor and four against (Australia, Canada, New
Zealand, and the United States). Since the vote, all
have changed their positions and support the Declaration in some form. Even with its limitations the Declaration is regarded a positive step because the concerns
of Indigenous Peoples can now be heard by the world
community.

If the UN Declaration on the Rights of Indigenous Peoples is to be meaningful in the global community, it is important that Indigenous Peoples abide

by international laws that accord respect for the rights of all other nations. The participation of Indigenous Peoples in the US-led invasion of Iraq has made these groups vulnerable to criticism by the international community since they were complicit (with the United States) in this illegal, unjust act of invasion and war; they are complicit in the violation of international law that prohibits regime change; and complicit in the miscalculations of the United States when it charged Iraq of having weapons of mass destruction and being associated with Osama bin Laden.

If Indigenous Peoples assert that it is their cultural right to maintain peace with other nations, the current UN Declaration on the Rights of Indigenous Peoples can help them avoid being coerced into participating in the illegal wars of colonizing nations. If Indigenous nations had condemned the Iraq War (before or after it ended) and called for the withdrawal of all Indigenous troops from Iraq (before it ended), they would have been in close moral and political step with the majority of the international community. However, if they did not object to the war and failed to withdraw their troops while the opportunity existed, they can be regarded as having supported the internationally condemned war policies of the Bush administration.

ACTIVITY:

Would condemning the Iraq War have increased or decreased Indigenous Peoples' standing in the international community? Why?

_____

_____

_____

_____

Should Indigenous nations consider themselves independent nations within the international community and abide by the laws of the United Nations rather than the dominant colonial society? Why or why not?

_____

_____

_____

_____

F. The Effect of the War on Iraqis

The Iraq War has caused intense suffering and exorbitant deaths among Iraqis. It now appears that as of 2010 over one million Iraqis have died as a result of violence due to the US invasion. On January 28, 2008, the Opinion Research Business (ORB), an independent polling agency located in London, published an estimate of the total war casualties in Iraq that numbered 1,033,000 deaths. In an earlier count, in October of 2006, *The Lancet* medical journal reported that the death toll among Iraqis was estimated to be 655,000.[12] While there is a large difference between these two sources due to the counting methods used and the time of the second estimation, it is anyone's guess how many deaths have actually occurred. Many believe that the rates are even higher than reported.

What is certain is that a great deal of violence and suffering has taken place in Iraq. One stream of horrible events that occurred during and after the invasion of Iraq was the systematic and illegal torture and abuse of Iraqi detainees by American soldiers, interrogators, and guards in Iraq at Abu Ghraib prison, Guantanamo Bay Naval Base (on the southeastern end of Cuba), and Afghanistan. Numerous reports have found that many of the detainees died as a result of the interrogations, most of which constitute torture under international law. Hundreds of shocking, sickening, disgusting photographs taken by US military prison guards have surfaced to support the claims of abuse and torture. The treatment of Iraqi prisoners has been condemned by the world community and is considered by many to be a war crime and a gross violation of the Geneva Conventions. A second set of torture photographs that surfaced after the Abu Ghraib prison scandal has been said to be even more disturbing than the first. So much more so that President Barack Obama on May 13, 2009, reversed his decision to release them to the public, stating that they would inflame the theaters of war, jeopardize the safety of American troops, and make US progress in Iraq and Afghanistan more difficult. Obama's decision outraged many.

Death and suffering was a constant in the Iraq War since it began. In June 2006 alone, the United Nations reported that more than three thousand Iraqi civilians were violently killed. The organization Iraq Body Count[13] reported that according to all available sources, "March 2006–March 2007 has been by far the worst year for violence against civilians in Iraq since the invasion." For instance, "mortar attacks that kill civilians have quadrupled in the last year (from 73 to 289)" while "fatal suicide bombs, car bombs, and roadside bombing attacks have doubled in the last year, from 712 to 1476."

The war has left deep, gaping wounds on the mental well-being of numerous Iraqis. A national 2007 ABC News poll taken in Iraq indicated that seven in ten Iraqis report multiple signs of traumatic stress; more than half (53 percent) have a close friend or relative who has been hurt or killed in the violence; 86 percent worry about a loved one being hurt and two-thirds worry deeply. In November 2005, 63 percent of Iraqis felt very safe in their neighborhoods. Two years later just 26 percent said they felt safe. In Baghdad 84 percent felt unsafe.[14]

In a disturbing move, the United Nations reported that it did not include Iraqi civilian casualty figures in its human rights report that came out on April 25, 2007. These data have been regarded by many "as a rare, reliable indicator of suffering in Iraq."[15] The omission of these numbers can be traced back to the political pressure exerted by the current US-supported Iraqi government, which has often complained that the number of civilians reported killed in Iraq is too high, despite reports to the contrary.

In 2009 the UN Assistance Mission for Iraq (UNAMI) reported numbers for civilian casualties due to indiscriminate shelling and shootings, and random bomb and suicide attacks resulted in 1,841 civilian deaths and 4,797 injuries. In 2008 the UNAMI said that the Ministry of Health reported 6,787 persons killed and 20,178 injured.[16] Economic destitution is widespread. A 2007 report from UNAMI estimated 54 percent of the Iraqi population struggled to survive on less than one dollar a day; 15 percent lived in extreme poverty (less than fifty cents a day). Acute malnutrition doubled from 2003 to 2005, rising from 4.4 percent to 9 percent, while the official unemployment rate stood around 60 percent. Only 32 percent of Iraqis have access to clean drinking water, and health facilities lack critical drugs and equipment; 12,000 of 34,000 doctors have left since the US invasion; 250 doctors have been kidnapped and 2,000 have been killed.[17] In addition, a later UNAMI report showed that by December 2007 sectarian violence had displaced 4.4 million Iraqis (2.5 million inside Iraq and 1.9 million outside of Iraq). Many Iraqis who were displaced by the war have been moving back to their former homes and neighborhoods. Unfortunately, many are finding their possessions missing or homes destroyed.

Iraqi civilian deaths from US private security contractors continued to be reported until 2007. In one of the more well-known incidents seventeen Iraqi civilians were killed in September 2007 in the al-Mansour district of Baghdad by employees of the Blackwater security group. Violence continues to claim the lives of many women and children while professionals, government employees, and religious figures are targeted for killing. Numerous civilians continued to be killed by Multinational Force (MNF) operations. The situation for women is very poor with gender-based violence continuing to kill and injure many women, and incidents remaining greatly underreported. Many women have "expressed little faith in the ability of the judicial system to protect the lives and rights of abused women."[18]

What does this mean for tribal nations? War is rarely, if ever, a moral act, especially an imperial war such as the Iraq War, which the United States undertook on false evidence, lies, and more lies. The occupation, torture, mutilation, killing, and murder of innocent Iraqi people are atrocities. Many of these acts are so horrible that they are beyond comprehension. Contributing to the suffering and deaths of others is a major violation of the ethics and spiritual beliefs of many Indigenous nations. Many traditions include a belief in the great circle of life and consequences for violations to that circle (i.e., we are all connected, we are all related, what goes around comes around, and what is happening to the Iraqi people is what the United States and other imperial powers did to our ancestors). Participation in, and the failure to condemn, the suffering and death of Iraqi citizens due to this war diminishes any moral high ground that Indigenous Peoples may claim over the US government with respect to life.

ACTIVITY:

Should Indigenous nations care about what happens to the "enemies" of the United States? Why or why not? What do the traditions of your nation say about the illegal torture and killing of innocents in times of war?

_____

_____

_____

_____

G. The Effect of the War on Global Safety

When the United States invaded Iraq, the Bush administration asserted that its actions made the world a safer place. Contrary to this claim, several different American intelligence agencies have concluded that the US invasion and continuing occupation of Iraq has worsened the threat of global terrorism.[19] Moreover, when Iraqis were polled by international news agencies in a 2007,[20] few believed that the US and Iraqi security forces could change the terrible situation in Iraq; many felt that if the Americans left, things would improve; many felt that the United States was controlling most decisions about what the direction would be for a postwar Iraq.

The increase in terrorism caused by the US invasion of Iraq was an important issue in the 2008 US presidential election. On the fifth anniversary of the Iraq War, then US senator Barack Obama (D-Illinois) delivered a speech during his presidential campaign entitled "*The World Beyond Iraq*" in which he declared that although nearly four thousand Americans had given their lives and thousands more had been wounded fighting the Iraq War, "we are less safe and able to shape events abroad."[21]

The 2007 international news agency poll also found that "eighty percent of Iraqis report attacks nearby—car bombs, snipers, kidnappings, armed forces fighting each other or abusing citizens." A total of 78 percent opposed the presence of US forces on their soil, and in an expression of their resentment toward US troops, 51 percent said it was "acceptable" to attack US and coalition forces. In contrast, only 17 percent felt this way in early 2004. Finally, even though billions of US taxpayer dollars were sent to Iraq for post-war rebuilding, 67 percent of Iraqis said in the 2007 poll that postwar reconstruction efforts have been ineffective or nonexistent. Two years later, despite the fact that the United States had spent fifty-three billion to rebuild Iraq, many Iraqis still considered the effort to be wasteful. Iraqi prime minister Nuri Kamal al-Maliki has said that it will take another four hundred billion in construction costs, but it is uncertain where the money will come from.[22]

What does this mean for tribal nations? The threat of terrorist attacks in the world has increased as a result of the US invasion and continued occupation of Iraq. Many Iraqis have felt that the United States has controlled their nation and many wanted US troops to leave. Due to a difficult and protracted history of resisting colonization, Indigenous Peoples should know the extent to which occupying powers can destabilize tribal governments, economies, relationships, and lives. More than most, Indigenous Peoples should understand what it means when others want you out of their territories and when they do not make good on their promises to rebuild after invading.

ACTIVITY:

Do you (or does your community) believe that it was acceptable to invade Iraq based upon false information, to militarily occupy it for all these years, and not rebuild what the US military has destroyed? Why or why not?

_____

_____

_____

How does this relate or not relate to what happened to your own Indigenous nation?

_____

_____

_____

_____

_____

H. Lack of Support for the War

In 2010 a CNN/Opinion Research poll found that 60 percent of all Americans opposed the war with Iraq.[23] Other earlier polls indicated that Americans felt the Iraq War was more unpopular than the Vietnam War and 63 percent of Americans thought "the US made a mistake sending troops to Iraq."[24] World opinion of the Bush administration's war on terror has never been favorable. Shortly before the US invasion of Iraq in 2003, international polls showed that significant majorities in nearly all countries surveyed opposed the war without a UN mandate, while the view grew that the United States was an increasing threat to world peace.

National polls indicated that the majority of US citizens lost confidence in Bush's ability as a leader and his ability to handle the war, with one poll showing 71 percent of respondents believing the country was seriously headed in the wrong direction.[25] After Bush addressed the nation on Iraq on January 10, 2007, 65 percent of Americans opposed his plan for a surge of nearly 22,000 troops.[26] In 2007 one national poll showed that 69 percent of respondents thought that US efforts to bring stability to Iraq were going moderately or very badly.[27] In another poll 72 percent said Bush did not have a clear plan for handling the situation in Iraq, and 80 percent felt that the war had gone worse than the Bush administration had expected.[28]

The few other nations that joined the US-led war against Iraq wanted out before the war ended and continued to withdraw their troops and resources as it dragged on. Britain, the staunchest US supporter in terms of numbers of soldiers they had serving, began withdrawing troops long before the war would end. The overall number of British troops declined from approximately 50,000 in 2003 to under 12,000 in 2007, with all leaving Iraq by July 28, 2009.

What does this mean for tribal nations? The overwhelming and continual opposition—both national and international—to the Iraq War should have sent a clear message to Indigenous leaders and communities that their participation was not in the best interests of their nations. It is important that Indigenous Peoples take world opinion into serious consideration when deliberating their participation in wars such as this one. By failing to add their opinions about whether they agreed or disagreed with the US-led invasion of Iraq, Indigenous Peoples were in de facto agreement with the Bush administration's reasons for this war and the belief that President Bush had the capability to lead it. The trend continued with all nations pulling out of Iraq before US withdrawal, then only the cowboys (American soldiers) and Indians (Native American Indigenous soldiers) were left in a war that most of the world community condemned.

ACTIVITY:

If Indigenous nations are truly sovereign, could and should they have withdrawn their soldiers before the United States ended its major combat operations against Iraq on August 19, 2010? How does keeping troops there or withdrawing them support Indigenous nations' sovereignty?

_____

_____

_____

_____

_____

I. Ending Indigenous Peoples' Participation in Unjust Wars

Despite overwhelming international and national opposition to the Iraq War, few elected tribal political leaders or mainstream national Indigenous organizations and media publicly opposed the war in Iraq or the policies to continue the war. Conversely, many individual tribal citizens, activists, scholars, intellectuals, and non-mainstream Indigenous organizations such as the American Indian Movement condemned the US military invasion and occupation of Iraq. Following the September 11 attacks, when Bush decided to invade Afghanistan to drive out the Taliban and find al-Qaeda leader Osama bin Laden, various tribal political leaders and media across the United States vigorously spoke out in favor of this war. However, US public support for the Afghanistan war waned considerably since the United States first began bombing this nation. At the time, 94 percent of the US public supported the war, but by 2010 support for the war had dropped to 37 percent while 52 percent of those polled

said that the Afghanistan war has turned into another Vietnam.[29]

When the Bush administration decided to invade Iraq, very few US mainstream Indigenous groups spoke out publicly or issued statements in opposition. In fact, even after learning that the Bush administration's pretext for this war might be based on flawed evidence, the strongest statement that could be mustered came from a June 6, 2003 lead editorial in the newspaper *Indian Country Today.* The opinion stated, "If the threat that was supposed to exist, and upon which we bombed another country into submission, causing great loss of life, was exaggerated—perhaps even manufactured—how can the people of this great Indian country know who the enemy really is? How can we know how to protect ourselves? How can we know, truly, for which good cause did our soldiers die?"[30]

Indigenous Peoples became involved in the illegal US-led war against Iraq for several possible reasons, including their sense of loyalty to their warrior traditions, the lack of employment opportunities on tribal lands, the manipulation of Indigenous warrior cultures by colonial society, and the loss of tribal *principles of just war*. These complex realities of Indigenous life made it much less likely that politically elected Indigenous leaders would openly advocate for the withdrawal of their citizens from this war or condemn the pretext of this war and its planners. Moreover, since Indigenous Peoples have been pushed so far and for so long to the margins of colonial society, many have gravitated to military service because it provides the status they may not otherwise gain from colonial or tribal society.

> **Since many Indigenous soldiers participated in the war against Iraq and many of the horrible outcomes of this invasion contradict the ethical principles of many Indigenous communities, the US-led war against Iraq should be, and remain, at the center of a national debate for all Indigenous Peoples.**

What does this mean for tribal nations? Because Indigenous political leaders could not speak out against the Iraq War, it is important that the tribal elders, youth, women, veterans, educators, activists, peacemakers, and others strongly encourage the organization of critical debates and the creation of tribal principles of just war. Time is of the essence since on any day a war could be launched against Iran, Venezuela, or another US "enemy," which would further entangle Indigenous soldiers in the web of the excessively flawed wars on global terror.

ACTIVITY:

Was the US-led war against Iraq just or unjust based upon your traditional principles? Why did Indigenous nations not prevent their citizens from joining this war? Why did they not pull them out before it ended? Why were there no strong condemnations of the Iraq War by Indigenous governments?

_____

_____

_____

_____

_____

J. Solutions

Indigenous Peoples can avoid being led into future unjust wars by engaging in in-depth discussions about these two issues. Assessing each situation will help formulate specific and independent perspectives that reflect tribal cultural beliefs, values, and survival.

To maximize success, all Indigenous constituents (citizens) must be evenly represented in these deliberations in order to encompass—to the greatest extent possible—the views, opinions, and ideas of all the people.

What Is War?

The Stanford Encyclopedia of Philosophy says, "War should be understood as an *actual, intentional* and *widespread* armed conflict between political communities. Thus, fisticuffs between individual persons do not count as a war, nor does a gang fight, nor does a feud on the order of the Hatfields versus the McCoys. War is a phenomenon which occurs *only* between political communities, defined as those entities which either are states or intend to become states...."[31] To be clear this definition is a Eurocentric view and does not consider Indigenous concepts of war. For instance, some tribal nations declared war according to their own standards, which could mean that the whole nation was involved or that some bands and villages within the nation may or may not support or participate in the war, and individuals could choose whether or not to participate.

The following list serves as a suggested set of steps that can assist tribal communities in gaining a critical perspective on participation in war.

For the Iraq War:

1. Assign committees to gather all evidence, stories, and reports that will provide an honest, objective perspective on the US-led invasion of Iraq.

2. Draft tribal resolutions calling for the immediate assembly of all tribal members to participate in an in-depth examination of the Iraq War to determine where it converges or departs from tribal values, ethics, and beliefs.

3. Discuss the principles of just war (see pages 171–173) in terms of how it does or does not meet the standard of an Indigenous Peoples' just war.

4. If in opposition of a war, draft a tribal resolution calling for the immediate withdrawal of all Indigenous soldiers from Iraq.

For future wars:

1. Tribal discussions can center on what each community chooses as its definition of war and peace in light of tribal values and beliefs, and how this definition is similar and dissimilar to that of the United States and other nations of the world.

2. Based on their own unique tribal just war standards, tribal communities may undertake a critical review and listing of all the reasons they will fight in a war.

3. Tribal war and peace committees can be formed in every Indigenous community to hold seminars and consult with other Indigenous communities on these topics, and create as many opportunities for education as appropriate.

4. Tribal nations are sovereign nations and, therefore, Indigenous Peoples' response to war may be that of a legitimate national government. Tribal governments can codify a formal, legislative response to war and peace in their tribal constitutions. For instance, what proportion of the membership must agree to go to war? What are the justified reasons the nation will go to war? And how will the tribal government approach the six stages of war (see page 170).

5. Tribal communities can develop their own "Principles of Just War" declaring a precise and culturally defensible criteria for justly participating in a war (*Jus ad Bellum*), waging war (*Jus in Bellum*), and ending war (*Jus post Bellum*) (see pages 171–173).

6. Tribes can develop compulsory community courses and curriculum that enable tribal youth and adults to study the origins, causes, effects, and prevention of war.

7. Tribal communities can train selected members of their tribes to be official emissaries of understanding and diplomacy to other nations of the world.

8. Tribal communities can institute war and peace councils to interview and screen tribal members who want to enlist in the US military, in order to

understand their motivations for "joining up," provide them with alternatives to military service, and ensure that those who do enlist are well educated and committed to tribal just war principles.

9. Tribal communities can train and assign their own war correspondents to the war fronts to cover the reality of war.

10. Tribal communities can maintain an official war and peace Internet blog to continually update tribal nations on the topics of war and peace.

The Stages of War

Because Indigenous communities constitute sovereign nations it is important that each have an appropriate political and moral code that is adhered to when considering the following stages of war: (1) how to prevent war; (2) when the use of force is appropriate; (3) when all attempts at peace fail, how war can be waged in an honorable and humane manner according to the beliefs and values of the nation; (4) how and when war can be ended; (5) what can be done to keep peace following war; and (6) how to honorably reconcile with the former "enemy."

What Is Just War?

Just war theory examines the question and context concerning what constitutes legitimate reasons to go to war. According to the United States Catholic Conference, "The just-war tradition begins with a strong presumption against the use of force and then establishes the conditions when this presumption may be overridden for the sake of preserving the kind of peace which protects human dignity and human rights. In a disordered world, where peaceful resolution of conflicts sometimes fails, the just-war tradition provides an important moral framework for restraining and regulating the limited use of force by governments and international organizations."[32] It is important to note that this particular definition mentions only the interests of humans and not the rights that must be accorded to all living beings such as plants, animals, lands, and waters. Many Indigenous Peoples would agree that these entities are sentient and have rights,

and that a war has been carried out against them through human activities and policies.

Although just war theory and principles are often credited to the early Greeks and Thomas Aquinas, Indigenous Peoples around the world practiced various forms of just war before their contact with colonizing powers. For instance, "counting coup," which involved touching the enemy during battle to display a combatant's bravery, was a non-lethal war practice used by various tribes on the Great Plains. Of course if an enemy tribe did not practice or respect this form of warfare, the individual counting coup could be killed or injured in a retaliatory act.

Several tribes used stickball games (or "stickball diplomacy") rather than warfare to settle their differences. Although the games were fierce and many could be injured, few were actually killed. In the case of those who might be killed, retaliatory acts were not common because the rules were agreed upon in advance by the contestants. For some tribes, killing on the battlefield was avoided when individuals from two "enemy" tribes were members of the same sacred tribal society or fraternity. For instance, an Arikara (Sahnish) warrior named Bull Head and the Dakota chief Sitting Bull, who were members of warring tribes, were both members of a sacred organization called the New Dog Society. Because the society made them brothers, during a battle between the Arikara and Dakota, Sitting Bull prevented other Dakota warriors from harming Bull Head when he was rendered helpless on the battlefield.[33]

Whether a just war can actually be waged is questionable since what transpires in combat or hostilities depends on human behavior on the battlefield. If one side practices indiscriminate killing of all, including the defenseless, it is more likely that the other side will follow suit. Although opposing sides have limited control in a war, it is important for Indigenous nations to examine the following principles of just war, in order to determine how each may be used to create principles that are appropriate and relevant to Indigenous Peoples. The examples below are meant to be a guide. Just war principles can be further studied through various books, websites, articles, videos, and DVDs.

The just war tradition's criteria for entering into war (*Jus ad Bellum*)[34] are:

1. **Just Cause:** There must be a real danger to innocent life and to the conditions necessary for decent human existence and the protection of human rights. Wars of retribution are not justifiable.

   For tribes: Is there a real threat or injury to tribal lands, resources, peoples, and culture that will compromise life and well-being? Have all efforts at diplomacy and peacemaking failed?

2. **Competent Authority:** The use of force is always related to, and in service of, the common good. War can be declared only by those who have responsibility for the common good.

   For tribes: Who actually decides whether the citizens of the tribal nation should go to war? Is it the leader of the colonial power? Is she or he a competent authority to decide what is best for your nation? Is it the legislative body of government? Are they competent and worthy of Indigenous Peoples' trust and loyalty? Or is it an Indigenous leader, legislative government, or the citizens of the nation?

3. **Comparative Justice:** In the absence of an agreed upon global moral or judicial authority, all nations must recognize that their claims to having a just cause are relative and must be compared honestly and fairly to the claims of their opponents.

   For tribes: It is important that the principles and claims of Indigenous Peoples to their just cause are made clear to the rest of the world and are not filtered or confused with those of the United States. To compare their claims to that of other nations, Indigenous Peoples can study the moral, economic, racial, political, and cultural issues, beliefs, and values of other nations of the world and assess the degree to which the comparability of justice between themselves and others exists.

4. **Right Intention:** The intention for entering war must be to protect human life and human rights. Its ultimate goal must be peace and reconciliation, which can be achieved only by avoiding massive destruction or punitive sanctions.

   For tribes: When entering a war on behalf of the United States, Indigenous Peoples must ask themselves, is the United States starting or participating in this war for the best intention of all living beings and is it in accord with an Indigenous code of just war? Will our participation cause more harm than good? Does the use of weapons of mass destruction against the enemy correspond with our tribal beliefs? Who is going to benefit and lose most because of the war? What mechanisms are in place to ensure that Indigenous Peoples can fully participate, as sovereign nations, in the processes of peace and reconciliation after war?

5. **Last Resort:** All peaceful alternatives must have been explored and exhausted before war can be justified. Nations of the world should be working together to strengthen the capacity and the moral authority of the United Nations to mediate and/or prevent conflicts.

   For tribes: Did the Indigenous nation send appropriate peace delegations to interact with the "enemy" to advocate for peace? Did Indigenous nations work with or through the allies of the "enemy" in order to make peace? How closely did Indigenous governments work with the United Nations or national and international bodies to avoid war?

6. **Probability of Success:** When entering war will clearly result in disproportionate suffering or obvious defeat, it must be rejected.

   For tribes: Indigenous Peoples should do all in their power to avoid the disproportionate suffering of their "enemy." They can determine for themselves if a war they are entering will be won easily without much bloodshed and suffering. Indigenous nations should ask themselves what the obvious defeat will do to the well-being of innocent non-combatants. They can ask themselves if they will be spiritually, economically, politically, and culturally better or worse off than before, and whether the mass killing and suffering of another nation are consistent with Indigenous Peoples' values and beliefs.

Once the decision has been made to enter into war, the just war criteria governing how to wage war (*Jus in Bello*), are:

1. **Proportionality:** The question of proportionality in war is slightly different from the question of proportionality in deciding whether or not to enter into war. In war, the principle of proportionality requires that the response to aggression not exceed the nature of the original aggression.

   For tribes: In the past this principle was well understood. If someone injured or killed another from a different tribe, elders, spiritual leaders, peacemakers, and chiefs would often enter into council with the aggrieved party to negotiate a settlement for the violation to avoid all-out war. For instance, payment of goods and services to the family who lost the member might be sufficient to close the matter. Or there may be agreement between tribes that the violator was on his own and could be killed by the aggrieved family without retribution from the violator's tribe.

   With respect to the Iraq War, first, this nation did not attack the United States, which makes war against this sovereign nation totally unjustified according to various tribal beliefs and values. Second, if any nation unjustly attacks any group of Indigenous Peoples and kills a particular number, the response must be the same and no more. If the attacking nation did not use chemical, biological, or nuclear weapons, cluster bombs, or napalm, none of these should be used in the retaliatory attack.

2. **Discrimination:** This principle requires that acts of war be directed *only* against unjust aggressors, *never* against innocent people caught up in a war they did not create and could not have prevented.

   For tribes: Tribal nations must completely instill in their warriors the necessary skills and compassion on the field of battle to avoid all acts of aggression against the innocent and unarmed non-combatants.

Ending a war: *Jus post Bellum.*[35]

1. **Just cause for termination:** A state may terminate a war if there has been a reasonable vindication of the rights that were violated in the first place, and if the aggressor is willing to negotiate the terms of surrender. These terms of surrender include a formal apology, compensations, war crimes trials, and perhaps rehabilitation.

   For tribes: Tribal leaders must maintain close and continuous negotiations with the leaders of the attackers throughout the conflict, constantly seeking ways to end the war following the admission of the wrongful violation of the attacker. In the case of the US-led war against Iraq, cause for termination should have occurred long ago since it was the United States that was the violator that illegally and unjustly prosecuted this war with false information and regime change goals that are illegal under international law.

   With respect to the illegal, unjust attack on Iraq, according to this principle it is the United States that should surrender, issue a formal apology, make compensation, put US leaders on trial for war crimes, and restore Iraq to its prewar state.

2. **Right intention:** A state must terminate a war only under the conditions agreed upon in the above criteria. Revenge is not permitted. The victor state must also be willing to apply the same level of objectivity and investigation to any war crimes its armed forces may have committed.

   For tribes: There must be a willingness to apply the same criteria to Indigenous governments and combatants for their role in any unjust war. If Indigenous soldiers commit war crimes, they must be tried by an international war crimes tribunal and not hide under the protection of the United States, which refuses to abide by international law or the laws of other nations.

3. **Public declaration and authority:** The terms of peace must be made by a legitimate authority (such as the recognized government) and the terms must be accepted by a legitimate authority.

> **For tribes:** Using formal Indigenous government processes, peace must be made by the legitimate leadership with the legitimate leadership of the nation with which war had been waged.

4. **Discrimination:** The victor state is to differentiate between political and military leaders, and combatants and civilians. Punitive measures are to be limited to those directly responsible for the conflict.

> **For tribes:** Tribal governments must decide what measures are appropriate punishments or how to apply "punitive justice" according to tribal values, beliefs, and customs.

5. **Proportionality:** Any terms of surrender must be proportional to the rights that were initially violated. Draconian measures, absolutionist crusades, and any attempt at denying the surrendered country the right to participate in the world community are not permitted.

> **For tribes:** Tribes must use their tribal traditions to help heal and bring the surrendered nation back into the global community (i.e., the great circle of life). Gestures of peace, economic assistance, and understanding are crucial at this stage.

K. The Roles That Indigenous Citizens Can Assume

There are many roles and duties that can be assumed by different sectors of Indigenous society to assist their individual nations to avert participation in any further unjust wars. Perhaps most important is that Indigenous governments regard themselves as legitimate political bodies within the international community who must participate in all affairs that concern the well-being of all nations on the planet. Long before colonizers invaded the territories and lives of Indigenous Peoples, these groups waged many wars according to their own unique principles of just war. Some wars were just and others were not. Although

colonizing governments continue to control the lives of Indigenous Peoples on many fronts, these groups still maintain inherent powers of self-government that they can turn to, seeking goodwill and practicing justice, respect, and healthy interactions with the world community.

Tribal Leaders and Elders

With their invaluable experience and insight, tribal leaders and elders have a crucial role in helping their communities examine the relationship between Indigenous Peoples and the military. For example, they can:

- Act to immediately help in the recovery or re-creation of principles that will guide the community's actions according to cultural beliefs, values, and ethics before, during, and after a war.

- Help balance the over-emphasis of warrior culture and military service in the tribe by assisting in the recovery of peacemaking and peacekeeping traditions, and can help identify ways that those who seek a warrior's life can contribute directly to the protection of the Indigenous community.

- Remind tribal political leaders that the over-reliance on the US military as a major employer for tribal members will not fix the problems of unemployment and will continue to make youth dependent on this source for their educational and training needs.

- Remind tribal political leaders and parents that using military service as a socializing mechanism to give meaning, structure, and order to the lives of young Indigenous women and men will undermine that function within the Indigenous community social system. Young men and women should not be socially and culturally initiated by forces outside the community; that duty must come from within healthy Indigenous women's and men's societies.

- Counsel political leaders and tribal membership to understand that silence with respect to war is often perceived as agreement by non-Indigenous society.

- Remind political leaders that the service of Indigenous men and women in the unjust wars of the United States creates a negative perception of Indigenous nations by the international community.

- Remind political leaders that many of the wars of the United States have been directed at other Indigenous Peoples and tribal groups due to greed, feelings of cultural supremacy, and dishonesty.

- Remind political leaders that our tribal governments have the sovereign powers to enter into negotiations with other nations for the sake of peace, have the power to declare war, and can deploy their tribal members out of any conflict or war at any time they deem culturally, morally, and politically appropriate.

Tribal Parents

Parents whose children have joined the military, or are contemplating joining, must carefully consider the consequences of enlisting:

- Remember that your children who participate in wars, whether just or unjust, will be affected by the numerous horrors of the experience.

- Remember that your children will be asked to do things (sometimes very vile and repulsive things) that are incompatible with family and cultural beliefs and values.

- Remember that the lives and well-being of your children will be sacrificed for the interests of the colonial powers. It is important to understand what these interests are, what their underlying reasons are, and who benefits the most from them.

Indigenous Activists, Teachers, Intellectuals, and Academics

Those involved with education and activism can use their skills to facilitate community participation on this issue. They have a duty to:

- Assist their communities to launch truth-seeking forums to critically discuss war and peace.

- Use their academic skills to discover all the hard evidence for the reasons and costs of war.

- Help their communities to employ critical thinking skills to analyze war and peace.

- Help political leaders to conceptualize all the dimensions of war and peace.

- Develop courses and curriculums that focus on war and peace.

Tribal Youth and Young Adults

The voices of Indigenous youth and young adults (the next generations of critical thinkers, peacemakers, and keepers of tradition) are needed more than ever at this time. The well-balanced, decisive thinking, ethics, "deep knowledge," and "strong actions"[36] of those untainted by the myths and glories of war will act as a first line of defense to counter unjust wars and promote legislation and education that is needed to prevent the occurrence of future unjust wars. In this regard you have certain rights:

- The right to know the true costs of war on the individual and community levels.

- The right to an education that rigorously assesses all aspects of war and peace.

- The right to learn and employ peacemaking and peacekeeping strategies in order to avoid war.

- The right to employment and training opportunities that are not centered on war and military service.

- The right to attend Indigenous government-sponsored classes with a curriculum that examines all factors and theories leading to war and peace.

- The right to consult with youth and young adults from other nations for the purpose of promoting understanding, peace, and cooperation between one another.

Tribal Veterans

Those who serve in the military now, or have served in the past, have a responsibility to:

- Counsel non-veterans about all the realities of military service and war.

- State how military service and war are compatible or incompatible with tribal values and beliefs of war and peace.

- Remind political leaders that war is only one way to solve differences.

- Help political leaders to articulate Indigenous just war principles.

- Assemble tribal war and peace committees.

- Be the first line of defense against unjust wars.

- Teach others about how warrior service can and should benefit Indigenous Peoples if warriors are putting their lives on the line.

Freedom from war and conflict is possible in this lifetime.

L. Resources

Books

Ahmed, Mosaddeq Nefeez. *Behind the War on Terror: Western Secret Strategy and the Struggle for Iraq.* Gabriola Island, BC: New Society Publishers, 2003.

Butler, Smedly D. *War Is a Racket: The Anti-War Classic by America's Most Decorated General.* Los Angeles: Feral House, 2003.

Churchill, Ward. *On the Justice of Roosting Chickens: Reflections on the Consequences of U.S. Imperial Arrogance and Criminality.* Oakland, CA: AK Press, 2003.

Clark, Ramsey. *The Fire This Time: U.S. Crimes in the Gulf.* 3rd ed. New York: International Action Center, 2005.

Hedges, Chris. *War Is a Force That Gives Us Meaning.* New York: Anchor Books, 2003.

Hillman, James. *A Terrible Love of War.* New York: Penguin Books, 2004.

Johnson, Chalmers. *Blowback: The Costs and Consequences of Empire.* 2nd ed. New York: Holt Paperbacks, 2004.

Lowen, James. *Lies My Teacher Told Me: Everything Your American History Textbook Got Wrong.* 2nd ed. New York: Touchstone, 2007.

Nardin, Terry, ed. *The Ethics of War and Peace: Religious and Secular Perspectives.* Princeton, NJ: Princeton University Press, 1996.

Nelson, Deborah. *The War Behind Me: Vietnam Veterans Confront the Truth About U.S. War Crimes.* New York: Basic Books, 2008.

Power, Samantha. *A Problem From Hell: America in the Age of Genocide.* New York: Basic Books, 2002.

Rai, Milan. *War Plan Iraq: Ten Reasons Against War with Iraq.* New York: Verso, 2002.

Roy, Arundhati. *War Talk.* Cambridge, MA: South End Press, 2003.

Saito Taylor, Natsu. *From Chinese Exclusion to Guantanamo Bay: Plenary Power and the Prerogative State.* Boulder, CO: University Press of Colorado, 2007.

Sallah, Michael, and Mitch Weiss. *Tiger Force: A True Story of Men and War.* New York: Bay Books, 2006.

Suskind, Ron. *The One Percent Doctrine: Deep Inside America's Pursuit of Its Enemies Since 9/11.* New York: Simon & Schuster Paperbacks, 2007.

Walzer, Michael. *Arguing About War.* New Haven, CT: Yale University Press, 2006.

———. *Just and Unjust Wars: A Moral Argument with Historical Illustrations.* 3rd ed. New York: Basic Books, 2000.

Waziyatawin. *What Does Justice Look Like: The Struggle for Liberation in Dakota Homeland.* St. Paul, MN: Living Justice Press, 2008.

Zinn, Howard. *Passionate Declarations: Essays on War and Justice.* New York: Harper Collins, 2003.

Websites

Addicted to War: Why the U.S. Can't Kick Militarism (http://www.addictedtowar.com/).

AntiWar.com (http://www.antiwar.com).

Carnegie Council (http://www.carnegiecouncil.org/education/index.html).

Just War Theory.com (http://www.justwartheory.com).

Resources on Just War Theory (http://ethics.sandiego.edu/Applied/Military/Justwar.html).

Rethink Afghanistan (http://rethinkafghanistan.com).

Stop the War Coalition (http://www.stopwar.org.uk).

"Teacher's Guide for the Fog of War, An Errol Morris Film." http://www.choices.edu/resources/detail.php?id=55.

Documentaries

Body of War. Dir. Ellen Spiro and Phil Donahue. Film Sales Company, Sept. 2007. http://www.bodyofwar.com.

Gulf War Syndrome: Killing Our Own. Dir. Gary Null. Gary Null Productions, 2007. http://video.google.com/videoplay?docid=8061307149260436858&ei=u72jS90BBYGClgfc4PmODQ&q=us+foreign+policy#docid=-475226309740846580.

Hearts and Minds. Janus Films. Dir. Peter Davis. The Criterion Collection, 1974. http://video.google.com/videoplay?docid=-8502739857306070849#.

In the Year of the Pig. Dir. Emile de Antonio. Home Vision Entertainment, 1968. http://www.youtube.com/watch?v=GQhwEGVVGS4.

Remember My Lai. Producers Kevin Sim and Michael Bilton. Frontline, PBS, 1989. http://www.pbs.org/wgbh/pages/frontline/programs/info/714.html.

Rethink Afghanistan. Dir. Robert Greenwald. Brave New Foundation, 2009. http://rethinkafghanistan.com/videos.php.

Soldiers of Conscience. Dir. Catherine Ryan and Gary Weimberg. P.O.V. PBS, 2008. http://www.socfilm.com.

The Fog of War. Dir. Errol Morris. Sony Pictures Classics, 2003. http://amazon.imdb.com/video/screenplay/vi1995571481/.

The Oil Factor: Behind the War on Terror. Dir. Gerard Ungerman and Audrey Brohy. Free-Will Productions, 2004. http://video.google.com/videoplay?docid=1130731388742388243&ei=DcKjS43FNIyFlgeksdmRDg&q=war#.

War Photographer. Dir. Christian Frei. Icarus Films, 2001. http://www.war-photographer.com/en/.

What I've Learned About U.S. Foreign Policy: The War Against the Third World (CIA Covert Operations and US Military Interventions Since World War II, What You Didn't Learn in School and Don't Hear on the Mainstream Media). Ed. Frank Dorrel, 2000. http://video.google.com/videoplay?docid=-6171375275571061709&ei=uN2jS7m3EqbCqQKV6aHRCA&q=what+i%27ve+learned+about+u.s.+foreign+policy#.

Where War Has Passed: The Legacy of Chemical Warfare in Vietnam. 1999. http://www.youtube.com/watch?v=-Ug0btt9aoU.

Why We Fight. Charlotte Street Films. Dir. Eugene Jarecki. Sony Pictures Classics, 2005. http://www.youtube.com/watch?v=SWyhOKbqdEQ&feature=fvwrel.

A number of excellent war documentaries can also be found at the American Friends Services Committee Video and Film Lending Library: http://tools.afsc.org/bigcat/video-film.htm.

Notes

1. "Activists Dye River Red for Iraq War Anniversary." Chicago Press Release Services, March 19, 2010. http://chicagopressrelease.com/press-releases/activists-dye-river-red-for-iraq-war-anniversary.

2. "Thousands Rally on the Anniversary of the Invasion of Iraq." Fox News.com, March 21, 2010. http://www.foxnews.com/politics/2010/03/20/thousands-rally-anniversary-invasion-iraq.

3. Allen Breed. "7th Anniversary of Iraq passes with little notice at home." LJWorld.com, March 20, 2010. http://www2.ljworld.com/news/2010/mar/20/7th-anniversary-iraq-war-passes-little-notice-home/.

4. Iraq: Thousands Dead, 747 Billion Spent. Brave New Foundation, n.d. http://rethinkafghanistan.com/sevenhundredbillion.php.

5. Ziauddin, Sardar, and M. W. Davies. *Why Do People Hate America?* New York: The Disinformation Company, 2002, 13.

6. Merriam-Webster's Collegiate Dictionary, tenth edition. Springfield, MA: Merriam-Webster, Inc., 2000, 1326.

7. General Petraeus' Testimony to the Senate Armed Services Comm. Real Clear Politics. http://www.realclearpolitics.com/articles/2008/04/gen_petraeus_testimony_to_the.html.

8. International Law Aspects of the Iraq War and Occupation. Global Policy Forum. http://www.globalpolicy.org/security/issues/iraq/attack/lawindex.htm.

9. The United Nations Charter prohibits "the threat or use of force against the territorial integrity or political independence of any state, or in any other manner inconsistent with the Purposes of the United Nations." http://www.lcnp.org/global/iraqstatement3.htm.

10. "Former weapons inspector: Iraq not a threat." CNN.com/World. Sept. 9, 2002. http://archives.cnn.com/2002/WORLD/meast/09/08/ritter.iraq/index.html.

11. Steven C. Perkins. Researching Indigenous Peoples' Rights Under International Law. Annual Meeting of the American Association of Law Libraries, 1992. http://intelligent-internet.info/law/ipr2.html#Permanent%20Forum%20on%20Indigenous%20Issues.

12. Sarah Boseley. "655,000 Iraqis killed since invasion." *The Guardian*, Oct. 11, 2006. http://www.guardian.co.uk/Iraq/Story/0,1892888,00.html.

13. Year Four: Simply the worst. March 18, 2007. http://www.iraqbodycount.org/press/pr15.php.

14. Gary Langer. "Voices From Iraq 2007: Ebbing Hope in a Landscape of Loss." National Survey of Iraq. ABC News http://abcnews.go.com/US/story?id=2954716&page=1.

15. "UN: Next human rights report to omit civilians." *Lawrence Journal World*, April 22, 2007: 9A.

16. United Nations Assistance Mission for Iraq (UNAMI). Human Rights Report. Jan. 1–June 30, 2009. http://www.uniraq.org/documents/UNAMI_Human_Rights_Report15_January_June_2009_EN.pdf.

17. United Nations Assistance Mission for Iraq (UNAMI). Human Rights Report Jan. 1–March 31, 2007. http://www.uniraq.org/FileLib/misc/HR%20Report%20Jan%20Mar%202007%20EN.pdf.

18. United Nations Assistance Mission for Iraq (UNAMI). Human Rights Report July 1–December 31, 2007. http://www.uniraq.org/FileLib/misc/HR%20Report%20Jul%20Dec%202007%20EN.pdf.

19. Mark Mazzetti. "Spy Agencies Say Iraq War Worsens Terrorism Threat." *The New York Times,* Sept. 24, 2006. http://www.nytimes.com/2006/09/24/world/middleeast/24terror.html?pagewanted=all.

20. Iraq: Where Things Stand. ABC/USA TODAY/BBC/ARD Poll. http://abcnews.go.com/images/US/1033aIraqpoll.pdf.

21. Barack Obama. "The World Beyond Iraq." Speech, March 19, 2008. http://www.realclearpolitics.com/articles/2008/03/the_world_beyond_iraq.html.

22. Timothy Williams. "U.S. Fears Iraqis Will Not Keep Up Rebuild Projects." *The New York Times,* Nov. 20, 2009. http://www.nytimes.com/2009/11/21/world/middleeast/21reconstruct.html.

23. Iraq. PollingReport.com. http://www.pollingreport.com/iraq.htm.

24. Opposition to Iraq War Reaches New High. Gallup, April 24, 2008. http://www.gallup.com/poll/106783/Opposition-Iraq-War-Reaches-New-High.aspx.

25. Gary Langer. "State of Union: Unhappy with Bush." *ABC News*, Jan. 22, 2007. http://abcnews.go.com/Politics/PollVault/story?id=2811599&page=1.

26. Susan Page. "Most Say No to Iraq Buildup." *USA Today*, Jan. 8, 2007. http://www.usatoday.com/news/washington/2007-01-08-gallup-poll_x.htm.

27. CNN/Opinion Research Corporation Poll, June 23–24, 2010. http://www.pollingreport.com/iraq2.htm.

28. Susan Page. "Most Say No to Iraq Buildup." *USA Today*, Jan. 8, 2007. http://www.usatoday.com/news/washington/2007-01-08-gallup-poll_x.htm.

29. Michael Krebs. "Poll: Support for Afghan War hits new low." Digital Journal, Oct. 16, 2010. http://www.digitaljournal.com/article/299010.

30. "Doubts on Iraq war: reason or pretext?" *Indian Country*, June 6, 2003. http://www.indiancountry.com/content.cfm?id=1054910559.

31. Brian Orend. War. Stanford Encyclopedia of Philosophy. Fall 2008. http://plato.stanford.edu/entries/war/.

32. The Harvest of Justice Is Sown in Peace. A Reflection of the National Conference of Catholic Bishops on the Tenth Anniversary of The Challenge of Peace. United States Catholic Conference. Nov. 1993. http://www.usccb.org/sdwp/international/justwar.htm.

33. O. G. Libby, ed. *The Arikara Narrative of the Campaign Against the Hostile Dakotas: June 1876.* New York: Sol Lewis, 1973, 47–48.

34. James E. Hug. "Just War Principles." Center for Concern at 40: Seeing the World Anew, Feb. 2, 2006. https://www.coc.org/node/1463.

35. Just War Theory. Wikipedia. http://en.wikipedia.org/wiki/Just_War.

36. The terms " Deep knowledge" and "Strong actions" are from Taoist traditions, cited directly from *The Book of Balance and Harmony* by Thomas Clearly, Boston: Shambala Publications, 2003.

Chapter 10

INITIATING THE PROCESS OF YOUTH DECOLONIZATION
RECLAIMING OUR RIGHT TO KNOW AND ACT ON OUR EXPERIENCES

Molly Wickham

A. Awakening from My Colonial Experiences

Most people in settler society take for granted that they will live a long life. Yet when I was a teenager, I could not imagine myself being older; this is a consequence of being in "survival mode." This term was added to my vocabulary through my experiences as an Indigenous young person. Slowly, I have begun the journey of discovering why I had been in survival mode for many years, and how I have come to feel empowered through a new understanding of those experiences. When I talk to youth these days, so many of them tell me they cannot imagine themselves being adults, or if they can, they cannot imagine themselves living to be old people. I understand many of their experiences and I know they are linked to the effects of colonization on Indigenous people all over Turtle Island.

As with many of the youth with whom I work, I also grew up with the inter-generational effects of residential schools, foster care, and displacement. My experiences of colonization as a Wet'suwet'en woman meant that we lived in poverty most of our lives, were disconnected from our culture and kinship networks, and experienced violence in our home. Drug and alcohol abuse were everywhere, including in our home on a day-to-day basis. I saw our family fighting all the time as a consequence of the disconnection between family members due to residential schools, foster care, and displacement from our lands. The only thing I knew about where we came from was that it was a place from which my mother desperately wanted to escape. I did not have the words to describe what was going on, so I turned the pain I was feeling inward. Not having an outlet for it, I held it in, distracted myself, and even hurt myself. Not knowing why these things were happening to my family caused anger and internalized racism. My mother did her very best to teach us that these things were not normal and that we should never allow these types of behaviors in our own lives as adults, but I could not help thinking that this kind of life existed because we were Indians. There weren't very many Indigenous families I knew that did not experience these same types of problems. I often felt frustrated at my situation, and disempowered. When I was younger these feelings led me to feel depressed and angry, and I did not have the words to express how I was feeling. As I got older and entered high school, these feelings were compounded by the racism and violence experienced at school. I reacted by being violent and numbing the pain with alcohol and drugs.

People who know what I used to be like always ask what saved me. I have spent countless hours trying to figure out the answer, and I have come to the conclusion that there is not just one. An important reason is that my mother loved us unconditionally and tried her best to educate us about her experiences. I also spent a critical part of my childhood learning my stepfather's cultural teachings, and I felt those teachings were always there supporting me in the background. I had positive experiences with very strong Indigenous people in ceremony and cultural settings, but that small pocket was not enough to save me from violence, drugs, and alcohol. Although I was conflicted, I was supported by the continuous praise of my mother. She always told my sister and me that many of our problems related back to her experiences in foster care. Furthermore, she always told us that we should be proud of being very strong, intelligent, Indigenous women. I attribute my survival to her teachings. I understand that I am fortunate to have had this kind of relationship with my mother. At a very young age I learned how valuable family was. However, the bulk of my decolonization process began when I learned about colonization itself. I was finally able to name what happened to my family. I became even angrier, but I no longer directed that anger toward myself or those whom I love.

Learning for me was a frantic attempt to counter all the negative impacts in my life. When I learned about residential schools, I locked myself in my house for weeks reading, crying, and healing. My grandparents were both victims of residential schools along with half of my aunts and uncles. I also learned, however, that this was just one part of the puzzle.

I finally had an answer. Now I had something to say about my history and knew how to respond to ignorant comments such as "They are just drunken Indians" and "They can't even raise their own kids." Not only did I finally have something to say, but I realized I was not the only one who was experiencing pain from colonization. I was not alone and neither was my family. When I realized that colonization is happening to all of us, I began to understand my family better. It was then that I first began realizing the importance of Indigenous solidarity and support. Still, it took me until I entered college at the age of twenty-two before I could name the trauma that happened to my family and People. My newfound understanding was born from a desire to learn and it was fuelled by anger. Now I use

> My newfound understanding opened up a very deep space where I had housed anger, shame, and pain. It was as if it all came rushing to the forefront and I had to know every detail of what had caused us so much pain. That deep anger had impacted my education, my relationships, my sense of self-worth and had created guilt and blame within me. Now I know that all those negatives do not come from me— they were imposed on me.

the anger to support young people who are experiencing similar effects of colonization. I know that using my own journey to understand what has happened to our people helps navigate my way into a healthy existence and that I have a responsibility to share this with others along the way. I did not work through this on my own, and I do not expect anyone else to either.

I no longer live my life in survival mode, which provides me the time and energy to share what I have learned with those who suffer the worst consequences of colonialism. I see it as my responsibility to share this understanding with youth who still can use their anger to empower themselves and their families, rather than internalize their anger and pain.

> I think about those years of suffering that came from the anger I had directed at myself and how easily it could have been me that ended up in jail, dead, or addicted to one of the many different kinds of drugs I used to numb the pain. Fortunately, I was never caught and I was taught to never give up.

B. Ongoing Suffering Under Colonization

As a young person I have been told, "You are a future leader." These words weigh heavily on young people attempting to survive the effects of colonization, in part because they have difficulty seeing themselves as future leaders. Fortunately, a growing number of educators and knowledge holders are teaching Indigenous young people their traditional values, language, and ways of being, and this helps alleviate the worst effects of colonization among those fortunate enough to be exposed to these teachings. Many more young people, however, are suffering the worst effects of colonialism without any recourse. This leads to internalized oppression and racism, resulting from a fragmented Indigenous identity.

In response to this suffering, social programs developed by governments focus on individualistic remedies that deny the greater context of colonization and imply that there is something inherently wrong with Indigenous youth. Surely, this is the experience that I had growing up, and continue to witness in every "white-stream" institution with which I have ever come in contact.

Even our own Indigenous organizations are often restricted by government funding regulations that dictate what approaches and programs should be implemented. Rarely, if ever, does support for Indigenous young people include educating them about colonization. Who on earth would pay Indians to educate themselves about how the state and church have in the past, and continue to, systematically rip apart our families, desecrate our lands, and undermine our leadership? Mainstream support not only omits this information, it also never links it to youths' behaviors. Similarly, healing programs focus on the individual rather than the colonial processes that keep Indigenous young people oppressed, in jail, or in foster care. Mainstream education focuses on assimilation—if you behave like white-stream Canada you will "succeed." Mainstream education fails to acknowledge other ways of knowing and labels youth as "slow" when they do not mould to white-stream criteria of what it takes to be a good citizen. Furthermore, cultural programming is often lacking a critical perspective, focusing on arts and crafts instead of what Waziyatawin, in *What Does Justice Look*

As many as twenty-seven thousand Indigenous children in Canada are in the care of the government, which is three times the number of children in residential schools at the height of the Residential School era. These traumas translate into rates of suicide five to six times higher than the settler population. Indigenous youth's involvement with gangs ranges from 58–96 percent in some provinces. In addition, there are approximately ten thousand incarcerated Indigenous youth in Canada.

Like: The Struggle for Liberation in Dakota Homeland, calls "truthtelling." For Indigenous young people, truthtelling is a critical way to gain understanding about the *truth* of their experiences—that colonization has affected every aspect of their way of life, and it accounts for the pain and anger they have turned upon themselves.

Until Indigenous people recover our land, languages, and ways of being, there will always be a need for decolonizing work. Given the overall objective of decolonization, one of the first steps in accomplishing this goal is to educate young people about colonization as it relates to their own lives so they can then begin to transform their thinking. Young Indigenous people are surely experiencing the effects of colonization on a number of levels simultaneously, and it is the responsibility of all Indigenous people to help facilitate their decolonization process and instill in them a sense of empowerment. This chapter is for Indigenous people who are committed to sharing their journey of understanding about how colonization affects Indigenous people, and upholding their responsibility to provide opportunities of empowerment for youth in the decolonization process.

C. Attacks on Youth and Families

Currently, colonial governments continue attacks on Indigenous families because families are at the heart of Indigenous nations. As a Wet'suwet'en woman, I know that kinship networks are the foundation of our traditional clan system and the lifelines of cultural transmission. Therefore, by allowing our most vulnerable populations to suffer in silence, we violate Wet'suwet'en laws that protect our children and were established for the survival of Wet'suwet'en People. Families have borne the brunt of colonial attacks for hundreds of years. Indigenous Peoples in Canada, for example, have faced cultural oppression through the continued forced removal of children to residential schools, the "sixties scoop"—the massive theft of Indigenous children placed in white homes following the decline of the residential schools—and the child welfare system where children have been, and continue

to be, severely abused physically, mentally, emotionally, and spiritually. In many cases children have even died either in the schools, or shortly thereafter, from the negative effects of abuse and dislocation. This dirties the government's hands with genocide. Meanwhile, the legacy of the residential schools and the current foster care system continue to affect the stability of families and communities.

Residential schools attacked every element of Indigenous being: spirituality, physical wellness, intellectual knowledge, and Indigenous ways of knowing, as well as causing the trauma of dislocation and disconnection from community and family. Residential schools were places of genocide on many different levels. However, when the atrocities were publicly identified, governments found new ways to steal Indigenous children.

Residential schools were followed by the sixties scoop from the 1960s to late 1980s. Like residential schools, mainstream Canadian foster homes do not speak Indigenous languages, do not teach Indigenous spirituality or culture, and promote Christian values. More importantly, children and youth are often disconnected from their families and communities, which necessarily disrupts cultural transmission and a sense of belonging. Children grow up learning that white people must care for Indigenous children because native families either cannot or do not want to care for their own children. Children grow up learning Western ways of being in the world because an Indigenous existence is seen as inferior. Consequently, confusion, hate, internalized racism, and anger are often emotions and feelings with which young displaced Indigenous people must contend.

Not much has changed in the last century in Canada. In fact, the theft of Indigenous children has increased. According to Kristine Morris, there are three times more children in foster homes today than there were children in the residential schools at the height of the Residential School era. An increasing number of children in care end up in youth detention centers, continuing the colonial attack. Furthermore, Indigenous youth are over-represented in the (in)justice system, and have obscenely high rates of suicide. Suicide has been linked to identity loss and is among the most devastating effects. Suicide not only affects youth but also affects whole communities by denying cultural transmission. Parents suffer the devastating losses of their children, elders no longer have young people to mentor, and generations to come will continue to feel the effects of devastation if we don't act now!

Even for those who do not experience foster care, mainstream Canada has the cards stacked against them. For example, young Indigenous people have to deal with the media's destructive interpretations of Indigenous people, as well as an education system that does not value Indigenous ways of knowing or being. Colonial countries assert white superiority at every turn. Jim Silver, in *In Their Own Voices: Building Urban Aboriginal Communities,* says, "The result can be and often is an undermining of young Aboriginal people's sense of self-worth and self-identity." For young people attempting to form a sense of self and a place in the world, this devaluing and racist culture can be traumatizing. We are still fighting the struggle for our freedom. Freedom for youth begins with an understanding that their experiences are tied to colonization and hope lies in decolonization.

D. Decolonizing Through Relationships

As previously discussed, many Indigenous youth experience extreme displacement and traumatic experiences leading to internalized anger and self-destructive

> It is time that we name these traumas as the colonial assaults they are; it is time that we release our anger upon the colonial system instead of upon the bodies and minds of our young people.

behavior. To counter these effects of colonization, Indigenous people must actively engage young people, modelling respectful relationships built on Indigenous revitalization and ways of being in the world. It is the responsibility of every Indigenous person to actualize these Indigenous ways of being. For instance, each one of us must first critically evaluate our own lives under colonial rule and then creatively think about engaging in decolonization work. At the same time that we are working on ourselves, there is something we can be doing to support our families and young people. Many of the teachings that have provided me support were given to me by people who were also struggling, showing me the value in determination and persistence. I have a responsibility to my family as a Wet'suwet'en woman, and I must balance that responsibility with the rest of my life under colonial rule.

Traditionally, extended family was considered critical to Indigenous nations. For example, Wet'suwet'en governance systems are based on kinship networks. Children are raised with a particular role in the community. If something were to happen to the parents of the child, the father's clan would step in and assist the family. This occurred wherever the need arose. Today, it is still understood that the young people must be nurtured and taught well for the survival of the nation. But since our kinship networks are often dismantled, others must step in to take on these roles of supporters and educators. Consider how your relationship to children and youth has been affected by colonization and how you can change that relationship.

> Each person may be engaged in a different way with the decolonization process, which means that each personal best will be different. If you are not ready to engage youth in decolonization, support someone who is. We all have a role to play.

ACTIVITY FOR YOUTH WORKERS:

How were children reared in your nation prior to colonization? If something happened to the parents, who would care for the children and raise them?

_____

_____

_____

_____

Are there ways we can begin to restore those relationships? In your work with Indigenous youth, what role can you help to play?

_____

_____

_____

_____

After such aggressive attacks on our families by colonial society, Indigenous nations are left with missing children and broken families. Consequently, nations are not always able to find and protect their own children. This is why it is necessary for all Indigenous people to take up this responsibility. Bonita Lawrence, in _"Real" Indians and Others: Mixed Blood Urban Native Peoples and Indigenous Nationhood_, asserts that "[M]ixed blood urban native people are Native people for one clear reason: they come from Native families, that is, from families that carry specific histories, Native histories." These children would carry forward their histories, culture, and familial ties except that many of these relationships have been severed through the colonial process. Without relationship to culture and Indigenous knowledge, the importance of bloodlines becomes lost, as does the young person who carries them. Unfortunately, we all share similar histories of colonization and cultural genocide. We can use these shared histories, however, as tools to build healthy relationships. We must show young people how to care for one another so they can become rooted or find their way back home. Whatever the case may be, young Indigenous people need to see that the Indigenous community cares for their well-being and can model healthy relationships. This will directly counter internalized racism and alienation and is necessary for the survival of both young people and Indigenous nationhood.

Interconnectedness requires respectful relationships and these relationships must be built upon traditional cultural foundations in order for communities to thrive. For example, my relationships with youth shape the knowledge I accumulate about youth and my own position in relation to them. The same applies to information relayed to youth by adults. Our relationships with youth are connected to how they perceive this information and how they use it. Indigenous scholars Taiaiake Alfred and Jeff Corntassel consider relationships to be "the spiritual and cultural foundations of Indigenous Peoples." In order to survive we must strengthen these relationships and nurture to health our young people who have fallen, so that they can grow up understanding the colonial processes that affect them and find healthy ways to resist. In *The Book of Elders*, Janet McCloud teaches us that if Indigenous people want their children to have a better future, they had better remember that children learn by imitating, thus we must all be the teachers. If Indigenous people want the next generation to resist the colonial system and to live healthy lives, we must show them what that looks like. Let us not assume the strength of the colonial system. Let us focus on our own strengths as Indigenous people. These relationships must nurture all elements of Indigenous being—mental, emotional, and physical.

E. Themes from Decolonizing Youth in Custody

Recently, a group of Indigenous adults have taken on the task of educating youth residing in a custody center about the effects of colonization and how to counter those effects (decolonization). The program was initially based on relationship building, land, spirituality, and families, and has since included topics such as healthy relationships and mixed-blood identity. For six weeks, two or three volunteers each week developed an interactive session designed to engage youth on a particular topic using real life experiences, to discuss decolonization initiatives, and to model healthy relationships and decolonizing behavior. This programming was developed entirely by Indigenous people who have direct experiences

with these topics. In the following discussion I will outline the purpose and content of the first six sessions of the program and how they worked to offer youth in custody an Indigenous perspective on their experiences, in addition to providing an alternative discourse to the one provided by an oppressive and unjust system. These examples and techniques could be used for other youth groups and altered to fit the specific needs of Indigenous youth all over Turtle Island.

F. Step One: Building Relationships— "It Feels Good to Be Indian Today"

In the first session we worked on relationship building. By modelling relationships built on respect, we can show youth that community matters. If possible, invite a number of volunteers to be involved. By involving more people, youth will have increased opportunities to make a connection with one or more individuals, which will also create a stronger sense of community. Some youth continually ask for one particular volunteer while others immediately connect with someone else. Youth understand genuine caring and appreciate volunteers who spend time with them. We found that certain youth connected with certain individuals more easily based on shared experiences and personality. Bring food to share as this is customary for most gatherings and often occurs before any business begins. It is also important to model the behaviors that you would like to see, as well as to raise questions and explain why you are doing things in a particular way.

For example, if there are urban youth involved, or youth from another territory, it is proper protocol to invite an elder from the territory where you are located to open and close the session. Invite the elder to open with a prayer and a song and share stories about local culture and experiences of colonization. Show youth how to respect one another, the territory, and our elders. At this point it is important not to delve too deeply into the effects of colonization and why colonization happened, but to explain to the group that these sessions will be used to learn about colonization and decolonization using interactive forums.

ACTIVITY FOR YOUTH:

Developing Relationships:

(1) Ask the youth to introduce themselves and state where they come from. Asking what nation they come from can be upsetting to young people who are not aware of the proper name of their nation; however, by inviting those who do know their nation to share with the group, others will feel more comfortable to explore their own ancestry.

(2) Ask the group to think of a positive personal attribute, beginning with the same first letter of their name, to share with the group (e.g., Compassionate Cindy). If youth are modest, ask them to identify something about themselves that not many people know.

This activity can become a regular part of the group. I communicate to youth that I was not raised knowing I am a member of the Wet'suwet'en Nation, from the Gitdumden (Bear/Wolf) Clan. It has taken me a long time to become comfortable introducing myself in that way. Thus, each week we go around the circle after our opening prayer and we practice introducing ourselves by sharing our name and the nation we come from. I have watched proudly as youth who have never identified as being Indigenous before, share their familial ties with the group. It is especially fun to acknowledge the territory and then hear youth proudly state they are from that territory.

These activities can not only help youth workers gauge where a youth is in terms of knowledge about their Indigenous histories, but also allow workers to share their own history with youth. Leave enough time at the end of the session to invite youth to share a song with the group. This can get the group comfortable with singing and drumming together.

ACTIVITY:

"Check in, Check out" Activity:

During the first session ask the youth to make representations of themselves out of clay. This can be something that represents something they like to do (e.g., a sport they play or drumming) or their favorite animal; it is something that can be used repeatedly over the next sessions.

Ask youth to describe what they have made and why it is important. This can then be used at check-out time.

To do this, make a circle on a hard piece of cardboard and paint colors within the circle. You can do this in whatever format makes sense for your group of youth or your culture. This should be done before the session begins.

Ask the youth to place their representation on the color that best expresses how they are feeling at the end of the session, and to describe what they have learned over the session and how it has affected them.

This exercise allows youth to engage physical activity and visuals in describing their emotions and experiences within the group and in their everyday lives. In addition, the circle can be used as a basis for the next activity. Remember to do a "check in, check out" at the beginning and end of each session to gauge how the youth are processing the material and to identify any changes in format or content that may need to be made. During our very first session, we invited local elders to attend and we all shared food, songs, and stories. We did not talk much about what colonization was but spent most of our time enjoying one another's company. When we did our check-out activity at the end of the session, everyone had really good responses. Most of the youth were pretty happy about the volunteers, and enjoyed the elders' stories, but I knew we were headed down the right path when one youth said, "It feels good to be Indian today."

I know that it hasn't always felt good to be Indian, so we must also be aware of the anger that comes along with learning about colonization. It is crucial that each group of volunteers or workers consistently gauge how the youth are dealing with the information and the people who present it and that they become comfortable changing or adapting formats to fit the needs of the youth. For example, in our most recent relationship building session we ended up talking at length about anger. We shared with youth that anger was a natural emotion, and talked about how we have dealt with, and continue to deal with, our own anger, redirecting it toward positive resistance efforts. It was useful to acknowledge that the youth are experiencing anger and to open up communication on the topic.

G. Step Two: Introduction to Colonization

Colonization is a difficult topic to approach with youth. Each person has experienced the effects of colonization but may not be able to name the effects and connect them back to the colonizer. Often the oppression and racism that youth experience become internalized. This is the most dangerous effect of colonization on young minds. In *In the Footsteps of Our Ancestors*, Waziyatawin illuminates the problem by saying, "When the victims of horrendous crimes against humanity are blamed for their state of crisis, the colonizer's interests are served." This type of internalization is extremely harmful to all Indigenous people, particularly the young. Caught in this type of mindset, youth begin to engage in self-destructive behaviors, which often lead to other social ills. As a response to this internalization, Waziyatawin calls for truth telling as an important step in our own decolonization. This means that youth must be educated about our history of colonization as a transformative tool, challenging the oppressive state as well as the assumption that Indigenous people are to blame for their own state of crisis. When approaching this topic, it is best to use examples with which youth can identify.

ACTIVITY:

Begin by drawing an outline of the following sessions:

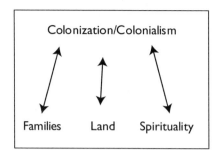

It is important to communicate that colonization is an ongoing process of domination over Indigenous life. Mainstream society advances the idea that colonial impacts are something of the past and need not be addressed; we can illustrate the falsehood of this through our own experiences. We want to show youth the ways colonialism has affected our families, land, and spirituality, as well as the ways colonization continues in our homelands. Communicate to youth that *colonialism* dominates Indigenous life and that *colonization* means the process of continued domination over Indigenous life. Use the following exercises to explore your own relationship with colonization and think about how you might respond to youths' relationships with colonization. Then pose these questions to the youth.

ACTIVITY FOR YOUTH WORKERS AND YOUTH:

What does colonialism mean to you?

_____

_____

_____

_____

What kinds of experiences in your life do you think are linked to colonization?

_____

_____

_____

_____

Since colonization is an extremely complex topic, it is useful to keep definitions clear and concise and focus on how it relates back to the youths' experiences. Identify tools of colonization that affect our lives in the present day so youth can connect the tools of colonization with their own experiences. In our most recent session we discussed how money (jobs), laws, land, ideas, and arms are used as tools of continued domination, and how these things affect our lives. For example, we talked about how arms were used to commit genocide on our people in an attempt to control the land, and how this control has shape-shifted into present day laws, which are enforced by the threat of violence and imprisonment. We shared ideas about how laws are used as a tool to control our access to hunting, fishing, and even housing on our own territories. Find examples of tools that affect all Indigenous people and then use an example from your community. You can then write these words or phrases under the existing headings or add new links under colonization. As an example, youth identified "fighting" as an experience of colonization. Violence could fit under families or could be its own branch of effects and tools. It is important to identify these branches as not only effects but tools that the colonizers use to continue domination (colonization). These are the same areas that youth identify as affecting their lives, which should be focused on later in decolonization discussions. Another aspect of this discovery is to attach an emotion to these experiences.

ACTIVITY FOR YOUTH:

If you had to attach an emotion to the experience of colonization, what would it be?

_____

_____

What are common reactions to these issues that you see in your life or community?

_____

_____

_____

Who benefits from these reactions?

_____

_____

_____

By attaching an emotion to the experience, youth can link what they are experiencing and feeling in their lives to the process of colonization. Again, it is important to normalize the emotions that colonized people may feel, such as anger and self-hate, and then discuss how to redirect the effects of those emotions. For example, it is perfectly normal to experience feelings of frustration and anger under colonial rule; however, instead of taking it out on one another, we can provide youth with alternative visions of using that anger to motivate direct action.

This is also an important activity to connect youth to one another and to the facilitators. For example, by drawing out these emotions and experiences, youth will clearly see that adults and other young people have shared experiences with them, which will help them feel less isolated. Remember, colonization affects us all negatively. Linking the tools of colonization to responses in communities creates awareness that all colonized peoples respond similarly, not just particular families or nations.

If youth are having trouble coming up with answers to questions, you may use your own life experiences as examples. It is critical that youth see that you understand their experiences and are willing to be honest and open with them. By using real examples from a specific territory and time period, we can remind the youth that colonization is ongoing and has real implications. For example, depending on how old the youth are, let them know when the last residential school was closed in their area, or research when the last Indian hospital was closed. You can also include dates of recent racist legislation that would have affected their parents or grandparents, like the banning of the potlatch or the reserve pass system. Use real life examples at every stage to engage youth's lived experiences with colonization or the experiences of their family members.

Once youth have been introduced to colonization, it is critical that they also be introduced to resistance efforts and decolonization. It is natural to have a lot of questions and anger when we face our experience of colonization. Be ready to respond to anger or confusion with resistance efforts and positive initiatives with which youth can engage. To engage youth with the idea of decolonization, ask them to identify representations of colonization and decolonization from resources around them like Indigenous magazines, newspapers, and other media.

ACTIVITY FOR YOUTH:

Using these materials (Indigenous magazines, newsletters, or any other relevant visual material including other art forms), pick something that represents what colonization is for you. What examples can you find?

_____

_____

_____

_____

_____

Look for representations of decolonization that could counter the effects of colonization? What examples did you find?

_____

_____

_____

_____

In doing this activity, youth will be considering how colonization affects their lives as well as identifying ways to resist it. By focusing on decolonization during each session, youth will also find hope in a colonial world, which can often feel hopeless. These representations can be glued onto the back of your "check-in/check-out" circle as a collage and can be used to identify how youth are feeling during check-ins. During our most recent introduction to colonization, we felt that youth had a great deal of understanding about how colonization affects their lives, so we focused our entire collage on decolonization efforts and positive ways to resist. Once youth are familiar with the topic, the following sessions can delve deeper into the effects on important Indigenous institutions like families.

H. Step Three: Family

Leroy Little Bear has taught us that traditional societies worked well because each individual was socialized with the values, customs, and philosophies of the group. The laws were the practical application of the philosophy and values of Indigenous Peoples. These values served as a means of social control and came directly from our families. Traditionally, kinship ties were the locus of social control, which meant that these interconnected relationships provided strength among the group. In Wet'suwet'en families, lineages were passed down through the mother's side, and our People were governed through the clan system, which was made up of kinship networks. Unfortunately, as a result of colonization our kinship networks are now often fragmented and fail to pass on the values and philosophies that would allow us to maintain a healthy existence.

Families are at the very heart of our governance systems and thus have suffered severe attacks. Not only have racist, sexist laws like Bill C-31 in Canada (or the nineteenth century removal and twentieth century relocation policies in the United States) displaced Indigenous families from their territories, but they have also served to disempower Indigenous women as powerful people in our communities. As a consequence, many women are forced to leave their communities, and their children are forced to grow up in a foreign, often urban, space where it is not only unsafe to be Indigenous, but the concept of belonging to a particular nation is often completely lost. Families in urban settings without the support of the kinship networks often face greater risks of poverty and violence. Violence on, and in, our families is a direct result of mainstream racist ideologies that say it is acceptable to violate and hurt Indigenous people, particularly Indigenous women. Thus, where there were once strong kinship networks of love and support, colonization has left us with families suffering the effects of violence, racism, displacement, and poverty. The colonial governments of the day use poverty to legitimate the theft of Indigenous children, furthering the devastation of our families. The cycles of dysfunction have been taught to our families for generations, and it is up to us to attempt to break those cycles.

A critical part of education around Indigenous families is to provide youth with an alternative. Many of our young people do not see an alternative way of living and have known only the worst effects of colonization. By providing them with a glimpse of a healthy way of life as an Indigenous person, they will be provided with hope for breaking the cycle. To do this, the facilitators should use their own life stories as examples of how we are striving to break the cycles of abuse and/ or cultural loss our own families have suffered. Youth have expressed the need to connect with people who understand their struggles. However, this topic can be extremely difficult to face and should be approached with caution, patience, and understanding. Many youth we've worked with have experienced extreme dysfunction within their families. Thus, talking about it can cause them discomfort and can even run the risk of traumatizing other youth and volunteers who are hearing about their experiences for the first time. Therefore, participants should be aware if a youth's emotions are escalating, and should always leave time to debrief.

It is difficult to navigate youths' relationships with their own families, particularly if one has a specific time limit. Another way to approach this topic is to use real life examples of how families have been affected by colonization and then focus on healthy familial relationships and how to break the cycle of broken families. In our groups, we often talk about our own experiences, and youth join in the conversation when they feel comfortable. If youth do not come from broken or displaced families, they may focus on what has kept their family strong, and how they will pass that strength on to their own children.

It is important to visually show youth how families have been torn apart, focusing on the loss of traditional values and ways of being such as kinship networks. This may be done by creating a flip chart diagram to show all the elements of a family. We used circles to illustrate this idea, placing the child at the center and then adding in circles of support such as the grandparents as the knowledge keepers, the parents, the child, and the kinship network (extended family or clan system). By seeing the kinship network physically represented, youth will be able to see that everyone around them has been affected by colonization. By seeing each kinship support systematically eliminated, youth can see how the process occurs on a more abstract level. As an example, tell a story (fiction or non-fiction) about a family impacted by colonization.

First, begin by discussing kinship networks and how they have been affected by the displacement from our homelands. For example, dislocation has occurred through the reservation systems and the urbanization of many of our families. In many instances, nations were forced into exile and could not possibly maintain a relationship with their homelands or relatives. Without our people and homelands, culture is lost; our culture is informed by our lands and the ways our Peoples were taught to survive and thrive on them. Furthermore, discuss how each generation has been negatively affected by harmful government policies and legislation. It is important to also emphasize how the loss of culture and language has permeated generations and how this has impacted the health of our families and the way Indigenous families function.

ACTIVITY FOR YOUTH:

Has your family been separated because of some of these circumstances? If so, what factors caused this disconnection? What impact has this had on your life?

_____

_____

_____

If your family has lost the use of your traditional language or aspects of your culture, when did that occur? How and why?

_____

_____

_____

_____

To represent the cultural loss and disconnection occurring after each generation has been eliminated or otherwise affected, cross them out or remove them from the diagram as the story progresses. You can also use markers or another method to systematically partially cover these kinship networks, representing the impact on them. For instance, perhaps the grandparents are affected by residential schools. For each violent colonial offense done to the grandparent, have the youth color in a part of that circle representing the systematic process of eliminating the ability of that grandparent to support the young person as he/she would have done so traditionally. Thus, even if a support person is not wholly eliminated, youth can see how these tools of colonization influence the ability of families to function. By doing this, youth can visually see the process through which their families have been destroyed or otherwise affected, and how this has made child rearing particularly difficult for parents. Discuss with the youth how each generation's child rearing practices have been affected. This can be done through the story as a way to apply the impacts of colonization to a real life scenario.

Finally, only the child will be left in the diagram. It is important to emphasize that the children and young people have now become less protected because of the process of colonization. Youth will be able to see that their family experiences have been directly affected by colonization. Once this happens, we must provide them with realistic decolonizing tools. Find some local examples of how communities are decolonizing by restoring family relationships. Then ask them to create a new diagram adding in all the elements that have been taken away.

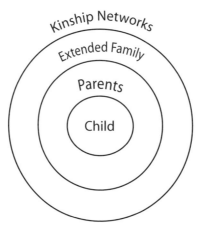

ACTIVITY FOR YOUTH:

What kinds of support do you need from family, and where might you find this support within a restored kinship network?

_____

_____

_____

_____

How can we add the parents back into this story?

_____

_____

_____

_____

How can we add in the role that grandparents played?

_____

_____

_____

_____

_____

Once major themes are identified as negative effects on families, youth can begin to think about alternatives. Show them that colonization has affected all Indigenous families negatively on a spectrum of how children are affected. By identifying alternatives to the normal reactions to colonization, youth can see that Indigenous people are working hard to break the cycles of abuse that plague many of our families. Youth also will be less likely to internalize any abuse or neglect that they themselves have experienced as a result of colonization. Youth will see that in addition to their negative familial experiences, without healthy families and kinship networks, culture is not transmitted and traditional governance is disabled. Familial ties are the lifelines of our nations, and we must find creative ways to re-create that same strength in the face of an onslaught of colonial tools working against us. Without strong family teachings, spiritual wellness also suffers.

I. Step Four: Spirituality

Through relationships with youth, spiritual practices can be reintroduced and strengthened. It is necessary for youth to understand what Indigenous spirituality is and how it has been affected by colonization. Alfred identifies spirituality as the root of the struggle; without grounding in a strong spiritual connectedness, successful recovery of our territories and political power will be meaningless to the survival of our people. Traditional spiritual practices will strengthen the spirituality necessary for a balanced life. Scholars Laurence Kirmayer, Cory Simpson, and Margaret Cargo say that "these traditions were displaced and actively suppressed by successive generations of Euro–Canadian missionaries, governments and professionals. Revitalizing these traditions therefore reconnects contemporary Aboriginal Peoples to their historical traditions and mobilizes rituals and practices that may promote community solidarity." It is critical that we spend an entire session on how our spirituality has been affected by colonization and explore ways that we can decolonize this aspect of our lives.

This can begin by discussing the role that spirituality plays within a traditional way of being. For example, spirituality has become disconnected from secular living and therefore also disconnects individuals from other life forms. Through residential schools, non-Indigenous adoptive and foster homes, as well as racist laws and ideologies, Indigenous people have been made to believe that their spiritual practices and ways of life are inferior and should be left behind. This aspect of colonization affects our relationships to the spirit world as well as our relationships to one another and, most importantly, to the land. Explain how, through colonization and displacement from our lands and traditions, people have lost the deep spiritual connections that guided our balanced existence with the rest of creation. Talk about the desecration to our homelands and the adoption of Christian values, such as man's obligation to establish dominion over all of creation, that continue to perpetuate destruction. Not only have our worldviews changed through our contact with settler society, but our ability to access our sacred sites has been eliminated as well. Link this desecration of lands to the overall health of our people. As a result of the loss of spirituality, people feel lost in a seemingly lifeless world. Remembering spirituality for what it actually is—a way of life—can guide youth toward an awareness of the richness of all our human and non-human relatives.

It is important to demystify spirituality for youth. It is not a question of whether or not they will understand what spirituality is, but that they see spirituality as a way of life instead of a religion. A good forum to discuss these issues is through storytelling. By engaging youth through a story, whether this is a real life story, fiction, or in the form of poetry, youth can begin to see how spirituality is situated within the context of everyday life. It is necessary to distinguish spirituality from religion so that spirituality does not remain a mystifying concept left to medicine people and old ones. We must learn why our spiritual practices have been lost but also have courage to reclaim a way of life that has sustained not only humansfrom but all of creation since time began. For Indigenous Peoples, spirituality was integrated into culture and our relationship to the land; it is imperative for youth to understand this concept and how our way of life is necessarily tied to our territory. But first, it is important that we work to unpack the differences between spirituality and religion.

ACTIVITY FOR YOUTH:

What does spirituality mean to you?

_____

_____

_____

_____

How is spirituality different from or the same as religion?

_____

_____

_____

What purpose do you think spirituality has in Indigenous societies?

_____

_____

_____

Then tell a story or read a poem to bring these issues back to our lived experiences. We read a poem to the youth called _Yuhh_ (The Place Where We Come From), by Jennifer Wickham:

Yuhh

Turn left on the Rocky Mountain road.
Follow your heart through this dark
time, let those family ties pull you in.
Call on your ancestors to light the way
along the rocky riverbed. Listen
for her voice in the waves, guiding you.

Remember, this fight upstream can get to you;
many have forged ahead on this lonely road
to freedom, free from having to listen
to their lies. Tricksters, laughing in the dark
distracting you from finding your way
through this city; back to _keyo_, in

the loving embrace of deciduous leaves, in
blankets of moss, down on your knees, you
remember when you were the stars. Way
back now; we have since forgotten the road
that brought us down, and further…this dark
dream caught so many, they won't listen

anymore. They have forgotten _how_ to listen.
The sweet song of loved ones as you come in;
beaten up, but not down, groping in the dark
your heart summons another beat, knowing if you
can make it around this bend in the road,
your people wait for you to find your way.

So few remember this lost ancient way.
The mountains mourn. Listen.
They long to feel your feet on the red road,
sing those songs—you carry them in
your blood. The words sung when you
were born, bringing light into the dark.

Keeper of the fire, memories of dark
places and stories untold, lead the way
back. Find your roots; wherever you
ended up, you are needed. Listen
to the old ones; they invite you in
with open arms. Waiting, watching the road

for a sign in the dark. If you listen,
your spirit guides the way, back through, and in,
to that place in you where you will find the road.

ACTIVITY FOR YOUTH:

What stands out for you in this poem?

_____

_____

What does that mean to you?

_____

_____

What parts of this poem contain spiritual elements?

_____

_____

How could you bring elements of spirituality into your everyday life?

_____

_____

_____

_____

The intent of discussing spirituality is not to direct youth in spiritual ceremonies but rather to initiate discussion and raise questions about their own spiritual experiences. If youth have been disconnected from spiritual practices, it is necessary for them to begin by becoming comfortable with spirituality, and then support them in their own processes of rediscovery. For example, at the beginning of each session we join hands in a circle and pray for good minds and good hearts. We also close every session this way, asking for the wisdom to take the information and use it in a good way; by doing this, youth can become comfortable with prayer and protocol. During our first six-week session we began and ended each day with prayer. Many of the youth were not comfortable with prayer or spirituality, and nervously laughed and looked away during these times. Each session, I would give them the opportunity to say the opening or closing prayer, and by the end of the six weeks several had volunteered. If this change can happen in six weeks, imagine the possibilities of long-lasting relationships with youth. However, we still have a lot of work to do. Since colonization, religion has become displaced from everyday life and people's lived experiences on their territories.

J. Step Five: The Land

All effects of colonization are tied to land precisely because land is tied to every aspect of Indigenous being. The physical effects of colonization that Indigenous youth have experienced are reflected in their health and the health of our homelands. The two are intricately interconnected. All of the above themes relate back to our physicality and land. It is not enough that we should physically survive and have control over our land base. As Alfred asserts, our disconnection from land has caused Indigenous people to become physically unhealthy and dependent on the state. The importance of land must be identified as one of the most important aspects of Indigenous identity. One of the major challenges that youth in custody face is that most come from urban environments and may not have an existing relationship with the land.

Although spirituality occurs within Indigenous Peoples, it is informed by land, just as culture is very much based within the context of homelands. Sean Kicummah Teuton, in *Red Land, Red Power*, asserts that without land it is difficult to hold the body of knowledge used to maintain cultural identity. This also includes language and the importance of coupling language with homelands. This means that it is critical for Indigenous Peoples to secure and protect our homelands in order for culture and language to survive. Indigenous Peoples have lived in harmony with the land and its beings since time began, which has necessarily affected our way of knowing and living. Therefore, land and culture are inseparable. Not only is it critical that Indigenous young people understand the negative effects caused by our displacement from our lands and the resulting anomie (departure from a structured social system resulting in grave social dysfunction and alienation), but we must also provide them with a sense of reconnecting. If young people do not have an investment in the land, they may not have a desire to maintain it.

It is critical that youth understand the role that land has played from the beginning of colonial contact to the current context. For instance, land is the prized possession of the colonizer. Currently our lands have not only been stolen, but they are continually attacked by government and industry. It is imperative that youth begin to see how Western "civilization" is unsustainable and how this lack of sustainability affects them now and in their future if our people fail to take action. As Waziyatawin points out in chapter 2, our lands are facing a critical threshold. Billions of people stand by while our lands are desecrated by logging, hydroelectric dams, mining, and oil and gas extraction, among a long list of other money-making, environmentally damaging endeavors. Thus, it is imperative for youth to make connections between how harmful these ways of life are to our lands and the impacts they have on our families, spirits, and nations. In contrast, Indigenous families have particular roles in caring for the land and keeping humans in harmony with our territories. In Wet'suwet'en homelands the clan and house groups are responsible for maintaining balance within our *yinta* (territory). Explain to youth how and why lands were managed in your territory. Most importantly, land must be seen as an interconnected aspect of all Indigenous life. Without it we would all cease to exist. It is at once life-giving and uniting. Despite our languages, spiritual practices, and protocols, all Indigenous Peoples share a deep relationship to land and have experienced the same effects of displacement from that land. This knowledge can give youth the hope and determination necessary to walk each day toward reclaiming not only our homelands, but the relationship to that land that has sustained us since time began.

A common tool used for decolonization and trauma work is to visually show how colonization makes Indigenous lands unhealthy and how, as a result, Indigenous Peoples are negatively affected.

To begin, place water in a jar or clear container. Use different colored food coloring to represent various negative effects on the land. For example, use green to represent how industries are harming Mother Earth, red to identify how Indigenous People are suffering from the desecration of the earth and her beings, blue to identify how the waters and air are being affected, and so on according to the issues relevant in your area.

ACTIVITY:

How has your homeland suffered from colonization? (Have the youth add a drop of colored dye into the water for each offender identified.)

_____

_____

_____

_____

How does this impact on the land affect people in your territory?

_____

_____

_____

_____

Be sure to prompt youth to identify the links between the desecration of land and negative effects on Indigenous Peoples and cultures. Use examples from your own territory or stories to identify these issues. For example, talk about impacts on water through industry pollution and how this affects our nations' abilities to fish and carry on with traditional uses of water in our territories, leading to unhealthy diets and bodies.

Throughout this process, use a small drop bottle of bleach to represent decolonization. Ironically, bleach is a toxic substance created by "civilized" society; however, this is representative of the challenges Indigenous people face in the decolonization process. Often we are forced to use the colonizers' own creations to advance Indigenous liberation. Most importantly, we must uphold our values and responsibilities by any means necessary. For every idea of how to decolonize our relationship to land, add a drop of bleach to the water. This will begin to clear the now murky water, representing the health of our lands and people. Remind youth that decolonization takes time and often much more work than it takes to make the water cloudy and unhealthy.

ACTIVITY:

In what ways can you counter these negative effects on your lands and Peoples? (Have the youth add a drop of the bleach into the water for each action identified.)

_____

_____

_____

_____

How can you begin to change your own relationship to the land?

_____

_____

_____

_____

Use real examples of ways that you are working toward decolonizing your relationship to the land. For example, if the pollution of water is an impact you are discussing, a counter action could be to actively pressure governments and industry to discontinue and rectify pollution caused by industry in your area. It is also important to identify how you can change your relationship with water. For example, my relationship to water is centered on its healing and life-giving value. I explain to youth that every morning I wake up and cleanse my body and spirit by drinking a glass of water. Other examples are spirit bathing and sweat lodges. Making a spiritual connection with water impacts what types of relationships we have with it.

Again, questions and focus can shift depending on the most critical issues your community is facing. Youth will be able to visibly see how our lands and bodies are affected by the continued colonization of our lands, while simultaneously identifying ways to alter that relationship. Certainly, the water will not miraculously become clear with one drop of bleach, just as our lands and Peoples will not become healthy again through one single action. Identify the need for ongoing healing and creative ways to restore our lands, thus strengthening our people and the opportunity for survival once this unsustainable civilization fails. We must remember that Mother Earth has her own ways of cleansing herself, and holds all the teachings we need to survive within her. Although the colonial state continues to desecrate our Mother and thousands of our relatives on a day-to-day basis, hope lies in the teachings and values that were given to us, and her survival depends on our ability to turn those teachings into action. We must learn to live in balance within our homelands, and we must ensure that *everyone* who impacts our homelands upholds a deep level of respect; it must begin within each individual and carry on through the youth.

K. Closing

For thousands of years young people were recognized as the future of our nations and were brought up with the knowledge they needed to thrive in our homelands. Immense attacks on the manifestation of this belief system have systematically hindered our nations' abilities to protect and provide guidance for our young people. Unfortunately, our young people suffer from the trauma this has caused; we all ultimately suffer the consequences.

Each and every person can influence how youth see themselves as Indigenous people. By engaging youth in our shared experience of colonization and providing them with the hope of decolonization, Indigenous Peoples can work together toward a common vision. By mentoring youth and building relationships, a positive sense of community will provide an alternative way of viewing their past experiences and help them imagine a different future. Through

questioning why they have similar experiences, new ways of approaching life can blossom and we can alter the course of internalized oppression and racism. Critical elements of an Indigenous existence can be discussed in a safe place with other people who have shared the same experiences. Land, spirituality, and families are critical to an Indigenous way of being in the world and to the survival of Indigenous nationhood. Without spirituality our relationships to other beings would be empty; without families our teachings and governance would not survive; and without land there would be nothing to hold the bodies of knowledge that have sustained us since the beginning of time. Isn't it time we provide our young people with the guidance to become our future leaders? After all, it is our responsibility.

L. Resources

Aboriginal Youth Suicide Fact Sheet. http://www.health.gov.bc.ca /mhd/pdf/fact_sheets/ab_youth_suicide.pdf.

Alfred, Taiaiake. "Colonialism and State Dependency." Prepared for the National Aboriginal Health Organization Project Communities in Crisis. *Journal de la Santé Autochtone*, Nov. 2009: 42–60.

———. *Peace, Power, Righteousness: An indigenous manifesto.* Don Mills, ON: Oxford University Press, 1999.

———. *Wasáse: Indigenous Pathways of Action and Freedom.* Peterborough, ON: Broadview Press, 2005.

Alfred, Taiaiake, and Jeff Corntassel. "Being Indigenous: Resurgences against Contemporary Colonialism." *Politics of Identity*-IX. Ed. Richard Bellamy. Oxford: Blackwell Publishing, 2005. http://www.corntassel.net/being_indigenous.pdf.

Carriere, Jeannine. "Promising Practice for Maintaining Identities in First Nation Adoption." *First Peoples Child & Family Review* 3 (2007): 46–64.

Johnson, Sandy. *The Book of Elders: The Life Stories of Great American Indians.* New York: Harper Collins Publishers, 1994.

Kirmayer, Laurence, Cory Simpson, and Margaret Cargo. "Healing Traditions: Culture, community, and mental health promotion with Canadian Aboriginal Peoples." *Australian Psychiatry* 11 (2003): s15–s23.

Lawrence, Bonita. *"Real" Indians and Others: Mixed-Blood Urban Native Peoples and Indigenous Nationhood.* Vancouver: UBC Press, 2004.

Little Bear, Leroy. "Jagged Worldviews Colliding." In *Reclaiming Indigenous Voice and Vision*. Ed. Marie Battiste. Vancouver: UBC Press, 2000.

Morris, Kristine. "Re-examining issues behind the loss of family and cultural and the impact on Aboriginal youth suicide rates." A Literature Review. *First Peoples Child & Family Review* 3 (2007): 133–142.

Preston, Jane P., Sheila Carr-Stewart, and Charlene Northwest. "Aboriginal Youth Gangs: Preventative Approaches." *First Peoples Child & Family Review* 4 (2009): 152–160.

Richardson, Cathy, and Bill Nelson. "A Change of Residence: Government Schools and Foster Homes as Sites of Forced Aboriginal Assimilation – A Paper Designed to Provoke Thought and Systemic Change." *First Peoples Child & Family Review* 3 (2007): 75–83. http://www.fncfcs.com/pubs/v013num2toc.html.

Silver, Jim. *In Their Own Voices: Building Urban Aboriginal Communities*. Halifax, Canada: Fernwood Publishing, 1996.

Sinclair, Raven. "Identity lost and found: Lessons from the sixties scoop." *First Peoples Child & Family Review* 3 (2007): 65–82. http://www.fncfcs.com/pubs/v013num1toc.html.

Taylor-Henley, Sharon, and Peter Hudson. "Aboriginal Self-Government and Social Services: First Nations: Provincial Relationships." *Canadian Public Policy* 18 (1992):13–26.

Teuton, Sean Kicummah. *Red Land, Red Power: Grounding Knowledge in the American Indian Novel*. Chpt. 1: "Embodying Lands: Somatic Place in N. Scott Momaday's *House Made of Dawn*." Durham, NC: Duke University Press, 2008.

Waziyatawin. *What Does Justice Look Like: The Struggle for Liberation in Dakota Homeland*. St. Paul, MN: Living Justice Press, 2009.

Wilson, Waziyatawin Angela. *In the Footsteps of Our Ancestors: The Dakota Commemorative Marches of the 21st Century*. St. Paul, MN: Living Justice Press, 2006.

Wilson, Waziyatawin Angela, and Michael Yellow Bird, eds. *For Indigenous Eyes Only: A Decolonization Handbook*. Santa Fe: School of American Research Press, 2005.

Chapter 11

DECOLONIZATION LESSONS FOR TRIBAL PRISONERS

George Blue Bird

A. Lakota Greetings

Hau (Lakota Greetings) to all our imprisoned people!

I am from the Pine Ridge Reservation and I was raised in the Pass Creek District. I speak and understand Lakota with a great passion. I am a self-taught artist and writer. I have been incarcerated in the prisons of Sioux Falls, South Dakota since October 1983. I am serving a life sentence without parole for first-degree manslaughter.

I wrote this chapter for all ground warriors and activists who struggle every day to protect our rights and ceremonies. These people are ingenious and efficient in the protection of our natural laws.

When I realized I would be spending the rest of my life in prison, I did not berate myself or become discouraged. I began listening to the words and advice of our spiritual leaders, singers, dancers, and people who are experts with our culture. I started a social network of tribal professionals from everywhere.

Prison life is a mental calculation of the hours that take us through the routines during the days and a different set of activities for the evenings and nights. The atmosphere of prison shuts freedom completely out of our minds.

Life in prison without parole is a harsh sentence. Time is different for us. In South Dakota, there is a system of inequality that I discovered when I started looking at the percentages of white prisoners serving the same sentence as mine, but who had received commutations and were returned home to their families on parole. This situation secretly mandates that we will ultimately die while incarcerated.

The hardest part of receiving my sentence was saying goodbye to my children. All of my dreams and ambitions for them ended on that day. Everything we ever wanted to do with our lives was pushed aside. We consoled each other until the last visit was finished. The police officers took me back to my cell. I was sad. My heart was broken. I already knew how to do time and so I began making plans for my entry into the world of concrete walls, steel cages, gun towers, barbed-wire fences, and prisoners from every background.

Information on death row in the United States from The Death Penalty Information Center:

- As of July 1, 2009, thirty-seven Native American prisoners resided on state and federal death row in the United States, which is 1.1 percent of the death row population.
- Seven states and the federal government hold condemned Indian prisoners.
- Since 1961, fifteen American Indians have been executed. Thirteen Indian prisoners were executed for killing whites and two were executed for killing other Native Americans.
- Between 1979–1999, whites killed 32 percent of the 2,469 Indians murdered, whereas Native Americans killed 1 percent of the 164,377 whites murdered.

---

and respectful. He and other long-term lifers told us as they made their cups of morning coffee: "Confront all of your fears. Be your own person and stay simple. Art and activism are the main sources for change in the world. Appreciate music from all cultures. Learn to be a reflection of creativity and passion. Never write your name on any prison wall. Liberate yourself. Life has a way of needing you." They believe in the powers of Ernesto Che Guevara, Nelson Mandela, Ho Chi Minh, Ingrid Betancourt, Benazir Bhutto, and other political fighters. Some of those men took care of jalapeño pepper plants they grew illegally every year along the walls of death row and the death houses where executioners killed many of their friends.

B. Dream

Dream of freedom in your mind. Walk the early morning route beside a river or into some hills with pine trees. Wear a green army fatigue jacket, blue jeans, a sweater, and black boots to symbolize who you are. Some scented oils will go well with your stature. Chop wood. Make a fire. Haul water. Pick chokecherries. Drink lots of wild peppermint tea. Find a dark colored stallion horse with long scraggly hair and ride him. Wait and watch for the full moon. Be inspired by great leaders. Let the rain and the thunders teach you their lessons. Study pictures. Allow your thoughts to carry you on many positive journeys. Search for the truth. Be strong spiritually, emotionally, mentally, and physically. Find a way out of prison every day. Dream.

"Our dreams imitate life and leave us suspended within the grips of something that needs to be answered," said one ninety-seven-year-old tribal lifer who began serving his sentence in 1958. His eyes were not afraid of anything and his disposition was keen

C. Indigenous People in Prison

Indigenous populations in the United States clearly suffer disproportionate rates of incarceration, second only to African-Americans. According to the Death Penalty Information Center, the incarceration rate for Native Americans is 38 percent higher than for non-Indigenous people. We currently have about 26,000 Indigenous people in the criminal (in) justice system. Like other minority populations, we also receive longer sentences and serve longer time

---

Be strong during your time in prison. Stay focused with our sacred pipes, sacred objects, ceremonies, and languages. They precede everything that we know. Our Indigenous ways were handed down to us by our ancestors.

> **Our people do not accept the concept of having to live in an environment of steel cages and concrete buildings as punishment for our wrongs and mistakes. We believe in forgiveness and this is vastly illustrated in our circles. Do not let prison further colonize you in any way.**

in the prisons. But there are other factors that affect our populations too. For example, we have a higher percentage of alcohol-induced actions resulting in incarceration. Once we arrive in prison, Indigenous prisoners are more likely to commit suicide. We are also more likely to be harassed or suffer abuse when we attempt to adhere to our cultural traditions. We continuously have to struggle to maintain even basic access to our spiritual practices that are guaranteed to other prisoners belonging to mainstream religions.

Given these circumstances, we have to consciously fight to stay strong and to support one another. We have to plan our survival in prison. The best way to describe how Indigenous people can successfully do time while helping to raise up one another can be seen in the example of a Lakota brother who helped all of us.

D. A Code to Live By: Eldred "Nisko" Iron Moccasin (May 9, 1951–November 5, 2007)

Nisko arrived in 1991 with Ron Two Bulls in the old prison in Sioux Falls and quickly established himself as our highest-ranking prisoner because of his dedication to our ceremonies and the responsibilities he took on as a result of his time in the federal prison system. Under his leadership there was a positive sense of confidence among all our brothers and relatives. He unified everybody and made sure that our circle was a priority every day. He was an important man. He was serious in everything he did.

Nisko spent twelve years with us. Four of those years were in the general and main populations, and he did a total of eight years locked away in administrative segregation and the special housing units, or the "hole" as it is called.

When he died, many of us went into a deep silence and did not speak to anyone for a long time. His death was hard to accept. We talked with him in our own ways and put offerings of food out for him. We loaded our pipes and smoked them for him and his family. But it was his life, which was an example for us all to live by, that I want to convey.

Nisko was a distinguished worker and promoter of better opportunities for all of us behind the walls of prison. He always wrote and talked to people he knew from our reservations and cities and they sent contributions of money and objects for our ceremonies. Some of these people worked exclusively for civil and Indigenous rights and he often asked them to speak to us about legal and spiritual cases that had been won in the courts.

His daily routine was simple but memorable. Each morning he cleaned his cell from top to bottom. He would sweep his floor, wash his walls, clean his sink and toilet with bleach, and scrub everything with soap and water. He was an expert at prison life. His coffee-pot would be boiling with fresh coffee grounds and his television would be on as he listened for the early edition of news and other events. His sheets and blankets on his bed were always tucked under his mattress with precision and he liked to have two pillows. All prisoners care about their laundry and their clothes have to be folded in a certain way. He made sure his laundry was clean and organized. Sometimes he would wash his own laundry by hand in his sink and hang it out to dry in his cell.

Generosity was one of Nisko's virtues. He would bring extra food out of his cell and feed whoever was hungry. He always kept a stash of canned meat, chili, potato chips, hot peppers, peanut butter, bread, cheese, crackers, and cookies. On some days, he would get a group of guys together and make sandwiches and burritos. It gave him great pleasure to see our prisoners eat. Just as people in our tribal communities enjoy giving away everything we have to those who do not have things in their homes, Nisko would do the same whenever he was transferred from one prison unit to another—he would give away all of his property to those who needed a radio, television, a new sweatshirt, commissary, scented oils, magazines, and a coffeepot. The prisons in Sioux Falls say we cannot do this, but he did not care. Giving was something he did and it came from the teachings of our people. The prisoners who received something from him always remembered him and spoke kindly about him.

There is something valuable about being poor that stays in our thoughts and never leaves us. It lets us know how precious water can be when we run out of food and commodities on our reservations. It tells us to be simple. We do not need things like a nice home, a brand new car, up-to-date clothes, expensive jewelry, money in the bank, and a retirement fund.

In emergency situations like the death of one of us or someone in our families, violence of any kind, a suicide, chaos, arguments, and misunderstandings, Nisko knew what to do. He always tried to find a solution to a problem or an answer to help us understand why something had occurred. If one of us got into debt and could not pay, he would cover the charges, especially if we were from Cheyenne River or Standing Rock. We did not have to pay him back. All he asked was that we help the next man in need. His blessings

Inmates are very weak individuals. They talk real loud and put themselves in places where they're not supposed to be. They have the potential to become informants.

Convicts are dangerous people. They know everything about prison. They carry a strict set of codes and look down at people who hurt women and children.

Prisoners keep themselves away from any drama and avoid all attention. They believe in honor and loyalty to all good things. Reading, writing, music, sports, and all forms of creativity exist in their lives.

and kindness will be passed on.

Carl E. Iron Shell Jr. was a traditional Sicangu Lakota prisoner who knew all of our ceremonies, and Nisko depended upon him to help us. Carl was from the Two Strike community on the Rosebud Reservation and was our Pipe Keeper for the Native American Council of Tribes (NACT) from 1981–1993. Nisko respected and admired him. They often talked about spiritual plans and what they could do to help our prisoners.

Administrative segregation—where Nisko spent a total of eight years—is a place where prisoners are locked up all the time, except for recreation and showers. All visits and passes to other areas of the prison must be done in handcuffs. All meals, commissary, library books, and small property items are passed through a "cuff port," which is a small security door on all cell doors that is kept locked. Shakedowns are random, and security guards conduct walk-throughs every day when prisoners are handcuffed, brought out of their cells, patted down, searched, and cells are checked for contraband. Mail is passed out daily except Sundays and holidays. Prisoners can have their small personal property. Living here requires everyone to have a strong mind.

Prisoners who are sentenced here must learn to live in a confined area with two men to each cell. Death row prisoners and others who cannot get along with anyone are housed in single cells. Survival in

Know your rights. We have legal, civil, human, and natural rights. Keep these in mind if you are ever taken away for questioning in any matter. It is best to consult with a lawyer and our outside tribal people who know what is going on. Prison officials will use intimidation and scare tactics to pressure us into talking.

prison means being a part of whoever is already there and adding respectability—kindness and politeness—to what happens all the time. Everyone usually sleeps all day and stays up all night doing beadwork, writing, playing guitar, singing, watching television, listening to their radios, telling stories, and working out. Some prisoners, though, have been in administrative segregation and the special housing units for decades.

The special housing units do not allow any kind of movement without handcuffs and ankle chains on prisoners. All the rules from administrative segregation are enforced here. Prisoners cannot have their property, and all privileges that exist in other parts of the prison are removed. Clothing is an orange jumpsuit, underwear, and shower shoes. Commissary is limited to hygiene products and writing material. Library books are allowed.

Listening to music, reading, writing, meditating, and pacing in their cells are the only things prisoners can do. Recreation and showers are allowed on certain days. A correctional officer will handcuff prisoners behind their backs and take them out. This is done every forty-five minutes.

It is important to have a "line" when doing time in administrative segregation and the special housing units. A line is made out of string or newspapers tied together, and is used to transport food, instant coffee, writing material, books, and notes with encouraging words to someone feeling bad. It can take a few minutes or several hours to move an item and it is all worth it. This is done through tiny openings under the door. Nisko always had a line with him.

Being in prison requires a positive mind-set and

> **Do something different every day. Stay away from the same thinking.**

> **A leader in prison will work to generate plans and ideas that will benefit everyone. They know how to get things done. Authority is delegated to all of our prisoners. A leader participates in all of our meetings. They must be prepared at all times to take criticism. Our leaders must be willing to establish a support system of people from our reservations and wherever they live. We have people who enjoy visiting us.**

the ability to work on getting out. Our Tribal-Prison Liaisons and spiritual leaders are allowed to visit our prisoners here with staff escort. This does a huge amount of good for us. Seeing our people relieves our heaviest burdens and gives us hope. Nisko did all he could to invite our people to come and visit us here. Communication means a lot to us.

He believed in our *Hunkakaġapi* (Making of Relatives) ceremony and carried this with him wherever he went. With sincere compassion he recognized our prison grandfathers, uncles, older brothers, younger brothers, sons, nephews, and all of our grandchildren. He knew that many of us came from broken families. Our prison families, at different intervals in life, are all that we have.

Nisko liked the beat and voices of our pow-wow drums and singers. His soul was touched with enjoyment and inspiration. Their abilities to perform for our gatherings reminded him of growing up in Eagle Butte. The Lakota people there are known for singing and dancing. They are taught at an early age to believe in these traditions and to pass them on. Nisko never forgot his people and the Lakota teachings they put into his life.

In the federal prisons no one gets out of line. The prisoners believe in unity, and their allegiance to one another begins with strict responsibilities that everyone must know. Troublemakers and anyone with bad politics do not make it out to the yard; they are checked into protective custody by other prisoners, for their own safety. Nisko did a lot of time in the federal system and he defended the prisoners' codes—the spiritual and cultural protection of our prison brothers.

Other races of prisoners do not attend their pow-wows and cultural events. Disrespect among prisoners is not tolerated anywhere. Federal prisoners are out in the yards all day and into the night—the only time they are locked up is for security counts and emergencies. Stereos, cassettes, compact discs, DVDs, and musical instruments are everywhere. Artists have access to a wide variety of supplies and mediums. Nutritious food is everywhere. Microwaves and vending machines are on all units. After their *inipi* (rite of purification, sweat lodge) ceremonies are over, they have a big meal of hot soup, frybread, other foods, and lots of things to drink. One of the brothers will cook. He has everything he needs.

"*Wicohan kin lena lila tewahilayelo!*" ("I really love these ways!") was a statement that Nisko always made about our ceremonies. Our eagle feathers, drums, gourd rattles, buffalo skulls, medicine bags, tobacco ties, altars, fires, prayers, songs, and the smell of sweetgrass burning were all things that put spiritual balances in his life.

Nisko believed that if something happened to one of us, then something happened to all of us. He reminded us with these words to keep everything negative away from us. He wasn't afraid of anyone from any prison administration or prison brotherhood who declared hate against our Indigenous prisoners. He was always the first person to step forward and confront people who did not like us. He did not want the company of liars, thieves, schemers, and anyone who could not pull their own weight.

Many of our leaders and hundreds of thousands of our people were killed in the 1800s by secret orders that were put in place by the US government, who wanted our homelands. These orders were carried out by white and tribal soldiers loyal to the US Cavalry. Different sums of money, whiskey, horses, and military rations were paid to those soldiers under a system of greed and corruption. Nisko knew these stories. He studied a lot.

He knew that different prison administrations would entice our prisoners to become informants, and through this arrangement many of our outspoken leaders—who the administrators did not like—were removed from the general population and shipped out to other prisons. He knew about slave labor and what the prison staff does to make a profit off of our prisoners by taking a percentage of their earnings.

Nisko was into sports. He liked to walk around and encourage our basketball players, weight lifters, boxers, sprinters, joggers, and horseshoe throwers. He was a devout fan of our fast-pitch softball games and cheered us on. His favorite NBA team was the Los Angeles Lakers. He stayed physically active by riding the stationary bicycles, stretching, lifting weights, and walking. He was the kind of person that everybody liked to be around. He was good at spades, dominoes, scrabble, and putting jigsaw puzzles together with anyone. He was a grown man and he loved to wrestle with our younger brothers on playful terms.

His laugh had its own personality. It would begin with a deepness and then pitch itself up to a sharpness in a matter of seconds. His laughter was a way of socializing. It drew people in. With funny situations and humorous jokes, he would laugh until tears came to his eyes.

Anyone serving a life sentence without parole or anything over twenty years must live with the bitter realities that are everywhere in prison. Visits are few and far between. Contact with the outside world fades in and

> Our time is not about magnificence, fame, having the best things, and living better than the next person. It is about how we take care of each other with food and coffee. It is about respect. It is about lifting ourselves up and away from the negative lifestyles and realizing our maximum capabilities. Different acts of kindness and humor can carry our prisoners for many years. Laugh a little. Laughing is a great invigorator that channels pure energy to our immune systems.

out. We grow old and live without the crucial elements of our families and people. Time becomes a yearly test of survival and hope. A movement for new laws and policies must be enacted by our legislators to begin freeing us. Nisko helped us understand this because he knew that because of discrimination in the judicial system, our people consistently serve more time in prison than all other races combined.

> Have the utmost respect for all female staff members, correctional officers, teachers, nurses, cooks, and general prison workers with whom we come into contact. These women have families to take care of and are not interested in doing anything wrong. We will pay the price for doing something we should not.

Prison is tough on a person's mind. Nisko understood that our wives and ladies would leave us for other men, temporarily or permanently, because of the mental pressures they experience as a result of our imprisonment. He knew that some of us could not handle doing prison time. Sometimes the monotony of prison causes a person to slowly break down, and suicide starts creeping in as a way out. Suicide is wrong and is not an answer. Leighton Rich and many others in prison and across our homelands have committed suicide. These deaths put a lot of hurt on their families and on the people who loved them. Their lives can never be replaced.

We have to decolonize all of the things that are destroying our people. Suicide is one of our top issues. Leighton was having difficulty living in administrative segregation. He needed help. Elroy Wabasha, one of our Isanti Dakota brothers, tried to help him by asking the staff if he could move in with him so he could have someone to visit with. They refused his offer.

Nisko and many of our prisoners developed a plan to immediately assist anyone contemplating suicide by talking with these individuals. We care about our people and this plan is the responsibility of all of us. We must always look out for our people in the prisons of South Dakota. Life is very valuable and it has to go on. Death is a friend to no one.

For political reasons, Nisko was blamed by informants and the prison administration for causing a riot in the old prison on May 5, 1993. Although Nisko had nothing to do with the riot, he was betrayed by prisoners who gave him up to the authorities. It was started by many younger prisoners who took advantage of being in the yards after we were locked out of the cell blocks when prison staff became afraid of our large numbers outside. There was a lot of tension in the days and weeks before the riot. No classes were being offered anywhere in the prison system for our tribal prisoners. Our younger prisoners were being harassed and ridiculed by various staff members. An outright attitude of discrimination existed for all of our prisoners with long hair and those of us who believe in our spiritual and cultural ways.

> Nisko was not perfect in this life. Nobody is. At the end of the day, he was content to know that all of our brotherhoods were safe from anything bad. He relied heavily on the tribal men incarcerated in both prisons of Sioux Falls. No decision was made without their knowledge and advice. When the political storms came crashing down to destroy our purposes, and the forces of immorality began attacking us, his powers as a leader would begin working to create alternative courses of perseverance and success. He always thought about our prisoners with a sense of prosperity and achievement.

The riot was started by all prisoners and every part of it was vicious. It happened instantaneously. Two guards were hit with softball bats; one was almost killed. The school and the work areas were broken into, every window was shattered, and heavy damage was done. A maintenance building was torched to the ground and fires burned all night. Prison guards, SWAT teams, state troopers, and various law enforcement officers had the whole place surrounded with guns and riot gear.

A meeting with all the prisoners was held in the basement of the school the next morning, and everyone decided to voluntarily end the riot by giving ourselves up. Armed police with rifles opened the West Hall gate, took us in one at a time, shut the gate, handcuffed us, searched us, and took us back to our cells.

In the months and years after the riot, all prisoners were held responsible for the destruction. All

> **Do not idolize anyone. When we do this, we fail to be ourselves. Seek out prisoners who are intelligent and learn what they know.**

art supplies, stereos, compact discs, permission for our immediate family members to come to pow-wows, and tobacco and tobacco-related products were removed from the general population. The prison began overcharging our phone accounts, taking our money from our general accounts for disciplinary fines, increasing commissary prices, and having a lower grade of food brought in by outside food companies. These things became routine. Our outside people and the South Dakota Peace and Justice Center worked hard to stop the overcharging of our phone accounts. We still pay disciplinary fines, commissary prices are high, the food is bad, and no Indigenous classes are offered.

Nisko never let us down. He always thoroughly followed through on his promises to us. The last time we saw him was May 2003 when he left us to finish some federal time in another prison. We never saw him again. His Lakota solidarity is with us.

> **Prison is all up to us. If there are not classes or areas of specific education in our places of confinement, there are books and other information that can be sent to us. Explore the world. Search for people who will help us to become better. Expand our opportunities. Learn what it takes to become someone with a degree or have knowledge about a particular job.**

ACTIVITY:

What important lessons can you take from the way Nisko lived his life in prison?

_____

_____

_____

_____

E. Anticipating Hardships

Our spouses will leave us because of prison. They will drift into the arms of other people. They may or may not tell us. We must be ready for this. Our hearts will start pounding with jealousy and anger. We will grow tense and weary. This negative energy will cut deep into our lives. We will not eat or drink anything for days. We will call them on the phone, write them letters, visit with them on bad terms, and blame them. The loss of our spouses and other relationships is a natural process. Stay strong. These words come from prisoners who have actually seen men hanging dead in their cells. They could not handle the hurt and emotional pain. Our prisoners will experience this vicious circle. Help them. Give them a reason to live. Things will get better. They always do. A new spouse or that significant other person will come along. Forgive everything. Think things through.

Convince our sons, daughters, friends, and other tribal members to not do the things we did. Steer them away from drinking, the chemicals, the crack pipes, syringes, and illusions of quick money. Our people may think it is righteous to be locked up. They may think prison is a place where one can be tough and have a reputation. In reality, prison for any amount of time breaks people down. The roads that lead into prison must be stopped. We have the ambition and confidence to do this.

Some prisoners will not change their ways. Drinking, using drugs, carrying weapons, criminal activities and behaviors, and extreme violence are all that they know. These are their lifestyles. They are programmed to party and not care about life. They have reached the darkest chapter of their lives and nothing can save or help them. No spiritual leader, counselor, judge, lawyer, doctor, nurse, man, woman, or child

> **Never pledge allegiance to the American flag, the US government, commemorations that celebrate American historical events, or things that are not ours.**

can reach them. The following three choices are all that are left for them:

- They will kill someone due to their own rage.
- Someone will kill them either in self-defense or in a bad situation.
- They will get out of prison, commit a crime or multiple crimes, and re-enter prison with such a long sentence they'll grow very old and possibly die behind the walls.

We need to be prepared to accept that we cannot help everyone.

F. Take Pleasure in Music

Music is a daily blessing of righteousness that inspires our thoughts and gives us unlimited determination and persistence. Whenever Nisko heard the *Wanbli Wakan Win* (Sacred Eagle Woman) Memorial Song, he remembered the family of eleven-year-old Kimberly Rose Means, and the pain they went through when she died. Kimberly was killed in 1981 by a white drunk driver while participating in the Run for Freedom, an annual event for tribal prisoners incarcerated in Sioux Falls. Her parents are Ted and Rita Means. This song was made by Severt Young Bear Sr. and will stay with our people for all time to come.

Nisko called Kevin Locke and Brian Akipa "our masters of flute playing" within our homelands on the northern plains and around the entire world. Those men perfected this highly spiritualized art, performing for millions of people. Any kind of tribal music got Nisko going. The voices of Buddy Red Bow and Rita Coolidge illuminated his appreciation for our music, and when he listened to their music his thoughts would travel to his friends in Rapid City. The music of Jackson Browne, Neil Young, Stevie Nicks, and Diana Ross—who all sang about activism, opposition to the Vietnam War, death, relationships, poverty, and our changing world—always gave him permission, it seemed, to look at his life as a man with many reasonable objectives.

Music helps all of us. "Do It Again" by Steely Dan lets us exit our prison atmosphere and alleviates any stressful thoughts. It explains our ambitions perfectly. Our lives become balanced with dignity and confidence. The lead singer must have friends who know what being locked up is all about. His words define our adversities and all undue burdens. "Stand Back" by Stevie Nicks is an all-time favorite that resonates confidence and inspires us to maintain our belief systems, our sense of anticipation, and our ability to maintain our vision of possibilities. Her velvety and textured voice creates worldwide excitement. She takes us to a place of contentment and dignity. The sound of the guitar strings and drums gives us a feeling of justice that no one can duplicate or claim as their own.

These songs can decolonize anything. They exemplify courage with a universal spirit of eloquence and loyalty. They prepare us for what is coming. They support our causes without any inhibitions. Steely Dan and Stevie Nicks deserve our gratitude and solidarity for giving us the right to be relentless and humble.

> Try not to break your parole. You will lose everything and have to start all over again. You will be moved into a cell with another prisoner who has a certain way of doing things. You violate their space. You return to the emptiness and hardship of prison starting from ground zero.

G. Decolonization

Look at yourself through the eyes of people in our circles, through the vision of life around us, through the perception of an individual who cares about us, and through your own introspection. We have the right to prize tribal conformity and Indigenous consensus as two of our opportunities for decolonizing ourselves. We have our own ways of life.

We are colonized by thoughts, situations, material goods, lifestyles, money, feelings, and power from other races of people and their cultures. These do not belong to us. We can decolonize ourselves and our lives can be made better. We start by changing the way that we think. We have valuable prisoners within our ranks and people on our reservations to make this happen. The first step is deciding you want to change your life and making a commitment to decolonization. If we recognize that colonization has destroyed Indigenous lives and helped to place us on this path to imprisonment, then we must learn to take a different path.

ACTIVITY:

Do you want to change your life? If you are ready to change your life, what has brought you to that decision? If not, why not?

_____

_____

_____

_____

How has your life been impacted by colonization?

_____

_____

_____

_____

How do your actions help the colonizers or colonizing institutions? How do your actions resist the colonizers or colonizing institutions?

_____

_____

_____

_____

Are you willing to work toward decolonization today? What does this mean to you?

_____

_____

_____

_____

In order to work toward decolonization, it is important for us to know ourselves and the people around us. It is also important to recognize whether our actions reveal the people we want to be. We help ourselves and become strengthened when we are good to others. For example, in Lakota tradition, when we want to honor someone we give things away in their name. We sing honor songs and dance in their honor. We publicly acknowledge the good things they do. It makes us feel good to honor our loved ones and it brings out the best in us. If you want to strengthen yourself, work to hold up your loved ones. For example, reward our women and other family members for raising our children. They nurtured them and paid the bills. Help our women with money, food, clothing, and support, and let them know you appreciate them.

ACTIVITY:

Write some words that describe who you are in this life. If you carry an Indigenous name, what does that name mean and how do you try to live up to that name?

_____

_____

_____

_____

Describe your spouse or partner. What do you value most about that person? How can you honor their contributions to your life?

_____

_____

_____

_____

_____

Describe your children and grandchildren. What do you value most about them? How can you honor their contributions to your life?

_____

_____

_____

_____

Describe your other family members. What do you value most about them? How can you honor their contributions to your life?

_____

_____

_____

_____

Describe your best friend(s). What do you value most about them? How can you honor their contributions to your life?

_____

_____

_____

_____

Colonization has brought out the worst traits in our people. Those ways are not traditional. In the past, living in the camp circle meant always striving to live in the most virtuous manner. To work toward decolonization, we need to live by the values and ways of our ancestors. Behind bars, this means holding tight to those values and ways, keeping them precious, and practicing them in order to keep one another strong.

H. Spirituality

Remember, our spirituality is there to help us stay strong in confinement. Our spirituality helped our ancestors endure tremendous hardships and it can help us survive imprisonment. We can use prayer to maintain our connection with the Creator, our ancestors, and all other spiritual beings. But we must never sell our sacred pipes, pipestone, ceremonies, eagle feathers, buffalo skulls, artifacts, and items we consider to be sacred. In addition, sex offenders and informants must never carry our sacred pipes and assume our spiritual duties. Sex offenders have raped and molested our women and children. They have terrorized them. To be an informant, hiding behind a sacred pipe, is also wrong.

ACTIVITY:

What is central to your spirituality?

_____

_____

_____

_____

Do you participate in our ceremonies and prayer times? If yes, how do these help you? If not, what do you need from our ceremonies, or where else could you find what you need?

_____

_____

_____

_____

Practicing our spirituality will help us stay strong, but remember that parole boards do not understand our Indigenous lifestyles. They will not accept our participation in our ceremonies and that our spiritual and cultural teachings are a vital part of our rehabilitation. Before going up for parole, make copies of your spiritual and cultural activities and ask a lawyer to have these placed in your central file. This is our right. When we appear before the parole board we have the right to have our tribal people represent us.

Never appoint yourself to any leadership or spiritual position within our circles. You will be ridiculed and dishonored. Let our prisoners select you. Some prisoners have fooled everyone into believing they are legitimate spiritual authorities. This is not right. To allow these prisoners the right to be Pipe Keepers is a total desecration against our people and our ceremonies. It is true decolonization to ask these prisoners to remove themselves from these sacred pipes and responsibilities. White prisoners, as well as all white people and non-Indigenous people, cannot possess eagle feathers, eagle plumes, medicine bags, tobacco ties, prayer flags, and sacred items that are protected under our jurisdictions. These possessions are illegal.

Federal prisoners are very strict in applying their codes. Pure tobacco for their ceremonies is important and protected by federal law. Sex offenders and informants are not allowed in their yards.

I. Becoming a Master

While in prison, use the time to master some skills and knowledge. When we understand and interpret the languages of other Peoples, in addition to our traditional languages, we will have a deep appreciation for their attitudes and values. We can become masters of our own lives in a way that lets us develop our source of endurance and personal creativity. We can foster an originality based on a highly principled way of being.

Our years ahead of us depend on what we know about things we have learned in prison. We have master artists, singers, dancers, beadworkers, speakers, organizers, historians, and sports enthusiasts. If you have skills, share them with others. If you want skills, learn from those around you. Strengthen and enrich yourself by developing your talents and learning new skills.

In addition, learn about our ancestors, creation stories, animal migrations, herbal plant medicines, customs, treaties, and why we must never give up our struggles for the return of our homelands. We are uniquely honored by what we do and what we give to our people. Some within our ranks will make themselves better people. Work to become a master.

ACTIVITY:

Among the people around you, who has skills you would like to learn or talents you would like to develop? How can you learn from them?

_____

_____

_____

_____

What skills or talents do you have that you could share or teach to others?

_____

_____

_____

_____

J. Indigenous Virtues

Decolonization involves recovering the ways of our ancestors that kept our men, women, and communities strong. When our families were intact, we operated according to a different set of values. Through colonization, we have lost many of those ways, and our families and communities have suffered as a consequence.

ACTIVITY:

Here are seven virtues that our people live by on a daily basis. Write seven of your own.

Generosity	1. _____	
Peace	2. _____	
Courage	3. _____	
Fearlessness	4. _____	
Bravery	5. _____	
Wisdom	6. _____	
Respect	7. _____	

Seven People to Always Remember to Pray for:
1. Our women
2. Our children
3. Our old people
4. Those not yet born
5. Our orphans
6. Our warriors
7. Our people in prison

How do you live by these virtues now? Why is this important?

_____

_____

_____

How can you live according to these virtues while imprisoned?

_____

_____

_____

_____

These values will help you cope with whatever comes your way and they will help you stay focused on the things that are important.

ACTIVITY:

Four great gains in our lives are the births of our children, finding the right spouse or soul mate, working toward decolonization, and finding freedom from prison and life's difficulties. What great gains are important in your life? What would you still like to accomplish?

_____

_____

_____

_____

Four great losses in our lives are the deaths of our children; the deaths of our mothers, fathers, brothers, and sisters; being surrounded by the enemy; and the loss of our homes. What great losses have you experienced in your life? How did you cope with those losses? How can you cope with future losses?

_____

_____

_____

_____

K. Survival

Everyone needs to be prepared for survival as our natural resources are depleted from the earth. People are killing people for control of their oil. Our water is polluted with radioactivity and other toxins. We will have to walk, ride horses, swim, and use boats for travel. Mass transportation will change. We will be confined to our families and certain areas in our countries. Survival means that we will have to go back to depending on our animals and nature for food, water, clothing, sustenance, and shelter. Our people will begin camping in large numbers.

Our prophecies tell us that the earth will grow angry about humankind's greed and the destruction of her elements. Many white buffalo and other white creatures have been born as spiritual messengers from the other world. Survival means that we must be ready.

For people imprisoned, survival means other things as well. I survive in prison by maintaining a rigid, disciplined schedule—running, playing basketball, participating in our ceremonies, singing, dancing, reading, writing, teaching our spirituality and culture, and being around positive people and situations. I promise myself each day that I will be freed from prison and return to my sons and daughters and all of my *takoja* (grandchildren). I have spent my entire time in prison helping to benefit our circles. I move from day to day, working with our prisoners who are highly motivated in leadership and organizing our brothers and relatives. These prisoners are artists, singers, dancers, and have multiple talents. They are experts with our laws, treaty rights, history, and customs. I stay away from people and prisoners who talk bad about everything and are dangerously self-centered.

To survive in prison in a righteous manner, tribal prisoners need to understand the long history of informants and snitches. Informants among our people go way back to the times when disgruntled warriors, filled with antagonism and hatred for our leaders and fighters, began collaborating with enemy warriors from other tribes and passing information about our activities to them. Many of these informants began working for the US government by providing intelligence in return for protection, weapons, money, and women. Millions of our people died and our homelands were stolen from us with this deadly system of violence and corruption. Snitches are ruthless people. They are not afraid to provide information to prison officials and law enforcement agencies about our brothers and sisters. They provide this information in a variety of ways: behind closed doors; with written statements; by telephone; and wearing listening devices.

Informants are often squeezed into a corner and threatened with being charged in court and spending more time in prison if they do not begin talking. They are not strong enough to withstand this bullying and bribery. These people begin infiltrating our circles and listening for information they can use against other prisoners. Their words, even made up stories, have put other prisoners away for a long time. Early release and recommendations for parole are used as incentives. A majority of confidential informants and snitches have exhausted all of their remedies in court with their cases and have no alternative plans for freedom. Some are shipped in from other prisons for safekeeping, and work within our ranks without being detected. Rapists, child molesters, and sex offenders fit very well into this category.

In the old days, informants and snitches, as well as all bad people, were banished from our camps. They began working as soldiers and interpreters for the US government and today they continue in our prison circles. We must protect our brotherhoods and sisterhoods from the ones who seek to harm us to benefit themselves.

L. Notes to Those on the Outside

When the mailman comes into our cell blocks he brings letters, newspapers, magazines, and postcards. These are connections from our families, life on the outside, business people, and friends. Letters from women who can cook a meal of homemade cheeseburgers, fried red potatoes, fried buffalo kidneys, pinto bean soup with bacon, skillet bread, commodity cheese, fresh onion slices, cucumbers, hot sauce, apple pie, and coffee boiled in a large pot give us strength and make us feel like we never left home. When we receive those letters we think better. Our dreams turn into conventional powers of determination and righteousness.

News from home, photos, money, and tribal greeting cards light our fires of happiness. We can begin planning on how we are going to write back. We like to write. We can sit for hours and think of what we are going to put into words. Some prisoners like to take a long walk and breathe in nature before writing. This helps them be more relaxed and expressive. Some like to listen to music with their televisions on. This creates a dual perception of adventure.

Tribal newspapers are passed around to a long

list of us who want to know what is happening on our reservations. Reading and seeing pictures spark our imagination. We come alive. On a weekly basis, eight hundred guys are waiting to read these newspapers, which are an important lifeline to us. We are proud of our people. It is seen in our eyes.

M. Remembrance, Tribute, and Activism

I am proud to be an activist for the memory of my uncle, Buddy Lamont, who was killed by a sniper's bullet from the US marshals at Wounded Knee in 1973. I will spend the rest of my life fighting for what he believed in. We must always remember our ancestors who were hunted down and killed by the US government, which came to steal our homelands. Our warriors were captured and executed, our women were raped, our children were sent off far away and sold into slavery, and our people suffered enormous pain. Our fingernails were pulled out, our hair was forcefully cut, pieces of our ears were sliced off, and we were deprived of food and water.

Remember the blood of our people that stained the faces, hands, boots, weapons, uniforms, and horses of the soldiers when they killed us. The soldiers were trained to destroy us, but not all of us died. Those of us who still lived became refugees under constant imprisonment. We saw torture and death every day.

Be free from calamity, intemperance, malice, doubt, exploitation, animosity, and vengeance.

Remember our people serving life sentences without parole. These men and women must be strong at all times. Every area of their lives must be conditioned with positive people and situations. Some of our lifers have been incarcerated for decades and some are just starting out.

Over the generations, we have become silent and effective activists and fighters. We have mobilized our people and have begun rebuilding our nations. The word *holocaust* is an accurate description of the crime perpetrated against us, yet we stay strong through our solidarity and support of Indigenous rights. We will never die.

We can best pay tribute to our ancestors by not only remembering their suffering but also working to stop the suffering of our people today. I am an activist for many reasons. I fight for our rights. I make sure white people and other races of people do not interfere with our business affairs. I remember our people who were killed by government snipers and secret agents. I work to expose discrimination issues and racism. I strongly believe that all government-run schools and Christian organizations should leave our reservations because these two entities represent a powerful money game with many documented cases of abuse against our people. I do not believe in the death penalty and I want to see it ended. I also want to see the day when the dictatorships and governments of the Indian Reorganization Act and the Bureau of Indian Affairs are ended. I believe in all indigenous herbs that grow everywhere in our homelands all over the world. I fight for our right to use tobacco in our ceremonies in prison. Finally, I want our original homelands to be returned to our people. I want our old ways of life to come back. These issues fuel my activism.

Tribal prisoners should study and thoroughly research our treaties, the maps of our original homelands and reservations, old pictures of our people, our family histories and names, lineal ancestries, sacred sites, massacre sites, creation stories, legal documents, and lawsuits that protect our rights. Keep a copy of these. Memorize them.

Prison administrations do not care about our rehabilitation and any of our rights. These are not necessary to them until we show them proof of the laws that have been passed by Congress and the courts. Prisoner officials do not think like us. They are more interested in placing a money system of taxes on our food, commissary, wages, disciplinary fines, health services, telephones, and our property items. Money to them is power. Money to us is nothing.

We have the right to question all monies that are collected from these taxes. Are they legal? Who uses the monies? Are they put into a benevolent fund? Is slave labor used? Are state and federal lawmakers fully aware of these taxes? Can we file lawsuits? Are people receiving secret kickbacks? Can prisons disperse our tribal monies that we receive from the US government and royalty payments from our lands into separate accounts without our approval? Is the Racketeer Influenced and Corrupt Organizations (RICO) Act being violated with the use of these taxes and monies?

Another important issue, especially for lifers, is what happens to our bodies upon our death. When our lives expire from natural causes or tragedy in prison, our bodies must not be cut open and tampered with in any way. It is the policy of prisons in America to transport our bodies to a morgue and have a coroner determine the cause of death through an autopsy. This is an extreme desecration to our people because we are cut open, our internal organs are removed, and we are bled out, only so they might determine the cause of death.

I ask our people and prisoners from wealthy tribes to help us set a legal precedence challenging this by finding lawyers who will get this issue into the courts and change this policy through a lawsuit. The courts can order prison wardens and their administrations to exempt tribal prisoners from this standard policy. We want our bodies to be put on dry ice and transported back to our families without any physical disturbance. The cause of our death can generally be determined without cutting open or removing any part of our bodies. Under current policies, our internal organs are sent to a landfill and the blood is drained down into sewers and lagoons. The coroners and the people with whom they work will make a profit from all of this.

After our bodies are returned home, we want our families to prepare us without any modern procedures. All traditional laws must be applied. We want to be dressed honorably without watches, modern jewelry, eyeglasses, hearing aids, and prosthetic limbs. We do not want caskets and the use of a hearse to move us.

With my people, our Lakota customs say that our dead bodies must be made into an offering to feed the insects of the earth, which in time become an offering of their own for the larger creatures in the greater cycles of life. This is done by wrapping our bodies in a buffalo hide, carrying us by hand, placing us up on a scaffold, and remembering us for the last time. This is all performed with our prayers, foods, songs, memories, tobacco, and the giveaway. Our warriors provide security.

My last words of advice are to know yourself and know those who work against you. This has to be a broad sentiment that we abide by at all times. All of our leaders from the times of Tecumseh, Little Crow, Sitting Bull, and Geronimo knew themselves and those who worked against them. Their main priorities were the protection of our people and our homelands. They carefully monitored the encroachment of white people onto our lands and into our camps. They were strategic thinkers and tactical fighters. So must we be. Leave no stones unturned.

N. Resources

Books

Davis, Angela Y. *Are Prisons Obsolete?* New York: Seven Stories Press, 2003.

Ross, Luana. *Inventing the Savage: The Social Construction of Native American Criminality.* Austin: University of Texas Press, 1998.

Websites

Critical Resistance (http://www.criticalresistance.org).

Dakota-Lakota-Nakota Human Rights Advocacy Coalition (http://www.dlncoalition.org/dln_issues/sdpsgdonations.htm).

Death Penalty Information Center (http://www.deathpenaltyinfo .org/native-americans-and-death-penalty).

From Residential Schools to Prisons. *Native Women's Association of Canada.* http://www.nwac.ca/sites/default/files/imce /WEBSITES/201104/insert1_final web english.pdf.

International Indian Treaty Council (http://treatycouncil.info /section_21151116.htm).

Prison Facts & Statistics (http://www.prisonjustice.ca/politics /facts_stats.html).

The Real Cost of Prisons Project (http://realcostofprisons.org/).

Sapawiyaka – Lakota, Dakota, Nakota Spiritual Group (http:// sapawiyaka.tripod.com/bio.html).

Chapter 12

KUA TUPU TE PĀ HARAKEKE
DEVELOPING HEALTHY *WHĀNAU* RELATIONSHIPS

Leonie Pihama and Ngaropi Diane Cameron

A. Opening with *Pēpeha*

Ko Taranaki te maunga	Taranaki is the ancestral mountain
Ko Waitara te awa	Waitara is the river
Ko Ngā Tai o Rehua tōku moana	Ngā Tai o Rehua is the ocean
Ko Tokomaru te waka	Tokomaru is the canoe
Ko Te Ātiawa, Ngāti Māhanga, Ngā Māhanga ā Tairi ōku iwi	My tribal groups are Te Ātiawa, Ngāti Māhanga ā Tairi, Ngāti Māhanga
Ko Ngāti Rāhiri tōku hapū	My subtribe is Ngāti Rāhiri
Ko Leonie Pihama tōku ingoa.	My name is Leonie Pihama
Ko Taranaki te maunga	Taranaki is the ancestral mountain
Ko Urenui te awa	Urenui is the river
Ko Ngā Tai o Rehua te moana	Ngā Tai o Rehua is the ocean
Ko Tokomaru me Takitimu ngā waka	The canoes are Tokomaru and Takitimu
Ko Ngāti Mutunga me Ngāti Kahungunu naā iwi	My tribal groups are Ngāti Mutunga and Ngāti Kahungunu
Ko Kaitangata me Ngāti Pahauwera ōku hapū	My subtribes are Kaitangata and Ngāti Pahauwera
Ko Raumati te whānau	Raumati is my extended family
Ko Ngaropi Cameron tōku ingoa	My name is Ngaropi Cameron

We have opened this chapter with our *pēpeha*. Pēpeha are ways through which our people introduce ourselves. These vary from tribe to tribe. The essence of pēpeha is that it links us to our tribes and all associated with it—our mountains, our rivers, our canoes, our ancestral lines. It links us to each other. It places us, as *Māori,* within a wider collective consciousness and set of relationships. It is important to highlight that the term Māori is a term that brings us together as Peoples. It is a term that our people have chosen to use as a means of unifying ourselves in the wake of the arrival of our colonizers. Prior to colonization all identification was done through our *whānau* (extended family structure), *hapū* (group of whānau connected though common ancestor/sub-groupings of *iwi*) or iwi (nations connected through common ancestor). Māori means to be "normal" or "pure," a fitting term for an Indigenous People. We have, however, also been active in maintaining our hapū and iwi identities, and it is through pēpeha that we can culturally share that identity with one another. Our people have been doing this for generations. And in spite of colonization seeking to undermine our cultural identity, many of us continue to do this.

Locating ourselves in relation to our natural world, our relations, and our lands is important to Māori. It acknowledges and affirms our cultural connections. It reminds us of our cultural obligations to one another, to the land, and all our relations who live with us on our lands. It recognizes the many generations that have come before us and gives those around us an ability to place ourselves within the Māori world. That is also important.

Often when our people recite their pēpeha in a gathering, you will hear responses within the group that indicate a close relationship. People will respond *kia ora whanaunga,* "Greetings relation," to make us

aware of the connection. Through this process we link to people whom we may never have met before. We link on an ancestral level. We link on a spiritual level. We link on a tribal level. These connections keep our relationships, our collectivity, our language, and our knowledge alive. And they remind us we are responsible for one another and for all we live alongside of on *Papatūānuku,* this great Mother Earth.

This knowledge has been passed down to us from our *tupuna,* our ancestors. It is exactly the knowledge and protocols that our colonizers sought to deny us. The systematic and unrelenting attacks on our language and culture have been deliberate. They are acts of denying our identity as *Tāngata Whenua* (People of the Land). For Māori, the suppression of our language and culture was key to the denial of Māori knowledge that enabled healthy relationships. As is the case on Great Turtle Island, violent attacks upon our language and culture aligned with acts of war and murder of our people. The importation of guns, alcohol, and the Bible brought about significant societal changes both within and between tribes.

B. Retaining Our Identity

The struggle to retain our identity as Indigenous Peoples is a part of a wider struggle to decolonize. Colonization has violently forced ways of being upon our communities that have changed our lives in ways that our ancestors could never have imagined. In our context within *Aotearoa* (referred to in colonial terms as New Zealand), Māori have been struggling for the past two hundred years to find ways to maintain those cultural protocols, language, and practices that enable us to hold our place as Indigenous on our own lands. The experience of family violence within our communities is a symptom of historical acts of genocide and ethnocide upon our Peoples.

ACTIVITY:

Are there particular ways that your People/nation introduce themselves or express their identity that affirm an Indigenous identity?

_____

_____

_____

_____

C. _Pūrākau_: Traditional Stories as Guidance

This is the story of Niwareka and Mataora, two well-known ancestors in Māori tradition who brought to our people the arts of _moko_ (Māori tattoo forms) and _tāniko_ (a decorative form of weaving). This story, as is the case with Indigenous traditional stories, provides insights and messages for our people today.

Niwareka lived in Rarohenga (the underworld). She chose to go to the world above, to Te Ao Mārama (the world of light) to live amongst those _tangata_ (human beings) who live in this world. In the world of light Niwareka partnered with Mataora. Mataora was abusive to her and in response Niwareka returned to Rarohenga to be amongst her people who did not agree to such behavior. Mataora followed Niwareka and after overcoming many trials and challenges he came across her father, Uetonga, who was a great carver of moko. Mataora wore the painted markings of the human world on his face, but in his encounter with Uetonga he was told that the markings of Rarohenga were permanent, and in time Uetonga began to place permanent moko on the face of Mataora. During that time Niwareka became aware of the presence of Mataora in the underworld and went to

find him. Mataora spoke with Uetonga of his desire for Niwareka to return with him to the earthly world. Uetonga questioned the act of abuse, stating that, like temporary moko, that was not the way of their people. Mataora pleaded with Niwareka to return with him and, in doing so, agreed that by wearing the permanent moko of Uetonga he would take to his people both moko and the challenge to stop any abuse amongst his people. Niwareka agreed to return and she took the art form of tāniko weaving back to the World of Light to share with the people above.

This chapter is about relationships. It is about how our ancestors have passed to us knowledge about what is and is not acceptable amongst our people. It is also about how traditional ways and stories, in their many forms, provide us with guidance in this contemporary world as we live on our own lands that have been colonized by others. It is argued that there is a need to draw from traditional knowledge as a source of healing contemporary issues.

There is a growing focus on drawing upon traditional knowledge to support the revitalization of our language and culture. This has been difficult to achieve given the impact of colonial beliefs and practices upon our people. The denial of _te reo Māori_

(Māori language) through the imposition of English and the native schooling system has had a huge impact on being able to access knowledge. The attack on our language was part of a sustained process by which to advance the assimilation of colonial ways of being. Many of our people have been forced to live on tribal lands that are not theirs in order to find jobs and feed their families.

Colonization undermined Māori cohesion and relationships through acts that stole our lands and individualized the little that remained. The impact of the historical trauma associated with colonial oppression upon generations of our people is clearly evident. This chapter focuses on how we can draw upon traditional knowledge as healing in a contemporary context.

As Indigenous Peoples we have many ways in which our cultural practices inform us about many forms of relationships: family relationships, friendships, and intimate relationships. The story of Niwareka and Mataora, for example, is often recited as the genealogy of the beginnings of permanent moko to our people. It is generally referred to as "the story of Mataora." The bringing of tāniko as a weaving form, an art form, by Niwareka is rarely mentioned. The underpinning message of dealing with issues of abuse is often not even considered or is glossed over. There are many ways that meanings and teachings from traditional stories have been influenced by colonization, including the processes through which Indigenous languages are translated and the influence of colonial gender relations that privileged the place of men as the primary transmitters of our stories.

Linda Tuhiwai Smith (1999) has argued that

Di Grennell, a long-term worker in the area of family violence, has highlighted the importance of traditional knowledge to healing in her work:

Drawing on the wisdom of our tupuna (ancestors) and traditions is not to return us to a mythic past or golden age—our people have always adapted to new circumstances and experimented with new technology. Rather it is to understand and be guided by the symbols, values, and principles that can enhance our capacity to live together peacefully as whānau and communities. Our capacity for resilience as an Indigenous People is fed and nourished by our language, traditional practices, and oral traditions.

Indigenous People have for some time critiqued the ways in which our histories have been told from the perspective of the colonizer. This concern over the representation of Indigenous Peoples by our colonizers is held by many Indigenous Peoples around the world. Vine Deloria Jr. wrote that "for most of the five centuries…whites have had unrestricted power to describe Indians in any way they chose." What this means is that we must be vigilant in the telling of our own stories in ways that are grounded within our own cultural frameworks. It is also clear to Indigenous Peoples that the translation and interpretation of our stories through the colonizers' language can create both understandings and misunderstandings—the story of Niwareka and Mataora is often the victim of both. Dominant understandings of this story have tended to lean to the belief that Mataora is the central figure in the story and that he journeyed to bring to us the art of moko. Where that may be the case, it is clear that the art of moko came from the family of Niwareka, and that her actions contributed hugely to how moko came to be a part of our cultural practices and protocols in the Māori world. More importantly, however, is that this story clearly highlights her refusal to stay in a situation where she had experienced abuse, and that once was enough for her to leave Mataora immediately. As Indigenous Peoples we must be constantly aware of the ongoing obsession by our colonizers to translate and interpret our stories as if the only characters that count are the men. The danger of such colonial interpretations is that the roles of our women and of our female ancestors are dismissed and key messages about our people and our relationships are made invisible. Consequently, Māori women have had to fight for many years for our ancestral women to be more visible.

Although this particular story gives us a way of understanding the gifting of permanent moko and tāniko to our people, it is much more than that. One central lesson that is often missed is the critical role of Niwareka in this story. She is central to the messages that our ancestors have passed through this story, although her role is rarely acknowledged. Sadly, the marginalization of Māori women within our traditional stories is not uncommon. Colonial ethnographers and anthropologists actively denied the role of our women. They subjugated Māori women's roles in line with their own sexist and misogynistic belief systems and ideologies that deemed women as both inferior and property. These ideologies pervade both the interpretation of our histories and our roles, even to the extent of determining what stories were even considered worthy of being recorded. In many interpretations of this story, Niwareka is marginalized to solely "the daughter of" Uetonga or "the wife of" Mataora. She is not seen as an active, powerful ancestral woman who made a clear decision to leave an unhealthy relationship and return to her people. As such, the often neglected interpretation of this story is that it challenges abuse. In particular it is a story that challenges male to female violence. It challenges such abuse through the act of Niwareka removing herself from that situation and returning to her people.

D. Teachings about Relationships

Stories like that of the relationship of Niwareka and Mataora appear throughout our tribal histories as ways of providing us with understandings and guidance about relationships. They are stories that tell of what is, and what is not, acceptable within our whānau, our extended families. The story of Niwareka and Mataora is one that tells us that abuse is not acceptable. There is a clear message that abuse must be challenged. It is a story that provides insight into the traditional belief that historically whānau and hapū were expected to be safe spaces for Māori women and children. It is, therefore, a story that reminds us that we must take collective responsibility for such actions.

The return of Niwareka to her people tells us that the response to individual acts of violence or abuse must also be a collective response. Such a belief is grounded in our collective relationships, roles, obligations, and accountability. Therefore any acts of abuse were dealt with collectively as a form of intervention that worked to ensure that repeat incidents of violence did not occur. The response was both immediate and collective. Such a notion affirms that as individuals we are a part of a wider collective within our Indigenous worlds. That has always been the way of our ancestors. It is a cultural belief and practice that is documented throughout our stories. It is a value that has been handed down through generations of our people. It is also a value that was actively attacked through colonization.

ACTIVITY:

What are some examples of traditional stories within your community and tribe that talk about relationships and how we relate to one another?

_____

_____

_____

_____

For the past twenty years we have been honored to work alongside our people as a researcher (Leonie) and a service provider (Ngaropi) on projects that have both a decolonizing and transformative intent. This work came more closely together in the evaluation of the programs offered by Tū Tama Wahine O Taranaki, the organization headed by Ngaropi. The programs are grounded in the belief that in order to make change in the area of domestic violence for Māori there must be a *Kaupapa Māori* approach.

Kaupapa Māori, in general terms, refers to Māori philosophies, Māori approaches, and Māori ways of being. These are defined and controlled by Māori. Inherent to Kaupapa Māori theory, methodology, and practice is the notion of Māori as self-determining. Kaupapa Māori is a culturally defined approach that enables us as Indigenous Peoples to draw upon our own language and protocols to develop and operate a wide range of services and initiatives within our communities. It is not a singular approach, as tribal-specific ways of being and tribal dialects provide us with a multitude of possibilities, but rather a cultural and political framework that advances Māori aspirations and desires for our own people. In this regard, many Māori practitioners, counselors, and healers in the area of domestic, family, and sexual violence have worked to develop both prevention and intervention strategies that align with a Kaupapa Māori approach. Part of that process has been to challenge the notion that such violence impacts only the individual, and recognize that it impacts the entire whānau, the entire extended family unit.

Whānau is the building block of Māori society. It consists of at least three generations who live together as an extended family and ensures the inclusion of grandparent generations in the lives of Māori children. The term *whānau* relates to both "extended family" and "birth." The plural meaning of the word highlights its significance in a society that was, and is, reliant upon future generations. Whānau enables the raising of children by many adults. The parent generation is only one group caring for and raising our children. There have always been many adults

present in the lives of Māori children, especially elders, the grandparent generation.

The term *whānau* as "birth" also exists within the context of a wider cultural belief system concerning our relationship as people to Papatūānuku (Mother Earth.) The land for our people is known as *whenua*, which is also the word for afterbirth. When a child is born, the cultural process for our people is to return the afterbirth to the earth; it is buried within the Earth Mother. It connects us to our land. The whenua (afterbirth) is returned to the whenua (the earth). As noted in the opening of this chapter, we stressed the cultural means by which we as tribal people within the Māori Nation link to our tribal areas, to our mountains, our rivers, our lands. The practice of returning the afterbirth to the earth is yet another cultural practice that affirms those connections and affirms our collective relationships. Such is the centrality of whānau within Māori society. Whānau is about collective responsibility for the well-being of generations present and future. It is also the place where issues and problems could be addressed and resolved. This is highlighted in the story of the healing of the relationship of Niwareka and Mataora.

The story of Niwareka returning to her people is a story of returning to whānau after being insulted by her partner. The story of Mataora taking the journey to Rarohenga and seeking the return of Niwareka is a story about his accountability to her people. It was within the whānau that the abuse of Niwareka was discussed, with the resolution being intervention and future prevention. The return of Niwareka to her whānau was an act of transformation in their lives through collective responsibility. Mataora was called to task for his actions, not by Niwareka as an individual, but by her whānau as a collective. This is highlighted by moko expert Mark Kōpua:

> It is said that as Mataora journeyed through Rarohenga seeking Niwareka he came upon Uetonga, his wife's father, preparing to place a moko on the face of a man. It was here that the terms of Mataora's acceptance were discussed. However the final decision was made by Niwareka. It is said that upon hearing

Mataora's song of lament and love for her that she knew he would not mistreat her by speaking poorly of her again, and so she allowed Mataora to not only receive a moko himself but to learn the art of tāmoko for the overworld.

Māori society, like many Indigenous societies, has clear *tikanga* (traditional protocols and lore) indicating that collective well-being is central. Our stories, our protocols, our cultural ways, and our original instructions all highlight that our relations and relationships are interwoven not only between human beings but with all living things. This does not deny the individuals their place, but rather highlights that we are all relations, and as such are a part of a much wider collective. Our survival and well-being are dependent upon balanced relationships, roles, obligations, and accountabilities. Our survival as Peoples is also about ensuring the well-being of future generations. In order for that to be possible, specific ways of relating needed to be grounded in an understanding of the well-being of the collective, which in Māori terms means the well-being of whānau (extended family), hapū (subtribal groupings), and iwi (tribal groupings).

ACTIVITY:

What are the social structures for your People/nation? And how do those structures help to provide ways of protecting the collective well-being of your People?

_____

_____

_____

_____

Another example of such relationships is the term *mokopuna*, which is used for grandchild. Mokopuna can be broken down into two terms: *moko* and *puna*. Moko, as highlighted in the story of Niwareka and Mataora, relates to traditional tattoo forms and in this case can be seen as children being a representation of their ancestors. The term *puna* relates to a "spring" or "fountain." A mokopuna is then a spring or image of our ancestors; it is a living representation of those who have come before. The relationship between past, present, and future is embodied within that term and as such within that child. Elder and healer Rangimarie Pere states: *He taonga te mokopuna, ka noho mai hoki te mokopuna hei puna mo te tipuna ka whakaaro tātou ka noho mai te mokopuna hei tā moko mō te tipuna, he tino taonga rā tōna. He mokopuna rā tātou, he mokopuna anō hoki ngā tipuna.* (A grandchild is very precious, a fountain for ancestral knowledge and an everlasting reflection of those who have gone before. We are all grandchildren, as are our ancestors.)

This concept alone indicates the sanctity of children. Children are the embodiment of all past and future generations, and as such, to hurt a child, hit a child, or abuse a child is to hurt, hit, and abuse all past and future generations that link to that child. Acts of abuse and violence towards Indigenous children are then acts of abuse and violence upon all of our ancestors past and all those yet to be born. That is the extent of such violence. That is what our language, culture, and stories remind us.

Clearly then, family violence, in Māori terms, is not only about the abuse of a partner or another family member. Such acts of abuse are considered to be acts of violence against both the ancestors and future generations. To abuse a whānau member is an act of abuse against the entire whānau, it is an act of abuse against our past, present, and future relations. That was how our ancestors understood acts of abuse. To know that is to also understand the sacredness of whānau within Māori society. What is clear is that such knowledge and practices have been denied and marginalized through colonization. This has occurred in many of the violent processes through which colonizing forces have attacked Indigenous Peoples. One consequence of such colonial violence is seen in the huge impact that colonization has had on how we now see and practice relationships.

ACTIVITY:

What are the words or terms within your language that relate to family, children, grandchildren?

Family_____

_____

Children_____

_____

Grandchildren _____

_____

How do those terms position children within your People/nation?

_____

_____

_____

The impact of family violence upon whānau cannot be understated. The Second Māori Taskforce on Whānau Violence noted:

> Whānau Violence is understood by this Taskforce to be an epidemic because of the magnitude and serious nature of it for whānau, hapū and iwi and the way in which it is collectively spread and maintained. Whānau violence is intergenerational and directly impacts on *whakapapa* (genealogical links). It has taken several generations of learned behavior and practice to entrench whānau violence as the most devastating and debilitating of social practices. It will take time for whānau violence to be unlearned.

For over twenty years there has been a growing understanding about the underlying causes of such violence. The definition of whānau violence by the taskforce highlights that such violence happens not only within our whānau, but is perpetuated upon us by the state. That adds another layer of structural analysis to the issue of family or domestic violence. Such a definition brings to the discussion the wider issues of colonization, oppression, injustice, racism, and the many acts of violence of colonial states upon Indigenous Peoples.

The struggle to bring an end to whānau violence for Māori people is a part of a wider struggle of decolonization and self-determination. In order to fully understand the origins of the epidemic of violence within our whānau we must engage directly with the ways in which colonization itself has altered and disrupted fundamental relationships amongst our people. For example, in a cultural framework that recognizes and honors our *kaumātua* (elders), how can there be growing incidences of elder abuse within our families? It is clear that the denial of key knowledge and practices through colonization has had a significant impact on how we see ourselves and one another in a contemporary context. Understanding the link between colonial- and state-imposed violence and whānau violence is critical. The two are intertwined. Colonization and oppression are based upon beliefs that colonizers possess a cultural and racial superiority. Those beliefs provide the justification for acts of

genocide and ethnocide upon Indigenous Peoples.

For those working towards healing within whānau, it has become clear that a critical part of our call for self-determination, for sovereignty, for control over being Māori is the reclamation and maintenance of healthy relationships. That is the essence of this chapter.

E. Traditional Māori Society and Views on Family Violence

It is important to note that acts of violence within Māori society did exist. Intertribal disputes and wars occurred prior to colonization within a particular cultural framework and context, and included ways of resolution. They were not indiscriminate acts of violence. War and struggle between tribes was also significantly different from how warfare is operated within contemporary societies. For example, pre-colonization intertribal battles were in the form of hand-to-hand struggle whereby combatants could see "the whites of the eyes" of their enemies. Cultural practices often meant that few deaths occurred, and in many instances arranged partnerships were formed to lead whānau within tribes to forge new and long-term relationships. Such arrangements were agreed upon and referred to as *te tatau pounamu* (the greenstone door), because such politically arranged relationships acted as a door to peace between the tribes.

We are not seeking to be idealistic in our discussion within this chapter, but to show that in a society based upon extended family relationships, acts of violence were clearly not acceptable within that unit. Research tells us, in fact, that before colonization family violence was rare within Māori society.

Whānau are cultural structures that traditionally supported both prevention and intervention. They provided for collective responsibility, obligations, and accountability. As an extended family structure, whānau is based within whakapapa (genealogical) relationships. Whakapapa is not a linear relationship like that of our colonizers, as we are led to believe by white anthropologists and ethnographers. Whakapapa is literally about layers of relationships that are culturally complex. Those relationships are highlighted within *te reo Māori*, the Māori language. For example, the term for mother is *whaea*; the term for our aunties and other women of the same generation within the whānau may also be *whaea*. Likewise the term for father is *matua*, which is also the term for uncles or men of the *same* generation within the whānau (there are tribal dialects that may use different terms for mother). What this tells us is that it is not only birth parents who care for and nurture children. In fact, within Māori society the role of raising children was collective and inter-generational, often with birth parents having a lesser daily role than that of the grandparent generation. The point is that our relationships within whānau were multiple and about collective well-being.

Cultural values, protocols, lore, and worldviews ensured that there were mechanisms by which to acknowledge and care for each generation. There are many traditional sayings that tell us of the sanctity of people. One often-quoted saying from the Northern tribe Te Aupouri is:

Hutia te rito o te harakeke
Kei hea te kōmako e kō?
Kī mai koe ki ahau
He aha te mea nui o te ao?
Māku e kī atu
He Tangata, He Tangata, He Tangata

Pluck the centre shoot from the flax bush
Where will the Bellbird sing?
Ask me
What is the most important thing in the world
I will say
It is people, It is people, It is people

This saying draws upon the metaphor of the *harakeke* (the flax plant) as a symbol of the whānau. When harvesting harakeke for weaving, the center shoot of the plant must never be removed, as it is the core from which the entire plant grows. It is likened to the whānau, with the middle shoot being the new growth or child, the surrounding leaves being the parents, and grandparents being the outer leaves. To remove the center shoot will remove the ability of the plant to grow and flourish. The proverb relates directly to the desire for a particular relationship that, if denied, would mean that future generations would not flourish. The sanctity of future generations is clear.

Whānau violence within Māori worldviews is not viewed as only physical forms of violence. It includes violence that occurs on multiple planes. For example, in an oral tradition such as that of our ancestors, the power of the word is clearly articulated. The following two *whakatauakī* give examples of how our people view the power of language:

Ko te pūtake o te Māoritanga ko te reo Māori, he taonga tuku iho nā ngā tūpuna
The root of Māori culture is in the language, a gift from our ancestors.

He wero o te tao e taea te karo, te kī e kore e taea
The flight of the spear can be parried, the spoken word cannot.

The power of verbal insult is acknowledged within Māori traditions. Insults or transgression in regard to disrespectful ways of behaving towards whānau were considered unacceptable. There are many stories of both women and men leaving relationships and

> **Denise Wilson on the impact of violations to the womb:**
> Any violation of *te whare tangata* (that is the house of the people), such as abuse of the genital area and rape, has the potential to create distress amongst Māori women. This distress is not only physical or psychological in origin, but also spiritual and has multiple dimensions to it. Not only is this a violation of the woman herself, but also a violation of her *tupuna* (ancestor) and her future generations. Spiritual distress is often a dimension that is neither recognised nor acknowledged, but one that impedes recovery and healing.

returning to their own people after feeling aggrieved. One of our ancestors, Ruapūtahanga, left her partner Whatihua after being insulted by his behavior. She returned to our tribal lands in *Taranaki*, a tribal region on the West Coast of the North Island.

Acts of physical and sexual violence are violations of an entire people. Denise Wilson, a Māori woman working in health, notes that such acts were deemed traditionally as acts of violation against the entire whānau, hapū, and iwi. Within Māori society the womb is referred to as *Te Whare Tangata,* "The house of the people." The sacredness and status of the womb is central to providing us with an understanding of the key position of Māori women in Māori society. Any violation is therefore a violation of the people.

Māori activist and counselor Mereana Pitman provides a view of abuse as acts of transgressing *mana* (the status and dignity of people). It was therefore addressed directly with severe consequences. She highlights that sexual violence is also imposed more broadly upon Māori collectively, through the many forms of rape that occur through the act of colonization.

What is clear is that whānau violence was seen always within the context of wider relationships and dynamics. It was never seen as violence only against that individual. Balzer and others place family violence in this manner:

> A person was not believed to exist as an individual, but was linked through their whakapapa to their whānau, hapū, iwi, and ecosystem. A slight or attack on one member of a hapū would therefore be considered an attack on the whole hapū and collective retaliation might be considered warranted. On other occasions the whānau or hapū of the offender might be expected to impose sanctions of their own in order to save face with the offended group. Preservation of the people was paramount and the life-giving roles of land and women were therefore revered. It would appear that the ties to whakapapa, the need for the preservation of the people and the social order of Māori communities would, if not totally obviating violence against women, at least limit its occurrence.

In their report *Māori Family Violence in Aotearoa,* Balzer et al. note that when people transgressed boundaries, the response was swift:

In radical cases of violence they go to that person with a *whāriki* (mat) or coffin, have a *tangi* (grieving at death) to them and from there on treat them as they weren't alive and within months they would die… certainly *utu* (reciprocity) was really swift. If you abused someone in the old days then you were abusing the whakapapa, therefore the retributions were quite strong.

In the rare cases that such violence did occur, it was dealt with collectively and swiftly. Such cultural responses indicate that violence within whānau was not condoned or socially sanctioned, and that was reflected in the collective response to such actions. Our people speak of responses in regard to the well-being of not only the individual and whānau affected, but also of the need to protect future generations.

Mereana Pitman argues that dealing with such transgressions was grounded in cultural protocols and included:

> [The calling of] *Wānanga* (gathering for discussion) so all those affected by the transgression could vent their shame and their anger at the actions of the abuser(s). Resolutions were agreed upon and sacrifices were made through death, through the taking of land and resources as payment, the destruction of the mana through enforced exile from tribal home-lands, the holding of the abuser's *tangihanga* (funeral) while he still lived. And upon death the abuser's body being buried standing up or face down to always face the womb of Papatūānuku and wear the shame.

Reflecting on these examples of traditional

responses to family violence shows that it was deemed a cultural transgression that must be dealt with directly and severely in order to ensure the well-being of whānau and future generations.

ACTIVITY:

How were acts of violence within families and between partners seen and talked about historically for your people? What are some of the cultural mechanisms used to both prevent and intervene in such acts of violence?

_____

_____

_____

_____

F. Colonization and Family Violence

Both our traditional stories and our proverbs support the position taken by Māori specialists working in the area of whānau violence that such behavior was unacceptable prior to colonization. Rangimarie Turuki Pere puts it succinctly:

I te wā i haramai ngā mihingare mai i Ingarangai i ērā whenua. I tīmata mai ēnei tu āhuatanga i a rātou, kāore i hanga mai i a ngai tāua, te tamariki he ariki katoa, te tamariki he rangatira katoa kāore kē e pā atu i a rātou ringaringa, kāore rātou e tūkino ana i tēnei mea te tamariki. I te wā i tae mai te Pākehā, kātahi ka tā mata ki te whakaaro pai kare kei te raruraru tātou. Ngā tamariki mokopuna me whakatikatika ki a rātou i te kōrero a ngā mihingare me patua e koutou. Kāore e tika kia mahi pērā ngā tamariki mokopuna i tīmata mai i te wā i tae mai a tauiwi i tae mai ngā Pākehā ki tēnei whenua. Ka mutu!

This behavior came with the arrival of missionaries

from England. It did not exist in our culture, as children were revered. Children were considered chiefly and so we would never hit them or expose them to abuse. However, through colonization we experienced significant changes that have caused problem for us. Our children were chastised by order of the missionaries. It was not our way, but rather, it began with the arrival of Pākehā. That's it!

Colonial belief systems impacted Māori society in other major ways, as well. The imposition of the nuclear family unit has undermined Māori structures and consequently weakened traditional educational systems that were dependent on the whānau concept. As a unit, the nuclear family isolates Māori whānau from each other and from the nurturing, knowledge, and support provided within those structures.

The Land Wars instigated by the theft of Māori land were devastating to many hapū and iwi. Acts of legislation by settler governments saw the confiscation of lands of any iwi who were considered "rebels." Much of what land remained was created as Reserve lands and leased to settler families at minimal cost or put into individual ownership through various Native Land Acts. The idea of individual title and ownership of property, let alone women being treated as property, was completely foreign to Māori people. One intent of these acts of colonial oppression was to create instability within Māori structures as a mechanism by which to ensure the imposition of colonial rule through both violent and assimilatory means.

What is clear for Māori is that imposed colonial-centered values, beliefs, and worldviews have brought about major changes in the ways we relate to one another. Many of our beliefs in the sanctity of whānau have been undermined and replaced with practices that are both unhealthy and harmful. Living in a nuclear family structure has facilitated that process. The nuclear family as a supposedly "normal" family has both domesticated and privatized our ways of being. Living in houses that accommodate only immediate family has meant that the support and knowledge that comes with grandparent generations and wider whānau being present in a daily way is rarely experienced by our people. The idea of private relationships denies any form of collective responsibility and accountability. It is often asserted that what happens in one's home is "no one else's business." This provides an environment whereby violence and forms of abuse can be hidden and where it is difficult for others to intervene.

The nuclear family has served to undermine the collective relationships of whānau by creating an idea that the normal family is the colonial two parent and children unit that is separated culturally, economically, materially, and physically from the wider extended and tribal structures. The family, then, became defined by colonial gender beliefs whereby men were deemed the "head of the household" and "breadwinner," and women the "domestic servant" and sole child-rearer. These ways of believing what constituted a family actively undermined our collective relationships for many of our people.

One of the earliest moves to undermine whānau came with the establishment of Mission schools in 1816 and later the transfer to Native Schools in 1847. Linda Smith described Native Schools as "Trojan horses" within Māori communities. Native Schools promoted colonial ideas of family within Māori communities as the model of civilization. Missionaries preached the superiority of white men and actively denied Māori women's roles as *rangatira*, chiefly positions, within our tribal communities. The idea of God as white and male permeated all parts of colonial society both in ideas and in policy. The colonial view of women as chattels, as property of their husbands, was embedded in all colonial institutions including that of marriage; women were to succumb to the demands of their husbands and men had the right to beat their wives. The system of colonial rule was grounded in violence.

ACTIVITY:

Discuss and list ways in which colonial thinking has changed the roles of women and men within your People/nation.

_____

_____

_____

_____

What are some of the ways in which colonial settler schooling systems have impacted your People/nation?

_____

_____

_____

_____

The impact of colonization on our relationships is clearly seen in the current statistics related to domestic violence, family violence, and sexual violence within and amongst our people. There is no doubt that family and domestic violence has taken hold within our communities. Current data in the report "The Scale and Nature of Family Violence in New Zealand" highlights that Māori people are more likely to report all forms of domestic assault. Māori women are nearly twice as likely as non-Māori to report "intimate partner violence." It is also known that there is a high degree of violence within and upon our people that is never reported and therefore never appears in the statistics.

The Second Māori Taskforce on Whānau Violence, which was a taskforce of respected Māori people working in the area of family violence prevention and counseling, referred to whānau violence in our whānau, hapū, iwi, and urban communities as an epidemic. They used the term "epidemic" because of the "magnitude and serious nature" of such violence amongst Māori. This taskforce described whānau violence as both the violence amongst Māori whānau and also the violence that is imposed upon our whānau by the state. The impact of such violence on our people is devastating and is, in their view, a direct outcome of colonization.

It is clear that in order to deal with the impact of all forms of violent relationships within our whānau, within our Indigenous families, we must find ways to unlearn the behavior. We have to decolonize our relationships. We have to decolonize our practices towards one another. We have to stop abuse amongst our families, our whānau, our tribes, and our people.

In order to work towards decolonizing our relationships, it has become clear that we must explore key ideologies and practices through which the process of colonization imposed foreign values, language, and social structures upon our people. This has occurred on multiple levels in multiple ways, and therefore this chapter needs to be read alongside the other chapters in this book that explore a wide range of facets of our lives that need decolonizing attention.

One Māori social service provider organization, Tū Tama Wahine O Taranaki, grounds their work within the history of the Taranaki region. Tū Tama Wahine provides a range of counseling, mental health, and social services programs to support well-being for whānau. Being located within the Taranaki region means working alongside eight Iwi and a wide range of Māori who have come to the region from other tribal areas. The incidence of family violence amongst our people is disproportionately high, as is the case across Aotearoa. The history of Taranaki is one of invasion and confiscation. The impact of historical trauma shows itself daily amongst our people and tribes in the oppressive acts of successive national and local governments.

The name _Tū Tama Wahine_ was gifted by tribal elders Matarena Marjorie Rau-Kupa and Dr. Huirangi Waikerepuru. It is a name that affirms the position of women in Taranaki. Derived from the response of Taranaki women to the invasion of our people at Parihaka, it is a name that acknowledges and recognizes an act of historical trauma. It acknowledges the forced invasion, illegal arrests, and imprisonment of the men of Parihaka who were taken in chains on colonial ships to Dunedin in Te Waipounamu (referred to as the South Island), a great distance from their tribal homelands. The name derives from the proverb spoken by Te Whiti O Rongomai, a renowned leader of the Taranaki people and an advocate of peaceful resistance. The proverb *E tū tamawahine i te wāo te kore* was coined at the time of the invasion in acknowledgment of the role of our women to stand strong at the time of the removal of the men from the village. It may be translated as "Stand women in the time of the void," and relates to a state where women of the tribe took on all roles for the people in the absence of their male kin.

This history and tribal experience is the basis for the way in which Tū Tama Wahine was formed and now operates. It provides a foundation built on the words and actions of our ancestors. It promotes the central place of whānau. It promotes the philosophy of non-violent intervention. It affirms the place of women and children in the future of our people. These cultural beliefs and practices give those who work within the area of family violence a basis from which to act.

A report on family violence by Te Puni Kōkiri (Ministry of Māori Development) described Tū Tama Wahine's work:

> It is this historical commitment to whānau in a time of adversity, and an ethos of non-violence, which has shaped and guided Tū Tama Wahine o Taranaki. In today's contemporary world, staff see themselves as continuing the legacy of non-violence (that is, of stopping violence within whānau), caring for whānau and drawing practical strength and application from ngā mahi a ngā tūpuna me ngā tikanga o mua (from the deeds of ancestors and historical cultural practices).

In seeking whānau well-being, Tū Tama Wahine provides a range of programs and services that incorporate both individual and collective healing. One program focuses on providing a space for Māori men who are perpetrators of violence to come to terms with both their actions and what underpins their acts of violence against their whānau. The program is based upon traditional values and practices with a clear decolonizing intent.

We know that many of our people do not have access to Māori language and culture. We also know that to seek to understand our traditions we must also have an awareness of the depth of the impact of colonialism. We need to be able to identify those places and spaces within our culture that have themselves become reflective of colonial thinking. When dealing with whānau relationships, and in particular gendered relationships, Māori women activists have for some time cautioned us to be aware of the insidiousness of colonial beliefs about the roles of women. In the programs offered by Tū Tama Wahine, building such an awareness is critical. So too is developing a sense of both individual and collective responsibility amongst those Māori men who act in violent ways towards their own.

G. Tū Tika o Aro Tika

Tū Tika o Aro Tika is a program for Māori men who have been directed to attend by the courts under the 1995 Domestic Violence Act. The program has a strong Kaupapa Māori approach and uses a methodology that seeks to address violence from a Māori cultural worldview. It is structured around tikanga Māori, our cultural values and practices, which assist in facilitating learning and self-examination. The program is about bringing cultural understandings alongside the diverse experiences of the Māori men involved. There is an acknowledgment that the experiences of our men are diverse and varied as a direct result of colonial oppression in Taranaki.

The principles that inform the program are grounded in Māori knowledge. These principles are as follows:

Tikanga

Tikanga refers to our cultural practices. It is a set of beliefs, values, and principles that informs and guides actions and behaviors. It is also the application and use of cultural practices, which makes explicit the historical and contemporary relevance of tikanga. For example, the first session (Te Tīmatanga: The Beginning) includes the cultural practice of *whakatau* (a process of greeting) by which elders welcome the men to the program and *mihimihi* (introductions) are made by everyone. These cultural practices locate the program within a Māori context, and demonstrate and model the application of tikanga within the program.

The term *tikanga* is based on the word *tika* or what is correct. It is the practice of doing what is correct. Throughout the program, tikanga is presented as a valid, relevant, and correct way for participants to live and order their lives. Therefore, any deviation from doing what is right or correct, such as acts of violence, is a transgression of tikanga.

Whakapapa

Whakapapa relates to our genealogical lines. It defines, determines, and connects an individual with their whānau, hapū, and iwi. Whakapapa confirms an individual's membership in hapū and iwi and provides the means for learning about the history of their tupuna. Knowledge of whakapapa is important to engender a sense of pride and belonging through understanding the roots of one's heritage. Within the program, whakapapa is about participants knowing their identity and having pride in their identity as Māori because of their ancestral links.

Whānau

Whānau is the fundamental unit of Māori society into which a person is born and socialized. It is the means by which the rules and obligations around whānau functioning are conveyed, transmitted, and enforced. Within the program, much of the discussion focuses specifically on the importance of whānau and reinforces the centrality of whānau to Māori.

For some men, one of the causes of their violence could be attributed to a breakdown in their relationships with whānau. Participants are first shown how important the whānau is to the well-being of Māori and then they are shown ways in which they can attempt to take responsibility for their action and begin to re-establish the bonds that may have been broken as a result of their violence. Men are encouraged to look at the history of violence within their own whānau. This enables them to better understand

themselves through understanding what has occurred in their whānau.

For many of the men, their experiences of whānau have not always been positive, so key to this principle is an analysis and understanding of some of the reasons why violence occurs, how they gave expression to violence, and strategies to manage and change their behavior.

Whanaungatanga

Where whānau is the extended family relationship, *whanaungatanga* is a practice of how we relate to each other. Whanaungatanga embraces whakapapa and focuses on relationships. Whanaungatanga defines the relationships, obligations, and responsibilities between whānau members. Whanaungatanga within the program emphasizes the importance of whānau and whānau relationships. The men are asked to talk about their cultural identity—who they are; their whānau (immediate and extended); where they come from; their connections to the land; and how they are connected to others. It is about the knowledge the men have about themselves—their identity, their roles within their whānau, their knowledge of the Māori world, their tribal links, and their connectedness to all those things. Whanaungatanga is not just about the individual, but is about all those connections we each carry, and coming to understand those things. Whanaungatanga is not only about how people are related to each other, but it also encompasses how people relate to others, the way they express themselves, and the manner in which they interact. The principle of whanaungatanga is about constant building of relationships with your whānau and others, and with the land and environment to which we connect.

Taranakitanga

The term *Taranakitanga* literally encompasses all that it means to be of Taranaki descent and includes Taranaki protocols and practices, our ancestors, history, traditional stories, etc. The program draws on tribal knowledge to affirm participants' identity as Māori of Taranaki descent; it connects and links all to whānau, hapū, and iwi of the region. It highlights the historical deeds of our ancestors and links those deeds to a contemporary context. It identifies tribal focal points such as *maunga* and *marae* to reinforce a sense of pride and belonging in being Māori and being of Taranaki descent. The weaving of the history and stories of Taranaki fosters a sense of place, pride, and respect for what it means to belong to this land and its people, and to live amongst them. Through this principle are many opportunities to contextualize stories of Taranaki—its land and its people. The stories can relate to current times.

Mana

Mana is an external expression of achievement, power, and influence. In Māori terms we understand mana in a number of ways. It is that which is bestowed upon us at birth—in this sense it comes from whakapapa. Then there is the mana that comes from being descendants of tupuna, our ancestors, who are well-known for their actions and deeds. Some whānau are known for certain traits, abilities, and skills, which can bring mana to that particular whānau.

All people have mana. Mana can be enhanced by one's actions and achievements, and it influences the way in which people and groups conduct themselves.

Personal and group relationships are mediated and guided by the high value placed upon mana. To violate the mana of an individual is to violate the mana of the whole whānau, including your own inherent mana. Restoration of mana in a context of family violence is crucial. For men to take their rightful place as fathers, as partners, as grandparents, there needs to be a restoration of their mana so that they have a strong sense of who they are and the roles, responsibilities, and obligations that go with each of these positions in the whānau.

Personal Responsibility

Men taking personal responsibility for their actions is a key principle. Throughout the program the men are encouraged and challenged to stop blaming others within their whānau for what they do or have done. The key messages are that change is possible and that change starts with them once they own their behavior and stop blaming others. It is also a form of empowerment enabling them to embrace their actions and take full responsibility for themselves. Developing an awareness of the six aspects discussed above is key to taking personal responsibility and for seeing the collective impact of violent behaviors within whānau.

ACTIVITY:

Identify initiatives within your tribal nation that draw upon traditional knowledge and original instructions as the basis for healing in the area of family violence.

_____

_____

_____

_____

What are some of the key cultural practices and original instructions that can inform a process of decolonizing our relationships and support the prevention of family violence within your community?

_____

_____

_____

_____

The work of Tū Tama Wahine in this program focuses on sharing with Māori men knowledge of themselves, their people, their history, and their connections. Working from this point enables a grounding for understanding collective tribal relationships and a recognition that those around them also carry with them ancestors, histories, and connections. This awareness provides a basis from which to explore the impact of colonization on those relationships and collective responsibilities and to question the basis upon which these men have come to justify perpetrating violence against other family members.

To undertake such decolonizing work requires us to be aware of who we are, where we are from, and our presence in this world and on Indigenous lands as reflections of our ancestors, and to come to understand that for Māori any form of abuse on any of our whānau is an abuse of generations past and generations to come. We must come to know that to be healthy as a people we must be healthy within our whānau—in our relationships to all within our whānau and more widely to all our relations. We can no longer accept Western colonial family structures as the models for our way of living, but must return to relationships that carry with them collective caring and obligations that affirm that we are all related; affirm that we carry the status and dignity of our ancestors and that we pass that dignity to future generations yet to be born; affirm our right to be Māori, our right to be Indigenous, our right to be who we are fully on our own lands.

That is the work that is ahead for our people if we are to intervene in the occurrence of family violence and child abuse that plagues our people, and to prevent this behavior in the future. What is clear is that the approaches that have been taken by successive colonial governments in this country have done nothing to transform this context, and the reality is that they never will as they have no interest in our people affirming our language, our culture, and our cultural identity. The work remains with us as Indigenous Peoples globally to decolonize and reassert those cultural ways of being that will bring well-being to this and future generations.

Ehara taku toa i te toa takitahi, he toa takitini kē

My accomplishments are not mine alone, but are those of many.

H. Glossary

Aotearoa: Land of the long white cloud: The Māori name for New Zealand

Hapū : Groupings of extended families (linked through common ancestors, sub-grouping of Iwi); Pregnant

Harakeke: Flax plant

Iwi: Nation (linked through common ancestor); Bones

Kaumātua: Elders

Kaupapa Māori: Māori philosophies, Māori approaches, and Māori ways of being

Mana: Status/power/influence

Māori: Indigenous People of Aotearoa; Pure; Normal

Marae: Communal gathering place

Matua: Father, uncles, or men of the same generation within the whānau

Maunga: Mountain

Mihimihi: Greetings

Moko: Permanent cultural form of skin carving

Mokopuna: Grandchild

Papatūānuku: Mother Earth

Pēpeha: Proverbial saying of introduction

Pono: Faith/belief

Pūrākau: Traditional story

Rarohenga: The underworld

Tamariki: Children

Tāngata Wenua: People of the Land

Tāniko: A form of weaving

Taranaki: A region located on the West Coast of Te Ika ā Māui (North Island)

Taranakitanga: Practices and protocols related to the Taranaki region

Te Ao Mārama: The world of light

Te Reo Māori: Māori language

Te tatau pounamu: The greenstone door

Te Whare Tangata: The house of the People; Womb

Tika: Correct/right

Tikanga: Protocols/cultural practices

Tupuna: Ancestor

Whaea: Mother, aunties, and other women of the same generation within the whānau

Whakatau: Cultural process of greeting/welcome

Whakapapa: Cultural genealogical relationships

Whānau: Extended family

Whanaungatanga: Relationships

Whenua: Land and Afterbirth

I. Resources

Balzer, R., D. Haimona, M. Henare, and V. Matchitt. "Māori Family Violence in Aotearoa." A Report Prepared for Te Puni Kōkiri. Wellington, NZ, 1997.

Deloria, V. Jr. "Comfortable Fictions and the Struggle for Turf: An Essay Review of the Invented Indian: Cultural Fictions and Government Policies." *Native and Academics: Researching and Writing about American Indians.* Ed. Devon A. Mihesuah. Lincoln: University of Nebraska Press, 1998.

Grennell, D., and A. Pivac. "Amokura–Indigenous Innovations." 10th Australasian Conference on Child Abuse and Neglect. Wellington, NZ, Feb. 15, 2006.

Kruger, T., et al. *Transforming Whānau Violence—A Conceptual Framework.* Updated version of the report from the former Second Māori Taskforce on Whānau Violence. 2nd Edition. Wellington, NZ: Ministry of Health, 2004.

Lievore, D., and P. Mayhew (with assistance from Elaine Mossman). "*The Scale and Nature of Family Violence in New Zealand: A Review and Evaluation of Knowledge.*" Crime and Justice Research Centre & Centre for Social Research and Evaluation, Ministry of Social Development, Victoria. University of Wellington, 2007.

Mikaere, A. *The Balance Destroyed: The Consequences for Māori Women of the Colonisation of Tikanga Māori.* Unpublished Master of Jurisprudence thesis. University of Waikato, Hamilton, NZ, 1995.

Pihama, L., K. Jenkins, and A. Middleton. *"Te Rito" Action Area 13 Literature Review: Family Violence Prevention for Māori Research Report.* Prepared for the Ministry of Health and Te Rito Māori Advisory Committee. International Research Institute for Māori & Indigenous Education (IRI), University of Auckland. Auckland, NZ: Auckland Uniservices Limited, 2003: 35.

Pitman, M. "The Māori Experience." The Proceedings of Rape: Ten Years' Progress? An Interdisciplinary Conference. Ed. J. Broadmore, et al. Wellington, NZ: DSAC 1996: 301.

Smith, L. T. "Is 'Taha Māori' in Schools the Answer to Māori School Failure?" *Ngā Kete Wānanga : Māori Perspectives of Taha Māori.* Ed. G. H. Smith. Auckland, NZ: Auckland College of Education, 1986: 3–66.

———. *Decolonising Methodologies: Research and Indigenous Peoples.* London: Zed Books Ltd., 1999.

———. "Māori Women: Discourses, Projects and Mana Wahine." *Women and Education in Aotearoa 2.* Ed. S. Middleton and A. Jones. Wellington, NZ: Bridget Williams Books, 1999.

Te Puni Kōkiri. *Arotake Tūkino Whānau Literature Review on Family Violence.* Wellington, NZ: Government Printer, 2010.

———. *Rangahau Tūkino Whānau: Māori Research Agenda on Family Violence.* Wellington, NZ: Government Printer, 2010.

Wilson, D. *Family Violence Intervention Guidelines: Māori and Family Violence.* Māori Advisory Committee, Ministry of Health, Family Violence Project, School of Health Studies, Wellington, NZ: Massey University, n.d.

Documentary

Te Taonga o Taku Ngākau. Māori Television. Rose Rangimarie Pere, Māori and Indigenous Analysis Ltd., Auckland, NZ, 2008.

Chapter 13

REMAKING BALANCE
DECOLONIZING GENDER RELATIONS IN INDIGENOUS COMMUNITIES

Chaw-win-is (Ruth Ogilvie)

A. Introduction

B. Gender Oppression at the Hands of Colonialism

C. *Heshook-ish Tsawalk* (Everything Is One) and *Iisaak* (Respect)

D. Examples of Patriarchal Oppression

E. Decolonization Is a Program of Action

F. *Witwaak:* Traditional Conceptions and Current Realities

G. Thinking About Tradition Critically

H. Remaking Balance

I. Learning Through Stories

J. Conclusion

K. Glossary

L. Resources

A. Introduction

This chapter discusses decolonizing traditional Indigenous gender roles and remaking balance within our communities. Before I begin I will share a family chant and situate myself appropriately. Fundamental to the life of Nuu-chah-nulth *witwaak* (warriors—the singular for "warrior" is *wiiuk)* is preparation. It is more than just physical and more than strategies and tactics in times of war. Preparation includes physical, mental, emotional, and spiritual readiness. In seeking spiritual support Nuu-chah-nulth witwaak would often *tsiikshitl.* To tsiikshitl is to chant/pray with a *khuukhmin* (rattle), humbly asking *Naas* (All Creation/ Creator) for strength and spiritual guidance. Specific chants/prayers belong to specific families or *muhdii* (house or longhouse family). Before he began any endeavor of significance, Too-tah, my eldest known ancestor, would tsiikshitl to start things off in a good way. As a descendant of Too-tah, I choose to begin here with a translation as it holds meaning for our family by reminding us to be strong and clear-minded at all times, be they full of conflict or in a state of peace. It reminds us to readily accept our circumstances and to be prepared for any challenges that we may need to confront:

Peace and war,

I'm all for peace,

Peace and quiet.

When the world is calm,

I am for the world.

When it gets ugly

I'm prepared for War,

I am for the world

I'm all for Peace and War.

It is important that I situate myself in this discussion of traditional roles and gender in a contemporary Nuu-chah-nulth context. My name is *Chaw-win-is-uxsup*, which means, "Boulder on the Beach Woman," and I am a granddaughter of *Cha-chin-sun-up*, "Putting the Land in Order," the current *tyee wiiuk*, or highest ranked warrior of Checlesaht. My grandfather and I have roots in both Checlesaht and Tla-o-qui-aht, both of which are located at the northern end of what is now known as Vancouver Island, British Columbia.

In addition to these ancestral connections, I have a personal history of being outspoken against many political and economic initiatives undertaken by my home communities. It is my belief that many of the bureaucratized processes engaged in by our current leaders, such as the current British Columbia Treaty Process (BCTC) and various fishing and rights litigation, work only to undermine our traditional governance capacities and responsibilities. Some people would characterize me as a "troublemaker," while others in the community feel that I give voice to their unspoken and valid concerns about the co-optive actions of many of our leaders. I have experienced lateral and sexualized violence as a result of speaking out against the BCTC and corruption in elected leadership. This disclosure is important any time an Indigenous woman acts politically or changes personally. Her credibility is questioned and she may become a target for lateral or physical violence.

ACTIVITY:

Are there differences in the way women and men leaders are perceived and treated in your community? If so, what are they?

_____

_____

_____

_____

Is it safe to be an outspoken woman in your community? If so, how are outspoken women supported? If not, how are outspoken women treated negatively and who benefits from the silencing or suppressing of outspoken women?

Next I will address some of the issues facing Nuu-chah-nulth women today in relation to our traditional roles and positions.

B. Gender Oppression at the Hands of Colonialism

The women of Tla-o-qui-aht and Checlesaht are confronted with internalized oppression and sexualized violence every day, from the more overt instances of rape, incest, and beatings to less overt oppression like silencing. These acts of internalized violence are a direct reflection of persistent colonial and patriarchal conditions and influences. This means that colonialism is rooted in a society controlled and led by men. Without decolonizing, thereby unraveling these influences from within our communities, they continue to dominate the lives of both Indigenous women and men.

In a Nuu-chah-nulth context, all of these colonial forces have acted against our people, and our reactions have been consistently internalized. Although Nuu-chah-nulth people have not been in contact with the European settlers for as long as other Indigenous Peoples, like others in Canada and the United States we have felt the full brunt of colonial imposition and law, especially over the last 150 years. All members of Nuu-chah-nulth families are survivors of the Indian residential school experience.

For example, the Alberni Indian Residential School, located in Nuu-chah-nulth territory, was particularly notorious for its cases of physical and sexual abuse, but it is important to remember that these acts of individual abuse cannot be our only concern. As heinous as those crimes were, we cannot ignore the removal of Nuu-chah-nulth children from their families and the breakdown in personal, family, and community relationships that followed. Not only were traditional social practices and political institutions disrupted, but also in many cases Indigenous people were prevented from being able to develop healthy relationships with one another. This has had devastating effects on personal and community well-being that continues today. Today, as in the past, abuse is the most overt expression of these dysfunctional relations. We must also consider the subtler implications of colonialism, for they are what is underneath our attitudes and our actions towards one another and to this land. To use a Nuu-chah-nulth metaphor, Wickaninnish says that our people are *hoquotisht* (our canoe is tipped over) and we are disoriented, we have lost our way.

C. *Heshook-ish Tsawalk* (Everything Is One) and *Iisaak* (Respect)

The losses we have experienced make it difficult for Indigenous men and women to emerge with any clear sense of how to live according to Nuu-chah-nulth teachings and laws. Many of these teachings and laws are simple yet very important and rather complex. A foundational Nuu-chah-nulth principle is *heshook-ish tsawalk,* which literally means "everything is one." Another foundational principle is *iisaak*, or "respect." Together, heshook-ish tsawalk and iisaak provide a strong basis for how to act in the world, with respect for all creation and the knowledge of unity and interconnection. On a broader scale, if our current leaders took these principles seriously, we would not be overfishing, or overharvesting within our territories, and we would take our responsibilities seriously as well. Actualized in our practices, recognition of unity of, and respect for, all things requires that we ensure the sustainability of our territories. It means that we must also stop non-Indigenous people from disrespecting and exploiting our lands as well. It means that we treat each other with the same reverence we demonstrate when uttering these words: Heshook-ish tsawalk and iisaak.

Our conceptions of unity and respect have been shattered by the way colonizers have mistreated us, our lands, the animals, and all that we hold sacred. In Nuu-chah-nulth life this plays out in a number of ways. For example, the *ayts-tuu-thlaa* is a coming-of-age ceremony that teaches a woman her responsibility to family, community, and land. It also teaches the men in the community what their role is in relation to the women—who are called "givers of life"— that they are vital to community health and well-being. Connected to this teaching is the value of mothers. I have been taught that women are the foundation of our muhdii (house)—if they are content and healthy, then the rest of the family will be as well. I will add that "givers of life" not only means women who have or will have children. Women are givers of life in that they live and work towards solutions, settling business, and prioritizing needs in our communities. A Nuu-chah-nulth example of this is during the whale hunt, when often men were gone for weeks or months at a time. It was the women who knew what the needs of the community were and it was incumbent upon the men to directly consult with them.

Eurocentric patriarchal thinking sends a different message. In Europe and later Canada, women were regarded as the property of men and were not recognized politically or legally as persons until the early twentieth century. Today, our people live in confusion because patriarchal power is legitimized, despite decades of liberal feminist activism. We often mimic these behaviors uncritically within our own communities. Yet, because we have not completely lost our old ways, this all leads to a clash of colonial and Indigenous worldviews.

The Stop the Violence March took place in May 2006 in response to the brutal raping and beating of a young woman from Tla-o-qui-aht. The assault occurred just two weeks after her family held an *ayts-tuu-thlaa* ceremony for her. The women of Tla-o-qui-aht were outraged and decided to take action, organizing a march within their community to demand the stop of violence. As young people, each from different Nuu-chah-nulth communities, we took up our responsibility to carry this message throughout all of the fifteen Nuu-chah-nulth nations. This march was a living example of *haa-huu-pah* (sacred teaching/sacred stories) that evolved directly from the political organizing of the women of Tla-o-qui-aht and spread throughout our nations.

D. Examples of Patriarchal Oppression

How this all plays out in Nuu-chah-nulth territory is certainly detrimental to the overall health and well-being of our communities. I wish I could say brutal rapes were uncommon occurrences, but the sad reality is that they are not. Just a couple of weeks before several peers and I embarked on the Nuu-chah-nulth Stop the Violence March in 2006 in response to the rape of a young woman of Tla-o-qui-aht, another young woman was beaten by her boyfriend. They were both from the same Nuu-chah-nulth community. She joined us on the march with her head shaven by medical personnel when she needed stitches, and with her broken arm in a cast. Clearly, her participation in the march expressed her desire to move out and away from this place of internalized oppression and return to a place of hope.

The fact that these acts of internalized violence can still occur in Nuu-chah-nulth communities that are regarded by many as being "culturally strong" is very indicative of the prevalence of patriarchal values and the relative weakness of our culture at present to defend our most vulnerable community members. Therefore it is incumbent upon all of us to regenerate the ceremonies and teachings that show us how to live in reverence for all life and to have respect for women as well as respect towards one another; *hishiimstawalk* (the people are one). For example, after consulting with an older relative about the march, he insisted that we "give back" our teachings about women through the ayts-tuu-thlaa. He explained it was important to relay who we are and what our values are as Nuu-chah-nulth Peoples according to our original principles, and in that we would find that *traditionally* violence against women was never tolerated.

ACTIVITY:

Is gender violence common in your community? What forms does it take?

_____

_____

_____

_____

Thanks to anti-colonial intellectual Franz Fanon, we understand that decolonization must be a foundational layer in developing a movement towards freedom and justice for colonized peoples. But what form does decolonization for Nuu-chah-nulth People take? In the broader socio-political scheme we see that there are Indigenous People who participate in mainstream party politics and work within the confines of state-centric legal and political processes, including court cases, current treaty negotiations here in British Columbia, and economic development ventures in which we are sitting at the table with governments as "stakeholders," not as sovereign nations. Others pursue social programs and money, framing our problems primarily in socio-economic terms. To date, most of these processes have not achieved even their own modest goals of socio-economic equality, land claims, or Aboriginal rights and title recognition. These mainstream efforts have succeeded only in reinforcing the status quo within Indigenous communities.

My focus here is on a more radical program of decolonization, specifically located *outside* of state-centric processes, in an attempt to address the issues of internalized oppression, sexualized violence, and patriarchal gender relations within Nuu-chah-nulth communities. As Glen Coulthard writes, "The best of today's Indigenous movements articulate a far more substantive relationship between identity and freedom insofar as they are attempting to *critically reconstruct* and deploy previously disparaged traditions and practices in a manner that consciously seeks to prefigure a lasting alternative to the colonial present" [*emphasis added*]. For example, when we organized the Stop the Violence March in 2006, we consciously did so outside of state funding or support. Further, we did not go into the communities as counselors, offering our services in order to conduct anti-violence workshops. We believed those Western approaches to be highly individualized and certainly not grounded in Nuu-chah-nulth ways of healing. We simply went to each community abiding by our law to "never take more than what you need," bringing camping gear and enough money for food and gas for boats. We made the decision to do this in an attempt to break free of the colonial restraints that are often attached to funding and "help."

ACTIVITY:

What do you know about your community's traditional roles and responsibilities? How have patriarchal values impacted these traditional roles?

_____

_____

_____

With the idea of gender balance in mind, how might your traditions need to change?

_____

_____

_____

_____

E. Decolonization Is a Program of Action

If Indigenous Peoples recognize that decolonization is a program of action that can both unravel the negative effects of colonialism and restore the values and principles of our ancestors, then we must focus our energies on the social formation of our societies, including the decolonization of gender roles. If the women in my family are calling for the remaking of balance between men and women, then it is my responsibility to take up that task for the sake of my children and family. In this chapter I focus on my own Nuu-chah-nulth communities. I will refer to the Tla-o-qui-aht and Checlesaht communities more closely as my Nuu-chah-nulth family protocol requires of me.

The method or model moves from self, to family, to community.

Here are some present-day examples that I will examine more closely with a critical eye on our gendered traditional roles. The task of decolonization under our current conditions may require that we de-gender our traditional roles as we remake them. It is often expected that women's roles are defined within the home fires—in other words, cooking, cleaning, and child rearing are seen as nurturing roles and appropriate for women only. This narrow perception of a much broader term has been drilled into our families through residential schools where boys and girls were segregated and made to work strictly within what the church thought was appropriate work for boys and girls; girls learned domestic chores and boys learned about trades. It is because of this that I prefer to speak of "remaking" rather than "restoring" balance through a process of critical engagement of traditional Nuu-chah-nulth values and roles. Both of these examples come from a recent proliferation of *nuushitl* (potlatch or gathering), in which the roles of chief, beachkeeper, warrior, and spokesman for the chiefs are passed on. Currently, it is being taught that traditionally these roles were passed on to firstborn sons in our family. Some elders remind us that it was not always the firstborn son who assumed the responsibilities of a role or position. For a variety of reasons, these roles were passed on to "the most capable" person in the family.

In traditional Nuu-chah-nulth society all young people were raised with certain fundamental values and principles; however, those who were expected to assume greater community responsibilities were given very specific teachings to prepare them for their positions. Even if the firstborn son was given specific teachings, he may not have been the most capable. A younger sibling might be found to possess the appropriate qualities necessary to lead, including generosity, fair-mindedness, and humility. In other cases, the heir to a particular role might be inappropriate because he lived an unhealthy life or acted disrespectfully to others. We have *haa-huu-pah* (teaching stories, sacred histories) about chiefs who were greedy and unkind; each faced extreme consequences including death for this kind of negligence towards the *muschim* (people) and the land. Unlike today, leadership in a traditional context was accepted as being more about a serious responsibility than it was about prestige, popularity, or power.

ACTIVITY:

How were leaders generally selected in your traditional society? What traits were looked for in a leader? Were there exceptions to the general rules and processes? If so, under what conditions would exceptions be made?

_____

_____

_____

_____

A common example of the dilemmas currently faced by traditional leaders is as follows: A Nuu-chah-nulth man would like to pass on his position of leadership to his son. These traditional positions of leadership require commitment and time, as well as proper mental, spiritual, physical, and emotional health. Unfortunately, his son struggles with an alcohol addiction and unhealthy relationships with women. In other words, he is not ready or able. As tradition currently dictates, the leader must ask that the next in line take up that position for his brother. In many cases there may be no more sons and so a daughter is then asked to *hold* the position until a grandson is born and then ready to take on the traditional role of leadership in the family. In other words, this traditional leader's daughter is considered only on a temporary basis. Why? A woman in a similar situation said to me, "Today, the men at home only respect other men in leadership—they won't listen to me, even though this goes against our teachings about *hakuum* (respected women, leaders)." I explained that I understood the rampant violence and everyday sexism to be a deterrent for her to take this on.

She explained further, "Not only that, but what makes me not good enough to take this position on, instead of merely holding it—is it just because I am a woman?" Apparently it is. She went on to explain that currently in Nuu-chah-nulth communities there are a few women who hold positions of leadership until such a time that men are ready to assume the roles, but in holding these positions they are not empowered and are often dismissed or forgotten. I agreed. In another community, however, when the *tyee hawiilth* (hereditary chief, *ha'wiih* is the plural of this term) decided to pass his position on to his daughter, she refused to simply hold it until an appropriate man came along. As I have already indicated about preparation, appropriate men do not just come along; they are raised. In the absence of formal child-rearing practices that prepare our youth, she has emerged as the most capable person. It is encouraging that her family has decided to back her up.

Another example relates to the passing on of the role of tyee wiiuk (head chief warrior). For six generations our family has *earned* the position of tyee wiiuk in Checlesaht. As far as I know, witwaak have always been men. My grandfather, Cha-chin-sun-up, was the last one to earn that position, and in April of 2008, he decided it was time to pass on this position to one of his sons at the nuushitl. My uncle was at first hesitant to commit to this new role, and I was also skeptical, as he rarely participated in Nuu-chah-nulth ceremonies or gatherings. A recent conversation I had with him added more details to my understanding that are relevant here.

During a two-hour discussion with my uncle, we both raised concerns that we needed to deal with outside of the more public family meetings. I asked my uncle what Cha-chin-sun-up said about him taking on that position. He told me Cha-chin-sun-up reassured him that it "is just a title," that he didn't have to do anything with it. Although my grandfather may have been trying to alleviate some of the pressure for my uncle, I explained that I did not agree that it was just a title, that all the haa-huu-pah he had passed on to me about wiiuk meant more than symbolic representations. They represent a way of living and acting within communities and on the land. My uncle appreciated me explaining the history behind witwaak—that they are responsible for protecting the most vulnerable of our communities and for enforcing Nuu-chah-nulth laws.

As the conversation proceeded he explained further as to why he was experiencing conflicted feelings about taking on this role of tyee wiiuk. Underneath it all he was angry and frustrated with the silence around unresolved physical and sexual abuse in the family. I found out that recently another woman relative confided in him that she had been abused by a male relative as a child. This woman did not want to participate in the nuushitl because she did not want to run into this person for fear of further trauma and shame. There it was. The truth in my uncle's story is one of contradictions. It illuminated the fact that there are still women in our family who have been abused and are afraid of the consequences of coming forward about it.

He explained to me that as a man, he experiences rage and anger and does not feel that he is empowered to protect the family today. It struck me then to tell him that as tyee wiiuk, he does have the power to remove anyone from the nuushitl who is abusing any substances or any people, difficult as that may be. We both realized the potential for healing this might have for family members who have been living with the pain and silence of their abuse for years, some for thirty years or more. I explained this was the reason why tyee wiiuk could not just be a title, but must be an active role for justice and balance in our community.

My uncle explained that he felt better after realizing that the values and commitments of being wiiuk are consistent with his personal values of how his father taught him to be a "good man." I then brought up the fact that he must choose, in consultation with our chief Hyuushistulth, ten warriors to stand with him. I asked my uncle how he felt about some of the men who were up for the wiiuk positions. He replied, "Well some of these guys I wouldn't want to back me up. They are either addicted to alcohol or drugs, or wife-beaters." I asked if he thought that following tradition, in this case when wiiuk can only be men, made sense to him. He said, "If this is the culture, then I don't want anything to do with it!" I explained that I felt similarly, that I understood that focusing on gender rather than capability is a problem that our family needs to deal with. There are women in our family who are physically fit, educated, and actively decolonizing. At this point in time, these women are the ones most capable to back him up, even physically.

Near the end of our discussion, we considered that in order to properly heal, our family must address the issue of internalized oppression and sexual violence in an upfront, honest, and safe manner. We considered how it might affect everyone if we empowered the witwaak to prevent abusers from coming to the nuushitl—to physically block them and thus publicly shame them, and to make the behavior known and demonstrate by our actions that abuse is not okay and that we will not tolerate it in our family.

Now I must be clear here: people in our communities who have abused often have done so as a result of experiencing abuse themselves as an aftereffect of colonialism, especially those abused in residential school. This does not mean, however, that these individuals should be allowed to continue abusing or that they are somehow not responsible (although this often gets confused in our communities). This is where witwaak can be utilized to enforce our laws at the request of their chiefs and the people, especially at the level of the collective community. This, I am saying, is a place to begin. For my uncle, becoming our tyee witwaak is both empowering and full of possibility for change. I could see in the way he carried himself that day that he was relieved to see some light being shed on the issue of internalized oppression and violence and that he could have a positive impact on the lives of the women and men in our family.

ACTIVITY:

Do women in your community feel unsafe attending ceremonies or community events for fear of abuse? If you are a man answering this question and do not know, ask the women of your community. Do your current leaders take action to protect the most vulnerable in your community? If not, how could people in your community begin to address these issues?

_____

_____

_____

I understand that many of our people are affected by psychological, physical, mental, and spiritual colonialism and respond with token acknowledgments while ignoring real problems that can render our traditions as meaningless symbols of a mystical past. However, there are young women in our family who are strong, physically fit, and actively decolonizing their minds, bodies, and spirits. The fact that these positions are still being handed down to men who are unprepared (or to women to hold until an appropriate man is ready) is not only an indication of the unhealthy state of our communities and our social and political institutions, but also an indication that we must have the courage to challenge our traditions when necessary. Furthermore, we must not discourage critical reflection, especially among our young people who bear the burden of remaking balance in our communities.

Next I will describe what the Nuu-chah-nulth concept of witwaak is, generally. I intend to demonstrate, without divulging too much culturally specific information, a rudimentary understanding of the fundamental principles of being witwaak, and how they are connected to *huupukwanum* (Nuu-chah-nulth governance), and being *Quu'asminaa* (Indigenous or real human being). Second, I will articulate the issues in which gender currently dominates our attitudes towards roles within community, like witwaak. I will then conclude by proposing some ideas about what remaking balance in our communities means and might look like.

ACTIVITY:

Did divisions of labor between men and women make sense traditionally? Were there exceptions?

_____

_____

_____

_____

Do the traditional divisions of labor make sense now? Why or why not? How critical is truth-telling in questioning tradition?

_____

_____

_____

_____

F. *Witwaak*: Traditional Conceptions and Current Realities

In Nuu-chah-nulth territory, we still have access to our haa-huu-pah about women and men and the roles we held within our society. These haa-huu-pah are gleaned from the oral histories of our elders. Personally, I rely on my family elders who are often aunts, uncles, and my grandfather Cha-chin-sun-up. There are also many others who are not Nuu-chah-nulth who have influenced my understanding about these roles as well. The common link seems to be an underlying attitude of *common sense* and practicality, as well as a general understanding that *taking action* is fundamental to being wiiuk. This goes to the heart of what it means to be Indigenous—to be from a particular place on this land. Our actions must make sense in our homelands. What I describe here will not be exactly what you experience in your homelands, but we share many common traditions along with the experiences of colonization. If there is to be any aspect of our traditions that does not change, let it be a commitment to the land and respectful and reciprocal relationships with all our relatives.

A wiiuk is the culmination of the things a warrior does and the actions a warrior takes, not necessarily a warrior's gender. Witwaak were members of our society who faced their fears through constant ritual and practice (self-discipline), and they did so *unflinchingly*. This does not mean they do not feel fear, but that they willingly confront their fears, preparing themselves for any kind of conflict. Witwaak were an integral part of our communities. In the past there were no debates as there are today regarding the relevance and purpose of the witwaak in our societies. They worked with the *ha'wiih* (hereditary chiefs, respected people) to ensure the *hahuuthlii* (roughly translates to all the lands, waters, and resources within a ha'wiih's area of responsibility) and its Peoples were secure and they could live on the land for generations. At its root, wiiuk means to be brave or courageous; it means facing your fears. This requires that witwaak prepare themselves daily through physical and spiritual practices and in this way make themselves ready for whatever state the world is in, whether it is at peace or at war.

My great-grandfather Kaynaiya was pierced with a spear through the skin of his back in an initiation ceremony so he could become tyee wiiuk. The spear pierced the skin laterally through both sides and over-top his spine. At each end of the spear two witwaak grabbed on and held Kaynaiya steady as he danced around both fires of the longhouse. Cha-chin-sun-up remembers his father showing him the scars and hearing about this initiation ceremony. This ceremony was important to demonstrate his unflinching willingness to take on this responsibility as tyee wiiuk—to show that he could be relied on to fight to the death, endure great physical danger, and continue to abide by the laws of the hahuuthlii and to protect the muschim. Witwaak like Kaynaiya were strong mentally and strong physically, disciplined and rooted in the ways of the hahuuthlii. Although Kaynaiya was initiated and trained to be wiiuk, he did not engage in actual warfare with other nations. By Kaynaiya's time, paper and verbal negotiations with the colonialists became the struggle of the day.

This haa-huu-pah shows us how the witwaak carried themselves by demonstrating love, courage, strength, discipline, and honor, as well as always showing sensitivity to be willing to adjust their battle strategies to the present needs of the hahuuthlii and the muschim. From the haa-huu-pah I have gathered from my own family and community, the witwaak were usually men. There are no stories that have emerged around women witwaak that I have found. It is important to note that there is still no evidence to suggest that women cannot not be witwaak. Witwaak means living in a way that is pushing through fear, acting in a way that holds up the collective well-being of the community, and supporting the most vulnerable of our communities. None of these are exclusively male traits.

During our family's most recent nuushitl, I was assigned by my uncle to be witwaak, to provide security alongside the men at the nuushitl. I agreed without hesitation. As I stepped onto the floor to protect the sacred space on which the business was being done, I realized how much I had to work at being taken seriously. Men and women appeared to be uncomfortable with me, but children appeared to be quite open and young women appeared hopeful *for their own sense of place.* By the end of the day, those who were not accepting my presence as witwaak began to shift their attitudes, in part because I had proven myself on that day to take this role seriously and to act with dignity and iisaak. The men I worked with, the other witwaak, did not flinch either, but instead treated me as an equal. In order for women to take on these roles, both women and men have to rid themselves of many old ideas. This requires effort individually (as with this book) and in community. This is the question that applies to my family and our fulfillment of our roles and responsibilities. Can we truly afford to ignore a whole segment of relatively healthy, able, and willing warriors and leaders simply because they are women? It seems that today we have become comfortable with the status quo, that the internalized oppression has become normalized. If our situation warranted, I doubt that we would be so quick to tell women to stay in the kitchen and to put down a weapon. Currently we are lulled into thinking that our situations are not desperate, that we are not at war. This is dangerous in that what may actually underpin these assumptions is the desire to assuage our own guilt for not acting as warriors, for not acting on behalf of and in accordance to our laws in protecting our hahuuthlii and one another.

ACTIVITY:

What was the role of the warrior in your community? What was the name used in your language? What does it mean?

_____

_____

_____

_____

Why has the role of the warrior been cast aside? Is it no longer truly relevant? Or has it been re-cast as a soldier for our own colonizing nations?

_____

_____

_____

_____

Can women fulfill these roles? If yes, why? If not, why not?

_____

_____

_____

_____

G. Thinking About Tradition Critically

Tradition with rigid gender roles is one thing and we are warranted in re-examining their utility, but many have also observed the distortion of our traditions within a colonial context. Traditional beliefs often go unexamined as to their relevance in today's context. For example, we rarely ask whether we are in fact upholding a right-wing Christian ethic about women's roles rather than a traditional view of women and their place in community. This leaves women constrained, as it has with most of the women in my family. Today we adopt Western patriarchal attitudes towards leadership and sometimes we attach tradition to these notions of leadership and roles. For example, I remember an elder telling me that it was not traditional for women to speak or be involved in politics. This was *after* I had spoken publicly at a small event about the issue of violence in our communities. He explained that politics are too powerful for women to withstand and that the women stood behind the men who could withstand this powerful energy. Wow—I thought, then maybe I am in the wrong line of work! Joking aside, there have been many times when I have been "kindly" advised that I should not speak publicly, but I am aware that most of it has been because I am speaking out about something unjust. Yet I notice it is okay for women to speak when they are saying something nice. This has certainly been the case in Nuu-chah-nulth territory as both our men and women have

been influenced by the dominant society's culture, and religious and political institutions. Recently, a Nuu-chah-nulth woman took the floor at a tribal council meeting and spoke out passionately articulating the need for our elected leadership to stop ignoring the issue of violence against women in our communities. The fact is she had to take the floor because there was no space made on the agenda to address this pressing issue.

We need to think about tradition critically because of our current reality. Specifically, there are many forms of abuse of power connected to tradition that happen *because of colonialism and its effects*. The African-American scholar bell hooks writes, "In this society, power is commonly equated with domination and control over people or things." hooks further urges us to rethink our notions of power in forms that are non-domineering. This is necessary because we have adopted an imperialist notion of power, which centers on human beings and negates all other forms of life. A Western notion of power is also structured hierarchically, in which there are humans who are more human than others, and contrary to the principle of heshook-ish tsawalk. For example, when colonizers first arrived in Nuu-chah-nulth territory they declared the land as *terra nullius* or empty land, equating Nuu-chah-nulth people with animals. According to the colonial worldview of that time, Nuu-chah-nulth people were unworthy of even making a pretense of a treaty. As hooks reminds us, a Western notion of power depends on the subjugation of some humans over others, and over all non-humans and things. Internally, we mimic these processes through culture and tradition if we do not actively decolonize. For example, with the instance of witwaak, what is it that is fundamentally principled about witwaak for us to employ in today's context? "Whoever is the most capable" does not mean gender was or has to be the focus; it means that the most appropriate person is whoever can get the job done, do the work, or take the action that is required. Simply picking men for the sake of gender can potentially disempower these positions of leadership and law-keeping in our communities, because the people they choose are not ready or prepared to take the right actions that are required of them. It goes against the idea that commonsense thinking underlies our culture and ways. Commonsense thinking is tied to practicality, and practicality is connected to community and is what keeps a community working together towards balance.

ACTIVITY:

What are the challenges to thinking about tradition critically? How do critical insights about tradition affect the way we act? Why is this important?

_____

_____

_____

_____

H. Remaking Balance

If we begin with the premise that our contemporary worldviews are indeed jagged, where our two worlds are colliding, as Leroy Little Bear has stated, we must assume that we cannot completely restore traditions. Therefore, any claim to complete traditional authenticity should be met with skepticism. Second, tradition is tradition because it makes sense in a particular place and time. This is not to say that tradition can never be abusive or domineering, as recent history shows us it can. Our challenge then is to revive the good, let go of the bad, and forge ahead in a way that makes sense in this place and in this time. The reality of colonization today demands more people and resources than our people may have ever previously deployed. We are facing extreme events on the planet,

the depletion of oil, and the global desire for corporations to get their last fix of resources such as oil, diamonds, gas, and water before they are depleted. We need to become healthy, to overcome these obstacles of internalized oppression so we can fight these broader struggles as well.

Traditional interpretations of witwaak or gender roles in Nuu-chah-nulth societies are not sufficient by themselves to remake balance between the men, women, and youth of our communities. They are not because an effort to decolonize means we must be willing to wipe from our eyes the anthropological lens that dictates our current reality. Specifically, this means we must see our traditions as creations of living and present Quu'asminaa. We must not see our traditions as the anthropologists see them—fixed in time. The work then lies in identifying principles of witwaak that may serve our current and political realities today, which means gender may not play the kind of forefront role that it has for at least 275 years. We need to identify these principles, which are place-based, which are rooted in our responsibility to land or hahuuthlii. When these values, principles, and knowledge are so strongly rooted, they have the potential to become instruments with which we may measure our actions, as well as confront the argument about whether something is tradition. The fundamental aspects of our governance of self and community in relation to the world is common sense. Without it, we may remain stagnant and inept when it comes to decolonizing gender. Decolonizing gender is important because thus far we do not have the population numbers to afford the luxury of sitting back while the men fight (or do not fight, but instead become complacent) for our land, our rights, justice, and freedom. And let's face it, alone they have not achieved this. What has been achieved has been done only with the love, support, and actions of women working with the men in our communities.

Indigenous resistance springs from a desire to free our minds and bodies from the affects of the ongoing process of colonialism. Decolonization as a project or process will bring us closer to the goal of self-determination, to restore our rightful place on this land as nations, striving daily for balance with all life. The Nuu-chah-nulth principle of heshook-ish tsawalk is embedded in our huupukwanum. As a concept that is embedded within Nuu-chah-nulth laws, it therefore requires that its members live and act in ways that put the well-being of all beings, human and non-human, on an equal plane. It requires that we as Quu'asminaa be prepared for whatever is needed in our current reality. This is what the women of Tla-o-qui-aht and Checlesaht mean when they talk about restoring balance in our communities. To refine our acts of resistance in accordance with the needs of the day, like decolonizing gender roles, is a necessary move towards self-determination, freedom, and justice.

The 2006 Stop the Violence Movement offers a current example of this kind of resistance combined with action towards decolonizing gender roles. While we worked outside the imposition of state-created conditions, the young women who participated were empowered to speak against internalized violence and oppression. They were inspired to carry themselves with the respect, dignity, and honor they deserve.

I. Learning through Stories

In bringing this chapter to a conclusion I want to share the story of *Chaastims* (Mink) to illustrate how we might utilize tradition *and* decolonize our gender roles to meet the demands of contemporary Nuu-chah-nulth society.

The Story of Chaastims

Chaastims wanted to go visit his father up in the sky. He wanted to be a good son and take care of things up there while his father went on a vacation. His father was responsible for watching the fire in the sky, the sun. Chaastims assured his father he could watch the sun for him, not to worry. "Just go ahead and enjoy yourself and I'll take care of things here," he said.

So his father agreed and went maybe to Hawaii to smoke some cigars and relax with his feet up on its warm sandy beaches.

Now Chaastims was a handsome guy. You know how good-looking people can be sometimes.... So Chaastims set himself about to watch the fire, taking pains to have enough wood and watching that the flames didn't get too high. As time passed he grew bored of the constant effort and attention that fire tending requires. That was when he caught his reflection in a flame and was distracted by his own reflection. "Gee I really am handsome," he thought.

As you may know, fires take only a moment of neglect before they are roaring, and hungry flames leap out. Chaastims got scared, ran away, and hid as the sun's fire grew rapidly out of control. The fire ended up burning the whole *chuuk* (island, now known as Vancouver Island) down! The land turned to ash, covering the whole island. There was only the sea left. *Tushkoh* (Codfish) got so excited he swallowed the *huupathl* (moon) too. Today we call this *tushkyuuthl*, or what is referred to as a partial eclipse of the moon.

Now remember, this was a haa-huu-pah from the time before there were Quu'asminaa, just animals—winged ones, four-legged ones, and finned ones. There were a few chiefs who led the people then and as soon as this disaster struck they gathered the animals together to strategize what to do next. You see, we didn't like dwelling on what had been done and exasperating ourselves with why things happened—we simply needed to put our heads together to figure out the answer to the question, "where do we go from here?"

The Chiefs we remember today are *Boo-ah* (Halibut), *Ko-oshin* (Raven), and *Tlaymupt* (Woodpecker). They called all the people to gather around the shore. Halibut explained there was earth at the bottom of the sea. He called for volunteers to dive to the bottom to retrieve the earth while Tlaymupt produced two cedar baskets for the volunteers to carry the earth in. Boo-ah told the people that once the earth was retrieved he would call the two fastest runners, the two *qwayaatsiik* (wolves) named Aykutupis and Astaasapii, and they would be tasked with running around the entire island redistributing the earth so the regeneration of the hahuuthlii could begin.

The first volunteer was *Chims* (Bear). He growled he would get the earth. He seemed a logical choice as he was a great swimmer and very strong physically. He took the baskets and placed them on his shoulders and dove. The people and their chiefs waited and waited. They waited some more and then Chims popped up, shaking water droplets off his fur and panting. The baskets, however, were empty.

Boo-ah called for another volunteer. This time *Ahma* (loon) volunteered. He is known to be a great swimmer, so he took the baskets from Chims and dove nimbly into the water. The people waited and waited. They waited some more then Ahma popped up, panting, almost out of breath. The baskets were empty and so this went on for a while with different people volunteering, from the strong to the clever.

Even many of the seabirds volunteered and each

time they came up empty, without any earth in the cedar baskets. The people grew discouraged as the last few volunteers were unsuccessful. They began to lose hope and started to move away from the shore, despairing.

Then, there was a little voice that piped up—*Ko-ho* (target head duck). "Excuse me!" he said, "I'd like to try."

Boo-ah, Tlaymupt, and Ko-oshin were fair and gracious chiefs and so offered him the same chance to retrieve the earth. Some of the people snickered as he precariously perched the cedar baskets across his tiny shoulders. The chiefs ignored their snickers and earnestly encouraged the little duck to go on. The little duck dove neatly into the water and the people waited and waited. They waited and waited some more. The people started to feel alarmed, surely he had drowned! He'd been gone for too long and the people were discouraged and began to cry. As they cried they began walking away from the shore, their last hope left at the bottom of the sea—or so they thought. Suddenly, Ko-ho popped up and on his shoulders he carried two full cedar baskets of earth.

The three chiefs acted quickly and called forward the two fastest runners; the two qwayaatsiik. They then took a cedar basket each to redistribute the earth. The first one was named Astaasapii because he ran in one direction around the island, taking as much time as it takes for a cedar ember to burn on the longhouse fire. The other, Aykutupis, took the other basket full of earth and ran around the island in the other direction. Aykutupis took as much time as it takes for a drop of rain to fall from the longhouse eaves to the ground.

When they finished this, the earth began to regenerate. Eventually, everything grew green again. The animal people spent this time preparing themselves because they knew *Cha-chin-sun-up* (To Put the Land in Order) was coming—he was coming to turn some of the animals into people.

Chaastims is a haa-huu-pah Cha-chin-sun-up (we learn at the end of the story that my grandfather was named after this Great Being) shared with me while I was in my undergraduate studies ten years ago. It is a Nuu-chah-nulth-centered example of the potential that teachings and stories have in informing Indigenous-centered strategies for decolonization within resistance movements. They can provide us with concrete examples of our worldview and highlight innovative ways to approach present-day issues within communities. Simply put, they help to get us thinking Indigenous again. I will give some analysis of this story to highlight what I think are hopeful prospects for future strategies or ways of thinking that are outside the state-centric box.

Chaastims represents a time when non-human beings almost walked away from life itself after all seemed lost when the island burnt down. It represents a time of great change and even greater internal conflict. Today, we can see that humans and non-humans together are approaching a time when things are "burning down" all around us—oil and gas, water, air pollution, unjust wars, and so forth. As Indigenous Peoples we are either being forced to participate or enticed to follow the ways of imperialist and capitalist nations—literally cashing in while we can. This means humans this time are at the point the animals once

were; to the point of walking away from who we are and how we live as uniquely Quu'asminaa.

We have some difficult decisions to make in regard to how we will move forward, just like the chiefs in the Chaastims story. In searching for answers some of us are encountering troubling contradictions about gender. The story does not focus on gender, but on the value of strong leadership. It demonstrates that we must always be open to the potential that leaders are often not who we expect, like the target head duck, Ko-ho. Koh-ho was least expected to be capable of diving so deep to get the earth at the bottom of the sea, but he did it when no one else could. The act of getting the earth represents reaching for the very fundamental meaning or principles of our teachings of our stories, ceremonies, beliefs, and practices as they are connected physically to earth; to land and sea. They took what was needed from the bottom of the ocean, what was already there, minus the embellishments or other debris. The two wolves spread the earth around, to regenerate the land, to regenerate the teachings to ground us. After this the land became green again and our ancestor Cha-chin-sun-up came down to "put the land in order" and this is where the work really begins.

ACTIVITY:

Do you know your community's and family's stories? Who can you go to, to help you re-learn them? How are they applicable today?

_____

_____

_____

_____

J. Conclusion

Women, men, youth, and elders together must set a course of action. We can build strong leadership among our women if we hold each other up, gathering the strength we already possess to maintain our rightful places on our homelands. This means we must steer clear of any divisive state-centered politics, whether they are on the far right or on the left of the political sphere. This movement can begin with like-minded men who are also willing to decolonize gender within their own lives, and who are willing to take the kinds of actions that are truly liberating for Indigenous Peoples and lands. But the emphasis may need to begin more strongly with women first putting on the table what we feel are the needs of our communities today. Second, we women must then be willing to task the men to take action on what we have outlined and according to the needs we have prioritized, community by community, and family to family. This may be a beginning of remaking balance.

Additional Reflection Questions:

1. Take some time to look over your upbringing to the present time. What do you see? Do you recognize any sexism towards women? Look at your family: how has your family been affected by sexism and rigid gender roles?

2. In what ways do men and women condone this kind of sexism in your community? Expand outwards: do you see this in the home, in the workplace, schools, ceremonial life (that you participate in), etc.?

3. How many leaders in your community are women?

4. For the men: What are some ways you can redirect your relationship towards the women in your community? Can you start a men's group to address whatever issues are relevant to your community? What issues would you think are most relevant to address?

5. For the women: What are some ways you can redirect your relationship to women in your community? Can you start a women's group to address whatever issues you think are relevant to your community? What issues do you think are the most relevant at the moment? For example, some issues might be social, like the ways in which we suffer from the effects of colonialism; sexualized violence; health issues including ourselves and the health of our homelands; issues of self-sufficiency (as in considering how we are going to ensure the ongoing health of our homelands and communities); and political issues like land reclamation and governance.

It is important to think about a plan of action that starts with community members getting together and deciding what is relevant at the moment and how the community wants to resolve or begin resolving those issues. I will end with what I think is a very important teaching from my own people here on the West Coast, one that is not heard or taught as often as it needs to be today. When the men were out hunting or fishing they were gone sometimes for months at a time (our people caught whales and went as far as Alaska to catch fur seal). This meant that, for the most part, women ran our communities. They knew what families needed what, who was low on food, who was organizing a nuushitl or gathering, who lost a loved one, who would be getting married, etc. Therefore, when the men returned they had to consult with the women in order to understand what the needs of the community were. Once this was understood, the men had to go about bringing food, fixing someone's house, tending to loved ones, or whatever was needed. I think this history of the relationship between members of our communities tells us how efficiently we looked after ourselves. It also shows us that love is an action that is undertaken by all members of our societies towards each other and towards this land. If the work of decolonizing gender roles returns us to a way of life that is in agreement with a future for our Peoples on this land, then it is work that is worth doing.

K. Glossary

Ayts-tuu-thlaa: A young woman's coming of age ceremony

Haa-huu-pah: Teaching stories, sacred histories

Hahuuthlii: The land, sea, sky, and mountains that ha'wiih are responsible for

Hakuum: Respected woman, knowledgeable woman

Heshook-ish Tsawalk: Everything is one

Hishiimstawalk: The people are one

Hoquotisht: Our canoe is tipped over

Huupukwanum: Nuu-chah-nulth governance

Iisaak: Respect

Khuukhim: Ceremonial rattle used in chant or prayer

Muhdii: Longhouse family

Muschim: "The people" of the community

Naas: All Creation/Creator

Nuushitl: Potlatch, gathering/feast where gifts are given away

Quu'asminaa: Indigenous people, real human beings (to differentiate between human beings and all other non-human beings)

Tsiikshitl: To chant or pray with a khuukhim

Tyee Hawiilth: Hereditary chief (ha'wiih plural)

Tyee wiiuk: Head Chief Warrior

L. Resources

Coulthard, Glen. "Nuu-chah-nulth Struggles against Sexual Violence: Interview with Chiinuuks (Ruth Ogilvie) and Na'cha'uaht (Cliff Atleo Jr.)." *New Socialist: Special Issue on Indigenous Resurgence* 58, Sept.–Oct.(2006): 29–31. http://www.newsocialist.org.

Fanon, Franz. *Wretched of the Earth.* New York: Grove Press, 1963.

hooks, bell. *Feminist Theory: From Margin to Centre.* Cambridge, MA: South End Press, 2000.

Little Bear, Leroy. "Jagged World Views Colliding." *Reclaiming Indigenous Voice and Vision.* Ed. Marie Battiste. Vancouver, BC: UBC Press, 2000.

Index

C

Cacioppo, John T., 60

Caiete, Gregory A., 9

Cameron, Ngaropi Diane, 11–12

Canada: assimilation and mainstream education in, 181; continued attacks on Indigenous youth and families in, 182–183, 184; examples of military force and repression of Indigenous people, 103; rates of suicide for First Nation communities in, 119, 181, 183; residential schools and "sixties scoop" in, 182. *See also* British Columbia

Canku, Clifford, 135

capitalism: impact of on Indigenous youth, 130; and pending economic collapse, 5

Cargo, Margaret, 196

cause, and just war principles, 171

Chaastims (traditional story), 259–261

Chaw-win-is (Ruth Ogilvie), 12–13

"check in, check out" activity, and educating youth about colonization, 186–187, 191

Checlesaht (British Columbia), 246, 247, 259

Child, Thomas, 48

children, and traditional Māori society, 232. *See also* family

Christianity: impact of on mind and brain functions, 72; and Indigenous spirituality, 134–135; and views of women, 257

circle, of Indigenous education, 154–155

civil rights movement, 108

Clarke, Tony, 18

Clean Up the River Environment (CURE), 16

climate, and average annual rainfall of British Columbia, 44. *See also* global warming

clothing, and survival plan for environmental collapse, 31

CNN/Opinion Research, 166

coal, as energy source, 23

cognitive bias, 59–60

cognitive flexibility, 78

collaborators, and resistance movements, 111, 113

"colonial brain disorder," 80

colonialism: and continued attacks on youth and families in Canada, 182–183, 184; critical consciousness about impact of, 29; and distortion of history, 86; and empowerment through education, 147–148; and enlistment in armed services, 130, 159–161; and epidemic diseases in British Columbia, 42; and gender oppression, 246, 248–250, 257; and genocidal policies of governments, 34; impact on Māori language and culture, 227–228; and Indigenous political systems, 143–144; mental resources for overcoming oppressions of, 58, 65, 81; negativity and oppressions of, 59; orbital frontal cortex and belief in over-stated attributes of, 80; stresses of on mind and brain function, 64; survival mode and experience of youth under, 179–181; and violence in Māori society, 232; and war against Indigenous youth, 126. *See also* colonization; decolonization; neo-colonialism; state

colonization: and concept of progress, 17; and cultures of resistance, 29; definition of, 2–3, 188; and domestic violence in Māori society, 236–239; economic impact of, 140–142; and environmental degradation, 39; and identity of Māori, 226; internalized oppression and fragmented identity of youth, 181; long-term effects of, 148, 233; and mindfulness traditions/practices, 70; program for educating youth about effects of, 185–202; psychological effects of, 138–139; and rates of death in Indigenous community, 71–72; social effects of, 139–140; and views of Indigenous youth, 123–124; as war, 8, 99–121, 189. *See also* colonialism; cultural bomb; decolonization; historical trauma

coming-of-age ceremony, and Nuu-chah-nulth culture, 248

community: and culture of resistance, 113; gender roles in Nuu-chah-nulth, 262; and Indigenous approaches to education, 146, 150; individualism and contributions to, 131; survival plan for environmental crisis and cooperation of, 33–34. *See also* leaders and leadership

Community Supported Agriculture (CSA), 35

compassionate feelings, 59

Coolidge, Rita, 213

cooperation, in Indigenous education, 153

co-optation, of resistance movements, 108

Corntassel, Jeff, 7–8, 33, 54, 185

Coulthard, Glen, 249

Counterinsurgency Field Manual 3–24, 109, 119

Counter Intelligence Program (COINTELPRO), 107, 108

counting coup, and traditional warfare, 170

Cousins, Norman, 74

Crocker, Ryan Clark, 160

Cross, Terry, 125–126

cultural bomb, 2, 4, 137

cultural immersion camp, for Indigenous youth, 128–132

cultural mythos, 149–150

culture: and homelands, 199; and survival plan for environmental collapse, 27–28; and resistance movements, 29, 111–116; and survival preparation for Nuu-chah-nulth people, 51; traditional stories and revitalization of Māori, 227–229

psychological development, and Zuya Naka program for youth, 129, 138–139
Psychology Today (magazine), 60
psychoneuroimmunology, 73–74
public declaration, of just war, 172–173
public opinion, and support for Iraq War, 166

R

Racketeer Influenced and Corrupt Organizations (RICO) Act, 224
Raisin Exercise, and mindfulness, 74
Rampanen, John, 54
Rau-Kupa, Matarena Marjorie, 238
reconciliation, and impact of state actions on Indigenous communities, 91
Red Bow, Buddy, 213
religion. *See* Buddhism; Christianity; spirituality
remembrance, and life in prison, 223
reptilian brain, 60
reservation systems, and displacement from homelands, 193
residential schools. *See* boarding schools
resistance movements: colonization as war and building of, 106–109; and developing culture of resistance, 29, 111–116; development and phases of, 8; diversity of tactics for, 109–111; and educating youth about decolonization, 190; encouraging organization of, 13–14; and warrior societies, 116–119
respect: and characteristics of Indigenous education, 153; and gender relations in Nuu-chah-nulth society, 247–248
responsibility, and Māori society, 241–242
Rich, Leighton, 211
Ritter, Scott, 161
Room, David, 19
Ross, Diana, 213
Royal Canadian Mounted Police (RCMP), 103
Rystale, Richard, 76

S

safety: effect of Iraq War on global, 165; and survival preparation for Nuu-chah-nulth people, 51–53. *See also* security
"salt water thesis," 93
Savage Family (music), 2, 14
schedule, and life in prison, 222
Second Māori Taskforce on Whānau Violence, 233, 238
security: state and culture of, 107, 115–116; and survival preparation for Nuu-chah-nulth people, 51–53. *See also* safety; terrorism

self-awareness, 59
self-defense, decolonization as, 104–105
self-determination, of Indigenous people within state-centric systems, 7–9, 90, 93, 95, 97
self-sufficiency, building of lifeboats as metaphor for, 31–34
semi-agriculture, 49
Shakopee Mdewakanton Sioux Community (Minnesota), 35
Sharp, Gene, 110
Shell Oil Company, 19
shelter, and survival plans, 31, 44
Siegel, Daniel J., 76
Silver, Jim, 183
Simpson, Cory, 196
Simpson, Leanne, 54–55
Sitting Bull (Dakota), 170, 224
Six Nations Reserve (Ontario), 103
sixties scoop, and residential schools in Canada, 182
Smith, Andrea, 138
Smith, Benny, 86
Smith, Linda Tuhiwai, 228, 237
social movements, tactics of and building of resistance movements, 107
society: and decolonizing through social relationships, 183–187; and empowerment as goal of Indigenous education, 155–156; and social development in Zuya Naka program for youth, 129, 139–140; and traditional Māori culture, 227, 229–233
soils, agriculture and depletion of, 18
solar power, 23
South Dakota, 103, 205–206
sovereignty, and powers of state, 90
Soviet Union, 26
special housing units, in prisons, 209
spirituality: and life in prison, 217–219; and program for educating youth about colonization, 195–199; and survival plan for environmental collapse, 27–28, 35; and survival preparation for Nuu-chah-nulth people, 51; and Zuya Naka program for youth, 129, 134–136
state: and common historical myths, 92–97; and definition of war, 169; and renewal of roles and responsibilities of Indigenous people, 7–8, 97; and security culture, 107; Treaty of Westphalia and definition of, 89–92. *See also* colonialism; politics
state effects, and brain, 77
Steely Dan (music group), 213–214
stickball games, and warfare, 170